eighth edition

CROSSCURRENTS

editors' choice

edited by

MARK CHARLTON
St. Mary's University College

and

PAUL BARKER
Brescia University College

NELSON EDUCATION

NELSON / EDUCATION

Crosscurrents: Editors' Choice, Eighth Edition

Edited by Mark Charlton and Paul Barker

Vice President, Editorial Higher Education:
Anne Williams

Executive Editor:
Anne-Marie Taylor

Marketing Manager:
Ann Byford

Developmental Editor:
Katherine Goodes

Permissions Coordinator:
Sandra Mark

Content Production Manager:
Claire Horsnell

Copy Editor:
Helen Guri

Manufacturing Coordinator:
Loretta Lee

Design Director:
Ken Phipps

Managing Designer:
Franca Amore

Cover Design:
Trinh Truong

Cover Image:
Sunshine Pics/Alamy

Compositor:
Nelson Gonzalez

Library and Archives Canada Cataloguing in Publication Data

Crosscurrents : editors' edition / Mark Charlton, Paul Barker. -- Eighth edition.

A collection of essays compiled from three previous books: Crosscurrents,international relations; Crosscurrents, International development; and Crosscurrents, Contemporary political issues.ISBN 978-0-17-652337-4 (pbk.)

1. Canada--Politics and government--1993-2006--Textbooks. 2. Canada--Politics and government--2006- --Textbooks. 3. Canada--Social policy--Textbooks. 4. International relations--Textbooks. 5. Economic development--Textbooks. 6. Political development--Textbooks. I. Charlton, Mark, 1948-, editor of compilation II. Barker, Paul, 1953-, editor of compilation III. Title. IV. Title: Crosscurrents.

FC640.C763 2014   971.07
C2013-906449-4

ISBN-13: 978-0-17-652337-4
ISBN-10: 0-17-652337-5

CONTENTS

Contents

CONTRIBUTORS

Brian Ames is president and political and economic analyst at Ames Universal Inc., and past division chief and advisor at the International Monetary Fund.

George Ayittey is president of the Free Africa Foundation and a professor of economics at American University, Washington, D.C.

Paul Barker teaches political science at Brescia University College, London, Ontario.

Ward Brown is an economist with the International Monetary Fund.

Philip L. Bryden is dean of the Faculty of Law at the University of Alberta.

Gregory Conko is senior fellow at Competitive Enterprise Institute and vice-president and member of the board of directors at AgBioWorld Foundation.

Adam Davidson-Harden teaches in the Queen's University Global Development Studies department.

Shanta Devarajan is an economist with the World Bank.

Faron Ellis teaches politics at Lethbridge College, where he also serves as director of the Citizen Society Research Lab.

Anna Esselment is assistant professor of political science at the University of Waterloo.

Thomas Flanagan recently retired as professor of political science at the University of Calgary.

Ted Robert Gurr is the Distinguished University Professor emeritus at the University of Maryland and continues to consult on projects he established there.

Barbara Harff is professor emerita in political science at the U.S. Naval Academy.

John L. Hiemstra is a professor of political science at King's University College, Edmonton.

Dr. Mae-Wan Ho is the director of the Institute of Science in Society.

Gary Hufbauer is the Reginald Jones Senior Fellow at the Peterson Institute for International Economics.

Alejandro Izquierdo is a senior economist at the Inter-American Development Bank.

Harold J. Jansen is a professor of political science at the University of Lethbridge.

Kenneth Jennings is an associate at Norton Rose Fulbright Canada LLP and a member of the class of 2009 at the Dalhousie Law School.

Tasha Kheiriddin is a political analyst and columnist.

Paul Krugman is a professor of economics and international affairs at the Woodrow Wilson School, Princeton University.

A. Wayne MacKay is a professor of law at Dalhousie Law School.

Alex Marland is associate professor of political science at Memorial University of Newfoundland.

Robert Martin recently retired from teaching law at the University of Western Ontario.

Daniel McGruder is a corporate lawyer at WeirFoulds LLP.

Hugh Mellon is associate professor of political science at King's University College at the University of Western Ontario.

John Miller is a professor of economics at Wheaton College.

John Mueller holds the Woody Hayes Chair of National Security Studies, Mershon Center, and is a professor of political science at Ohio State University.

Moses Ochonu is an associate professor, History College of Arts & Sciences, Vanderbilt University.

C.S. Prakash is a professor in plant molecular genetics and the director of the Centre for Plant Biotechnology Research at Tuskegee University.

Dr. Eva Sirinathsinghji is a researcher at the Institute of Science in Society.

Hugo Slim is a senior research fellow at the Oxford Institute for Ethics, Law and Armed Conflict at the University of Oxford, where he is leading research on humanitarian ethics.

Joseph E. Stiglitz is professor of economics at Columbia University.

Roger Townshend is a lawyer specializing in Aboriginal issues at Olthuis, Kleer, Townshend LLP.

Peter Uvin is provost of Amherst College.

Nelson Wiseman is a professor of political science at the University of Toronto.

INTRODUCTION

In the first edition of *Crosscurrents: Contemporary Political Issues*, we developed a collection of readings that would not only challenge students to think through a number of contemporary political issues but also foster an understanding of and tolerance for the views of others. We felt that a text structured in the form of a debate or dialogue provided an ideal format. We find it gratifying that a number of our colleagues have shared our goals and have used the previous editions in their introductory political science or Canadian politics courses.

CHANGES TO THE EIGHTH EDITION

In preparing the eighth edition of Crosscurrents, we maintained the basic structure and format of previous editions. For each issue, an introduction provides the reader with the necessary background, placing the subject in the context of more general principles of concern to the study of politics. Two essays then present conflicting viewpoints. Finally, a postscript offers a short commentary on the debate and suggests readings for students to explore the topic further.

This edition includes topics from not only *Crosscurrents: Contemporary Political Issues*, but also *Crosscurrents: International Relations* and *Crosscurrents: International Development*. Although the topics themselves are quite varied, we have attempted to select those that raise broad theoretical or ideological issues relevant to introductory political science courses. The publisher is making available a more comprehensive database of articles, from the previous editions of all three titles, which can provide the basis for a custom text. These options will provide maximum flexibility for instructors to design packages of readings that best suit their courses.

A NOTE FOR FIRST-TIME USERS

In the introduction to the first edition of *Crosscurrents*, we set out our rationale for developing a reader using the debate format. We believe the rationale for using this format to teach introductory courses is as strong as ever and bears repeating for those who may be picking up this text for the first time.

There are three good reasons, we believe, for using the debate format. First, studies have shown that students learn and retain more information when they are engaged in an active learning process. Yet the reality in most Canadian universities is that students in introductory courses face ever larger class sizes, which militate against discussion and active student involvement. While students generally come to political science courses with a great deal of interest and enthusiasm, they frequently find themselves slipping into a pattern of simple note-taking and passive learning.

Second, most introductory political science courses must by necessity address abstract principles and concepts and cover a great deal of descriptive material concerning processes and institutions. At the same time, students come to these courses expecting that they will discuss and debate what is going on in the chaotic world of politics. Unfortunately, it is often difficult for them to relate the debates of everyday political issues to the broader and more abstract principles encountered in their introductory courses. Without a reference point, discussions of contemporary issues may seem more like interesting "current events" digressions, with little direct relationship to the overall propositions being dealt with in the lectures.

Third, students frequently bring to their readings an uncritical awe of the authority of the published word. When confronted with a series of readings by the leading authorities on each subject, there is a strong temptation for students to think that the text presents the "final" word on the subject. They assume that further discussion and debate can add little to the issue.

With these thoughts in mind, we have endeavoured to develop a collection of readings that will serve as a resource for a more interactive style of teaching, whether it be in classroom or tutorial discussion situations, or in a more formal debate setting. Because of the flexibility of the format, *Crosscurrents* can be employed in the classroom in several ways:

(i) Some may wish to assign the chapters simply as supplementary readings reinforcing material covered in lectures, and to use them as points of illustration in classroom lectures or discussions.

(ii) The readings may be used as a departure point for essay assignments in the course. To encourage the development of critical skills, students could be asked to write an assessment of the arguments and evidence presented in one of the debates. Alternatively, students could select one side of the debate and write an essay developing their own arguments in favour of that view.

(iii) Others may wish to use the readings as a means of organizing weekly discussion sessions into a debate format. On each topic, two students may be asked to argue the case for opposing sides, and these arguments could be followed by group discussion. This format requires students to adopt a particular point of view and defend that position. Because the necessary background material is provided in the readings, this format is very easily adapted to large courses where teaching assistants are responsible for weekly tutorial sessions.

ACKNOWLEDGMENTS

We would like to express our appreciation to the many reviewers who offered very helpful comments and suggestions throughout the years: Tom Enders, Grand Prairie Community College; Karen E. Lochead, Wilfrid Laurier University; Gerry Boychuk, University of Waterloo; Andrew Heard, Simon Fraser University; Susan Franceschet, Acadia University; Darin Nesbitt, Douglas College; Alexandra Dobrowolsky, St. Mary's University; John von Heyking, University of Lethbridge; Andrew Banfield, University of Calgary; Chris Kukucha, University of Lethbridge; Cheryl Collier, University of Windsor; and Ross Gibbons, University of Western Ontario. We are particularly indebted to those authors and publishers who have granted us permission to use their published work. In addition, we want to acknowledge the excellent support of Katherine Goodes in helping us to bring this project to completion. The careful and detailed work of Claire Horsnell, Content Production Manager, Helen Guri, Copy Editor, and Sandra Marks, Permissions Editor, was also much appreciated. Finally, we would be remiss not to mention the support of many others, not named above, who have contributed to this volume in different ways.

Mark Charlton, Langley, B.C.
Paul Barker, London, Ontario

Mark Charlton is vice-president academic and dean at St. Mary's University College, Calgary, Alberta. Professor Charlton received his Ph.D. in political science from Laval University, where he studied as an Ontario–Quebec Fellow. He is author of *The Making of Canadian Food Aid Policy* (1992), editor of *Crosscurrents: International Relations* and *Crosscurrents: International Development*, and co-author of the *Thomson Nelson's Guide to Research and Writing in Political Science* (2013). He has also published a number of articles in *International Journal*, *Études Internationales*, *Journal of Conflict Studies*, and the *Canadian Journal of Development Studies*.

Paul Barker teaches political science at Brescia University College, London, Ontario. Professor Barker received his Ph.D. from the University of Toronto. He has written articles on public policy that have appeared in *Canadian Public Administration*, *Canadian Public Policy*, and the *Canadian Journal of Law and Society*.

LETTER FROM THE PUBLISHER

Dear Professor,

We are pleased to announce the publication of the eighth edition of *Crosscurrents*, edited by Mark Charlton and Paul Barker. Since it was first published nearly thirty-three years ago, *Crosscurrents* has evolved into a series of three books: *Contemporary Political Issues*, *International Relations*, and *International Development*. For several years we have been asked to provide the debates from this series in a flexible format so instructors can pick and choose which ones they would like to use. In this edition Nelson is pleased to present two formats of the text, each taking the most popular readings from all three of the *Crosscurrents* texts: the *Editors' Choice* and the *Reader's Choice*.

The volume you have in your hands now is the *Editors' Choice*. Our editors have carefully selected fourteen debates that span a variety of issues across the discipline, providing you with a topical collection of provocative essays and readings designed to stimulate discussion on Canadian and international politics.

If you would prefer to select your own debates, you will want to consider the *Reader's Choice*. It allows you to select from our complete *Crosscurrents* database of debates, and gives you all the flexibility of a course pack without the hard work of putting one together. The end result for your students is a real book with pedagogical material, rather than a set of photocopied readings.

Please contact your local Nelson representative to learn how easy it is to create your own custom reader for your course.

Visit www.nelson.com/crosscurrents to see the list of readings and for more information on creating your own custom reader.

We look forward to your feedback on this exciting project.

Sincerely,

Anne-Marie Taylor
Executive Editor (Political Science)
Nelson Education Limited

Will Conservatism and the
Conservative Party Fail?

✔ **YES**
NELSON WISEMAN, "A Dead End: Conservatism and the
Conservative Party"

✘ **NO**
FARON ELLIS, "Twenty-First Century Conservatives Can
Continue to Succeed"

In 2003, members of the Progressive Conservative Party and the Canadian Alliance party agreed to combine their forces to create a new national political party. The two representatives of conservatism in Canada would be replaced by one single entity called the Conservative Party of Canada. Not surprisingly, the new party subscribed to beliefs and principles associated with modern conservative thinking. Government would be small; elected officials would be accountable; and individual rights and freedoms would be emphasized. Progressive social policies, such as health care and the environment, would be respected, but the well-being of the country would rest on the efforts of individual Canadians and not on government.

The genesis of the Conservative Party lay in developments that took place in the preceding decade. The Progressive Conservatives historically had been the standard-bearer of conservatism in Canada. But in the late 1980s, the Reform Party rose in an attempt to more accurately represent those with conservative views (and to better serve interests in the western provinces). The two parties tangled in federal elections, each frustrated in the belief that the other had divided the conservative vote. The result was easy victories for the Liberal Party of Canada. Faced with this situation, efforts were made to unite the two parties of conservatism. Initial efforts managed only to alter the makeup of the Reform Party and to give it a new name (the somewhat awkward Canadian Reform Conservative Alliance, shortened to Canadian Alliance). Eventually, the endeavour to unite the right led to serious discussions between the leaders of the two conservative parties and the creation of the Conservative Party of Canada. Canada would now have a single, united party dedicated to conservative principles and ready to govern.

The question was whether Canadians were ready to accept conservatism and its representative. Early indications certainly suggested that Canadians were willing to give the two a chance. In the 2004 federal election, the new Conservative Party won 99 seats and helped force the ruling Liberals into a minority situation. In the 2006 election, the Conservative Party of Stephen Harper won a minority government with 124 seats and, in 2008, another minority government with 143 seats. Then, in 2011, the Conservative Party achieved its goal: a majority government, with 166 seats. The rather quick ascendancy of the new party is impressive, but these gains have been achieved with little increase in the Conservative popular vote. Moreover, certain regions of the country—Quebec, most importantly—remain beyond the reach of Prime Minister Harper and his party. It seems that the election of Conservative governments, whether minority or majority, has not resolved the issue of whether modern conservatism has a future in Canada, but rather has only made it a more interesting question to ponder.

In the minds of some, Canada has never been and for the foreseeable future will never be suited to conservatism and conservative parties. In the past, conservatism was less hostile to government than its modern counterpart and more willing to respect traditions. But it largely lost out to the emerging liberalism and its focus on individualism and progressive policies that challenged past practices. In this environment, the Progressive Conservative Party experienced mostly failure and had to watch the triumphant Liberal Party of Canada become the nation's governing party. Modern conservatism differs from the old conservatism and indeed reflects some of the attributes of classical liberalism (for example, small government and a focus on economic freedoms). However, it seems that the country has moved on and is embracing a liberalism that provides for active government and that has little time for those with qualms about same-sex marriages, easy access to abortion services, and state support for regulated child care. In other words, modern conservatism fits uneasily, if at all, into the Canadian reality. Accordingly, the Conservative Party faces only disappointment.

There are others, however, who feel differently and believe that Canada is ready for a party that advocates limits on government and that reminds people of the importance of traditional institutions such as the family and church. The challenge is to ensure that the party plays to its strengths and resists the temptation to be all things to all people (which is the Liberal way). Already some believe that the party has pursued policies and actions little different from its Liberal predecessor. It must also ensure that extremists in the party—those who wish to use the state to impose moral choices on the citizenry—are unable to wield much power or gain much notice.

In the readings, Nelson Wiseman, a professor of political science at the University of Toronto, argues that modern conservatism and the Conservative Party have little future in Canadian politics. Faron Ellis, a political scientist at Lethbridge College and recently elected alderman on the Lethbridge City Council, makes the case that Canada is fertile ground for modern conservatism and that the Conservative Party can position itself to take advantage of this situation.

✔ **YES**
A Dead End: Conservatism and the Conservative Party
NELSON WISEMAN

This is a tale of two quite different conservative philosophies and two quite dissimilar Conservative parties that share the same label but differ in thought and development. According to our story, both variants of conservatism have failed. The fortunes of both Conservative parties relate to the shortcomings of the conservative ideologies that have infused them. The denouement to this account is—alas for conservatives and Conservatives—the continuing hegemony of liberal-social democratic values in Canada.

To be sure, the Conservative Party has had electoral successes. It racked up the largest parliamentary majorities in Canadian history in 1958 and 1984, tenuously triumphed in 2006, and won an outright majority in 2011. Periods of Conservative success have been relatively brief, however, best seen as temporary interregnums between long periods of Liberal rule. Conservative governments have served as a default option for the electorate when the Liberals have faltered. The conservative impulse, in both its older manifestation and its newer incarnation, is a minoritarian one in Canada. The overarching mainstream ideology—liberalism—has been the principal driver of Canadian politics and political thought. The periodic, transitory victories of the Conservative Party have come as reactive jerks to the Liberals when they appeared arrogant, tired, or disorganized. Chastened by the electorate from time to time, the Liberals once consistently bounced back, more effectively capitalizing on the evolving values and social composition of Canadians than did the Conservatives.

The older Canadian conservative tradition and Conservative Party are those of the nineteenth century. Rooted in British conservatism or Toryism, early Canadian conservatism reacted to American revolutionary liberalism. The conservative creed—carried to Canada by decamped and expelled American Loyalists—expressed itself earlier, in a Gallic manifestation, in French Canada's quasi-feudal structures and practices. The War of 1812 and Britain's imperial reach reinforced conservatism in Canada: for example, the early influence of a high Tory right in the form of Upper Canada's Family Compact and Lower Canada's Chateau Clique. In French Canada—which appeared more like pre-liberal, pre-revolutionary Old France than Europe's liberal, revolutionary New France—the ultramontane Roman Catholic Church came to hold sway a few decades after the Conquest. It deferred to British leadership in matters of state and economy. In exchange for its fealty to the British, the conservative clerical class was left at the commanding heights

---

of French Canada's separate, segregated culture and society. It was a mutually reinforcing division of labour: the economically dominant British—driven by a possessive individualist outlook—tended to industry, finance, and commerce protected by a strong centralized state, while the economically subordinate but proud French Canadians looked inward to their religion for spiritual inspiration to preserve their traditional conservative and rural ways. Canada's founders in 1867 were America's anti-revolutionary liberals—those with a Tory streak buttressed by their British connection—working with French Canadian conservatives.

The new conservatism—and the new Conservative Party—are that of the late twentieth and early twenty-first centuries. Unlike the old conservatism and the old Conservative Party, they are not repelled by America. Proximity and attraction to America's evolving neoconservatism (also known as "neoliberalism") pollinate the new conservatism. Both Canadian liberalism and the new Canadian conservatism have drawn heavily on American thought and models, while the older conservatism and Conservative Party had greater British impetus. A massive influx of nineteenth-century Britons who had experienced the rise and success of the anti-Tory and liberal British Reform Party bolstered Canadian liberalism as Upper Canada's population exploded from 77,000 in 1811 to 952,000 by 1851. British liberalism, streaked by Tory conservatism, was sustained in Canada by the opportunities afforded in an expanding frontier economy where land was free or cheap. Liberalism grew and further eclipsed Toryism because, while Old World social structures such as rigid class divisions and a state-sanctioned Anglican church could be wistfully imitated in Canada, they could not maintain their early hold. They were not native to, nor an organic part of, the North American reality and came to be rejected. Canada's conditions, however, favoured some Old World Tory notions, such as a respected and strong state. It was indispensable to the settlement of the Canadian West and the building of a national economy and culture using, among other instruments, Crown corporations.

Modern conservatism claims to reject Keynesianism, the liberal economic paradigm that took hold after the Second World War. In the Keynesian schema, the state guides macroeconomic supply and demand, that is, society's gross production and consumption. It does so by manipulating the levers of fiscal policy, public sector spending, and taxation. Modern conservatism, in contrast, emphasizes ardent support for free-market practices and laissez-faire. It wishes to shrink the state, privatize state enterprises, deregulate industries, liberalize trade regimes, outsource state functions to profit-motivated contractors, and cut back social entitlements.[1] This new conservative agenda seeks to downsize government and offload its activities. The new conservative focus is on what private enterprise, acting freely, can do to boost the economy, not on what the state can do to manage it. The state's role as a social engineer in the form of affirmative action and other programs for disadvantaged groups is rejected by neoconservatives and ridiculed as setting quotas. On some social issues, such as abortion and gay marriage, however, the new conservatism's partisans are divided. Some fear moral anarchy and are puritanical on matters such as gay marriage, abortion, drug use, pornography, and prostitution. Others adopt libertarian positions—the church of the self—on such issues.

Times change, ideas evolve, political parties reinvent themselves, and new groups of Canadians appear as older ones fade from influence and die off. Canadian society is always in flux but successful institutions, ideologies, and political parties outlive their competitors and shift with the changing temper of the times. The weakness of the old and new federal Conservatives has been, in part, a product of political geography: the key to federal power is to capture the larger cities consistently. There, the Liberals had dominated between the 1960s and 2011. In most provinces, in contrast, the road to provincial power lies in the rural and outlying districts, where Conservatives have been more successful.[2] The key to winning over the ever-changing electorate has been to change with it. Ontario's Progressive Conservatives did that during their unmatched dynasty of forty-two consecutive years in office between the 1940s and 1980s. The party bridged the Old Ontario and the New Ontario; it maintained its Anglo-Saxon rural/small town support and augmented it with those in the growing, more ethnically and ideologically diverse metropolitan centres. The party was by turns—sometimes simultaneously as need be—"progressive" and "conservative," a formula that worked.[3] In contrast, the federal Conservatives have largely acted as followers, not trailblazers, in the political and policy arenas. The opponents of conservatism successfully characterize the old and new Conservative parties, both their older Tory and newer neoconservative thinking, as reactionary and keen to perpetrate an inegalitarian status quo that serves established interests.

THE OLD CONSERVATISM

Classical conservatism or Toryism as articulated by Edmund Burke was receptive to change so long as society's fundamental institutions were preserved. In this view, organic change—where society's classes and groups worked together harmoniously for the beneficial maintenance of the whole system—was natural and welcome. Fundamentals were to prevail over innovations when they clashed. This older strand of conservatism harked back to the wisdom of the ages, and there is a quaint, archaic flavour to it. It warns of the dangers of experimentation and cautions people to do and think as their forebears did. It sees man as born flawed, he and his world as imperfect. Classical conservatism knitted together a number of interconnected and reinforcing principles. In addition to an adherence to tradition, they included the maintenance of social order through strong authority, authority that demanded and deserved deference. Order required protecting the weak as well as the strong and meant a muscular, but not necessarily big, government. Classical conservatism was less optimistic about human nature than classical liberalism or neoconservatism, which place less faith in government's wisdom and planning abilities and more faith in the individual's capacities.

Classical conservatism embraced hierarchical institutions as guarantors of stability. These institutions—such as the Crown, the church, the military, the patriarchal family, and other hierarchies such as corporations and universities—were organized and understood to provide reinforcement and direction for the community's common interests. Such institutions worked as partners, in collaboration; they neither competed with each other nor were internally driven. In this Tory cosmology, political society is a hierarchically structured organic-corporatist-communitarian entity comprised of unequal classes—some more privileged than others—all sanctioned by heredity and tradition and relating to each other cooperatively. It was a compassionate conservatism in that society's privileged were duty-bound to protect and aid the less fortunate out of a sense of noblesse oblige. Classical conservatism's collectivist and elitist elements were considered natural as well as necessary bulwarks against revolutionary chaos, class conflict, and anarchy. The old conservatism thus viewed democratic stirrings and unshackled individual freedoms with suspicions of "mobocracy."

The creation of the modern Canadian state was a conservative triumph over liberalism in that market logic, which dictated Canada's absorption by the American economic behemoth, was resisted on nationalist grounds. Politics trumped the economic allure of continental integration. Nevertheless, the old conservatism or Toryism was always a minoritarian impulse in the political culture; it infused Canadian liberalism but did not displace it as the dominant outlook. The state's Tory institutions were deployed in the interests of liberal acquisitiveness and economic expansion. The old conservatism, for example, underwrote private enterprise at public expense for national economic development and "national purpose" in projects such as the Canadian Pacific Railway.[4]

Joe Clark highlighted the old conservatism's notion of community when he portrayed Canada as a "community of communities." Brian Mulroney preached an aggressive market liberalism and reversed his Conservatives Party's historical protectionist posture vis-à-vis the United States, but he described Canada's universal social programs as a "sacred trust" not to be violated and "a cornerstone of our party's philosophy."[5] Socialists, however, had first championed such programs and the old Conservative Party opposed their implementation by welfare liberals. Perhaps one of the last gasps of the old conservatism came on the eve of the 2003 merger of the Progressive Conservative Party and the Canadian Alliance. Lowell Murray, a Progressive Conservative senator and former Mulroney cabinet minister, wrote that as a Progressive Conservative,

> We believe that government's job is to provide stability and security against the excesses of the market. Democratic politics must define the public interest and ensure it always prevails over more private ambitions. To that extent the forces of technology and globalization need to be tamed. . . . Reform [the new] conservatism which is what the Alliance [party] practises [sic] relies on people's fear of moral and economic decline. . . . It spoils all the good

arguments for the market economy by making a religion of it, pretending there are market criteria and market solutions to all of our social and political problems.[6]

Clark and others in the older Tory mould, such as former Progressive Conservative cabinet minister Flora MacDonald, left the party after the merger of the Progressive Conservative and Canadian Alliance parties, with the claim that the new Conservative Party had left them. MacDonald reportedly then voted for the New Democratic Party (NDP), possibly because it represented more of Toryism's communitarianism than the new Conservative Party's neoconservatism.[7]

THE OLD CONSERVATIVE PARTY

John A. Macdonald's old Conservative Party was undeniably successful; it won five of Canada's first six elections. The party, however, floated on the shaky foundations of a shifting coalition of forces rather than being constructed on solid pillars. Indeed, the very first Conservative government was actually a Liberal–Conservative one, bringing together anti-American Tories and Montreal-based English Canadian financiers and business liberals who sought to build an economic empire via railway construction. This alliance drew on the support of Quebec's conservative *Bleus* and some of Canada West's Reformers who were also tied to railway interests. The old Conservatives' triumphs lay in Macdonald's skill in organizing and dispensing bureaucratized patronage: Conservative constituency associations operated like employment agencies where individual party activists formally applied for government positions and traded on their financial or campaigning contributions. Such behaviour was considered normal and legitimate, based on the idea that "to the victor belongs the spoils."[8] Notwithstanding its brokerage orientation and pork-barrelling—traits shared with the Liberals—the old Conservative Party differed from the Liberals in that it was the carrier of what there was of the old conservatism.

The old Conservative Party's undoing was its failure to continue to broker successfully between the British and French on issues of language and religion. French Catholic Quebec was upset with the execution of Métis leader Louis Riel and the suppression of French language schooling in New Brunswick, Ontario, and especially Manitoba. The party appeared fiercely Protestant and British, and Quebec was lost to the Conservatives as they further distanced itself from the Québécois on issues of international empire, war, and conscription. The Conservatives could thus not muster enough support to win more than four Quebec seats in any of the four elections between 1917 and 1926; they won none in 1921. Six decades later, the story had not changed much. Only two seats in Joe Clark's governing caucus in 1979 were from Quebec and, in 1980, the party won but one. The Conservatives did not select a French Canadian leader (Jean Charest) until the party was in its death throes in the 1990s. John Diefenbaker's Conservative victory in 1958 and Mulroney's landslides in the 1980s had proved to be false indicators of Conservative viability in Quebec. The party had benefited from the fleeting tactical acquiescence of Quebec's old and new nationalists, the Union Nationale and the Parti Québécois, as well as, in Mulroney's case, the provincial Liberals.

Another source of the Conservatives' undoing was, paradoxically, their most notable policy accomplishment: the National Policy of 1879. The construction of a Trans-Canada railway, the settlement of the West, and the imposition of tariffs facilitated the development of central Canada's nascent industrial economy but the tariff, a regionally discriminatory transportation policy, as well as the power of financial institutions associated with the Conservatives of Montreal's St. James Street and Toronto's Bay Street, turned the West against the party. It became a Liberal stronghold and a wellspring for third-party protest (in the form of the Progressives, Social Credit, and the Co-operative Commonwealth Federation [CCF]). R.B. Bennett's Conservatives held power during the Depression but came to be blamed for it. Diefenbaker's Conservatives swept the West in 1958 in part because his populism and background were so different from those, like Ontario's Colonel George Drew, who preceded him as party leader. The party had anointed westerner John Bracken as its leader during the Second World War, but the country was not prepared to switch leaders then or in the war's aftermath. The challenge to the ruling Liberals then was from the left (the CCF) rather than the Conservative right. Bracken's singular contribution to the party was to change the "Conservative" brand to "Progressive Conservative," but the party did not live up to its new billing.

The chronic electoral weakness of the old Conservative Party was evidenced in the thirty elections between 1896 and the party's last outing in 2000: it won nine of them, but in only six did it win a majority of seats. In all three elections that returned Conservative minorities, the party attracted fewer voters than the Liberals. As the "government party," the Liberals held office in parts of all but twenty-five years between 1896 and the old Conservatives' demise in 2003. The old Conservatives served as the natural "opposition party." A telling sign of their vulnerability came in Canada's first multiparty election in 1921: they ran third behind the upstart, loosely organized Progressives, who themselves became a dilapidated annex of the Liberals. In all three elections between 1993 and 2000, the old Conservatives claimed that they were the only "national" alternative to the Liberals but they ran last in a five-party system. The relatively few Conservative victories in the twentieth century were more rebuffs for the perceived shortcomings of Liberal regimes than Conservative mandates. In only four of the twenty-six elections after 1921 have the Conservatives won with wide national support.

Unlike parties of principle like the Progressives, CCF–NDP, Social Credit, the Reform Party, and the Canadian Alliance, the old Conservative Party styled itself, like the Liberal Party, as a brokerage party. Its strategy was to build a tent large enough to hold Canadians from all strata of society. It operated as a cadre party—deferring to its leader and his entourage on major issues of policy. No Conservative convention or policy gathering, for example, debated or endorsed free trade or the GST before their institution by the leader. Gaining a few seats and a higher vote share is deemed a victory by a small party like the NDP, but Conservatives measured their leader by a higher standard: outright victory. The more they found themselves relegated to the opposition benches, the more a mindset of defeat and self-destructive tendencies set in. A "Tory Syndrome" took hold, where a weak election performance led Conservative partisans to attribute failures to their leader, which weakened him and his ability to take the party forward.[9] As a near-perpetual opposition party, the old Conservatives projected the image of naysayers with little or no experience in fashioning public policy or responsibility for public administration. More often than not, the party's Members of Parliament (MPs) appeared uncoordinated in their opposition roles, some working at cross-purposes with their leader. When they occasionally did hold office, as in the Meighen, Bennett, Diefenbaker, and Clark years, they offered incoherent and unsynchronized policy direction or struggled with crises beyond their control (for example, the Depression and skyrocketing oil prices in the 1970s).

The Mulroney Conservative victories in the 1980s were the fruit of a tenuous alliance of western Canadian rural and fiscal conservatives on the one hand and Quebec nationalists on the other. There had always been substantial Conservative support in Ontario and the Maritimes—the very creatures of Loyalism—but it had not been sufficient to propel the party to power. Quebec's francophone Conservatives were first and foremost nationalists whose nationalism transcended the liberal-conservative-socialist cleavage of English Canada. Once Quebecker Mulroney left the stage, the party plummeted in the province from sixty-three seats in 1988 to one in 1993 and reverted to its longstanding marginal position.

Socio-demographic change eroded the historic bases of support for the old Conservative Party in English Canada. The Maritimes' constantly shrinking share of the population in the twentieth century made the region count for less and less. Loyalist and early post-Loyalist rural Ontario was transformed into an increasingly urban, multicultural, kaleidoscopic society. The Liberals benefited. The outcome of the four minority elections between 1957 and 1965 reflected that change: southern, metropolitan Ontario's swing seats determined whether Conservatives or Liberals would come out on top as the rest of the country was in a state of electoral stasis with few seats changing hands. Immigrants, soon naturalized as citizens, were more favourably disposed to the Liberals, as was a rising class of young, upwardly mobile, urban professionals. These groups saw Liberal immigration and urban policies as more positive than those of the Conservatives. Old Tory Toronto, once a Conservative stronghold, became a Liberal bastion. The Conservatives' battles against bilingualism and the maple leaf flag (they fought to retain the Red Ensign with its Union Jack) did not resonate with either Quebeckers or Ontario's newer ethnic minorities. The Liberals reinforced their standing with these groups, and the Conservatives weakened theirs, on issues such as multiculturalism, affirmative action programs, and social policy. The old Conservatives represented the Old Canada, disproportionately those of British ethnic descent, Protestant, and rural/small town. They could not shake that image.

THE NEW CONSERVATISM

The new conservatism is a modern variant of the old liberalism. The new conservatism or neoconservatism assigns priority to the individual over the community, which is defined atomistically as the sum of its self-governing, equally free-willed individuals. Margaret Thatcher captured this sentiment with her observation, "There is no such thing as society." The new conservatism, unlike the old conservatism, is loath to use the state to protect the public good or for broad community interest at the expense of the private freedoms—the negative liberties—of its autonomous individuals. An exception is made for the state's war-making capacity and police functions. The new conservatism depicts society as a one-class citizenry rather than as a society of unequal classes, as both Tories and socialists do. Thus, the neoconservatives of the Reform/Alliance Party, until they came to power as the rechristened Conservatives, favoured an individual-based participatory form of democracy; they embraced the use of referenda and the potential recall of elected representatives and argued that elected representatives must serve as delegates who communicated their electors' unmediated views. The new conservatism claimed not to see politicians, as Burke and the old conservatism did, as trustees elected to exercise their personal judgment of what is best and held to account in elections based on stewardship.

Neoconservatives view the state as a constantly renewed and voluntary arrangement among contemporaries. This jettisons the Tory conceptualization of state and society as an inherited ancient bond that links past, present, and future generations. The new conservatism moves on popular impulse, operating on the principle that society is a compact among equal citizens. Hierarchical and monarchical institutions—like an appointed Senate and the Crown's residual prerogatives, which are exercised by the prime minister—were condemned by neoconservatives as outdated remnants of the old conservatism until the new Conservative Party came to power and exercised those prerogatives. The new conservatism lambastes the old conservatism for offering an unreal, inferior understanding of the existing socioeconomic order and how it should work. Neoconservatives indict the old conservatism as a reactionary vision of the future.

The new conservatives, however, are divided on the moral, as opposed to economic, sphere of human behaviour. Social conservatives abhor traditionally proscribed acts—homosexuality, abortion, suicide, drug use, and so forth—while libertarian conservatives tolerate them so long as such behaviour is freely chosen. Social conservatives, unlike libertarians, believe government must not remain neutral on moral issues and look to government to preserve and promote traditional values and institutions such as the traditional family and to do so in the schools, the law, and the media. They condone teaching religion in schools as part of education's bedrock function. In contrast, libertarians would leave the teaching of religious doctrines to the educational marketplace. It is a comment on its evolution that the old Conservative Party by the 1990s had come to look at abortion and gay rights more favourably than the Reform/Alliance Party's social conservatives who upheld the moral cudgels of an older Canada.

Where the libertarian and social conservative tendencies of the new conservatism merge is on rejection of state intrusion in economic matters, with the exception of state intervention in support of private enterprise. Their common objective goes beyond shrinking the state to reducing its very capacity to act. They would place much of the traditional public policy agenda beyond the reach of government and, consequently, beyond the reach of citizens who may wish to have their government steer a more collectivist course. Wedded to free-market solutions, the new conservatives would limit the instrumentality of government in pursuit of social justice objectives. This dampens the prospect for public embrace of the new conservatism because Canadians have become inured to and expect government action in the liberal reform tradition. For neoconservatives, a preoccupation with individual and corporate rights and unfettering the market economy towers over considerations of social and economic justice. But, "Like nature itself, the market order knows neither justice nor injustice," writes Cy Gonick. "Social obligation, the idea of solidarity between self and community, has no place..." in this logic.[10] Nationalism is a litmus test differentiating the old and new conservatism. Tory conservatism expressed itself in a certain anti-Americanism. Anti–free trade crusader David Orchard carried its banner in his bid for the old Conservative Party leadership in 1998 and 2003. Red Tories and old-style Burkean Tories had been nationalist communitarians who opposed class struggle and promoted a national identity to counter American influence. The Liberals' liberalism, in contrast, had not been philosophically or historically linked to statism or nationalism until Pierre Trudeau led them. The closer the new Conservative Party moves toward contemporary American conservatism, the farther it moves away from the Tory nationalism that had informed the old Conservative Party.

The last Conservative leader who underlined the links between his party and its British Conservative Party roots was Robert Stanfield; he cited both Burke and the pioneering factory legislation of Britain's Conservatives in the nineteenth century as part of Canadian conservatism's legacy. Stanfield justified restraint of the individual in the interests of the community's welfare as a whole. Melded to conservatism's elitism and its sense of noblesse oblige, his Tory sensibility led him to propose protection for the less secure. He became the first major Canadian political leader to endorse a guaranteed annual income in an election campaign.[11] Such a policy and the old Conservative Party's British political pedigree are alien to the new conservatism.

THE NEW CONSERVATIVE PARTY

There is no single genesis for the new Conservative Party: its roots lie in some elements of the populist agrarian revolt of the 1920s, the Social Credit phenomenon of the 1930s, the appearance of the Reform Party in the 1980s, and the demolition of the old Conservative Party in the 1990s. Social Credit, preaching the virtues of monetary reform, wedded it with messianic evangelicalism, its logo a green Christian cross on a white background. Ernest Manning, Alberta's premier for a quarter-century, reflected Social Credit's transmutation from assaulting to making peace with finance capital. He served as Alberta's anti-bank provincial treasurer in the 1930s but became a director of the Canadian Imperial Bank of Commerce in the 1960s when he urged the merger of Conservatives and Social Crediters into a new party that stressed "Social Conservative ideals and principles." He wrote of "the responsibility of governments to give first consideration to human beings as individuals (as persons) rather than to human beings in the aggregate." He deemed the family as the "most fundamental unit of human association," pointed to the public's "spiritual resources," and proclaimed "the Sovereignty of God." The "Social Conservative," wrote Manning, "will speak of a 'society of great individuals,' before he will speak of a 'great society,'" a term popular among welfare liberals and in the American Democratic administration in the 1960s.[12]

Social Credit disappeared but Manning's son Preston and his Reform Party resurrected the division among conservatives in the 1980s. Under Mulroney's old Conservatives, blatant favouritism for Quebec's aerospace industry at Manitoba's expense sparked Reform's creation and the new party smashed the old Conservative base in English Canada. The policy inclinations of Reform's activists, however, limited the party's appeal. A survey of the party's 1992 Assembly—attended by the elder Manning who termed it a "crusade"—showed that 99 percent agreed that government ought to reduce its deficit as much as possible, 96 percent thought the welfare state made people less willing to look after themselves, 98 percent opposed a constitutional veto for Quebec, and 97 percent opposed increased government efforts to further multiculturalism.[13] Reform and its successor, the Canadian Alliance, competed with the old Conservatives for the same minoritarian right-wing vote with failing results for both parties, but especially the old Conservatives, in the three elections between 1993 and 2000. Some policy convergence facilitated the parties' merger; electoral arithmetic compelled it. In 1997, the economic and fiscal planks in the old Conservative and Reform Party platforms were near carbon copies. Where they differed was on the recognition of Quebec's distinctiveness, bilingualism, immigration, and institutional reform. In the 2000 election, Clark's old Conservatives, with their only remaining electoral base in Atlantic Canada, somewhat tempered their market liberalism as they spoke of social safety nets and equalization payments.

The Conservative government's behaviour since 2006 betrays the new conservatism. Although they had denounced the Liberals as spendthrifts, Stephen Harper's Conservatives increased deficits and the national debt to unprecedented levels in an orgy of incontinent spending. The new Conservatives' first two budgets increased program spending by more than 7 percent annually at a time that inflation was running near 2 percent, and their spending continued to exceed inflation even before the recession of 2009. The Conservatives also expanded public sector employment at a higher rate than the Liberals had.[14] "Who would have thought that Harper, the former Reform MP, the noted fiscal hawk, the man who once led the right-wing National Citizens Coalition, would ever be the one who would recklessly plunge Canada into a sea of red ink?" lamented Gerry Nicholls, vice-president of the National Citizens' Coalition, which Harper headed before becoming the Conservative leader.

> It's no wonder Canada's conservative community, those Canadians who actually believe in things like minimal government and balanced budgets and fiscal prudence are currently in a state of shock... Stephen Harper was supposed to be their champion. He was the guy who was going to roll back the state, make government smaller and usher in a new conservative Canada. They expected Harper to be Canada's Ronald Reagan. What they got instead was Bob Rae.[15]

The new Conservatives have failed to instill a libertarian political culture in Canada. In opposition, they criticized the Liberals for keeping too tight a regulatory rein on banks, but as the world's financial system shook in 2008, the Conservatives praised those regulations. They offered huge subsidies to large corporate interests, which they had once condemned, took part ownership of General Motors and Chrysler, back-stopped banks on mortgage insurance, expanded the government's stable of regional development agencies, extended benefits for the unemployed, and, despite their criticisms of government-funded child-care spaces, increased funding for them.[16]

The Conservatives abandoned their putative populism and commitments to openness, accountability, and transparency. They closely manage the dissemination of information and govern in a top-down style more authoritarian and secretive than that of the Liberals whose behaviour on such issues they had castigated. Conservative MPs have acted as pawns of the party leader and not as delegates for their constituents. More than ever, cabinet ministers serve as the prime minister's servile minions, their every utterance vetted before delivery by his office. After condemning the patronage practices of the Liberals and pledging Senate reform, Harper appointed thirty-three unelected partisan Senators in less than five years. The Conservative promise of a public appointments commissioner has gone unfulfilled, and although the Conservatives created, as they had pledged, an ostensibly independent parliamentary budget office, it is leashed and starved for funding and staff.

Conservative policies flip-flopped across a range of issues. After he dismissed climate change and the Kyoto Protocol as a socialist fraud, Harper described global warming as "perhaps the greatest threat to confront the future of humanity today." After he beat the war drums on Canada's role in Afghanistan and vowed not to "cut and run," he asked a former Liberal foreign minister for policy direction and adopted the Liberals' position on military disengagement.[17] After he declared that his government would not sell out its human rights beliefs "to the almighty dollar" in dealing with China, he made improving ties with it a high priority and dispatched four ministers to kowtow there on four separate occasions in the space of four months in 2009.[18] The re-imagined Canada of the new conservatism's populist discourse had challenged the "politics of cultural recognition" with the principle of "universal citizenship"[19] and Harper's Reform Party had denigrated special status for Quebec, bilingualism, multiculturalism, Aboriginal self-government, and existing levels of immigration. He, however, moved a parliamentary motion to recognize the Québécois as a nation, requires all ministers to include French in their speeches, zealously courts ethno-religious communities, and has boosted immigration to record levels, not reduced it.

THE FUTURE: A DEAD END

In the 2006 election, the Conservatives eked out a plurality of seats and formed a minority government, but they only lurched ahead of the Liberals after the RCMP launched an investigation into a leak of the Liberal government's tax policy. Benefiting from the failings of the Liberals—in particular, the "sponsorship" scandal documented in a scathing judicial report—the Conservatives came to office not by virtue of their neoconservative philosophy but in spite of it. They made further gains in 2008 and in 2011, but their victories have been shallow in terms of changing the philosophical and policy inclinations of Canadians.

Despite the advantages of incumbency and their triggering an election in 2008 in violation of the spirit of their fixed-election date law, the Conservatives increased their support by only just over 1 percent from 2006. In 2011, they increased it by a further 2 percent. Their greatest strength lay precisely in those areas where Social Credit, Reform, and the old Conservatives had been strongest, the West. They are weakest where Reform and the old Conservatives since the 1960s had been weakest, the cities and Quebec. This suggests continuity, not dramatic change.

In the 2011 election, the Conservatives captured less than 40 percent of the vote. The four parties critical of neoconservatism and that elected MPs won about 60 percent. The number of Conservative voters in 2011 increased by over 600,000 over 2008, but the number of voters endorsing the social democratic NDP swelled by two million. A poll in the immediate aftermath of the election revealed that Conservative support had not increased—a usual occurrence for a party in the wake of an election victory—while NDP support grew to within three percentage points of the Conservatives.[20] To be sure, polls fluctuate but a Conservative Party that cannot attract more of the electorate will not easily reconfigure Canadians' values. The Conservatives have failed to persuade a majority of Canadians to embrace the neoconservative tonic of limited government. The party's philosophy will continue to fail unless more women, urban residents, and Quebeckers flock to the party's banner. The liberal-social democratic ethos of the other parties will continue to overwhelm neoconservative thinking, especially among women.

A majority election victory for the new Conservative Party is a necessary, but not sufficient, condition for the new conservative philosophy to prevail. As new Canadians settle in the New Canada of cosmopolitan, polyethnic, metropolitan cities, the Conservatives' Old Canada base—rural/small town, Protestant, English Canada—continues to shrivel. The Conservatives have potential for few further gains in English Canada's suburban and the exurban areas. In the 2008 election, they squandered their prospects in Quebec with their funding cuts for culture, their crime and punishment agenda, and their attack on Québécois nationalists as separatists. In 2011, they elected the fewest Quebec MPs of any governing majority party in Canadian history. "Canada is not yet a conservative or Conservative country," wrote Tom Flanagan, the 2004 Conservative national campaign director. Notwithstanding the Conservative victories of 2006 of 2008 or of 2011, "neither the philosophy of conservatism nor the party brand comes close to commanding majority support."[21] Citing Burke, Flanagan urged Harper's government to pursue "moderation," "inclusion," and "incrementalism." This revealed both a lingering touch of the old conservatism and the need to imitate liberal-social democratic ways as the path to electoral success.

Conservatism and the Conservative Party have had an embedded place in Canada's political culture, but the new conservatism of the late twentieth- and early twenty-first centuries appears to have stalled. Perhaps it has been a passing phenomenon. The appeal of the new conservatism is limited so long as Canadians invest in defining themselves by who they are not—Americans—and so long as the new conservatism is driven by similar ideas and demographic forces as those that drive American neoconservatives. The new Conservative Party's prospects only brighten when they behave as the opportunistic Liberals once did.

NOTES

1. Stephen McBride and John Shields, *Dismantling a Nation: The Transition to Corporate Rule in Canada*, 2nd ed. (Halifax: Fernwood, 1997), p. 18; and John Shields and B. Mitchell Evans, *Shrinking the State: Globalization and Public Administration "Reform"* (Halifax: Fernwood, 1998).

2. Timothy L. Thomas, "An Emerging Party Cleavage: Metropolis vs. the Rest," in Hugh G. Thorburn and Alan Whitehorn, eds., *Party Politics in Canada*, 8th ed. (Toronto: Prentice-Hall, 2001), ch. 30.

3. John Wilson, "The Red Tory Province: Reflections on the Character of the Ontario Political Culture," in Donald C. MacDonald, ed., *The Government and Politics of Ontario*, 2nd ed. (Toronto: Van Nostrand Reinhold, 1980).

4. Reg Whitaker, *A Sovereign Idea: Essays on Canada as a Democratic Community* (Montreal: McGill-Queen's University Press, 1992), p. 20.

5. Quoted in Colin Campbell and William Christian, *Parties, Leaders, and Ideologies in Canada* (Toronto: McGraw-Hill Ryerson, 1996), p. 52.

6. Lowell Murray, "Don't Do It, Peter," *The Globe and Mail*, June 23, 2003.

7. Thomas Walkom, "Still Feeling Jilted after Right-Wing Marriage: Many Unhappy with PC-Alliance Union," *The Toronto Star*, November, 12, 2005.

8. Gordon T. Stewart, "Political Patronage under Macdonald and Laurier, 1878–1911," *American Review of Canadian Studies* 10, no. 1 (1980), pp. 3–26.

9. George C. Perlin, *The Tory Syndrome: Leadership Politics in the Progressive Conservative Party* (Montreal: McGill-Queen's University Press, 1980).

10. Cy Gonick, *The Great Economic Debate* (Toronto: James Lorimer, 1987), p. 130.

11. Robert L. Stanfield, "Conservative Principles and Philosophy," in Paul Fox and Graham White, eds., *Politics: Canada*, 8th ed. (Toronto: McGraw-Hill Ryerson, 1995), pp. 307–311; and Rodney S. Haddow, *Poverty Reform in Canada, 1958–1978: State and Class Influence in Policy Making* (Montreal and Kingston: McGill-Queen's University Press, 1993), p. 167.

12. E.A. Manning, *Political Realignment* (Toronto: McClelland and Stewart, 1967), pp. 65–70.

13. Keith Archer and Faron Ellis, "Opinion Structure of Party Activists: The Reform Party of Canada," *Canadian Journal of Political Science* 27, no. 2 (June 1994), Table 5, pp. 295–297.

14. Bill Curry, "Performance Pay for Senior Bureaucrats Up Sharply," *The Globe and Mail*, August, 13, 2010; and Statistics Canada, "Employment and Average Weekly Earnings (including Overtime), Public Administration and All Industries," available at http://www40.statcan.gc.ca/l01/cst01/govt19a-eng.htm. Accessed Sept. 29, 2010.

15. Gerry Nicholls, "Et tu, Stephen?: Fiscal Conservatives Feel Betrayed by the Man They Thought was Their Champion," *The Gazette (Montreal),* February 4, 2009, available at http://www2.canada.com/montrealgazette/features/viewpoints/story.html?id=60fe5fd6-9f0e-49b3-804d-0b8f0d9788e9. Accessed Sept. 7, 2010.

16. James M. Flaherty, *The 2007 Budget Speech: Aspire to a Stronger, Safer, Better Canada* (Ottawa: Dept. of Finance, March 19, 2007), p. 6.

17. Quoted by Lawrence Martin, "Unlike George, Steve Keeps God to Himself", *The Globe and Mail*, July 5, 2007; and CBC News, "Canada Committed to Afghan Mission, Harper tells troops," March 13, 2006, available at http://www.cbc.ca/world/story/2006/03/13/harper_afghanistan060313.html. Accessed September 24, 2010.

18. CTV News, "Cda. Won't Appease China on Human Rights: Harper," November 15, 2006, available at http://www.ctv.ca/CTVNews/CTVNewsAt11/20061115/china_snub_061114/; and CBC News, "Harper Urged to Talk Human Rights with China," December 1, 2009, available at http://www.cbc.ca/world/story/2009/12/01/harper-china-visit.html. Accessed September 24, 2010.

19. Steve Patten, "The Reform Party's Re-imagining of Canada," *Journal of Canadian Studies* 34, no. 1 (Spring 1999), pp. 27–51.

20. Bruce Cheadle, "Poll Suggests NDP Election Day Support has Solidified," *Winnipeg Free Press*, June 2, 2011, available at http://www.winnipegfreepress.com/canada/breakingnews/123025923.html. Accessed June 2, 2011.

21. Tom Flanagan, *Harper's Team: Behind the Scenes in the Conservative Rise to Power* (Montreal and Kingston: McGill-Queen's University Press, 2007), p. 275.

✗ **NO**

Twenty-First Century Conservatives Can Continue to Succeed
FARON ELLIS

> In order that our free will may not be extinguished, I judge that it could
> be true that fortune is the arbiter of half our actions, but that she lets the
> other half, or nearly that, be governed by us.

> —Niccolo Machiavelli, *The Prince* (1513) XXV

Included in Machiavelli's message to sixteenth-century princes is advice that
contemporary political parties should heed: although they cannot control their
entire fate, they can control some of it. By making provisions to help with-
stand the ravages beset upon them by their opponents, they are better armed
to accomplish their primary goals: to guide public policy, voters, and public
discourse toward their objectives and away from their opponents'. For conservatives, this includes establishing a set of core principles that, after considerable
compromise by all the disparate and divergent interest that makes up the loosely
knit Canadian conservative movement, they can agree to champion as the best
way to achieve some of their objectives. For the Conservative Party of Canada,
the overall task is similar, but complicated by the structural requirement of
building those common objectives into an organization capable of fulfilling its
primary purpose: to successfully compete for votes in a manner that affords it
the opportunity to form a national government and implement policies based
on conservative principles. Ideologically, Canadian conservatism has been composed of an often fractious, complex mix of seemingly contradictory ideological
streams. Elements of Toryism, business liberalism, nationalism, and populism,
among others, have all enjoyed periods of support,[1] making Canadian conservatism, like most ideologies, a very amorphous entity. The Conservative Party of
Canada, on the other hand, is a political party, and parties are first and foremost
organizations. As organizations operating within a larger institutional context,
parties have different demands placed on them than do movements or ideologies.
As such, parties are subject to different pressures for accommodating the wide
variety of perspectives that underpin their overall electoral constituency. They are
also subject to standards of compromise and cooperation that are unique to them
as organizations, including deciding what constitutes their core ideology, values,
or principles. They must determine how much of each competing sub-ideology

will be represented and how far the organization will go in accommodating more peripheral elements. Attempting to accommodate too many peripheral elements often comes at the expense of fulfilling the party's ultimate purpose: successfully competing for votes.

The founding liberal-pluralist political culture in this country dictates that Canadian parties cannot afford to become too ideologically doctrinaire in either their policies or their leadership selection, at least not if their intentions are to form a national government. To a certain extent, this is what three-time Harper campaign manager Tom Flanagan expresses in his "Ten Commandments" of Conservative campaigning.[2] In particular, he advocates *moderation* because "Canada is not yet a conservative or Conservative country."[3] Citing game theory, he reminds Conservatives that if they veer too far to the right of the median voter they will not win elections. Note Flanagan's somewhat hopeful use of the term *yet*. He does not say that Canada will never be a conservative country, only that in 2007, it has not *yet* become one. In order to move the median voter closer to conservatism, Flanagan advocates an *incrementalism* in which conservatives must be satisfied with making progress in small, practical steps. In allowing that "sweeping visions have a place in intellectual discussion," he is unequivocal that they are "toxic in practical politics."[4]

There is considerable truth in Flanagan's analysis. In particular, it is true that practising politicians must effectively mediate competing political demands much more so than do even the most practically minded academics writing from the somewhat detached isolation of academe. Also, minority governments must be particularly cautious given their precarious existence. But it is also important to remember that neither can parties become so amorphous, or unfocused, as to be devoid of any tangible identity onto which voters can grasp and thereby attach their partisan and voting loyalties. In acknowledging that Conservatives cannot be seen as straying too far to the right, they also cannot attempt to extend their support base so broadly as to appear to have no principles at all, a real risk the editors of this book have alerted us to in previous editions, and exactly what *Maclean's* national editor Andrew Coyne accused the Harper Conservatives of doing during their first five years in government.[5] So complete has been the betrayal of conservative principles, argues Coyne, that "conservatism is not just dead but, it appears, forgotten."[6] Others, including *Maclean's* national affairs columnist Paul Wells tends to agree more with Flanagan. In conceding that the Conservatives have not adopted as many traditionally conservative principles as many of its core supporters may have hoped for, Wells argues that during their first five years in government the Conservatives have nonetheless made progress by "chipping away at the foundations of the idea of government the Liberals built over decades."[7]

It will be argued here that although the Harper Conservatives have indeed made progress, for a variety of reasons—their minority government status, the need for incrementalism as opposed to revolution, and the vast conspiracy of enemies, to mention but a few—they have not yet fully defined their core identity. If they choose to do so based on libertarian-conservative principles, by more forcefully championing a limited-state that promotes not only economic liberty, but also moral and social liberty, they will be in an even better position to deflect charges such as those levelled by fellow conservatives like Coyne, as well as those from their more traditional foes. Further, subscribing to a clearly defined core identity need not come at the expense of electoral success. Here, it is important to remember that even when attempting to win a majority of seats in the Canadian House of Commons, a party need not command majority support within the voting electorate. That is, it need not dilute its core principles to the point of confusion and inconsistency in order to appeal to a grand coalition of voters. A minimal winning coalition is not only all that is required, as evidenced by the 2011 election results,[8] but they also tend to be more manageable and stable over the long term. The Liberals demonstrated this thoroughly throughout the last half of the twentieth century and acutely from 1993 to 2000 when they won three consecutive majority governments, never once achieving more than 42 percent of support among the roughly two-thirds of eligible Canadian voters who chose to cast ballots.[9]

There is also considerable truth in Professor Wiseman's arguments, so much so that we can begin by conceding half, or nearly that much, of his position. He is correct in his assertion that conservatives fail when they pursue an Old Canada vision with values rooted in the nineteenth century and that survive primarily in rural Canada. He is also correct in his assertion that conservatism will continue to be at best a default option for voters who tire of corrupt or arrogant Liberal governments if Conservatives continue to be united by no greater principles than their mutual distaste for Liberal regimes. As long as Conservatives refused to embrace the overriding, mainstream, liberal political culture of contemporary Canada, including the primacy of pluralism and individual rights, they were destined to suffer from a schizophrenia that exposed their unreadiness to govern. Denying that liberalism is the foundation of Canadian political culture, and is here to stay, was a prescription for failure, while simply attempting to rebuild previously failed coalitions would have been as irrational as it had been unproductive.

But the continuing hegemony of liberalism in Canada need not necessitate continued Liberal Party hegemony. As Wiseman correctly concedes, the Canadian Liberal Party has shown itself to be at best a liberal–social democratic pretender. To that we can now add that it has been exposed as such and therefore rejected by voters seeking the real thing in the NDP. The Liberals have also become overly statist at a time when many middle-class Canadians are questioning the limits of a purposive state. In their quest to provide continuing rationale for a strong national government, and federal powers more generally, Liberals have been seemingly obsessed with providing Canadian voters with statist responses to most social, economic, and political issues, real or imagined. In the process, the federal Liberals have become so illiberal that they can no longer legitimately claim the mantle of liberty's defenders. These conditions all but necessitated a libertarian-conservative response to Liberal party electoral hegemony.

It is here where Conservatives can continue to succeed. By consistently following a few simple principles, albeit most involving ongoing tough choices, considerable discipline, and tremendous resolve, Conservatives can complete the project of building a mainstream party around a core set of libertarian-conservative principles that will enhance their ability to consistently compete for power in the twenty-first century. This has required a leap of faith for some. But as the evidence and rationale that follows will demonstrate, accommodating Canadian liberalism's new manifestations in a complex, urban, pluralistic polity is not as radical a transformation for Conservatives as it may have first appeared. The libertarian core of both the former Reform and Alliance Parties, as well as the disparate remaining non-Tory elements of the Progressive Conservative Party have several common foundational elements upon which a natural governing party can be built—and to which many mainstream voters can be recruited. Quite clearly, the Harper-led Conservative governments have gravitated toward some of these principles in the short term. As discussed below, their securing of a majority government in the 2011 federal election has some analysts already describing them as Canada's next governing dynasty.[10] While one majority victory does not a dynasty make, they have won three successive elections and made significant gains in areas and among voters once thought to be far out of reach for conservative parties. What remains to be seen is whether or not the Conservative Party of Canada has the vision and discipline to continue building an enduring political institution upon those foundations.

VARIOUS KINDS OF CONSERVATISM

All the forms of conservatism that have emerged in all the federal and provincial party systems over the years can be distilled down to three:

1. Toryism of the nineteenth century—combining a reverence for tradition with support for state maintenance of an ordered and structured society—that in various incarnations sputtered through the twentieth century.

2. Libertarian conservatism in the form of nineteenth-century liberalism—with its emphasis on economic liberty, free markets, capitalism, and a limited state—that reappeared in the late twentieth century as neoconservatism or neoliberalism.

3. Social conservatism of the nineteenth century—with its emphasis on traditional, primarily religious moral values and opposition to advancing liberal pluralism—that manifested itself in the late twentieth century as the religious right.

Innumerable hybrids of one or more elements of each have appeared in the various parties, movements, and factions that have called themselves conservative over the past 150 years.

The most important dimensions of conservatism at the beginning of the twenty-first century revolve around the relative unity of conservatives in support of fiscal conservatism and the need for dismantling late twentieth-century state-sponsored "left-wing" social engineering public policy. There exists, however, a wide gulf between libertarian and social conservatives on moral issues, and each has recently taken up common cause with populists in an effort at improving their fortunes. Each errs in doing so, but for different reasons, which shall be elaborated upon later.

Conservatives should relegate Toryism, with its accompanying statism, to the dustbin of history or to the Liberals and their socialist allies. Social conservatism should be tolerated, in the same manner in which all competing ideas should be tolerated. It should not, however, be adopted as part of the defining identity of the national Conservative Party. Hybrids must also be rejected for practical and strategic reasons; most important among these being the propensity for hybrids to be so amorphous that they provide conservatism's enemies with frequent, numerous opportunities to distort and mischaracterize the Conservative Party. Only by defining a core libertarian-conservative identity will Conservatives find the ideological consistency necessary to maintain a successful, enduring national electoral coalition.

REFLECTIONS ON THE WISEMAN "DOOMED TO FAILURE" THESIS

Many grains of truth are contained in Nelson Wiseman's review of Canadian conservative history. Most students of Canadian politics are introduced early in their undergraduate studies to the Hartz-Horowitz "Tory touch" fragment thesis and to Wiseman's application of the thesis to the study of Canadian prairie political culture.[11] Both continue to serve as exemplary readings when conceptualizing and teaching Canadian political culture, as much for their utility in engendering critical thinking as for their other virtues. The thesis posits that political cultures in new societies are primarily fragments cast off from the European ideological dialectic. Separated from the original dialectic, new societies lose the impetus for change and remain frozen fragments of the prevailing ideology that existed at the time of their founding. Having been founded when liberalism dominated, Canadian and American political cultures are primarily liberal. But because Canada contained a quasi-feudal French element as well as an English Tory element, the Canadian political culture, although primarily liberal, is touched with Toryism, thereby making a synthesis to socialism a possibility. Because a full critique of the thesis is outside of the parameters of this debate, readers are directed to previous rebuttals[12] and the commentary here will be restricted to how this historical thesis impacts on the contemporary debate about the future of conservatism and the Conservative Party of Canada.

Initially, pining for the virtues of a mythical Toryism, while at the same time portraying all libertarian elements of conservatism as inherently vicious, is in keeping with the standard statist attack on the "new right." It is typically the pur-view of hostile academics and media pundits, but not necessarily that of Canadian voters. It is no coincidence that the death of the Progressive Conservative Party, and by default the "Tory touch" mythology, was bemoaned far more by the former than the latter. After all, without a party vehicle to which the myth can remain attached, the Tory element of the dialectic appears more difficult to substantiate and the Marxist tautological house of cards begins to collapse. In effect, without Toryism, the desired end state of socialism becomes unattainable. Liberalism's triumph leaves Toryism a relic of the past, and socialism a never-to-be-achieved fantasy. But the next generation of Marxist academics need not despair. They will likely find enough anti-American and statist Toryism within the Liberals and NDP to keep the myth alive. The fact that a wide variety of left-wing pundits see so much to mourn in the death of the Progressive Conservative Party should give conservatives cause for celebration. For it was the Tory element of the coalition that failed conservatism in the 1980s and has been at least partially responsible for keeping them from succeeding since. Conservatives should bid a fond farewell to the vanguard of former Progressive Conservative "red Tories" and rejoice at the prospect of extinguishing them and their fellow travellers from their ranks.

Secondly, it is correct to assert that if the new Conservatives were to have remained geographically anchored in the West and rural ridings, they would have likely been destined to perpetual opposition. But as demonstrated by the results from last three federal elections, history need not dictate a predetermined future. Canadian voters are characterized by a number of traits and among these is their well-deserved reputation for vote switching.[13] The persistent shattering, rebuilding, or creating anew of electoral coalitions and partisan alignments is one of the most enduring features of Canadian party systems.[14] Not only do Canadian voters regularly realign their partisan attachments in tectonic shifts that shatter the old order, they also exhibit a high degree of vote switching between non-monumental elections. Wiseman implies this when he states that Toronto used to be a Conservative bastion but is now a Liberal fortress. Or at least it was until the 2011 election when the Conservatives won nine of twenty-one seats within the city, and swept all but one of the GTA's suburban ridings on their way to winning over two-thirds of the provinces' seats. They did so by appealing to large num-bers of voters who have tired of bearing an increasingly disproportionate burden for the multiplicity of statist schemes designed to address issues that affect them only marginally, or not at all. Given that the Conservatives offered voters who were suffering most from the economic crisis the least statist economic plan, and although it may be premature to declare Ontario a conservative province, voters there have clearly indicated their willingness to "experiment" with becoming a Conservative province.

Not surprisingly, many who switched to the Conservatives were previous Lib-eral voters. Evidence abounds suggesting that the Liberal coalition, although consistently the largest, was increasingly the most susceptible to erosion while Conservative voters tend to be much more loyal. For example, while the Conservatives brought 83 percent of their 2004 voters back to them in the 2006 election, the Liberals retained only 53 percent of their 2004 voters. Further, the 2006 pattern was not simply a temporary manifestation of the Liberal's misfortunes. Since 1993, the Liberals consistently retained less than two-thirds of their former voters between elections while the Reform-Alliance-Conservative parties have consistently retained over 80 percent of their voters.[15] This should also give pause to those who believe the Conservative coalition would be most susceptible to fracturing under various hypothetical electoral reform or party competition scenarios.

With that said, if the new Conservatives do not succeed in defining a libertarian-conservative vision for these voters, but instead allow their opponents to define conservatism as inhospitable to the individual and collective ambitions of central Canadian urbanites, Conservatives will not continue to succeed. Opponents will use simplistic but often effective guilt-by-association tactics such as those marshalled against Reform (familial and/or ideological: what former Alberta premiers Aberhart and Manning stood for in the 1930s is equivalent to what Preston Manning stood for in the 1990s);[16] the Canadian Alliance (operational and/or ideological: Stockwell Day is not competent at least partially because he is beholden to the religious right);[17] and the Conservatives (dictatorial and/or conspiratorial: Steven Harper is a control mongering thug[18] who is quite likely under the influence of the vast, U.S.A.-based, religious, right-wing conspiracy).[19] Attempting to equate what Preston Manning advocated in the 1990s to what his father or Aberhart advocated in the 1930s and 1940s stretched credibility too far to be effective.[20] But Day's use of social conservative activists and their organizational muscle in his Alliance leadership campaigns legitimized the "too scary" stigma, adding significantly to his inability to establish a positive public image of his own making.[21] And although Harper's electoral prospects suffered from the "vast right-wing conspiracy" attacks more in the 2004 election[22] than in 2006,[23] 2008,[24] or 2011,[25] the overall political problem remains: until very recently, conservatism's opponents have been more successful at defining conservative parties' identities than have conservatives. The "reactionary agents of their own privilege" case has been repeatedly made, and it has repeatedly stuck. When supported by frequent, often outlandish public comments made primarily but not exclusively by undisciplined Members of Parliament, an image of Reform and the Alliance emerged that often didn't mesh with members' and voters' core values. In both cases, the parties tended to be mischaracterized as much more socially conservative, more pro-American, and more anti-French than were either their memberships or their voting bases.[26]

Professor Wiseman's selective use of the attitudinal data that Archer and I collected at the 1992 Reform Assembly is instructive on these points. He correctly points out that virtually all Reform delegates thought the federal government should seek to reduce its deficit as much as possible—neither a surprising nor unreasonable finding given the soft question (standard at the time) and the fact that the federal government was continuing to borrow between $30 and $40 billion annually on its way to building a half-trillion dollar national government debt. He also quite correctly characterizes Reformers as fiscal conservatives. But little evidence exists to support the characterization of Reform as antiabortion and therefore upholding the "moral cudgels of the Old Canada." Clearly, Reformers held solidly libertarian, not social conservative, positions on the abortion choice issue by a two-to-one margin (61.5 percent agreed abortion choice is a private matter to be decided by a woman, 30.9 percent disagreed, and 7.5 percent were uncertain).[27] Opinion structure among delegates attending the Alliance's only convention in 2002 was also clearly pro-choice and not significantly different from Reform (56.2 percent agreed, 34.8 percent disagreed, and 9 percent were uncertain).[28] Delegates to the 2005 Conservative convention adopted as policy, by a margin of 55 percent to 45 percent, the most libertarian position possible by committing the party to not restricting abortion choice.[29] Post-convention survey results indicate that the majority of Conservative delegates in all provinces except Saskatchewan were pro-choice.[30] During the 2008 election campaign, Harper reinforced the convention delegates' position by clearly stating that his government "will not open the abortion debate and will not allow another opening of the abortion debate." He has consistently repeated that message in every election campaign since and has lived up to that commitment for the first five years in government.

Yet the mischaracterizations continue, are strategic, and aptly demonstrate the challenges faced by Reform and the Alliance. The Conservatives have only begun to address the challenge of positively defining a vision for conservatism before the many entrenched interests—who correctly view conservatism as a threat to their state-sponsored privilege—define conservatism's public image negatively. The fact that their opponents' tactics are as predictable as they are transparent makes that task somewhat easier for Conservatives than it was for either Reform or the Alliance.

Finally, despite his general characterization of libertarian conservatives as atomistic hedonists with no collective consciousness, and the corresponding implication that socialists have a monopoly on what constitutes social justice, Wiseman is correct to state that conservatives tend to be relatively united on economics but divided on moral matters. More problematic is his inclusion of "the role of the state" on his list of "conservatives' common objectives." While it is true that general agreement exists about reducing the state's capacity to excessively engage in socialist economic engineering, the various factions within conservatism are bitterly divided over the state's role in legislating moral issues—a point Wiseman concedes about the moral divisions but not about the state's role in defining or regulating moral decision making.[31]

The problem for libertarian conservatives, and many voters who are intrigued by but have not yet voted for conservative parties, is their suspicion that social conservatives want to simply replace left-wing economic social engineering with right-wing moral engineering. Libertarian conservatives are as opposed to the latter as they are to the former. They share these sentiments with growing legions of Canadian voters who have become either suspicious of or hostile to forty years of statist public policy and the corresponding price tag, but have repeatedly demonstrated that they are more distrustful of right-wing moral engineering than they are of left-wing social engineering. Which brings us to the choice Conservatives face: which type of party and which vision of conservatism are they prepared to champion to Canadian voters over the long-term? The contention here is that a libertarian-conservative vision within the mainstream of Canadian liberalism offers the most effective strategy for continued Conservative success. While this analysis will not presume to prescribe what specific policy measures Conservatives should adopt, it will conclude by offering a few suggestions as to the direction their policy positioning should take as the party continues to define its identity and its electoral constituency. It will also review and evaluate a selection of the initial steps the party has taken toward (or away from) achieving that goal.

In essence, Conservatives need to clearly articulate and begin implementing fiscally conservative, non-statist economic policy. They need to define a libertarian core vision that includes drawing a line in the sand across which social conservatives will not be allowed to drag the party. And most importantly, they must avoid the *populist trap* by setting clear limits on the party's use of populist decision-making mechanisms.

ESTABLISHING LEGITIMATE FISCAL CONSERVATIVE CREDENTIALS

The Harper Conservative governments have at best a mixed record on establishing legitimate fiscal conservative credentials. After inheriting an enviable fiscal situation from the Liberals, the first Harper government appeared to view successes in battling the evils of annual deficits as a victory in the war on socialist fiscal policy and was therefore satisfied with simply using unanticipated surpluses to marginally reduce the national debt. They have not yet presented Canadians with a comprehensive, bold, or clear fiscally conservative economic platform that includes substantial, broadly based middle-class income tax cuts. Spending increases in its first three budgets rivalled that of the previous three Liberal budgets.[32] Despite rhetoric to the contrary, the government did not deliver broad-based income tax cuts. They instead offered up a 2 percent reduction in the GST and a series of selective "boutique" tax cuts in attempting to win over targeted voters. But in order to finance these minor reductions, and the laudable further reductions in business taxes announced in the government's October 2007 *Economic Statement*, Canadians' personal tax burden is increasing and is projected to rise to its highest level in fifteen years by 2012–13.[33] This is far from satisfactory given the prominence fiscal conservatism plays in uniting the various conservative factions.

The Conservative's most noteworthy fiscally conservative pronouncements came in its ill-fated November 2008 economic statement that contained no massive stimulus program similar to what other national governments were planning during the initial stages of the 2008–2009 economic crisis.[34] However, in a post-election fit of strategic hubris, the government attached a clause to the economic statement that would have eliminated per-vote public subsidies to political parties. By the time the government regained its footing after having come close to being defeated and replaced by an unconventional coalition of the combined opposition parties, the full international efforts to forestall an economic collapse were well underway. The Conservatives too became Keynesians, offering up a generous stimulus package that included bailouts for the North American auto sector, support for Canadian banks (although they didn't need it), and massive infrastructure spending, all financed by deficits originally predicted to exceed $30 billion per year for two years and eventually rising above $50 billion.[35] The net result was too much for conservative critics such as Coyne, who declared the death of conservatism in Canada,[36] but was rationalized by others, including Wells. Citing the Conservatives' cancelling of the Liberals' statist child care plans and expensive Aboriginal policies in the Kelowna Accord as evidence, Wells deployed the last arrow in supporting conservatives' quivers: that the situation would have been much worse under a Liberal government and that indeed the Conservatives were making real, albeit modest, policy changes that were incrementally shifting the political culture to the right.[37] A corollary can be added that it would have been unreasonable to expect any Canadian government to willingly pay the political price of standing on the sidelines while the American government bailed out its auto sector and other G20 countries engaged in an orgy of economic stimulus.

Be that as it may, by focusing, (or being forced to focus) on achieving strategic, short-term electoral gain, the Conservatives have not yet provided a comprehensive vision for a limited state that most of its core supporters agree should underpin a conservative economic agenda. Although the Harper governments should be given credit for not being reckless, and thereby partially inoculating themselves against charges of extremism or of harbouring a radical right-wing economic agenda, their fiscal policies have not been nearly bold enough to meet even minimum expectations from most of their core electoral base. Conservatives should rise to the challenge of living up to their rhetoric about Canadians being overtaxed and provide meaningful evidence that they take their sloganeering seriously. If public opinion is not yet fully onside with this agenda, it is incumbent upon Conservatives to convince more voters of the wisdom contained in their vision rather than shirk from it and yield the economic agenda to their competitors. Conservatives should emulate past successes

where they have led rather than followed public opinion on conservative economic policy. The battles against deficits and the fights to achieve free trade
should serve as reminders of how voters have handsomely rewarded politicians
who demonstrate leadership.

Conservatives must also be cautious about being further distracted in their
economic policy development by national unity or regionalism issues. Most
importantly, they must resist the temptation to adopt "special case" exemptions
from the limited-state agenda for the sake of vote buying, traditionally in Quebec
or Atlantic Canada but now also in Ontario.[38] The mobilization strategy for all
regions of the country should be based on conviction of principle and the consistency and comprehensiveness of the vision rather than opportunistic piecemeal
regional graft. Dedication to the rule of constitutional law, including respect
for the division of federal powers, is consistent with a libertarian, non-statist
approach to economic issues, with an overall agenda of reducing centralized
social engineering, and in support of provincial equality and autonomy. Corporate
welfare in the form of subsidies to regionally based industries, hugely disproportionate equalization asymmetry, and regionally structured employment insurance
programs should be as anathematic to Conservatives as are billion-dollar gun
registry bureaucracies and affirmative action agendas.[39]

DEFINE THE CORE LIBERTARIAN IDENTITY

Conservatives should adopt social and moral policies that are consistent with their
economic positions. That is, if Conservatives can justify limiting the state from
excessively interfering in Canadians' economic lives, they should also be able to
justify, with equal conviction, the legitimacy of limiting the state from excessively interfering in Canadians' personal lives. By boldly articulating the moral
legitimacy of individual liberty, the rule of law, political freedom, responsive and
accountable governing institutions, and free political expression, Conservatives
can succeed in defining an identity for themselves that is consistent, principled,
and enduring. Social conservatives need to be assured that they are welcome in
the coalition,[40] but they also need to be reminded that the planned dismantling of
left-wing social engineering will not be accompanied by a corresponding increase
in right-wing moral engineering. Ensuring that this libertarian core philosophy
is established and clearly communicated is both honourable—in that it will allow
social conservatives to make informed decisions about their participation—and
necessary to continue attracting moderate voters who are still repelled by the
possibility of a social conservative hidden agenda. Social conservatives need to
understand that by remaining within the mainstream of the Conservative coalition they are likely to achieve about half of what they want, or nearly that much.
But social conservative zealots who refuse to defer to party policy, or who plan to
continue championing their moral causes at the expense of the greater electoral

good of the party, should be thoroughly, swiftly, and efficiently extinguished from the ranks of the Conservative Party.

Conservatives began making progress toward libertarian principles and away from social conservative principles at their 2005 policy convention.[41] The Harper government quickly followed up with its tactically brilliant and strategically adroit handling of the same-sex marriage issue. Given that opinion among party activists was running three-to-one against same-sex marriage,[42] and Harper had committed to campaign in support of those opinions during his speech at the party's first policy convention, he had little option but to include opposition to the Liberal's same-sex marriage legislation in the 2006 election campaign. But the way in which he approached the issue should be considered a textbook example of how to achieve both short-term tactical electoral advantage and long-term strategic positioning. In announcing on the first day of the 2006 election campaign that his government would hold a free vote on the same-sex marriage issue, Harper achieved the former by defusing the issue early. But even more impressive was the decision to hold a free vote on the issue, virtually guaranteeing that the motion would be defeated, allowing the Conservatives to put the issue behind them. The transparency of the tactical decision was obvious to all but the most zealous social conservatives. To ensure that the motion would not succeed, it was written to include enough seemingly contradictory provisions to allow MPs on either side of the issue vote against it based on one or another of its provisions. When the parliamentary vote was held in December of 2006, Conservative MP support was sufficiently muted that the caucus was correctly accused of "merely going through the motions" of fulfilling an election promise.[43] The Prime Minister then put the issue to rest by declaring that the "decisive result" had determined the issue once and for all, and that he did not anticipate "reopening this question in the future." Harper also poured cold water on any hope of a compensatory motion to strengthen religious freedoms. Ardent social conservatives such as the Canadian Family Action Coalition were predictably outraged, and reacted to the government's "betrayal" of social conservatism with declarations that "their" party had abandoned them. Those reactions enhanced an already successful strategy by further distancing the Conservatives from organized social conservative interests and their overall policy agenda. Further evidence of how far Conservatives have moved on this dimension came during the 2011 election campaign, when several prominent social conservatives publicly bemoaned their exclusion from the Conservative's election agenda and therefore from the campaign issue matrix more generally.[44]

The Conservatives have also made considerable progress in attracting voters from formerly inhospitable enclaves such as new and ethnic Canadians.[45] Libertarian conservatives should follow up on this successful political strategy by making an articulate case for the moral legitimacy of pluralism. Although Canadian conservatives have succeeded in making their opposition to state-sponsored social programs well known, because their opposition extends to programs that are targeted at identifiable groups they have been much less successful at defending themselves against charges that their lack of support for government sponsorship of specific groups equates to hostility toward the groups themselves. It is here where libertarians have failed Canadian conservatism most: by not countering the charges of intolerance with a staunch defence of the diversity that is by definition a necessary component of pluralism.

Liberal pluralism entails a diversification of power and the existence of a plurality of organizations that are both independent and non-inclusive. Central to this is a limited state that leaves individuals free to voluntarily enter into multiple associations with others. But it is yet more. Pluralism entails not only the recognition and articulation of diversity or differentiation: it assumes a particular belief content that contains its own morally authoritative claim on legitimacy. In other words, pluralism is a normative as well as a descriptive concept. Pluralism asserts that not only do differences exist, but also that difference itself is a moral good. Difference rather than likeness, dissent instead of unanimity, and choice above conformity are all fundamental to pluralism. Advocating for the liberty to voluntarily enter into non-inclusive associations without state interference requires the recognition of competing associations with which one may choose not to associate. Libertarians need to further argue that these choices and associations are private and that the state should not be making decisions about which groups are to be publicly sponsored and which are not. But in advocating for private choice, a diversity of competing perspectives is assumed. Libertarians owe it to conservatism to firmly establish that Conservatives are as supportive of diversity and choice in private moral matters as they are supportive of private religious or economic associations. Libertarians must begin to vigorously counter all charges to the contrary from both within and outside of the conservative movement.

For the most part, Prime Minister Harper has taken the lead on this dimension, albeit incrementally and primarily on the international front. Examples include his government's unyielding support for Israel at the expense of its non-liberal democratic neighbours, his hectoring of China over its human rights record, and his lectures to Latin and South American political leaders.[46] Even after his approach was credited with Canada losing its 2010 attempt to reassume a temporary seat on the UN Security Council—the first rejection of a Canadian bid in the organization's history—during a visit to Eastern Europe Harper stuck to his principles and denounced the authoritarian tendencies of the new Ukrainian president. All of this makes a speech he delivered to a Manning Centre for Building Democracy conference in 2009 that much more curious. In addressing fellow conservatives, the Prime Minister attacked libertarians as he attempted to enunciate his vision of conservatism based on the "3-Fs" of freedom, faith, and family. He situated his brand of conservatism somewhere in the moderate middle between big-spending Liberals and near-anarchist (in his view) libertarians. Although clumsily reasoned and delivered, inconsistent with his previous publicly stated principles, and easily refuted by libertarians who until that moment thought they were kindred with the Prime Minister's true philosophical dispositions, the speech did serve to illustrate two important features of the current state of libertarianism within Canadian conservatism. Initially, as well articulated by the *National Post's* Terence Corcoran, the speech signalled that Harper viewed libertarians as a greater threat to his incrementalist approach than are social conservatives.[47] Further, the swift and widespread negative reaction to the speech by many conservatives who do not typically describe themselves as libertarian—but began to do so as a result of this challenge—demonstrates the potential for growth if conservative principles are packaged in libertarian logic and rhetoric. This point was not lost on several erstwhile successors to Harper, including Conservative cabinet minister Maxime Bernier.[48]

AVOID THE POPULIST TRAP

Both social conservatives and libertarians have periodically attached themselves to populism. In doing so, the various elements of conservatism created a populist trap that had the effect of limiting their electoral success. Social conservatives frequently embraced populism in the naive hope that direct democracy mechanisms would somehow help them stem the tide of an increasingly secular, liberal political culture. Libertarians, although philosophically opposed to social conservative moralizing, did not fear the consequences of putting their differences to the test of a populist dispute-resolution mechanism because doing so usually wasn't much of a risk on the policy front. Libertarians know that under most direct democracy scenarios, they will come out winners when the mainstream liberal-pluralist political culture expresses its collective will in favour of rights, autonomy of individuals, freedom of choice, and liberty. A referendum on same-sex marriages today would likely maintain the status quo. A vote on abortion would be a slam-dunk in favour of choice. But in not fearing the outcome of populist decisions, libertarians too often and too easily surrender the moral legitimacy of their principles at the same time as they seemingly abandon their very legitimate concerns about the potential for majority tyranny. By legitimizing the populist dispute-resolution mechanism, libertarians legitimize the majoritarian principles contained in them, and thereby legitimize the potential for the suppression of individual rights, autonomy, choice, and liberty; so long as it is done democratically. Libertarians should stop surrendering to populist expediency and begin a concerted defence of libertarian pluralism.

Populism has also been thought to offer conservatives an escape from having to take firm stances on moral issues so as to not alienate one or the other key elements of the contemporary coalition.[49] And herein lays the populist trap. It is a function of both excessive cleverness and cowardice to not adopt firm positions on divisive policy domains. By substituting populist direct democracy decision-making mechanisms for firm policy stances, conservatives institution-alize unknowns into their platforms and their parties' identities. By definition, direct democracy contains a quality of the unknown, for if a party's policy plat-form dictates the eventual public policy outcome, the direct democracy decision-making exercise is meaningless. Conversely, institutionalizing direct democracy decision making severely restricts the party from taking firm positions on con-troversial issues when needed, most importantly during election campaigns. The latter creates uncertainty in the minds of voters. No one can say for sure what the party stands for because, prior to consulting the people, it does not know itself where it stands. More importantly, the institutionalized uncertainty affords the party's opponents ample opportunity to fill in the unknowns with negatives, especially when supported by the often-extreme utterances of undisciplined party members. It also serves to deny Conservatives the ammunition needed to defend their positions with any certainty, clarity, or conviction. No party can afford to turn over the definition of its own identity to its opponents. New parties with high levels of unknown quantities can afford it the least.

The populist trap plagued Reform in its attempt to expand its base outside of western Canada. It helped turn much of the Alliance's 2000 election campaign into a fountain of comedic material and political ridicule. Harper has so far successfully avoided building a populist trap of his own making—witness the noticeable lack of advocacy for a referendum to resolve the same-sex marriage or abortion issues—but to some extent he has suffered from a residual populist trap hangover from the Reform/Alliance era. It stalled Conservative momentum in the 2004 election and quite possibly was the single biggest issue to forestall their ascension to government at that time. Since then Harper has increasingly adopted a libertarian position when discussing populism. His September 2007 speech to the United Nations Council on Foreign Relations is instructive both for its critical, and at times hostile treatment of populism as well as for its messaging. At one point he all but equates "political populism and authoritarianism." And while the content of the speech was primarily directed toward Latin American nations, he concluded by admonishing the North Americans in the audience that this is not simply a problem for the developing countries: "[T]here is nowhere in the hemisphere that those forces [populism, nationalism, and protectionism] can do more real danger than those forces in the United States itself," and by extension, also in Canada.[50] This speech provides the best example to date of what many conservatives believed to be the real Steven Harper, at least in as much as it is illustrative of his thinking and public pronouncements while he was an opposi-tion MP and while he served as president of the libertarian-conservative National Citizens Coalition.[51]

The Conservative Party would be wise to carefully consider their leader's words and limit their proposed use of referenda to only constitutional or other grand institutional changes. Free parliamentary votes can remain a symbolic aspect of the overall platform, but should not be relied on so frequently that it delegitimizes using the "whip" when important and often divisive matters of core principle need to be acted upon. As the Harper government has demonstrated, its Members of Parliament and other party officials must exercise the discipline necessary to act as a cohesive organization, thereby providing Canadians with the assurances that they are competent enough to continue governing. Doctrinaire populists, and those willing to use populism as an excuse for a lack of discipline, should be told respectfully but firmly that their opinions would be better expressed through advocacy groups than from within a party organization, and their presence within the Conservative party should be extinguished.

As part of this process, Conservatives must judiciously avoid the temptation to enlist help from mercenary interest groups: social conservative, populist, or otherwise. They tend to be the most undisciplined of all associates, will tarnish the party's image, and will abandon it when their most zealous pursuits are not realized. Their potential for short-term electoral help is dwarfed by the detriment they cause to the long-term objectives of establishing a broadly based coalition built upon a libertarian-conservative core. And once associated with their causes, it is difficult for the party to overcome the negative impression that will have been implanted in the minds of many voters. Trying to extricate the negativity by purging itself of these associations at a later date will likely also prove futile. Few elections have been won on the slogan "You can trust us…now that we have turned on our former friends."

CONCLUSION

In the short span of only eight years since the merger of the Canadian Alliance and the Progressive Conservative Parties, Stephen Harper and the Conservatives have fundamentally altered the federal political landscape in Canada. To their credit, they have done so by successfully avoiding the populist trap and resisting the temptation to enlist social conservative mercenaries. Work remains on building the libertarian-conservative identity while even more effort is needed to establish legitimate fiscal conservative credibility. But they have built the most successful and effective political machine in Canadian federal politics on their way to establishing one of the most stable electoral coalitions any Canadian conservative party has cobbled together in generations.[52] They turned marginal gains in voter support into maximum seat gains in the 2011 election and clearly demonstrated that the Conservative Party of Canada has taken another important step toward building the foundations for an enduring and competitive national political party. They won seats in every province and increased their vote in each of them except Quebec on their way to winning their first majority government. They continued to gain support from new Canadians and penetrated deeply into most urban centres outside of Quebec, including Toronto. Indeed, so successful were the Conservatives that even Andrew Coyne was among the plethora of commentators marvelling at their accomplishments,[53] with some venturing to call them the next natural governing party.[54]

Rather than denying the continued progression of liberal pluralism in Canada, Conservatives have succeeded by incrementally embracing it. They have staked out reasonably clear positions in defence of individual liberty while their leader has consistently and articulately promoted the virtues of pluralism. By and large, they have sided with individual choice in opposition to an expanded state presence in the day-to-day lives of Canadians. By more fully eschewing both left-wing social engineering and right-wing moral engineering, by standing in defence of liberty in moral as well as economic affairs, Conservatives can further define a place for conservatism in the mainstream of Canada's liberal-pluralist political culture. If carefully organized and executed with discipline, the Conservative Party of Canada has the potential to end Liberal Party hegemony and establish themselves as legitimate contenders to become Canada's natural governing party for the twenty-first century.

NOTES

1. For a concise introduction to these and other issues involving ideology and parties in Canada, see Faron Ellis and Heather MacIvor, *Parameters of Power: Canada's Political Institutions*, brief edition (Toronto: Nelson, 2008), in particular, chs. 1, 4, and 5.

2. For a list of "Ten Commandments for Conservative Campaigning," see Tom Flanagan, *Harper's Team: Behind the Scenes in the Conservative Rise to Power* (Montreal & Kingston: McGill-Queen's University Press, 2007). Important among Flanagan's "Ten Commandments" are unity, moderation, incrementalism, and policy.

3. Ibid., p. 278.

4. Ibid., p. 282.

5. See Andrew Coyne, "Do Nothing, Say Nothing Politics Rule Ottawa," *Maclean's*, September 16, 2009, available at http://www2.macleans.ca/2009/09/16/do-nothing-say-nothing-politics-rule-ottawa/. Accessed August 14, 2010.

6. Andrew Coyne, "An Empty, Almost Flippant Budget," *Maclean's*, March 4, 2010, available at http://www2.macleans.ca/2010/03/04/the-government-delivers-an-empty-almost-flippant-budget/. Accessed August 14, 2010.

7. Paul Wells, "Harper's Got Us Just Where He Wants Us," *Maclean's*, August 5, 2010, available at http://www2.macleans.ca/2010/08/05/harpers-got-us-just-where-he-wants-us/. Accessed August 14, 2011.

8. See Jon H. Pammett and Christopher Dornan, eds., *The Canadian Federal Election of 2011* (Toronto: Dundurn Press, 2012).

9. In the last half of the twentieth century, only in 1949 (49.2 percent) and 1953 (48.8 percent) did the Liberals approach majority popular vote territory. In most of their other election victories, they garnered less than 45 percent of the popular vote.

10. See Lawrence LeDuc and Jon H. Pammett, *The Evolution of the Harper Dynasty*, in Pammett and Dornan, *The Canadian Election of 2011*.

11. For concise versions of each, see Gad Horowitz, "Conservatism, Liberalism and Socialism in Canada: An Interpretation," pp. 90–106; and Nelson Wiseman, "The Pattern of Prairie Politics," pp. 351–368; both in Hugh G. Thorburn and Alan Whitehorn, eds., *Party Politics in Canada*, 8th ed. (Toronto: Pearson Education Canada, 2001).

12. See Nelson Wiseman, "Canadian Political Culture: Liberalism with a Tory Streak," pp. 56–67; and Janet Ajzenstat and Peter J. Smith, "The 'Tory Touch' Thesis: Bad History, Poor Political Science," pp. 68–75; both in Mark Charlton and Paul Barker, eds., *Crosscurrents: Contemporary Political Issues*, 4th ed. (Scarborough: Thomson Nelson, 2002).

13. See Harold D. Clarke, Jane Jenson, Lawrence Le Duc, and Jon H. Pammett, *Absent Mandate: Interpreting Change in Canadian Elections*, 2nd ed. (Toronto: Gage Educational Publishing Company, 1991).

14. See R.K. Carty, "Three Canadian Party Systems: An Interpretation of the Development of National Politics," in Hugh G. Thorburn and Alan Whitehorn, eds., *Party Politics in Canada*, 8th ed. (Toronto: Prentice Hall Canada, 2001), pp. 16–32; and R.K. Carty, William Cross, and Lisa Young, *Rebuilding Canadian Party Politics* (Vancouver: UBC Press, 2000).

15. For evidence, see Ellis and MacIvor, *Parameters of Power,* ch. 5 and in particular the table entitled "Canada by the Numbers 5.4: Voter Loyalty 1988–2006," p. 198.

16. See Sydney Sharp and Don Braid, *Storming Babylon: Preston Manning and the Rise of the Reform Party* (Toronto: Key Porter, 1992). For a critique of these early analysts, see Tom Flanagan, *Waiting for the Wave: The Reform Party and Preston Manning* (Toronto: Stoddart Publishing Co., 1995).

17. Trevor Harrison, *Requiem for a Lightweight: Stockwell Day and Image Politics* (Montreal: Black Rose Books, 2002).

18. Lawrence Martin, *Harperland: The Politics of Control* (Toronto: Viking Canada, 2010).

19. Marci McDonald, *The Armageddon Factor: the Rise of Christian Nationalism in Canada* (Toronto: Random House Canada, 2010).

20. Faron Ellis and Keith Archer, "Reform at the Crossroads," in Alan Frizzell and Jon H. Pammett, eds., *The Canadian General Election of 1997* (Toronto: Dundurn Press, 1997), pp. 111–133.

21. Faron Ellis, "The More Things Change…The Alliance Campaign," in Jon H. Pammett and Christopher Dornan, *The Canadian General Election of 2000* (Toronto: Dundurn Press, 2001), pp. 59–89.

22. Faron Ellis and Peter Woolstencroft, "New Conservatives, Old Realities: The 2004 Election Campaign," in Jon H. Pammett and Christopher Dornan, eds., *The Canadian General Election of 2004* (Toronto: Dundurn Press, 2004), pp. 66–105.

23. Faron Ellis and Peter Woolstencroft, "'A Change of Government, Not a Change of Country': The Conservatives and the 2006 Election," in Jon H. Pammett and Christopher Dornan, eds., *The Canadian Federal Election of 2006* (Toronto: Dundurn Press, 2006), pp. 58–92.

24. Faron Ellis and Peter Woolstencroft, "Stephen Harper and the Conservatives Campaign on their Record," in Jon H. Pammett and Christopher Dornan, eds., *The Canadian Federal Election of 2008* (Toronto: Dundurn Press, 2009), pp. 16–62.

25. Faron Ellis and Peter Woolstencroft, "The Conservative Campaign: Becoming the New Natural Governing Party" in Pammett and Dornan, *The Canadian Election of 2011.*

26. For an analysis of Reform opinion structure, see Faron Ellis, *The Limits of Participation: Members and Leaders in Canada's Reform Party* (Calgary: University of Calgary Press, 2005). For a comparison of attitudes of party members in Canada with specific analysis of ideological divisions, see William Cross and Lisa Young, "Policy Attitudes of Party Members in Canada: Evidence of Ideological Politics," *Canadian Journal of Political Science* 35, no. 4 (December 2002), pp. 859–880.

27. See Keith Archer and Faron Ellis, "Opinion Structure of Party Activists: The Reform Party of Canada," *Canadian Journal of Political Science* 27, no. 2 (June 1994), pp. 277–308.

28. Faron Ellis, "Canadian Alliance Party Profile: Results of the 2002 Alliance Convention Delegate Study," Citizen Society Research Lab Seminar Series, March 15, 2005, Lethbridge College.

29. See Conservative Party of Canada, "Results of the March 17–19 2005 Founding Policy Convention."

30. Faron Ellis, "Conservative Party Profile: Results of the 2005 Conservative Party Convention Delegate Study," Citizen Society Research Lab Seminar Series, November 9, 2007, Lethbridge College. Overall, 55.5 percent agreed that abortion is a matter of private choice, 38.1 percent disagreed, while 6.4 percent were uncertain.

31. See Cross and Young, "Policy Attitudes of Party Members," for a comparison of differences between Alliance and Progressive Conservative members' attitudes.

32. See Department of Finance Canada, *Budget 2008: Responsible Leadership for Uncertain Times*, available at http://www.budget.gc.ca/2008/home-accueil-eng.html. Accessed August 14, 2010.

33. See Dale Orr, "1: Income Tax Cuts," *National Post*, November, 15, 2007, FP15; and the federal government's October 2007 *Economic Statement* available at www.fin.gc.ca/budtoce/2007/ec07_e.html. Accessed August 14, 2011.

34. Department of Finance Canada, *Economic and Fiscal Statement: Protecting Canada's Future*, November 27, 2008, available at www.fin.gc.ca/ec2008/ec-eng.html. Accessed August 14, 2011.

35. Department of Finance Canada, *Budget 2009: Canada's Economic Action Plan*, available at www.budget.gc.ca/2009/home-accueil-eng.html. Accessed August 14, 2011.

36. Andrew Coyne, "The End of Canadian Conservatism: How Harper Sold Out to Save Himself," *Maclean's*, January 29, 2009 available at http://www2.macleans.ca/2009/01/29/the-right-in-full-retreat/. Accessed August 14, 2011.

37. Paul Wells, "Does Harper Have a Plan?" *Maclean's*, October 4, 2010, available at http://www2.macleans.ca/2010/10/04/does-harper-have-a-plan/. Accessed August 14, 2011.

38. See Federal Economic Development Agency for Southern Ontario at www.feddevontario.gc.ca.

39. As of the end of 2010, the Conservatives had failed in multiple attempts to dismember the national long gun registry but had begun a review of affirmative action policies within the federal bureaucracy. Their 2011 majority victory all but ensures the end of the gun registry.

40. For further thoughts on these matters see Flanagan's "Ten Commandments," (1) Unity, and (3) Inclusion, in *Harper's Team*, pp. 277–281.

41. See Ellis and Woolstencroft, "A Change of Government," pp. 62–65.

42. The formal vote on the issue at the 2005 Montreal convention resulted in 74 percent of delegates voting to uphold the traditional definition of marriage.

43. Janice Tibbetts, "Same-sex Debate's Over, Harper says: MPs Soundly Defeat Motion 175–123," *The Gazette (Montreal)*, December 8, 2006, p. A1.

44. See Ellis and Woolstencroft, "Becoming the New Natural Governing Party."

45. See Stuart Soroka, Fred Cutler, Dietlind Stolle, and Patrick Fournier, "Capturing Change (and Stability) in the 2011 Campaign," *Policy Options* (June 2011), pp. 70–77.

46. See for example, Stephen Harper, "Prime Minister Harper Signals Canada's Renewed Engagement in the Americas" (speech delivered in Santiago Chile, July 17, 2007); or "Prime Minister Harper Concludes Meetings with CARICOM Leaders," (Bridgetown, Barbados, July 19, 2007). Both these and many other of the Prime Minister's speeches are available in multimedia format on the government's web pages at http://pm.gc.ca/.

47. Terence Corcoran, "No Room for Libertarians in Harper Conservatism," *National Post*, April 30, 2009, available at http://network.nationalpost.com/np/blogs/fullcomment/archive/2009/04/30/terence-corcoran-no-room-for-libertarians-in-harper-conservatism.aspx. Accessed August 14, 2011.

48. Don Martin, "True Blue Believer Bernier Squares Off with Jim 'Deficits' Flaherty," *National Post*, October 14, 2010, available at http://fullcomment.nationalpost.com/2010/10/13/don-martin-true-blue-believer-bernier-squares-off-with-jim-deficits-flaherty/. Accessed August 14, 2011.

49. See Ellis, "Limits of Participation," for an analysis of Reform's approach to wrestling with this dilemma.

50. Steven Harper, "PM Addresses the Council on Foreign Relations," New York, September 25, 2007, available at http://pm.gc.ca/eng/media.asp?category=2&pageId=46&tid=1830. Accessed August 14, 2011.

51. Harper served first as vice-president (1997) and then as president (1998–2002) of the National Citizens Coalition, an advocacy organization that has as its slogan "More freedom through less government."

52. See Tom Flanagan, "The Emerging Conservative Coalition," *Policy Options* (June 2011), pp. 101–103.

53. See Andrew Coyne, "A New Power Couple: The West is in and Ontario has joined It in an Unprecedented Realignment of Canadian Politics," *Maclean's*, May 16, 2011, pp. 60–63.

54. See Adam Daifallah, "Rescuing Canada's Right: Five Years Later," *Policy Options* (June 2011), pp. 109–112.

POSTSCRIPT

In his article, Nelson Wiseman sees dim prospects for modern conservatism and the Conservative Party in Canadian politics. Though there are many reasons for this expected fate, the main one appears to be that modern conservatism is out of step with the beliefs of most Canadians. The tendency of the Harper government to act in a manner quite similar to its Liberal predecessors is seemingly only one manifestation of this assertion. Yet the claim can be questioned. In Wiseman's view, most Canadians supposedly believe in a government that takes a leading role in shaping society and providing service; but there are signs that Canadians appear less deferential to elected officials and more willing to challenge their actions. Wiseman also points to what many think to be the Achilles heel of the Conservative Party—namely its potential to support reactionary or extreme stances on moral issues. But the party has so far been able to steer well clear of positions that would limit access to abortion services or marginalize gays and lesbians. And as for Wiseman's belief that certain elements of the electoral map—large cities, certain regions of the country—are beyond the grasp of the Conservative Party, it can be argued that Canadians are more than capable of switching their allegiances. For supporting evidence, one need only look at the 2011 federal election. Nothing in Canadian politics is set in stone.

For his part, Faron Ellis is much more positive about the chances of conservatism and the Conservative Party. Indeed, it seems that Conservatives need only be themselves and electoral success will come their way, a belief seemingly proven with the results of the most recent federal election. But, as with Wiseman, there are questions. Ellis himself raises important queries. An important element of conservatism and the Conservative Party is a fiscally responsible state; yet Ellis suggests that the Harper government has fallen well short of this goal. The same might be said of the wish for a more libertarian party, which seems to have been frustrated by the prime minister and his push for electoral success. Perhaps more interesting is the possibility that the Liberal beast has been slain only to be replaced by a new liberal beast—the Conservative Party of Canada.

For an understanding of the new Conservative Party of Canada, one might start with Faron Ellis and Peter Wollstencroft's contribution in Jon H. Pammett and Christopher Dornan, eds., *The Canadian General Election of 2004* (Toronto: Dundurn Group, 2004). This article discusses the origins of the party and contains references to documents necessary for appreciating the position of the Conservative Party. A follow-up to this article is another piece by Ellis and Wollstencroft in Jon Pammett and Christopher Dornan, eds., *The Federal General Election of 2006* (Toronto: Dundurn, 2006). For a more detailed examination of the Conservative Party and its electoral experiences, students should see Tom Flanagan, *Harper's Team: Behind the Scenes in the Conservative Rise to Power*, 2nd ed. (Montreal and Kingston: McGill-Queen's University Press, 2009). This exciting text also includes much on what is central to the debate on the fate of conservatism and the Conservative Party, namely the appropriate strategy for the new Conservative Party.

Flanagan has recently added to his thoughts on strategy in Tom Flanagan, "The Emerging Conservative Coalition," *Policy Options* (June/July 2011).

With this understanding of the party, students might wish to back up and acquire a better picture of the overall party system in Canada, as well as predecessors to the Conservative Party. For these insights, Hugh Thorburn and Alan Whitehorn's *Party Politics in Canada*, 8th ed. (Toronto: Prentice-Hall Canada, 2001), is the place to go. Also useful is James Bickerton and Alain-G. Gagnon, "Political Parties and Electoral Politics," in James Bickerton and Alain-G. Gagnon, eds., *Canadian Politics,* 4th ed. (Peterborough: Broadview Press, 2004). For some deep history on conservative parties in Canadian politics, a good source is Dan Azoulay, *Canadian Political Parties: Historical Readings* (Toronto: Irwin Publishing, 1999).

The debate addresses not only the Conservative Party but also the ideology of conservatism. For information on conservatism and the competing ideologies in Canadian politics, a good place to start is Colin Campbell and William Christian, *Parties, Leaders, and Ideologies in Canada* (Toronto: McGraw-Hill Ryerson, 1996). There are also some useful chapters on this topic: David Bell, "Political Culture in Canada," in Michael Whittington and Glen Williams, eds., *Canadian Politics in the 21st Century*, 7th ed. (Scarborough: Thomson Nelson, 2008); and Neil Nevitte and Mebs Kanji, "New Cleavages, Value Diversity and Democratic Governance," in James Bickerton and Alain-G. Gagnon, eds., *Canadian Politics*, 4th ed. (Peterborough: Broadview Press, 2004). Nelson Wiseman's book, *In Search of Canadian Political Culture* (Vancouver: UBC, 2007), should also be consulted, as should Travis Smith's insightful article on conservative thinking, "Why Canada Needs Conservatives, Though It Tends to Imagine Otherwise," *C2C: Canada's Journal of Ideas* 1, no. 1. Finally, Hugh Segal has written a recent book on the history of conservatism in Canada from pre-Confederation times to the present: Hugh Segal, *The Right Balance: Canada's Conservative Tradition* (Vancouver/Toronto: Douglas & McIntyre, 2010).

A number of books have been written about conservative parties in Canadian politics that preceded the formation of the Conservative Party of Canada. These include Jeffrey Simpson, *The Discipline of Power: The Conservative Interlude and the Liberal Restoration* (Toronto: MacMillan, 1980); George Perlin, *The Tory Syndrome: Leadership Politics in the Progressive Conservative Party* (Montreal and Kingston: McGill-Queen's University Press, 1980); Tom Flanagan, *Waiting for the Wave: The Reform Party and Preston Manning* (Toronto: Stoddart, 1995); Trevor Harrison, *Of Passionate Intensity: Right Wing Populism and the Reform Party of Canada* (Toronto: University of Toronto Press, 1995); and Faron Ellis, *The Limits of Participation: Members and Leaders in Canada's Reform Party* (Calgary: University of Calgary Press, 2005). Books have also been written on Stephen Harper and the Conservative Party of Canada: William Johnson, *Stephen Harper and the Future of Canada* (Toronto: McClelland & Stewart, 2004); Bob Plamondon, *Full Circle: Death and Resurrection in Canadian Conservative Politics* (Toronto: Key Porter, 2006); and Paul Wells, *Right Side Up: The Fall of Paul Martin and the Rise of Stephen Harper's New Conservatism* (Toronto: McClelland & Stewart, 2006).

Can Native Sovereignty Coexist with Canadian Sovereignty?

✔ **YES**
ROGER TOWNSHEND, "The Case for Native Sovereignty"

✘ **NO**
THOMAS FLANAGAN, "Native Sovereignty: Does Anyone Really Want an Aboriginal Archipelago?"

In Canada, the subject of Aboriginal rights has generally never been high on the political agenda. Most Canadians have a vague awareness of the deplorable living conditions on many Indian reserves, but that is about all. The demands of Native people for land, greater autonomy, and even self-government have received little sustained public attention. More "immediate" issues such as constitutional reform, Quebec separatism, western alienation, free trade with the United States, or economic recovery from recession have usually pushed Native issues off the list of urgent public issues, especially at election time.

However, dramatic events will occasionally push Native issues to the forefront of media attention. One such case was the Oka crisis of 1990, which, at the time, probably did more to change the public perception of Native issues than any other single event. Reacting to municipal plans to expand a local golf course onto traditional Native lands, armed Mohawk Warriors began erecting barricades in an effort to stop the work. The protest soon escalated into a full-scale confrontation between the Quebec provincial police and the Mohawk Warriors, in which one police officer was killed. Soon a second set of barriers was erected on the Kahnawake reserve near Montreal as a demonstration of support. As the situation appeared to become more violent, Quebec Premier Robert Bourassa called in the Canadian armed forces to restore order to Oka. For the first time in twenty years, Canadian troops were deployed against fellow citizens.

For federal and Quebec officials, the issue was straightforward. The Mohawks, in using arms and barricades to press their case, had broken the law and needed to be brought to justice like any other citizens who had committed illegal acts. Land claims and other grievances would be settled only when arms were surrendered and the lawbreakers brought to justice. But the Mohawks rejected this view. It was not just the matter of land claims that was at stake. It was, the Warriors claimed, a question of sovereignty. The Mohawks occupied sovereign territory that had never been surrendered to any British or Canadian government. Thus, the Mohawks had every right, as any other sovereign nation, to take up arms to defend themselves. It was the police and army who were acting illegally.

At the heart of Native grievances is the *Indian Act*, 1876, which set the tone for successive federal government dealings with Native people. Under this act, elected Indian band councils, not traditional political institutions, deal with the Department of Indian Affairs and Northern Development. Band councils are granted limited powers, but all financial decisions are ultimately subject to the approval of the minister responsible for Indian Affairs. Thus, sovereignty remains undivided and concentrated in the hands of Ottawa. Band councils are like fledgling municipal governments, able to exercise only those powers specifically delegated to them.

Native leaders have long argued that this relationship is humiliating and paternalistic. The real aim of the *Indian Act*, they argue, has been to use the band councils as an instrument for destroying traditional Native institutions and for assimilating and integrating Native people into the larger Canadian society. For moderate Native leaders, the solution has been to negotiate some greater delegation of powers to the band councils. But for a growing number of Native leaders, this is not enough. Only when the full sovereignty of Indian nations is recognized will Native people be able to overcome their degrading colonial status.

In the wake of the Oka crisis, Native issues were suddenly given a more prominent place on the Canadian political agenda. The government of Brian Mulroney appointed a Royal Commission on Aboriginal questions and gave Native leaders an increasingly prominent role in discussions leading up to the constitutional proposals of 1992. The Charlottetown Accord appeared to address many Native concerns. The accord included a recognition of the inherent right of Aboriginal people to self-government and the commitment to make these Aboriginal governments one of three orders of government along with Ottawa and the provinces. Federal and provincial governments committed themselves to negotiating self-government agreements with those Native bands that wished to do so, while a series of future First Ministers' Conferences were promised to give ongoing consideration to Aboriginal constitutional issues.

However, many remained skeptical of the accord. Non-Native critics wondered what a third order of government meant. What form would Native self-government take? How would it mesh with the notion of a sovereign Canada? At the same time, many Native people felt that the accord had not gone far enough. After all, the accord stated that Aboriginal laws could not be inconsistent with those Canadian laws that are deemed essential to the preservation of peace, order, and good government. This was hardly a recognition of Native sovereignty.

With the defeat of the referendum, many of the questions surrounding the issue of Native sovereignty were left unresolved. In October 1996, the Royal

Commission on Aboriginal Peoples published its five-volume report. Although the commission made more than four hundred specific proposals, the report has quietly passed from public attention. This complacency was due in part to the lukewarm response of the Liberal government, which stated that the estimated $30 billion cost of implementing the report's recommendations was too great to accommodate in the present economic circumstances. Instead, the Liberal government introduced the *First Nations Governance Act,* which the government stated was designed to ensure financial and political accountability and to "modernize" the old *Indian Act.* Many Native groups opposed the pending legislation, arguing that, rather than being a step forward, the legislation would in fact turn Aboriginal communities into the equivalent of municipalities and open the door to the expansion of provincial powers in Native affairs. When Parliament was prorogued in December 2003, the *First Nations Governance Act* was allowed to die on the order paper and has not since been reintroduced. In 2010, the Conservative government of Stephen Harper proposed making some amendments to the *Indian Act*, but these too died when Parliament was prorogued. However, in 2011 the Assembly of First Nations released a document proposing the replacement of both the department of Aboriginal Affairs and the Indian Act. In response, Peter Penashue, the Conservative government's Minister of Intergovernmental Affairs, suggested that the Harper government was willing to consider scrapping the *Indian Act* if that were the wish of the First Nations chiefs.

In the following essays, two specialists in Native issues debate the meaning of Native sovereignty and its relationship to the concepts of a sovereign Canada. Roger Townshend, a lawyer who has done extensive work on Native land claims and Aboriginal constitutional issues, sets out the case for Native sovereignty. Thomas Flanagan of the University of Calgary argues that the demand for Native sovereignty as it is posed by Native leaders is incompatible with the continued existence of Canada.

✔ **YES**
The Case for Native Sovereignty
ROGER TOWNSHEND

There is a great divide in perceptions between Aboriginal people in Canada and non-Aboriginal people. The average non-Aboriginal Canadian takes as self-evident the legitimacy of the Canadian state and its jurisdiction over Canadian territory. The average Aboriginal person, on the other hand, views much of the power exercised by the Canadian state as illegitimate, oppressive, and infringing on Aboriginal governance powers. To the extent that non-Aboriginal Canadians are aware of this perception among Aboriginal people, they are likely bewildered by it and have trouble seeing either a reasonable basis for it or any practical ways in which such a view could be acted on. Yet it is precisely this divergence of views that has caused and will continue to cause confrontations in the political arena, such as those regarding constitutional amendments, and confrontations on the ground, such as at Kanesatake (Oka), Ipperwash, and Caledonia.

Although non-Aboriginal Canadians rarely question the legitimacy of the Canadian state, most thoughtful people would likely be distressed at how flimsy the logical justification for Canadian sovereignty indeed is. There is no question that, prior to European contact, Aboriginal nations in North America had stable cultures, economies, and political systems, and that many (if not all) of these were of amazing sophistication in adaptation to their environment. What is sometimes not recognized is that different Aboriginal nations had cultures and economies that were vastly different from one another. They still are.[1] However, European peoples were often blinded by preconceived notions of Aboriginal culture and mistook difference from European lifestyles for inferiority. Some Euro-Canadians still do. But to view as inferior cultures that, for example, had the technology and organization to hunt whales on the open ocean, build large permanent houses, or create sophisticated political confederacies is surely untenable.[2]

Pre-contact Aboriginal nations unmistakably exercised full control or "sovereignty" over their traditional lands, although in somewhat different ways than did European nations. It would be arrogant and ethnocentric to recognize only a European model of political organization as capable of possessing sovereignty. It would also be deeply ironic, since European political theorists took a significant interest in the Haudenosaunee (Iroquois) confederacy and its structure influenced the drafters of the U.S. Constitution (the latter was acknowledged by the U.S. Senate in 1987).[3]

In their initial contact with Aboriginal nations, Europeans generally treated them as allies or as enemies, but in any event, as nations to be treated as equals with European states. How then did this change? International law then and now recognized changes in sovereignty based on conquest, discovery and settlement, or treaty. There is nothing in Canadian history that could qualify as a conquest in the international law sense. Treaties with Aboriginal nations fall into two rough categories. There are "peace and friendship" treaties, which, if anything, reinforce the concept of the equal nationhood of Aboriginal nations. There are also treaties that read as land transactions, which by their silence concerning matters of jurisdiction would seem to provide little help in rooting a claim that they are a source of Canadian sovereignty. Furthermore, there are vast areas of Canada where there are no historic treaties whatsoever. Thus, the invocation of treaties is wholly unsatisfactory as a foundation of Canadian sovereignty. What is left is the doctrine of discovery and settlement. The difficulty with this is that it was intended to apply only to lands that were vacant. Its initial application to a claim of European jurisdiction required the step of considering the Aboriginal people as legal nonpersons. In fact, the "discovery" of the Americas sparked lengthy theological and judicial debates in Europe about whether indigenous people indeed were or should be treated as humans. Thus, the only justification for Canadian sovereignty (inherited from British sovereignty) that has an air of reality to it requires, as a precondition, a judgment that Aboriginal people are not really human for legal purposes. This is surely repugnant to thinking Canadians.[4]

Despite the logical flimsiness of its assertion of sovereignty, the British (and later the Canadian) state, after an initial period of nation-to-nation dealings, has treated Aboriginal people as subjects and indeed as less than equal subjects. Since the onset of European settlement, Canadian "Indian" policy has been aimed at assimilating Aboriginal people into Canadian society. This integration was to be achieved on an individual level and preferably by entry into the working-class level of society. Efforts of Aboriginal people to interact as a group with Canadian society or to integrate at a non-working-class level of Canadian society met with suppression. For example, for many years an Aboriginal person who graduated from university automatically ceased to be an "Indian" in the eyes of the federal government. The policy of assimilation came to a head in 1969 with the notorious White Paper, which called for the termination of "Indian" status. This document was resoundingly rejected by Aboriginal people and in fact became the catalyst for the creation of Canada-wide Aboriginal political organizations. This policy of assimilation has been a complete and utter failure. The political resistance of Aboriginal peoples to assimilation into Canadian society has never been stronger. Most Aboriginal people, in a fundamental way, view the Canadian government as a foreign government and not one that is "theirs." This should hardly be shocking, since it was only in 1948 that the Inuit gained the right to vote in federal elections and in 1960 that status Indians living on reserves were given this right. Neither have Aboriginal communities lost their social, cultural, and economic distinctiveness. The Canadian government has tried long and hard to change this, but it has failed. Its attempts have only created much human misery. The residential school system, where Aboriginal children were separated from their families, forbidden to speak their language or practice their religion and culture, and were physically, psychologically, and sometimes even sexually abused, is one of those attempts. Another attempt was the criminalizing of traditional Aboriginal religious ceremonies. Also, the Aboriginal traditional economy has in many parts of the country been seriously impaired both by the environmental effects of development activities and directly by legislation restricting hunting rights. Yet the attachment of Aboriginal people to the land remains unbroken.[5]

So what options are open? The dismal social conditions in which many Aboriginal people in Canada live are the result of failed assimilationist policies of the Canadian government. Most Aboriginal people firmly believe that the political key to a better future is the recognition of jurisdiction of Aboriginal governments. This must be a jurisdiction that goes well beyond a municipal-government type of jurisdiction, which would allow and encourage the development of new types of structures that would reflect the distinct cultural, political, economic, and spiritual aspects of Aboriginal society. This must be a jurisdiction that is provided with sufficient resources to be viable. It would indeed mean a fundamental restructuring of the institutions of the Canadian state or, perhaps more accurately, a rolling back of the jurisdiction of the Canadian state to allow Aboriginal institutions to flourish. It is this approach that could allow for a just and peaceful coexistence of Aboriginal peoples in the Canadian state.

The defeat of the proposed constitutional amendments in 1992 was a missed opportunity to begin to pursue this path. These amendments were rejected by the majority of both non-Aboriginal and Aboriginal people. However, it must be realized that they were rejected for very different reasons. The rejection of the Charlottetown Accord by non-Aboriginal people seems to have little to do with the Aboriginal proposals in the accord. To the extent that these were a factor, non-Aboriginal Canadians were probably disposed to view them as giving too much to Aboriginal peoples. Most Aboriginal people, on the other hand, rejected the accord because it was too small a step in the direction they wanted to go.

It is puzzling that the idea of Aboriginal sovereignty should be so threatening to non-Aboriginal people. The very nature of the Canadian political system involves a division of powers between federal and provincial governments. It is but an easy step in theory to implement another order of government and provide for an appropriate division of powers. This would not be a challenge to the very essence of Canada, since the sharing of jurisdictional powers between different government institutions is already part of the essence of the Canadian state. Canadian sovereignty is also leaking at the other end with increasing globalization and trade agreements. It becomes confusing, then, why Canada should be unwilling to share jurisdiction with Aboriginal governments if it is indeed willing to modify its sovereignty with relation to the provinces and also at the international level. Nor would the idea of Aboriginal sovereignty within a federal state be an uncharted course. In the United States, a country hardly known for being progressive, it is an established legal doctrine that Indian tribes are "domestic dependent nations." The implementation of this concept extends to separate tribal justice and court systems.

Many non-Aboriginal Canadians may be troubled by the idea of Aboriginal sovereignty, since they feel that Aboriginal people should be able to achieve their social and economic goals by participation as individuals within Canadian society. This misses the entire point of Aboriginal difference. Most Aboriginal cultures have a distinctive and tangible collective nature that goes well beyond the sum of the individuals that constitute them and that would be destroyed by assimilation on an individual basis. The failure of many non-Aboriginal Canadians to appreciate this reflects only that liberal individualism is such a pervasive ideology in Canadian society that it is barely recognizable as an ideology at all and often viewed as ultimate truth. This appears to be the position taken by Thomas Flanagan in the opposing article. He uses "liberal democracy" as a touchstone. The definition of "liberal democracy" has contentious points, but the sense in which Flanagan appears to be using it, and in which I am using it for the purpose of this article, is a political system in which individual rights are considered paramount and equality is measured as formal equality of agency (that is, as the lack of state restraint on an individual's actions) rather than measured by whether the result of political and economic forces leads to substantively equal results. The economic aspect of a "liberal democracy" in this sense is an unrestrained free market, which by this definition is the pinnacle of economic equality, despite resulting in extremes of wealth and poverty.

By definition, a group with a culture that differs in significant points from liberal individualism cannot be accommodated within a purely individualistic framework, particularly when any integration with a larger society can take place only on an individual basis. It is true that a society that permits or encourages interaction on a collective basis is not a "liberal democracy" in the sense explained above. In this sense, many Canadians are not "liberal democrats" and few nations are "liberal democracies."[6]

The point is, a "liberal democracy" is not an acceptable political structure for most Aboriginal people. Fortunately (in my view), Canada has never been a "liberal democracy" in a strong sense. As Flanagan notes, French–English duality and ethnic diversity (both of which include collective aspects) challenge the basis of "liberal democracy." For that matter, whether or not "liberal democracy" is a meaningful term is questionable, since the concepts of liberalism and democracy can come into sharp conflict (for example, when a majority wishes to suppress rights of a minority).

Others may view the kind of structural diversity advocated in this article to be impractical. As Flanagan admits, it is not unprecedented—he cites the Ottoman Empire as an example. There are also analogies less unfamiliar to Canadians—the position of Indian tribes in the U.S. system is one.

The practicality of political structures that could accommodate Aboriginal diversity was studied extensively by the Royal Commission on Aboriginal Peoples. The commission operated from 1991 to 1996, collected thousands of briefs, generated tens of thousands of pages of transcripts of hearings, and commissioned an extremely comprehensive set of research papers. The commissioners included a retired Supreme Court judge and a Quebec Superior Court judge. The report of the commission is more than 3,200 pages long. The underlying research papers are many times that long.

The commission recommended sweeping changes to relations with Aboriginal peoples. The report sets out the following:[7]

- First, Aboriginal nations have to be reconstituted.

- Second, a process must be established for the assumption of powers by Aboriginal nations.

- Third, there must be a fundamental reallocation of lands and resources.

- Fourth, Aboriginal people need education and crucial skills for governance and economic self-reliance.

- Finally, economic development must be addressed if the poverty and despondency of lives defined by unemployment and welfare are to change.

The commission emphatically saw the needs for political restructuring and social initiatives as mutually dependent—neither could succeed without the other. The commission also went into great detail about processes and structures. For example, it saw the right of self-determination as vested in Aboriginal nations, not individual local communities (e.g., First Nations). The commission made detailed recommendations about how such nations could be encouraged to reconstitute, for example, as aggregations of local communities. It also suggested a number of options for the integration into this structure of off-reserve and urban Aboriginal people. This vision of fairly sizable Aboriginal nations having the right of self-determination responds to concerns about the practicality of hundreds of First Nations or similar communities, some very small, having powers similar to those of provinces. With the issuance of the commission's report, it should no longer be enough for those opposing Aboriginal self-determination to simply object that hundreds of small Aboriginal communities could not possibly be able to be self-governing, except perhaps in the municipal sense. To be made fairly, any such objections need to engage with the many and detailed recommendations of the commission about how to make Aboriginal self-determination work.

The alternatives to recognizing Aboriginal jurisdiction must be examined realistically. The commission also looked at this question in considerable detail and concluded that the economic cost of doing nothing exceeded, in the long term, the cost of implementing its recommendations.[8] Flanagan's alternative is to do more consistently what the Canadian government has been trying to do for a century. This has failed utterly and has created much suffering and resentment in the process. What is there to lose in trying something different? Demands for the recognition of Aboriginal jurisdiction are not going to go away. If "legitimate" avenues for advancing these demands are shut down, other means may be sought. The continued peace and security of Canada may well depend on accommodating Aboriginal jurisdiction.

Respect for the cultural distinctiveness of Aboriginal people requires the recognition of institutional forms of Aboriginal governments, with sufficient resources to exercise jurisdiction meaningfully. The sad history of the treatment of Aboriginal people by the Canadian state also cries out for redress in the form of recognition of Aboriginal sovereignty. Such recognition should not be viewed as completely impractical or as entailing the very destruction of the Canadian state.

NOTES

1. See, for example, the descriptions of five distinct pre-contact Aboriginal cultures in *Report of the Royal Commission on Aboriginal Peoples* ("RCAP") 1 (Ottawa: Minister of Supply and Services, 1996), pp. 46–90.

2. For whaling practices, see, for example, G. Monks, A. McMillan, and D. St. Claire, "Nuu-chah-nulth whaling: Archaeological insights into antiquity, species preferences, and cultural importance," *Arctic Anthropology,* 2001. Aboriginal nations on the Pacific coast built large permanent houses (*RCAP* 1, p. 73). The Haudenosaunee (Iroquois) had a sophisticated political confederacy (*RCAP 1*, pp. 52–61). Thomas Flanagan, in the article opposite, characterizes pre-contact Aboriginal cultures as "Neolithic" hunting–gathering societies, incapable of possessing sovereignty. "Neolithic," if understood in the technical anthropological sense of agricultural peoples settled in large villages with domesticated plants and animals, fairly accurately describes the economies of some pre-contact Aboriginal cultures. "Hunting–gathering" (if interpreted to include fishing) describes the economies of some others. However, "Neolithic hunting–gathering society" is a contradiction in terms. See, for example, P. Driben and H. Herstein, *Portrait of Humankind: An Introduction to Human Biology and Prehistoric Cultures* (Boston: Pearson Custom Publishing, 2002), pp. 347–351. Further, Flanagan appears to be using anthropological vocabulary in a value-laden way to disparage Aboriginal cultures and has ignored the fundamental rejection by anthropology of any kind of ethnocentrism, including conceptual ethnocentrism (Driben and Herstein, p. 359).

3. See *RCAP* 1, p. 53 and related endnotes, and Dale Turner, *This Is Not a Peace Pipe: Towards a Critical Indigenous Philosophy* (Toronto: University of Toronto Press, 2006), p. 34.

4. For more detail on the international law aspects of this, see, for example, O. Dickason, "Concepts of Sovereignty at the Time of First Contact," in Dickason and Green, eds., *The Law of Nations and the New World* (Edmonton: University of Alberta Press, 1989). See also a brief summary in *RCAP* 1, pp. 43–46.

5. For more examples of the failure of the policy of assimilation and Aboriginal resistance to it, see, for example, Diane Engelstad and John Bird, eds., *Nation to Nation: Aboriginal Sovereignty and the Future of Canada* (Concord: House of Anansi Press, 1992), and the revised edition by John Bird, Lorraine Land, and Murray MacAdam, eds. (Toronto: Public Justice Resource Centre and Irwin Publishing, 2002).

6. The U.S. would amount to a liberal democracy in this sense, although "liberal democrat" in U.S. political parlance means something completely different.

7. *RCAP* 5, pp. 2–3.

8. *RCAP* 5, pp. 23–89.

✘ NO

Native Sovereignty: Does Anyone Really Want an Aboriginal Archipelago?

THOMAS FLANAGAN

"... words are wise men's counters, they do but reckon by them: but they are the money of fools...."

—Thomas Hobbes, *Leviathan* (1651), I, 4

In the spirit of Hobbes, we should be clear on what we are talking about before we try to debate Native sovereignty. I have elsewhere defined *sovereignty* as "the authority to override all other authorities." More specifically, it is

> ... a bundle of powers associated with the highest authority of government. One is the power to enforce rules of conduct.... Another is the power to make law, [also the power of] raising revenue, maintaining armed forces, minting currency, and providing other services to society. In the British tradition, sovereignty also implies an underlying ownership of all land.... Finally, sovereignty always means the power to deal with the sovereigns of other communities as well as the right to exercise domestic rule free from interference by other sovereigns.[1]

That is the abstract meaning of *sovereignty* in the vocabulary of political science. In this sense, it is a conceptual property of the states that make up the international state system. Almost all of the entities that possess sovereignty are members of the United Nations (192 members in 2007).

In this frame of reference, sovereignty can pertain only to states. It makes no sense to speak of sovereignty unless there is, as in the classical definition of the state, an organized structure of government ruling over a population within defined territorial boundaries. Native societies in what is now Canada did not possess sovereignty before the coming of the Europeans; neither the concept nor the underlying institutions were part of the Neolithic cultures of their hunting–gathering societies. Of course, hunting–gathering societies have political processes that assign rank and dominance within communities and involve conflict between communities, but the political processes of stateless societies are not the same thing as statehood and sovereignty.

As a way of increasing their political leverage in contemporary Canada, Native political leaders have adopted the classical language of statehood to describe their communities. What used to be called bands or tribes are now called "nations," and these nations are said to have possessed sovereignty from the beginning and to possess it still.[2] This strategic use of language has served Native leaders well in their struggle for greater power within the Canadian polity, but politically effective assertions should not be confused with intellectually persuasive analysis.

When Native leaders in Canada now claim to possess sovereignty, they typically mean one of two things, each of which is related to a particular political situation. In what follows, I will argue that both of these meanings are incompatible with the continued existence of Canada and the maintenance of essential Canadian political traditions. It is not that words alone can destroy Canada; words in themselves do not accomplish anything. But words such as *Native sovereignty* are the verbal symbols of political projects that cannot be reconciled with Canadian institutions.

1. Some Native leaders, for example those from the Mohawk communities of Kahnawake and Kanesatake in Quebec, speak of sovereignty in the robust sense described above, that is, the international sense. They hold that the Mohawks on their territory constitute a sovereign, independent state not part of Canada or the United States. This sovereign state should be admitted to the United Nations and in other respects become part of the international community. A Mohawk elder told the Royal Commission on Aboriginal Peoples in March 1993, "You have no right to legislate any laws over our people whatsoever. Our lands are not yours to be assumed. You are my tenant, whether you like it or not."[3] Many times since then, some (not all) Mohawks have acted as if Canadian law did not apply to them, as in the occupation, beginning in 2006, of a construction project in Caledonia, Ontario.[4]

   While I respect the honesty of this position, I do not take it seriously as a political proposition. In the ten provinces, Canada has over six hundred Indian bands living on more than 2,200 reserves, plus hundreds of thousands of Métis and non-status Indians who do not possess reserves. These scattered pieces of land and disparate peoples are not going to be recognized as independent sovereign states, now or ever. They are simply not viable as sovereign states paying their own way and defending their interests in the international community. Nor is there any practical way to weld them into a single sovereign state. Native peoples are deeply divided by language, religion, customs, and history and in no way constitute a single people. They are not seeking emancipation from the tutelage of Indian Affairs in order to lose their identity in some supra-tribal bureaucracy.

2. The concept of sovereignty, as originally formulated by the philosophers Jean Bodin and Thomas Hobbes, was thought to be a set of powers located in a single seat of authority—perhaps the monarch, perhaps the parliament, but in any case one sovereign. However, sovereignty can also be divided. Indeed, the classical definition of *federalism* implies a system of divided sovereignty, in which two levels of government each have shares

of sovereign power guaranteed in a constitution that cannot be changed unilaterally by either level of government acting alone. In such a context, it is at least verbally meaningful to speak of giving Native peoples a constitutionally entrenched share of sovereign authority.

This is more or less the political theory contained in the failed Charlottetown Accord. According to that document, "[t]he Constitution should be amended to recognize that the aboriginal peoples of Canada have the inherent right of self-government within Canada," and Aboriginal self-governments should be recognized as "one of the three orders of government in Canada."[5] Although the terms *federalism* and *sovereignty* were not used, the most straightforward way to interpret the scheme proposed by the Charlottetown Accord was as an extension of divided sovereignty in a federal system from two to three levels. Although none of the details were worked out, the accord would have endowed Aboriginal self-governments with many of the attributes of provinces: an entrenched constitutional basis of authority, participation in constitutional amendment procedures, representation in the Senate, a role in fiscal federalism, broad legislative jurisdiction, and so on.

Even though the Charlottetown Accord was defeated in a 1992 referendum and never adopted, its proposal for a limited form of Aboriginal sovereignty cannot be dismissed on a priori grounds. There is no self-evident reason that federalism must be based on only two levels of government. Why not a "third order"? There are in fact many reasons why not, but they are more practical than conceptual.

As mentioned above, there are in Canada over 700,000 status Indians belonging to more than six hundred bands on more than 2,200 reserves scattered across all provinces. No one has proposed a workable mechanism by which this far-flung archipelago could be knit together into a single level of government. On the contrary, it was widely assumed in the debate on the Charlottetown Accord that the focus of self-government would be the band, or perhaps small clusters of closely related bands organized into tribal councils. Indeed, one of the widely touted advantages of the third order of government is its alleged flexibility, which would allow different bands or groups of bands to have their own institutions of government, criminal justice systems, schools, and so on.

But surely realism must intervene at some point. We are talking about six hundred bands with an average population of little more than a thousand, many located on small, remote pieces of land without significant job opportunities, natural resources, or economic prospects. There would be virtually no revenue base, let alone a pool of human skills necessary to operate modern public services. How are such small, isolated, and impoverished groups of people supposed to support and operate an untried system of government incorporating a degree of complexity not seen since the Holy Roman Empire of the Middle Ages?

This is only the initial objection. Hard as it would be to harmonize 2,200 reserves into a workable third order of government in a multi-tiered federal system, the problem is actually much more difficult than that. At any given time, about half of Canada's status Indians live off reserve. They reside almost everywhere in the rest of Canada, from remote wilderness areas to the city centres of Vancouver, Toronto, and Montreal. In addition to status Indians, there are several hundred thousand (the true number is impossible to ascertain) Métis and non-status Indians, that is, people of partly Indian ancestry who are not registered under the *Indian Act* but have some degree of identity as Native people. A small number of Métis live in territorial enclaves (the Métis settlements of northern Alberta), but most are mixed in with the general population of Canada. Again, there is every conceivable kind of social situation. There are Métis hunters, trappers, and fishermen in the northern forests; Métis farmers on the Prairies; and Métis business owners, professionals, and workers in Winnipeg and other major cities.

How could one create a third order of government embracing all Aboriginal people, as the Charlottetown Accord purported to do, when most of these people do not live in defined territories? Since no one, thank God, was talking of forcibly relocating populations to create separate territories, the only other approach would be to create a racially defined system of government for Aboriginal people no matter where they live.

There is a historical model for such a system, namely the Ottoman Empire that ruled the Middle East and southeastern Europe from the fifteenth century until it was dismembered after the First World War. Throughout this immense territory, members of numerous Christian churches (Maronite, Coptic, Chaldean, Greek Orthodox, Armenian Orthodox, etc.) lived alongside the adherents of several Islamic sects (Sunni, Shi'ite, Druze, etc.). There were also important Jewish populations in most parts of the empire. Ethno-religious communities were allowed a substantial degree of autonomy, including not only religious freedom but also their own systems of private law, regulating matters such as marriage, family, and inheritance within their separate communities.

It was in some ways an admirable system, ruling a colourful, polyglot population for five centuries—no mean achievement in itself. But I doubt it is a model Canadians want to imitate, for it was in no sense liberal or democratic. There were no elections or other institutions of representative government. The sultan was theoretically an autocrat, but in fact rule was carried out by the imperial bureaucracy. The empire existed to collect taxes, keep internal order, and wage war against the neighbouring Persian, Russian, and Austro-Hungarian empires.

Like all liberal democracies, Canada is based on an entirely different set of political principles, most notably the twin concepts of the rule of law and equality under the law. The legal equality of all citizens is what makes democracy possible. As John Stuart Mill argued cogently in his *Considerations on Representative Government*, people cannot participate peacefully and cooperatively in one political system unless they feel themselves part of a single community: "Free institutions are next to impossible in a country made up of different nationalities."[6] A territorial definition of the polity is essential to the existence of liberal democracy. Political and civil rights must be contingent on residence within a specific territory, not membership in a specific race or ethnic group.

Admittedly, Canada as a liberal democracy is challenged by the linguistic cleavage between English and French as well as the ethnic diversity of our Aboriginal and immigrant populations. But, at least prior to the Charlottetown Accord, the solutions toward which we groped were always liberal democratic ones based on legal equality within defined territorial jurisdictions. The French fact in Canada was recognized by creating the province of Quebec, which, although it happens to have a French majority, is a province similar in principle to all the others. The same is true of the largely Inuit province of Nunavut. It is a territory within which an Inuit majority controls a liberal democratic system of government, not an Inuit ethnic polity.

The Aboriginal self-government provisions of the Charlottetown Accord would have changed this by authorizing an ethnically defined third order of government to sprawl across existing territorial jurisdictions. It was a departure from, not an extension of, our federal system of liberal democracy. It is so incompatible with our system that it probably would not have worked at all. But to the extent that it had any effect, it would have encouraged the segmentation of Native people. Wherever there were appreciable numbers of Indians and Métis in our cities, they would have been encouraged to develop their own schools, welfare agencies, justice systems, elective assemblies, and other paraphernalia of government. Instead of being encouraged to take advantage of the opportunities of Canada's urban society and economy, as so many immigrants from the Third World are now doing, Native people would have been led to withdraw further into a world of imaginary political power and all too real dependence on transfer payments.

Finally, even if they could have been made to work in their own terms, the Aboriginal self-government provisions of the Charlottetown Accord would have set up unacceptable pressures to create segmented arrangements for other groups. In addition to setting up the third order of government across the country, the accord provided for unique Aboriginal participation in national political institutions: Aboriginal senators, possibly with a "double majority" veto over legislation on Aboriginal matters[7]; Aboriginal members of the House of Commons;[8] and Aboriginal nominations to the Supreme Court, as well as a special advisory role for an Aboriginal Council of Elders.[9] It would not have been long before other groups demanded similar treatment: women's organizations, visible minorities, the disabled, gays and lesbians, and so on. Indeed, demands of this type were heard during the referendum on the accord. Reservation of Senate seats for women was a major issue in certain provinces, notably British Columbia; and Joe Clark promised to revisit the situation of the disabled once the accord was passed. Even if Canada's liberal democracy could have survived the distinct society for Quebec and the third order of government for Aboriginals, it could not survive if every identifiable group set out to entrench its political power in the Constitution. It would be the end of equality before the law, and ultimately of liberal democracy itself.

Up to this point, the tone of my essay has been unavoidably negative, because I was asked to argue the negative side in a debate about Native sovereignty. Let me take the opportunity in closing to state my views in a more positive way.

Status Indians in Canada have certainly failed to thrive under the regime of the *Indian Act* and the Department of Indian Affairs. Bureaucratic socialism has been a failure wherever it has been tried, whether in Eastern Europe or North America. In my view, Indian bands should receive full ownership of their reserves, with the right to subdivide, mortgage, sell, and otherwise dispose of their assets, including buildings, lands, and natural resources. This more efficient regime of property rights would accelerate the trend to Aboriginal entrepreneurship that is already evident on some reserves. Politically, reserves should assume the self-government responsibilities of small towns or rural municipalities. What happens afterward should be up to them. This kind of devolution of power is already possible under federal legislation; it has taken place in a few cases, such as the Sechelt band of British Columbia, and is being negotiated by other bands across the country. It does not require an elaborate metaphysics of sovereignty.

However, a large and ever-increasing majority of Native people do not live on reserves and never will, except for occasional visits. For this majority, neither self-government nor sovereignty can have any meaning except to the extent that they, as Canadian citizens, participate in the government of Canada. For them, the political illusion of self-government is a cruel deception, leading them out of, rather than into, the mainstream of Canadian life. Their future depends on fuller participation in the Canadian society, economy, and polity. They are, for all intents and purposes, internal immigrants, and for purposes of public policy, their problems are fundamentally the same as those of other recent immigrants.

It is now thirty years since Pierre Trudeau became prime minister of Canada. One of his government's early projects was the famous White Paper on Indian affairs, which articulated an approach similar to the one stated here, namely to encourage the social, economic, and political integration of Natives into Canadian society. Sadly (as I see it), Native leaders totally rejected the White Paper and set off along the opposite path of emphasizing separate institutions and political power, pursuing the elusive goals of land claims, Aboriginal rights, self-government, and sovereignty. As far as I can tell, thirty years of this political approach have produced hardly any beneficial results. There are more Native politicians and lawyers than there used to be, but economic and social conditions seem to have improved very little. We still read every day about unemployment rates of 90 percent on reserves, of Third World standards of housing and health, of endemic alcoholism, drug addiction, violence, and family breakdown.

What the black economist Thomas Sowell has written of the United States is equally true of Canada:

> Political success is not only relatively unrelated to economic advance, those minorities that have pinned their hopes on political action—the Irish and the Negroes, for example—have made some of the slower economic advances. This is in sharp contrast to the Japanese-Americans, whose political powerlessness may have been a blessing in disguise, by preventing the expenditure of much energy in that direction. Perhaps the minority that has depended most on trying to secure justice through political or legal processes has been the American Indian, whose claims for justice are among the most obvious and most readily documented .... In the American context, at least, emphasis on promoting economic advancement has produced far more progress than attempts to redress past wrongs, even when those historic wrongs have been obvious, massive, and indisputable.[10]

More concisely, but in the same vein, the Tsimshian lawyer and businessman Calvin Helin has written, "It is time for indigenous people to stop dwelling on the rancorous injustices of the past ... we cannot do anything about history. Our actions now, however, can impact the future."[11]

Helin's words point in the direction of a different understanding of sovereignty, as when political philosophers talk about "popular sovereignty" or economists talk about "consumer sovereignty." These usages refer not to statelike systems of organized authority but to people making decisions for themselves, either as groups (popular sovereignty) or as individuals (consumer sovereignty). They are more or less synonymous with "self-determination."[12] As Helin argues, Native people have to take control of their own lives. They have to find and hold jobs, get better education for their children, and run their own communities more openly and efficiently. None of this requires an elaborate apparatus of government and vocabulary of sovereignty; it is more a matter of change at the individual level.

Native people probably don't value my advice, because I'm not a Native person and haven't experienced what they've experienced. So let me close by quoting Calvin Helin again:

> Aboriginal citizens must take ownership of [their] problems and assert control over their own destinies. We must look immediately to opportunities that are available to generate our own sources of wealth and employment that ultimately could lead to the Holy Grail of rediscovered independence and self-reliance. It is time to re-take control of our lives from government departments, bureaucrats, and the Indian Industry. To do this, we have to create our own wealth, develop a focused strategy to educate youth, and control our own purse strings. Reasserting control with a strategic plan for

moving forward should ultimately lead to more basic personal happiness. The object is to ensure that larger numbers of Aboriginal people are leading more enriched, rewarding lives. Wealth (or money), although needed to provide opportunities, in itself is not the goal, but only a means to this greater end. Successfully implemented, this process in turn should pay huge economic and social dividends for Canada as a country.[13]

NOTES

1. Mark O. Dickerson and Thomas Flanagan, *An Introduction to Government and Politics: A Conceptual Approach,* 7th ed. (Toronto: Thomson Nelson, 2006), pp. 30–31.

2. See Menno Boldt and J. Anthony Long, "Tribal Traditions and European-Western Political Ideologies: The Dilemma of Canada's Native Indians," *Canadian Journal of Political Science* 17 (1984), pp. 537–553; Thomas Flanagan, "Indian Sovereignty and Nationhood: A Comment on Boldt and Long," ibid., 18 (1985), pp. 367–374; Boldt and Long, "A Reply to Flanagan's Comments," ibid., 19 (1986), p. 153.

3. Debbie Hum, "Ottawa Has No Right to Impose Its Law on Natives: Mohawk," *The Gazette* (Montreal), March 18, 1993.

4. *Wikipedia*, "Caledonia Land Dispute," available at http://en.wikipedia.org/wiki/Caledonia_land_dispute.

5. Charlottetown Accord, s. 41.

6. John Stuart Mill, *Considerations on Representative Government* (Chicago: Henry Regnery, 1962; first published 1861), p. 309.

7. Charlottetown Accord, s. 9.

8. Ibid., s. 22.

9. Ibid., s. 20.

10. Thomas Sowell, *Race and Economics* (New York: David McKay, 1983), p. 128.

11. Calvin Helin, *Dances with Dependency: Indigenous Success through Self-Reliance* (Vancouver: Orca Spirit Publishing and Communications, 2006), p. 264.

12. Terry L. Anderson, Bruce Benson, and Thomas E. Flanagan, eds., *Self-Determination: The Other Path for Native Americans* (Stanford, CA: Stanford University Press, 2006).

13. Helin, *Dances with Dependency,* p. 39.

POSTSCRIPT

The main purpose of the article by Roger Townshend is to demonstrate that Native claims to sovereignty have a strong historical and moral basis. Moreover, the author argues that there is plenty of room to accommodate broader notions of Native sovereignty that would not lead to the destruction of the Canadian state as Thomas Flanagan suggests. Nevertheless, even if we accept his argument, there still are a number of nagging practical questions that remain. Would all of the more than 600 tribal bands in Canada be given equal sovereign status? Or would sovereignty be granted to some kind of pan-Indian confederation? Would such a body constitute a third level of government as envisaged in the Charlottetown Accord? If sovereignty is recognized, and outstanding land claims resolved, would federal and provincial governments, preoccupied with deficit reduction measures, simply withdraw access to all services currently provided? Would small and dispersed Indian bands be able to fund and staff the social, economic, and governmental programs that self-government would necessitate?

One intriguing response to some of these questions has been put forward by Thomas Courchene and Lisa Powell in a volume entitled *A First Nations Province* (Kingston: Institute of Intergovernmental Affairs, 1992). They suggest that instead of creating a third order of government, a First Nations province could be created that would represent Native aspirations, providing the powers, institutions, and ability to carry out intergovernmental relations in largely the same manner as provinces presently do.

The notion of a third level of government was taken up by the Royal Commission on Aboriginal Peoples. In its final report, the commission recommended that an Aboriginal order of government, which would coexist with the federal and provincial orders of government, be recognized. According to the commissioners, "The governments making up these three orders are sovereign within their own several spheres and hold their powers by virtue of their inherent or constitutional status rather than delegation. They share the sovereign powers of Canada as a whole, powers that represent a pooling of existing sovereignties" (p. 244). Although the commission found that Aboriginal communities may choose from one of three different models of Aboriginal government, it recommended that a House of First Peoples be created as a third chamber of Parliament. The House of First Peoples would have power to veto certain legislation that "directly affect[s] areas of exclusive Aboriginal jurisdiction . . . or where there is a substantial impact of a particular law of Aboriginal peoples" (p. 418). Although Aboriginal responses to the report were positive, government complacency and the ongoing preoccupation with unity issues relating to Quebec have ensured that these recommendations have largely been ignored. Some fear that it will take further Oka crises to put the issue of Native sovereignty back at the top of the public policy agenda.

Not everyone sympathetic to Native concerns feels that these demands should be pressed in terms of claims to sovereign statehood. For example, Menno Boldt and J. Anthony Long point out that sovereignty is really a Western European concept based on notions of territoriality and hierarchical authority that are foreign to traditional Native culture. In their article "Tribal Traditions and European-Western Political Ideologies: The Dilemma of Canada's Native Indians," *Canadian Journal of Political Science* 17, no. 3 (September 1984), pp. 537–555, Boldt and Long argue that reliance on the concept of sovereignty has led many Native leaders to reinterpret their own history in a selective way that actually legitimizes European-Western philosophies and conceptions of authority: "The legal–political struggle for sovereignty could prove to be a Trojan Horse for traditional Indian culture by playing into the hands of the Canadian government's long-standing policy of assimilation" (p. 548).

Although Native issues have been ignored for so long, a number of excellent books on the subject have appeared in recent years. *Pathways to Self-Determination: Canadian Indians and the Canadian State,* edited by Leroy Little Bear, Menno Boldt, and J. Anthony Long (Toronto: University of Toronto Press, 1984) is a useful set of essays (many written by Native leaders) for beginning to explore these issues. *Nation to Nation: Aboriginal Sovereignty and the Future of Canada,* edited by John Bird, Lorraine Laud, and Murray MacAdam (Concord: House of Anansi Press, 2001), contains a series of thirty essays that deal with the issues surrounding sovereignty, land claims policy, and Native/non-Native relations. Also useful are the following volumes: J. Frideres, *Native People in Canada: Contemporary Conflicts,* 3rd ed. (Scarborough: Prentice-Hall, 1988) and B. Morse, *Aboriginal Peoples and the Law: Indian, Métis and the Inuit Rights in Canada* (Don Mills: Oxford, 1984). Another good resource, Tim Schouls's recent book, *Shifting Boundaries: Aboriginal Identity, Pluralist Theory, and the Politics of Self-Government* (Vancouver: University of British Columbia Press, 2003), focuses on the importance of the question of formation and protection of Aboriginal identity to the notion of self-government.

Perhaps the most detailed resource on this issue is the five-volume Report of the Royal Commission on Aboriginal Peoples. Especially useful on the issues of sovereignty and self-government is the volume titled *Restructuring the Relationships* (Ottawa: Report of the Royal Commission on Aboriginal Peoples, Volume 2, 1996). For a critical perspective on the issue of Native sovereignty, see Melvin Smith, *Our Home or Native Land?* (Victoria: Crown Western, 1995).

Two of Canada's noted political scientists have published books on Aboriginal policy from quite different perspectives. Tom Flanagan published *First Nations? Second Thoughts* (Montreal and Kingston: McGill-Queen's University Press, 2000), which sets up to refute what he sees as the primary "myths" surrounding the debate over Aboriginal rights. Alain Cairns, in *Citizens Plus: Aboriginal Peoples and the Canadian State* (Vancouver: University of British Columbia Press, 2000), looks at ways in which the gap between Aboriginal people and non-Aboriginal people can be bridged in a way that respects the distinctive needs of First Nations peoples. While he thinks that Aboriginal nations will not opt for a form of sovereign independence that exceeds their capacity to govern, Cairns encourages Canadians to seek ways to improve the living conditions of Aboriginals and give them greater control over their daily lives while recognizing that a certain degree of integration into modern society, an option he calls "citizens plus," is essential. Cairns concludes, "So the choices that we have to make for territorially based nations are the nature and extent of Aboriginal self-government and how we organize our common life in the areas beyond the reach of self-government" (p. 212). For an assessment of Cairns's argument, see Heidi Libesman, "In Search of a Postcolonial Theory of Normative Integration: Reflections on A.C. Cairns' Theory of Citizens Plus," *Canadian Journal of Political Science* (December 2005).

Is the Canadian Charter of Rights and Freedoms Antidemocratic?

✔ **YES**
ROBERT MARTIN, "The Canadian Charter of Rights
and Freedoms Is Antidemocratic and Un-Canadian"

✘ **NO**
PHILIP L. BRYDEN, "The Canadian Charter of Rights and
Freedoms Is Antidemocratic and Un-Canadian: An Opposing
Point of View"

Do terminally ill patients have the right to a doctor-assisted suicide? Should women have unrestricted access to abortion without fear of criminal penalty? Does freedom of expression include the right to produce and distribute pornography? Are Sunday shopping regulations a violation of freedom of religion? Should people be able to marry same-sex partners? All of these questions raise difficult issues regarding the relationship between individual citizens and their government. In essence, they each pose the same questions: What civil rights does an individual have, and how are they to be protected from the intrusive arm of the state?

In choosing to establish a system of parliamentary government on the "Westminster model," the founders of Canada adopted a British solution to this problem. Parliament would be supreme and would act as the ultimate guarantor of individual rights and freedoms. This solution reflects an implicit trust in both Parliament and the basic democratic values of civil society. It assumes that civil liberties are so deeply ingrained in the national political culture that parliamentarians and citizens alike would never seriously consider using the power of government to infringe upon them. Public opinion and tradition would act as a powerful constraint against any violation of the fundamental civil and political liberties that are considered to be an inherent part of a democratic system. With the establishment of a federal system in Canada, courts were given the task of deciding whether federal and provincial legislatures were acting within their respective jurisdictions, not whether their actions violated civil and political liberties. There was no perceived need to give such rights special judicial protection that put them outside the reach of legislators.

Not everyone was happy with this solution. They pointed to a long history of both provincial and federal governments' trampling of the rights of citizens. In the early part of the twentieth century, British Columbia passed laws denying Asians the right to vote in provincial elections. During the Second World War, the federal government arbitrarily seized the property of Japanese Canadians and placed them in internment camps without due process of law.

These experiences, and others, convinced many Canadians that greater protection of civil rights was needed. The Americans provided an alternative solution: define the rights of citizens in a written constitutional document that is beyond the reach of the legislature. The courts, through the power of judicial review, can then pass judgment on whether the legislation passed by a government infringes on civil liberties. John Diefenbaker began to move Canada in this direction in 1960, when his government passed the Canadian Bill of Rights. But this bill was simply an act of Parliament and applied only to the federal government. As a result, Canadian courts made only limited use of the Bill of Rights.

With the adoption of the Canadian Charter of Rights and Freedoms as part of a larger constitutional package, the government of Pierre Trudeau brought in a new era in 1982. With the entrenchment of the Charter in the Canadian Constitution, not only were Canadians given an explicit definition of their rights, but also the courts were empowered to rule on the constitutionality of government legislation.

There is little doubt that the adoption of the Charter has significantly transformed the operation of the Canadian political system. Since the adoption of the Charter over a quarter of a century ago, the Supreme Court of Canada has been involved in virtually every issue of any great political significance in Canada. As a result, there has been a growing public awareness about the potential "political" role that the Supreme Court now plays in the lives of ordinary Canadians. Canadians now primarily define their needs and complaints in the language of rights. More and more, interest groups and minorities are turning to the courts, rather than the usual political processes, to make their grievances heard. Peter Russell has described the dramatic impact of the Charter on Canadian politics as having "judicialized politics and politicized the judiciary."

Has the impact of the Charter been a positive one? Has the Charter lived up to its promise to enhance Canadian democracy through the protection of civil liberties? Robert Martin, a former law professor at the University of Western Ontario, feels that the impact of the Charter has been largely a negative one. In particular, he argues that the Charter has had an antidemocratic effect on the country and has accelerated the Americanization of Canada. In contrast, Philip Bryden, dean of the Faculty of Law at the University of Alberta, argues that the Charter plays an essential role in protecting and enhancing the quality of Canadian democracy.

✔ YES

The Canadian Charter of Rights and Freedoms Is Antidemocratic and Un-Canadian

ROBERT MARTIN

INTRODUCTION

On April 17, 1982, the Canadian Charter of Rights and Freedoms became part of our Constitution. Everyone who has written about the Charter agrees its effect has been to change profoundly both our politics and the way we think. Most of the commentators have applauded these changes. I do not.

I believe the Charter has had decidedly negative effects on Canada. It has contributed to an erosion of our democracy and of our own sense of ourselves. It is time for a serious and critical stocktaking.

Let me be clear that I am not suggesting the Charter itself has actually done any of this. A central problem with the Charter has been its contribution to our growing inability to distinguish between the concrete and the abstract. The Charter is simply words on a piece of paper. What I will be addressing are the uses to which the Charter has been put by human beings. I will look at the antidemocratic effects of the Charter and then turn to an analysis of its un-Canadian character.

THE CHARTER IS ANTIDEMOCRATIC

By their nature, constitutions express a fear of democracy, a horror that the people, if given their head, will quickly become a mindless mob. As a result, constitutions, all constitutions, place enforceable limitations on the powers of the state and, more particularly, on the lawmaking authority of the people's representatives.

Prior to 1982, the Canadian Constitution did contain such limitations. Our central constitutional document, the British North America Act of 1867, divided lawmaking authority between Parliament and the provincial legislatures and, thereby, limited that authority. But these limitations were purely functional. The authority to make laws about education, for example, rested with the provinces. Ottawa could not make laws about education, and if it attempted to do so, the attempt could be struck down by the courts. The courts had no authority to tell the provinces how to exercise their authority over education, to tell them what kind of laws they should make about education.

This is what changed in 1982. The federal division of powers remained, but for the first time, substantive limitations were placed on lawmaking authority.

The judges were given the power to strike down laws that, in their opinion, were inconsistent with the Charter.

It is crucial to understand basic distinctions between legislators and judges. Any Canadian citizen over the age of eighteen is eligible to be elected to Parliament or a provincial legislature. Elected members are directly accountable to their constituents. They must face reelection at least once every five years. By way of contrast, to become a senior judge in Canada, you must be a lawyer, and you must have been one for ten years. You are appointed until age seventy-five through a closed process that a former chief justice of Canada described as "mysterious," and you are made constitutionally independent, directly accountable to no one.

The defining feature of representative democracy in Canada has been that it is up to the elected members of our legislatures to resolve issues of social, economic, and political policy, subject, of course, to the approval or disapproval of the people, which is expressed at periodic elections. This has changed since the adoption of the Charter. Judges can now overturn deliberate policy decisions made by the elected representatives of the people where those decisions do not accord with the way the judges interpret the Charter. This is undemocratic. Some of our commentators call this "counter-majoritarian," but the phrase is pure obfuscation.

We seem to be experiencing great difficulty today in grasping this simple truth about the antidemocratic nature of judicial review of legislation. One explanation for our difficulty is that we have forgotten that liberalism and democracy are not the same thing. Liberalism is about individual rights, about the ability of individuals to do as they please without interference from the state. Liberalism makes protection of the autonomy of the individual more important than the promotion of the welfare of the collectivity. Democracy is, and always has been, about the interests of the collectivity, about majority rule, about power to the people.

There is an inherent and irreconcilable tension between liberalism and democracy. This tension has always been built into our political system, a system that is ordinarily described as liberal democracy.

The Charter is a liberal document. It sets out fundamental notions about the rights of the individual that have always been at the core of liberalism. More to the point, the Charter has led to a shift in emphasis in Canadian liberal democracy. The balance has been tilted in favour of liberalism and away from democracy.

Members of the judiciary, led by the Supreme Court of Canada, have shown little restraint in arrogating to themselves a central policymaking role. In 1984, they conferred upon themselves the distinction "guardian of the Constitution." They haven't looked back.

Our judges have not hesitated to substitute their views of acceptable or desirable social policy for those of our legislators. When the judges have not agreed with the policy decisions of our elected representatives, they have invalidated the legislation that expresses those decisions. But the judges have been prepared to go further. They have shown themselves willing to write legislation, to even go to the point of imposing financial obligations on the state.

The willingness to interfere with the traditional policymaking functions of leg-islatures has not been restricted to the courts. Administrative tribunals now sit in judgment on the validity of legislation, and boards of inquiry set up under human rights acts rewrite legislation and create new legal responsibilities for individuals.

We have become more and more inclined to seek to resolve the central ques-tions agitating our society in the courtroom, rather than through the political process. The result of this is to surrender to lawyers control of the social agenda and of public discourse.

In a similar vein, the Charter has given a great boost to interest-group politics. Indeed, an active judicial role and interest-group politics seem made for each other.

Interest-group politics is antidemocratic in two respects. It erodes citizenship, the essential precondition to democratic politics. People are induced to define themselves according to their race or sex or sexual preference or some other ascriptive criterion, rather than as citizens. And, in practice, interest-group politics has meant seeking to use the courts as a means of short-circuiting or bypassing democratic processes.

The Charter has thus, in an institutional sense, had an antidemocratic effect. But it has also reinforced ideological currents that are antidemocratic. The most important of these stem from our growing obsession with "rights."

Our fascination with rights has been central to a process through which we seem to have come to prefer the abstract over the concrete. "Rights" appear to be more attractive than real things such as jobs or pensions or physical security or health care. We have been persuaded that if we have "rights" and these "rights" are enshrined in a constitution, then we need not concern ourselves with any-thing else. It is difficult to describe as "democratic" a public discourse that avoids addressing actual social and economic conditions.

Rights discourse itself encourages antidemocratic tendencies. The inclination of persons to characterize their desires or preferences as "rights" has two unfortu-nate results. First, there is an inevitable polarization of opposing positions in any debate. And, second, the possibility of further discussion is precluded. If you assert that something is your "right," my only possible response is, "No, it isn't."

Finally, the interest in rights has done much to promote individualistic and, therefore, antisocial ways of thinking. My impression is that many people view their rights as a quiver of jurisprudential arrows, weapons to be used in waging the ceaseless war of each against all.

THE CHARTER IS UN-CANADIAN

It is difficult to imagine any single event or instrument that has played a more sub-stantial role in Americanizing the way Canadians think than has the Charter. The Charter clearly did not begin this process, but it has, since 1982, been central in it.

The basis for my assertion about the Americanizing effects of the Charter is a recognition that, historically and culturally, the Charter is an American document.

This truth is seldom adverted to. As a technical drafting matter, the Charter, it is true, was the creation of Canadian lawyers. But the document's roots lie elsewhere. The idea of enshrining the rights of the individual in a constitution and then protecting those rights through judicial intervention is uniquely American. It may well be a good idea, but no one who had the slightest acquaintance with our history could call it a Canadian idea.

"Life, liberty, and the pursuit of happiness" are not simply words in the Declaration of Independence; they are essential notions defining the American experience. Up until 1982, the central Canadian notions were profoundly different. Our social and constitutional watchwords were "peace, order, and good government."

That has changed. I now teach students who are convinced that we did not have a Constitution, that we were not a proper country until we adopted the Charter. We have worked diligently to abolish our own history and to forget what was once our uniqueness. We are now told that the Charter is a basic element in defining what it means to be Canadian. And many Canadians do appear to believe that we can understand ourselves through our approach to the constitutional protection of rights.

The Charter has promoted our Americanization in other ways besides helping persuade us that we don't have a history. We have, as has already been noted, become more individualistic in our thinking and in our politics over the last decade. Again, it would be foolish to see the Charter as the only cause of this, but it is noteworthy that the first decade of the Charter saw an increase in the concrete indications of social alienation—crime, marital breakdown—as well as in more subtle forms—incivility, hostility, and so on. There was a time when one had a palpable sense, on crossing the border, of entering a different society. This is no longer true.

The Charter has led us to forget our uniqueness as Canadians and to disregard our history. It has had an incalculable effect in Americanizing both the way we think and the way we see ourselves. We have become incomparably more individualistic. Our collective sense of ourselves, and our idea of responsibility for each other and the society we share, has been seriously weakened.

Like Americans, we now believe there must be a legal remedy for every social ill. Like Americans, we put "me" first.

CONCLUSION

Many Canadians have contrived to forget that most of the things that once made Canada a fine country—physical security, health care for all, reasonably honest and competent government, sound education—came about through the political process, not as gifts from beneficent judges.

The fact is that, during the period the Charter has been part of our Constitution, ordinary Canadians have seen a steady erosion of their standard of living.

Unemployment is high and rising. Social services, health care, and pensions are threatened. Not only has the Charter not been of any help in preventing this erosion; it has served to distract our attention from what has been going on.

The great beneficiaries of the Charter have been the lawyers. They are consulted on issues of public policy, they pronounce on the morality or desirability of political and social beliefs and institutions, their advice is sought in a vast array of situations. The number of lawyers grows exponentially as does the cost of retaining their services.

The Charter has, to judge by media commentators, become the basis of our secular religion. And the lawyers are the priests. At some time, Canadians will decide to take control of their agenda back from the lawyers. That is when we will begin to give serious thought to repealing the Charter.

✗ **NO**

The Canadian Charter of Rights and Freedoms Is Antidemocratic and Un-Canadian: An Opposing Point of View

PHILIP L. BRYDEN

Robert Martin's essay launches a two-pronged attack on the Canadian Charter of Rights and Freedoms. The Charter is, according to Professor Martin, both anti-democratic and un-Canadian, and the sooner we Canadians come to our senses and realize that our lawyers have hoodwinked us into believing that the Charter is a good thing, the better off all of us (except maybe the lawyers) will be. My own view is that Professor Martin's essay presents a caricature of both the Charter and modern Canadian democracy, and that when we put the Charter in a more realistic light, we will see that the Charter can, and does, make a valuable contribution to Canada's democratic system of government.

The more powerful of Professor Martin's criticisms is his argument that we should get rid of the Charter because it is antidemocratic. Its attraction is that it contains a germ of truth. Like most half-truths, however, it hides more than it reveals.

In its simplest terms, the argument that the Charter is antidemocratic rests on the superficially plausible idea that if nonelected judges are empowered to over-turn the decisions of elected politicians, the document that gives them this power must be antidemocratic. The usefulness of the argument lies in its reminder to us that the greatest challenge for a court that has the kind of authority granted by our Charter is to interpret the vague but meaningful generalities on which this authority rests—ideas such as freedom of expression, fundamental justice, and equality—in a way that is consistent with our commitment to democratic govern-ment. Where the argument begins to mislead is when its proponents assume that because some judges have had difficulty meeting this challenge in the past, the whole enterprise is doomed to failure.

More specifically, two myths that underpin the notion that the kind of judicial review created by our Charter is inherently antidemocratic need to be exposed. The first myth is that the decisions of our elected legislators and the will of the majority of the electorate are one and the same. Democratic government as it is currently practised in Canada bears little resemblance to the workings of the Athenian polis or a New England town meeting. That observation is neither a disavowal of our current system of representative democracy nor an assertion that the way we presently govern ourselves stands in no need of improvement. It is, however, a reminder that when skeptics examine the record of judicial review using our Charter and point out some court decisions that deserve criticism, we should be evaluating that judicial performance against the reality of parliamentary government in Canada today and not against some romanticized portrait of government of the people, by the people, and for the people.

The second (and ultimately more damaging) myth is that majority rule is, or ought to be, all that modern democratic government is about, and it is in perpetuating the myth that "there is an inherent and irreconcilable tension between liberalism and democracy" that Professor Martin makes his most serious error. My point is not simply that we need a Charter to protect us from the tyranny of the majority, though I think it is dangerously naïve to believe that our fellow citizens are somehow incapable of tyranny. Rather, I want to suggest that democratic government as we should (and to a significant extent have) come to understand it in Canada consists of a complicated web of commitments to each other, only one of which is the commitment to government that in some meaningful way reflects the will of the people.

A belief that important decisions can be taken only after a free and public discussion of the issues, a willingness to abide by a set of rules that govern the way we make authoritative decisions, an acceptance of significant constraints on the use of force—these and many other commitments, some contained in the Charter and others not, are not mere side effects of modern Canadian democracy. They lie at the very heart of democratic government in Canada. And they are part of the reason that the Canadian system of government—notwithstanding all its shortcomings—is respected by people around the world.

This is, I freely acknowledge, a liberal conception of democratic government. Moreover, I recognize that there are other visions of democracy—the kind of Marxist democracy practised by Chairman Mao's Red Guards during the Cultural Revolution, for example—that leave no room for special protection of those who are not able to identify themselves with the will of the majority. For very good reasons, however, Canadians have accepted a liberal notion of democracy, and our commitment to this version of the democratic ideal was firmly in place long before we adopted the Charter.

The real issue is not whether placing some constraints on our legislators is inherently antidemocratic—it isn't. Instead, we ought to ask whether Canadian judges using the Charter can play a useful role in enhancing the quality of our democracy. The answer to this question is not obvious, but I believe that our judges can play such a role, and that by and large our experience during the first few years of the Charter bears this out.

Robert Martin leaves the impression that the Charter has fundamentally undermined the power of our elected representatives to shape the laws that govern our society. If we take a closer look at both the structure of the Charter and the judicial record in interpreting the Charter, however, I find it very difficult to see how that impression can be substantiated.

Because of the types of rights it does (and does not) guarantee, the Charter has little relevance to large and important areas of our political life, notably economic and foreign policy. The judiciary did not bring us free trade with the United States—our political leaders did. And our elected representatives, not our judges, will decide the shape of any new trade pact we may enter into with the United States and Mexico. Our elected representatives decided to commit our troops in the Persian Gulf War, and they, not our courts, will decide what role we play in other trouble spots around the world.

Where the Charter has had some potential to conflict with social policy, our judges have tended to be rather reluctant to accept claims that individual rights should override important governmental interests. Thus, our Supreme Court has decided that provincial Sunday closing laws reasonably limit freedom of religion and that Criminal Code prohibitions on hate speech and obscenity are acceptable constraints on freedom of expression. We may or may not agree with the wisdom of these and other decisions upholding the right of our politicians to pass laws that place reasonable limits on our constitutionally protected rights and freedoms, but this is certainly not the record of a judiciary that is attempting to undermine democratic government in Canada.

This is not to say that Charter litigation is meaningless because the government always wins. Our courts have made important decisions upholding the rights of refugee claimants, of people accused of crimes, of women, gays and lesbians, and many others. Once again, many of these decisions have been controversial, but I believe they have raised our sensitivity to the concerns of people whose interests are not always well represented through our political process. And in so doing, I would argue, they have enhanced the quality of Canadian democracy.

Professor Martin seems to believe that the Charter has undermined our sense of ourselves as a collectivity and contributed to the rise of a political life that is alternatively characterized by narrow interest-group politics or pure selfishness. To the extent that this description of contemporary Canadian politics has an aura of authenticity about it, however, I think it confuses cause and effect. The popularity of the Charter (indeed much of the need for a Charter) arises from the fact that Canadians understand the diversity of their interests and want to incorporate into their democratic system of government a recognition of the vulnerability of some of those interests.

This diversity of interests was not created by the Charter, and getting rid of the Charter is not likely to usher in a return to a mythical golden age of harmony and communitarian spirit. Throughout our history, Canadians have recognized and sought to give legal protection to our diversity on regional, linguistic, religious, and other grounds, and I suspect that only someone from Ontario could imagine characterizing this as an erosion of citizenship.

Again, the problem of the fracturing of our sense of ourselves as a political community that Professor Martin identifies is a real one, and it is a challenge for supporters of the kind of political ideals that the Charter represents to realize their goals in a way that does not irreparably undermine other political values that are important to us. What Professor Martin fails to do, in my view, is make a convincing case that it is not possible for us to meet this challenge or that it is not worthwhile for us to try to do so.

Professor Martin's second criticism of the Charter is that it is un-Canadian, by which he seems to mean that the Charter contributes to the "Americanization" of Canadian political life. It would be foolish to deny the influence of the United States Bill of Rights on both the content of the Charter and the political will that animated its adoption. In my view, however, Professor Martin is wrong in his attempt to characterize the Charter as a species of cuckoo in the Canadian political nest that seeks to supplant domestic institutions and traditions with unsavoury ideas from south of the forty-ninth parallel.

In response to Professor Martin, I would begin with the rather obvious point that even if some of the important ideas embedded in the Charter were imported into Canada from abroad, so is much of the rest of the apparatus of Canadian government. Canada's parliamentary and common law traditions were imported from England; our federalism was imported (albeit in a substantially altered form) from the United States in 1867; and our civil law traditions were imported from France. In each instance we have made these traditions our own, in some instances by performing major surgery on them in the process.

The Charter itself follows in this tradition of domesticating foreign political ideas and structures. For example, a central element of the American Bill of Rights is the protection of the right to private property. The drafters of the Canadian Charter (wisely in my view) decided that our normal political processes were adequate for the protection of the rights of property owners and that judges should not be given this responsibility under the Charter. In addition, the Charter recognizes certain rights of French and English linguistic minorities, expresses a commitment to our multicultural heritage, and contains approaches to equality and other rights that set it off as a document that is quite distinctive from the American Bill of Rights. The Charter's roots may lie in American soil, but the tree that springs up from those roots is distinctively Canadian.

The more subtle but significant point on which Professor Martin and I disagree is that he seems to use the term "Americanization" as a sort of shorthand for most of what he doesn't like in contemporary Canadian political life. No doubt there are plenty of Canadians who prefer the kind of life we had in the 1970s (or the 1950s for that matter) to the kind of life we have today. What is unclear to me, however, is how unemployment, family breakdown, the consequences of massive public-sector debt for our social welfare programs, and the other things that trouble Professor Martin about life in Canada in the twenty-first century can be laid at the door of the Charter.

In fairness, Professor Martin does not ascribe these social ills to the Charter itself, but he says that the Charter has "served to distract our attention from what has been going on." If the Charter has served to distract Canadians from thinking about the problems of high unemployment and threats to the continued viability of our present schemes for delivering social services, universal health care, and pensions, this is certainly news to me. And I dare say it would come as news to those who took part in the 1993 federal election campaign that revolved around these very issues. Professor Martin is probably correct when he states that the Charter is not going to be of much help in addressing these problems, but nobody ever claimed that it would. More important, we shouldn't assume that because the Charter doesn't address these important problems, the issues the Charter does address are somehow insignificant.

The Charter does not represent the sum of Canadian political life, any more than the American Bill of Rights represents the sum of political life in the United States. From a political science standpoint, what the Charter represents is a special way of addressing a limited range of issues that we feel are unlikely to get the kind of attention they deserve in the ordinary process of electoral politics, and a formal commitment to ourselves that the ideals such as freedom, justice, and equality that the Charter enshrines deserve a special place in our democratic political life. I think this was a commitment that it was wise for us to make in 1982, and that Canadians are right to be proud of this new and distinctive feature of our democracy.

POSTSCRIPT

The debate between Robert Martin and Philip Bryden on the Charter of Rights and Freedoms dates back to 1994. Robert Martin has more recently expanded his critique of both the Charter and the role of the Canadian Supreme Court in a strongly written book entitled *Most Dangerous Branch: How the Supreme Court Has Undermined Our Law and Democracy* (Montreal and Kingston: McGill-Queen's University Press, 2004). In this book, Martin writes, "As someone who is committed to the maintenance of constitutional democracy, I cannot avoid seeing the Court as a collection of arrogant and unprincipled poseurs, largely out of control."

But Martin is not the only one to express serious reservations about the impact of the Charter on Canadian political life. One of the most caustic critiques of the Charter has been written by Michael Mandel. In his book *The Charter of Rights and the Legalization of Politics in Canada,* rev. ed. (Toronto: Wall and Thompson, 1994), Mandel argues that the Charter has led to the "legalization of politics in Canada." Because the scope of interpretation of the Charter is very broad, judges make highly political decisions. They are not just interpreting the law according to some technical, objective criteria but are actually making the law, usurping the role traditionally reserved only for elected legislators. Because of the high cost of litigation, the legalization of politics, according to Mandel, leads to a conservative, class-based politics that works against socially disadvantaged groups.

Like Martin, Seymour Lipset, a noted American sociologist, argues that the Charter threatens to erase the cultural differences between Americans and Canadians by transforming Canada into a "rights-centred" political culture. See his *Continental Divide* (New York: Routledge, 1990). Christopher Manfredi argues that part of this Americanizing influence is reflected in the frequency with which Canadian judges cite American precedents when making their decisions.

Because of the growing importance of the Charter to Canadian politics, there has been a steady flow of books on this subject in recent years. In addition to the works cited above, students will find the following helpful: Rainer Knopff and F.L. Morton, *Charter Politics* (Scarborough: Nelson, 1992); Patrick Monahan, *Politics and the Constitution: The Charter, Federalism and the Supreme Court* (Toronto: Carswell, 1987); and David Beatty, *Putting the Charter to Work* (Montreal and Kingston: McGill-Queen's University Press, 1987). A book written by a civil rights activist who supports Philip Bryden's arguments is Alan Borovoy's *When Freedoms Collide: The Case for Our Civil Liberties* (Toronto: Lester & Orpen Dennys, 1988). See also Janet Hiebert, *Charter Conflicts: What Is Parliament's Role?* (Montreal and Kingston: McGill-Queen's University Press, 2002); Christopher Manfredi, *Judicial Power and the Charter, Canada and the Paradox of Liberal Constitutionalism,* 2nd ed. (Toronto: Oxford University Press, 2001); Peter McCormick, *Supreme at Last: The Evolution of the Supreme Court of Canada* (Toronto: Lorimer, 2000); and Rory Leishman, *Against Judicial Activism: The*

Decline of Freedom and Democracy in Canada (Montreal and Kingston: McGill-Queen's University Press, 2005).

If we accept Martin's argument that we should be concerned about the impact of the Charter, what can be done? Martin's closing suggestion that many Canadians may begin thinking about repealing the Charter seems unlikely now that a whole new generation has grown up with the Charter as an accepted fact. Perhaps a more likely development is that Canadians will begin to take a more careful look at the record of individual judges and to demand more say in their appointment. This has led some to argue that Parliament should review the appointment of Supreme Court judges as the Senate does in the United States. However, would such a move be a positive step or lead only to a very politicization and Americanization of the Canadian judicial system?

Is a Majority Government More Effective Than a Minority Government?

✔ **YES**
ALEX MARLAND, "The Case for a Functioning Majority Government"

✘ **NO**
ANNA ESSELMENT, "The Case for an Effective Minority Government"

A natural experiment has arisen that allows for resolving a crucial issue in parliamentary politics—which is preferable, a majority or minority government? The former type of government is formed by a political party with a number of legislative seats that exceeds 50 percent of the total number. The latter type has no party with a majority of seats. In 2004, 2006, and 2008, Canadians refused to give any of the federal political parties more than half of the seats in the House of Commons. Accordingly, political scientists, interested observers, and anyone else with a passing interest in politics were given a chance to see a minority government in action. But now a political party—the Conservative Party of Canada—has been awarded a majority government, which offers an opportunity to compare minority and majority governments. The fact that the majority follows the minority governments permits us to assume that any differences in the performance of the national government in the next few years—good or bad—can be attributed largely to the change in the type of government (because most other major factors affecting political life will have changed little—hence the notion of a *natural* experiment). The patient ones with an interest in politics will wait until the next election (in four years) to decide which type is preferable. But others, less patient, will want to begin their assessment early. Among this latter group will be political science students who, aside from being inquisitive about any matters political, may know that a question on majority and minority governments is a good candidate for inclusion in a final examination. And the way to begin investigating this issue is to look at the relevant evidence and arguments on both sides.

A number of arguments favour majority governments. The great fear in parliamentary systems—at least for the party in power—is the loss of a legislative vote. In this situation, conventions of parliamentary government require the dominant party to step down. But with a majority in hand (coupled with party discipline), a government can avoid this situation and accomplish, theoretically, many good things. For one, it can make longer term plans, because it is almost guaranteed a four-year term. Planning requires that a government have the time to think about their intentions, something that is often unavailable to minority governments obsessed with their precarious existence. Some retort that this may be fine, but also say that majority governments can afford to ignore any criticism. This possibility may detract from the quality of policy, but supporters of strong majorities in turn claim that majority situations are not necessarily without effective opposition forces. Finally, there are the supposed failings of a minority government that can be avoided with a majority—the game-playing, the short-run policy focus, and above all the constant posturing by the opposition to force an election in the hope that they can become the government.

The other side accepts some of the criticisms of minority governments, but suggests that these shortcomings can be remedied. For instance, the posturing mentioned above takes place largely because the electoral system—the single-member plurality (SMP) system—allows for significant shifts in seats to take place with insignificant shifts in the popular vote. In the SMP system, seats are allocated based on who wins in each of the ridings, so close contests tempt parties to try again in the knowledge that a swing of a small number of voters from one party to another may change the results. But the adoption of a proportional representation system in which the percentage of seats is roughly proportional to the percentage of votes would end this (a shift of a few percentage points in the popular vote, say, 30 percent to 33 percent, would have little effect on seat allocation). More important, say supporters of a minority government, the absence of a majority in the legislature produces significant benefits. One is that government action is not the result of often imperious majorities, but the product of a consensus built on the contributions of all parties. As well, a minority government gives individual Members of Parliament (MPs) a greater role because the government needs them to survive, which is not the case with a majority government supported by party discipline. And perhaps most relevant, minority governments are hardly aberrations or freaks of parliamentary government. Canada has a history of minority governments and so do other parliamentary democracies.

With their contributions, Alex Marland, a professor at Memorial University, and Anna Esselment, a professor at the University of Waterloo, guide us through the arguments for majority and minority governments.

✔ **YES**

The Case for a Functioning Majority Government

ALEX MARLAND

Canada's parliamentary system follows the principle of responsible government. This means that the executive branch, featuring a cabinet of appointed parliamentarians from the party of the prime minister, must be supported by at least half of the elected members of the legislature. So when a single party holds over 50 percent of the seats, there is minimal risk of cabinet being defeated on bills, on budget matters, or on a motion of nonconfidence. The planning stability, efficiency, and smoother operation of the state that results is generally preferable to the opportunism, political games, partisan conflict, and information secrecy that characterizes a government run by a party with less than 50 percent of the seats.

SUPER MAJORITY VERSUS FUNCTIONING MAJORITY

There are at least two types of majority governments. One is seriously problematic. Recent experience suggests that the other type is a better form of government than a minority. Let's dispense with what can be called a "super majority." This is when the support of the governing party has been so exaggerated by the single-member plurality (SMP) electoral system that there are too few opposition members to provide healthy debate or to participate in legislative committees. This sometimes occurs at the provincial level of government. Some extreme examples are the New Brunswick Liberals, led by Frank McKenna, who held all fifty-eight of that province's seats after the 1987 election; the Liberals, led by Gordon Campbell, who won seventy-seven of British Columbia's seventy-nine electoral districts in 2001; and the Progressive Conservatives, led by Danny Williams, who occupied forty-four of forty-eight seats in the Newfoundland and Labrador House of Assembly after the 2007 election.

A super majority should be actively guarded against. It raises serious concerns about flaws in the electoral system; about the fusion of the executive and legislative branches; about the supremacy of the head of government; and about the health of democracy. Political leaders tend to want freedom from limits on their power,[1] which is not always a bad thing, but a super majority results in superficial scrutiny of the political executive and it undermines responsible government. That super majorities are achieved in provinces, where premiers already have far more localized power than the prime minister of Canada could ever aspire to,[2] is distressing. Yet even then the political executive still faces constraints, such as the division of federal and provincial powers, the monitoring role of press galleries, and the dominance of the rule of law. A good government therefore faces enough opposition members that it is held accountable—but not so many opponents that its work grinds to a halt. When one party has more than half the seats, but does not have a super majority, we can refer to it as a "functioning majority." Functioning majorities tend to be fairly common due to the SMP electoral system. A recent example is the 2011 federal election that saw the Conservative Party of Canada, led by Stephen Harper, win 166 of 308 seats (54 percent) in the House of Commons on 39.6 percent of the popular vote. The Conservative government faces scrutiny from the Official Opposition New Democratic Party (103 seats) and the Liberal Party (34 seats). Two other parties, the Bloc Québécois (4 seats) and a lone Green Party MP, also monitor the government.

Recent experience suggests that a functioning majority is more desirable than when no party controls at least half of the seats in the legislature, that is, a minority government. Federal elections in 2004, 2006, and 2008 all produced minorities, the first headed by Liberal Paul Martin and the latter two by Harper. During this period there was so much political bickering, gamesmanship, and partisan threats to bring down the government that any romantic who hoped that a spirit of cooperation would emerge was bitterly disappointed. Former NDP national director Robin Sears described those governments as "childish, high-volume, low-achievement exercises that have driven more and more Canadians to distraction and dismayed them about the state of Canadian politics."[3] Consequently a 2009 public opinion survey found that Canadians wanted a majority government instead of a minority by nearly a 3:1 ratio;[4] another poll pegged the ratio of majority to minority supporters at 4:1.[5] After the negative experiences of the early 2000s, returning to the relative serenity of majority governance in 2011 was a welcome relief.

THE DISADVANTAGES OF A MINORITY GOVERNMENT

Opportunism and Instability

To establish the benefits of a majority government we first need to acknowledge that there are considerable problems with a minority government. Foremost among these is that the governing party is so constantly threatened with losing power that it cannot deliver good government. It weaves from vote to vote in the legislature, the executive has difficulty planning, and to survive it must emphasize short-term political strategies and tactics. Parliament is shut down more often through prorogation (which ends a session and puts the assembly in recess) or dissolution (which ends the assembly and an election must be held to elect new representatives). When this happens, bills and motions "die on the order paper" and the work must be restarted when Parliament is reconvened.

The possibility of a snap election means that political parties behave as though they are in a permanent election campaign. There are rancorous Question Periods and committee meetings. The governing party groups many bills into a single omnibus bill, daring the opposition to defeat major legislation over smaller issues, and behaving as though it has a majority without such a mandate.[6] Members of non-government parties may skip votes to allow a government bill to pass to avoid triggering an election but they still criticize the governing party's decisions. Premiers and interest groups lobby for special treatment, and their threats carry more weight. For instance, between 2004 and 2008, Danny Williams openly exploited the weaknesses of minority prime ministers. He ordered Canadian flags be removed from provincial buildings to pressure Prime Minister Martin to give Newfoundland more money, and then Premier Williams ran an "Anything but Conservative" campaign against Prime Minister Harper when he didn't get his way. Given this ongoing conflict, minority governments tend to last less than two years before another election is required, and such a short duration is evidence of how unworkable they are in practice.

The one time that minority governments are thought to work is when a Liberal government is propped up by a third party.[7] Such deal making involves post-election negotiations between party elites, as opposed to such choices being vetted by voters, or following known conventions.[8] The 1963–1968 Liberal minorities, led by Prime Minister Lester Pearson with the support of the New Democrats, are often cited as a productive period that produced grand programs such as medicare, the Canada Pension Plan (CPP), and interest-free student loans. Supporters of those parties, of progressive government, and of big spending therefore say that minority government is good. Yet this ignores that much of Canada's social welfare framework, including old age pensions, employment insurance (EI), the family allowance, and the equalization program, had been set by Liberal majority governments. With backroom deals it also becomes difficult to sort out which political parties deserve credit and who should be blamed. Politics being what it is, many parties say that they alone are responsible for good ideas, and are eager to point the finger at others for unpopular decisions.

These grand programs are expensive and are a reflection of ministers in a minority prioritizing proposals that may win votes in the next election. This can produce policy that is poorly researched and/or that contributes to overspending. J.S. Hodgson, who has written about the implications for government staff, observed that

> [l]egislation and programs involving payments or benefits to individuals therefore take on special attraction....A minority government is prone to spend, but because of its relative weakness it is much less likely to impose tax increases. It is therefore likely to incur budgetary deficits.[9]

The need for a minority government to spend money to stay alive goes against the Conservative Party's philosophy of cautious government spending. There are three infamous cases in Canadian federal politics of the instability of Conservative minority governments: the King-Byng crisis of 1926, the Clark budget defeat of 1979, and the Harper coalition crisis of 2008. Each illustrates that the Conservative Party's lack of a political dancing partner is a critical shortcoming of minority governance.

The difficulty of the parliamentary system of government prioritizing parties ahead of leaders, even though Canadians prioritize leadership over partisanship,[10] was exemplified in the mid-1920s. The oddity of a party leader "winning" an election and not becoming prime minister occurred in 1925 when the Arthur Meighen-led Conservatives more than doubled their seat count to 115 (46 percent of the 245 House seats at the time). Prime Minister Mackenzie King's Liberals were reduced to 100 MPs, the Progressive Party was reduced to 22 MPs, and other parties and independents held 8 seats. King himself was even defeated as an MP—and yet he stayed on as prime minister of a minority government by negotiating the support of the Progressives (totalling 122 seats, so nearly 50 percent) and by persuading a Liberal MP to resign so that he could win the seat in a by-election. This led to the King-Byng crisis of 1926 when the prime minister, facing a spending scandal, sought an election but Governor General Viscount Byng instead appointed Meighen as prime minister to avoid yet another election. The Conservatives were promptly defeated on a confidence vote in the House of Commons, and King went on to campaign in 1926 against the "chaos" of minority government in favour of a stable majority government, which electors awarded him.

The short-term decision making that characterizes a minority government is best exemplified by the period after the 1979 federal election. Joe Clark's Progressive Conservatives grew to 136 seats (of 282 at the time, so 48 percent) and replaced Pierre Trudeau's Liberal government, which was reduced to 114 MPs. The Progressive Conservatives' first budget tackled high inflation, ballooning spending, and deficit financing in part by seeking to cut programs and increase taxes on gasoline. John Crosbie, the Minister of Finance, explained this as "short term pain for long term gain,"[11] meaning that sometimes governments need to make unpopular decisions in the best interest of its citizens. But because austerity is not possible in a minority situation, the Liberals and NDP voted down the budget, triggering an election just nine months after Clark had been elected. Trudeau was returned with a majority government.

The most blatant example of Canadian political parties' opportunism in a minority government was the coalition crisis. In October 2008, amid global economic turmoil triggered by the collapse of the American housing sector, the Harper Conservatives were reelected with a larger minority of 143 seats (46 percent of 308). Liberal leader Stéphane Dion announced that he would step down as soon as a replacement could be selected. The finance minister tabled an economic update that contained a provision to eliminate some of the party financing that the Conservatives' opponents depended upon.

Six weeks after the election the Liberals (77 MPs), Bloc Québécois (49 MPs), and NDP (37 MPs) announced that they would bring the government down. They said the lack of stimulus spending to strengthen the economy was unacceptable; in private, they were outraged that Harper was trying to cut their government funding. Sensing the fragility of their hold on power, the Tories removed the controversial proposal, but it was too late. The leaders of the three opposition parties signed an agreement whereby Dion would become temporary prime minister of a coalition government that would include a handful of NDP MPs in a Liberal cabinet. The Liberals and NDP together had fewer seats than the Tories, but with the support of the separatist Bloc Québécois, they would control the House of Commons with 163 MPs (53 percent of seats). The minority government was in crisis. The Governor General rushed back to Canada from a trip abroad; Conservative advertising demonized a "separatist coalition"; supporters and opponents organized competing rallies across Canada; Harper and Dion delivered national televised addresses. Public anger, excitement, and confusion reigned.

Neither a coalition nor eliminating the party subsidies had been debated in the election campaign. Governor General Michaëlle Jean allowed cooler heads to prevail when she agreed with Harper's request to prorogue parliament. Within days the Liberal Party installed MP Michael Ignatieff—who was lukewarm to the coalition idea—as its new leader and the next month the Tories introduced a budget with stimulus spending. The Conservatives then prioritized spending in their own MPs' districts,[12] promoted a so-called "economic action plan" with millions in government advertising, and registered record deficits that the opposition decried. The lesson? That in a minority government, especially in situations when strong leadership is needed, we can expect political parties to put their own interests first, to stir public unrest, and to generally behave poorly.

Political Games and Information Secrecy

In a minority situation the opposition keeps the government unbalanced and under relentless attack. A political entertainment industry emerges to keep track of the games on Parliament Hill. The press speculates about the possibility of an election over and over. Pundits analyze strategic manoeuvring and reporters race to reveal the latest partisan tactics. The drama of by-elections to fill seat vacancies is magnified, questionable decisions are amplified into major scandals, and critics become media stars. Opinion polls keep score of which party or leader is "winning" and who is "losing."

In an effort to neutralize attacks the governing party tries to control the availability of information. The Harper minority era (2006–2011) was hypersensitive about going off message—though this was equally a reflection of the trend toward the centralization of the executive branch and of Harper's leadership style. Secrecy and toeing the party line was deemed essential to his government's survival. For example:

- Access-to-information processing was delayed, and documents that were released were redacted (blacked out) to avoid arming the opposition, most notably information about when the government knew that some prisoners in Afghanistan were being abused.

- People holding senior government positions were replaced for speaking out, such as the president of the Canadian Nuclear Safety Commission, or they resigned, including the Chief Statistician of Canada.

- Party communications were disparaging, most notably the Conservative Party's television ads that relentlessly attacked Liberal leaders, branding Dion as "not a leader" and then Ignatieff as an elitist who "didn't come back for you."

Legislative committees are an important check on government power, but in a minority government, they can become the scene of partisan jockeying. Committees are the small groups of MPs from different parties who scrutinize government bills, spending, and topical issues. In a minority situation, the presence of more non-government members does not lead to more effective committee work,[13] and members may be more prone to grandstand. In 2007, Conservative committee chairs followed a guidebook with instructions on "how to favour government agendas, select party-friendly witnesses, coach favourable testimony, set in motion debate-obstructing delays and, if necessary, storm out of meetings to grind parliamentary business to a halt."[14] Such shameful behaviour was defended as necessary amid a fragmented minority Parliament.

It was a lack of transparency that led to a legislative committee finding the Harper minority government in contempt of Parliament. The Standing Committee on Procedure and House Affairs (SCPHA) investigated the Harper administration's refusal to provide a finance committee with the costs of airplane purchases, of hosting international summits, of reducing the corporate tax rate, and of reforms to the justice system. In denying this request, the Conservatives invoked the privilege of "Cabinet confidence," referring to the fact that some high-level government decisions must be kept secret in order to govern. Eventually additional information was released, but in 2011, the Speaker of the House (at the time, a Liberal MP), who oversees legislative proceedings, ruled that this was insufficient and the committee concluded that "the government's failure to produce documents constitutes a contempt of Parliament." The SCPHA's Conservative members dissented by stating that the main report was "simply a piece of partisan gamesmanship."[15] The contempt ruling was the final straw and led to the minority government's defeat on a non-confidence motion. This parliamentary derision was a re-occurring theme during the ensuing election, and Harper countered by repeatedly positioning the solution as a "strong, stable national Conservative majority government."

Short-Term Public Policy and Inefficient Public Administration

Under minority rule the civil service operates on a temporary basis, and public servants become "like a man treading water because he is free neither to swim nor to come ashore."[16] Planning is complicated by the difficulty of implementing a Throne Speech and the annual budget, which end up reflecting a Frankenstein of ad hoc priorities promoted by various opposition parties, special interests, and premiers. Serious decisions are put off until clarity and permanence can be achieved. There is less time to develop good public policy and a need to fast-track program implementation. The heightened centralization of decision making, such as budget planning between the prime minister and the minister of finance, comes at a cost of excluding other members of cabinet and delaying even basic decisions.[17] Public servants are scared of routine actions or inactions that could get them into trouble and time pressures increase the number of decisions that are made based on hunches rather than guided by data.

In a minority era, money for invisible government operations is harder to come by, and people with party connections put more pressure on bureaucrats to make exemptions to administrative policies. Senior policy advisors are more likely to have any controversial proposals rejected and to find that ministers will not follow their recommendations. They may be tempted to save face by advocating only courses of action that are likely to be adopted. David Good of the University of Victoria identifies the negative implications of a minority Parliament on public administration this way:

> ...the singular focus of minority governments on their short term electoral prospects has significant consequences for the public service. The scope for the public service to adjust previously announced campaign commitments is sharply reduced; budgetary decision-making and public communications is more centralized; expenditure reductions fall more heavily on the public service; pressure for speedy and error-free implementation of policies increases; ministerial demand for longer term policy analysis evaporates; and the risk of political interference in administrative matters increases.[18]

THE ADVANTAGES OF A MAJORITY GOVERNMENT

Stability, Efficiency, and Smoother Operations

One of the most significant advantages of a functioning majority is that government policy can be improved. This is because it can be designed over a four-year cycle rather than on a three-month survival basis. The governing party's campaign platform, its Throne Speech, and the annual budget provide a more truthful indication of the government's direction. Officials close to the prime minister face less pressure to interfere with ministers and their departments. International planning, trade negotiations, and meetings with other country's representatives can be more fertile. The result is a better government that is still held to account in the House of Commons and which has a record that voters can pass judgment on in the next election campaign.

Whereas leaders of minority governments are in constant crisis, a leader who controls a majority of seats in the legislature can choose between running an activist government to effect major change, or can opt to be a steady hand over the country's political affairs. Mackenzie King, often considered to be Canada's most successful prime minister, governed with caution, sought to overcome differences, and infamously said that "it is what we prevent, rather than what we do, that counts most in government."[19] Prime Ministers Wilfrid Laurier, Louis St. Laurent, and Jean Chrétien likewise ran managerial governments, and electors consistently returned them to office with a majority of seats. Other leaders, such as John A. Macdonald, Pierre Trudeau, and Brian Mulroney have been visionaries who used their majorities to profoundly shape Canada. A democracy needs debate and scrutiny, but public policy should not be merely a popularity contest. We depend on leaders to make difficult decisions, especially in unwinnable "dirty hands" scenarios, and to think beyond next week. It was under majority governments that the Canadian Constitution was amended and the Charter of Rights and Freedoms was adopted. Strong leadership has been needed to deal with national security matters, such as handling the Front de libération du Québec (FLQ) terrorism crisis, leading Canada's response to the 9/11 terrorist attacks, and making the subsequent decision not to send Canadian troops to Iraq. Long-term financial initiatives would not have been possible without strong majority governments, such as the North American Free Trade Agreement (NAFTA), the goods and services tax (GST), and the deficit/debt reduction of the 1990s. The Conservatives' 2011 election platform[20] also featured some domestic and international policy pledges that would be difficult in a minority situation but which are viable with a majority government, such as

- long-term fiscal planning, as evidenced by the party's plans to reduce government spending to eliminate the deficit and balance the budget;

- major international negotiations, notably the completion of a free trade agreement between Canada and the European Union and a Canada–India free trade deal;

- creating Canada-wide standards, such as establishing a national securities regulator to replace the thirteen regulators in the provinces and territories who govern investing in the stock market;

- reforming government, including passing legislation to limit the term in office for members of the Senate; and,

- ending the party subsidies that had triggered the coalition crisis in 2008.

With less than half of the seats, the opposition wields little power over the governing party but a hardworking group can nevertheless hold a functioning majority responsible for its actions. There is time to scrutinize, time to research, and time to produce viable alternatives that are less prone to partisanship, populism, or sensationalism. There are plenty of examples of good opposition during majority governments, such as the Liberal "rat pack" that dogged the Mulroney Conservatives in the 1980s, or the Reform Party pressuring the Chrétien Liberals to reduce spending in the 1990s. Ministers were still held to account and pressured to resign. But with the temperature lowered, MPs from different parties can work behind the scenes together with the understanding that the governing party has the final say. Committees still hold hearings to listen to stakeholders' testimony and may recommend amendments to a bill.[21]

Parliamentarians and lawyers have more time to scrutinize draft legislation that, if necessary, can pass through the three reading stages with fewer delays. Freed from daily firefighting, opposition parties have an opportunity to recharge and rebuild through internal discussions about viable policy alternatives, candidate recruitment, and campaign planning. The public at large also benefits from a functioning majority. Businesses and non-governmental organizations can plan based on reasonably predictable monetary policies and commercial regulations.[22] Citizens are able to get answers to their questions faster because civil servants have clear direction.[23] A majority government can increase the recruitment and retention of talented and/or well-meaning candidates. It also provides stability for the hundreds of political staffers in Ottawa and in constituencies, many of whom are young university graduates who face less angst about suddenly losing their job.

ARE CRITICISMS OF A MAJORITY GOVERNMENT FAIR?

There is a fine balance between a government's right to govern and the opposition's right to hold it accountable. Given all this there is a strong case to be made for a functioning majority government, especially for people who believe in government efficiency and for those who recognize that in practice, party politics is a rough game. Nevertheless two criticisms should be addressed.

One of the biggest critiques of majority government is that is unfair. This is because the SMP electoral system creates what scholar Peter Russell calls "false majorities."[24] This is when the governing party wins a majority of the seats even though more than half of voters actually voted for a different party, as was the case with the Harper Conservatives in 2011. Minority government is said to be more fair, and advocates of a proportional representation (PR) system would agree. In theory this makes sense; however, in practice a minority government can be unworkable, especially under a Conservative regime. Moreover the SMP electoral system tends to grossly overstate the support of smaller regional and/or ideological parties, such as the Bloc Québécois, which gain even more clout in a minority situation as opposed to being held in check by a majority government. Changing the electoral system might be desirable, but until then, functioning majorities offer more stability than fragile minorities do.

Another critique is that the head of government has too much power in a majority government. This is a valid concern and is why super majorities must be avoided; but even in functioning majorities there is much talk about the prime minister becoming a "friendly dictator," as Jean Chrétien was described.[25] Such notions are a gross exaggeration and have been debunked by some political scientists.[26] The prime minister's powers are constrained by federalism, by central agencies, by the auditor general, by government reporting and access to information, by televised proceedings, by the press gallery, and possibly by the Senate or Governor General. There are also the premiers, public opinion polls, the courts and, increasingly, citizen activists such as bloggers and online mobilizers. Internationally the prime minister's policy options are limited by global agreements and diplomacy. There is also the ever-present risk of internal party revolt, including from aspiring party leaders. The issue of the prime minister having too much power is mostly related to the rigidity of party discipline in Canada, a problem that exists in both majority and minority parliaments, and yet is also a source of leadership strength.

CONCLUSION

The recent era of minority government was characterized by instability, short-term decisions, and political games. The record shows that leaders with a minority of votes in the legislature become biased toward increasing government spending and avoiding difficult decisions. Supporters of this form of government tend to draw upon evidence from other countries, to complain about the electoral system, and to cite the Pearson era as the glory years.[27] If Canadians need minority governments it is for two reasons: first, as a warning to political parties, leaders, and cabinet ministers that they must not get too comfortable with the levers of power and, second, to remind voters how much they prefer the comparative tranquillity of life under a majority government.

A functioning majority can provide a strong, stable government and a leader who is able to calmly manage government business or who may actively implement reforms. The governing party can make decisions on behalf of an electorate that is less divided and less agitated. It reflects a democratic compromise of selecting a leader in an election every four years and the ability of that leader to balance short-term and long-term decisions for the good of society as a whole. Given the evidence, it seems clear that a majority government is, all things considered, better than a minority government.

NOTES

1. Peter Aucoin, Jennifer Smith, and Geoff Dinsdale, *Responsible Government: Clarifying Essentials, Dispelling Myths and Exploring Change* (Ottawa: Canadian Centre for Management Development, 2004).

2. Graham White, *Cabinets and First Ministers* (Vancouver: UBC Press, 2005).

3. Robin V. Sears, "Minority Government: From Productive to Dysfunctional," *Policy Options* (October 2009), p. 31.

4. Harris Decima, "Canadians Say It's Time for a Majority Government," July 12, 2009, available at http://www.harrisdecima.com/sites/default/files/releases/071309E.pdf. Accessed August 17, 2011.

5. Nik Nanos, "Canadians Don't Want a Fall Election; Majority Preferred but Minority Expected," *Policy Options* (October 2009), pp. 16–20.

6. Anna Esselment, "Market Orientation in a Canadian Minority Government: The Challenges of Product Delivery," in Alex Marland, Thierry Giasson, and Jennifer Lees-Marshment, eds., *Political Marketing in Canada* (Vancouver: UBC Press, forthcoming).

7. C.E.S. Franks, *The Parliament of Canada* (Toronto: University of Toronto Press, 1987), p. 50.

8. Peter H. Russell, *Two Cheers for Minority Government: The Evolution of Canadian Parliamentary Democracy* (Toronto: Emond Montgomery, 2008), p. 95.

9. J.S. Hodgson, "The Impact of Minority Government on the Senior Civil Servant," *Canadian Public Administration* 19, no. 2 (June 1976), p. 234.

10. Elisabeth Gidengil and André Blais, "Are Party Leaders Becoming More Important to Vote Choice in Canada?" in Hans J. Michelmann, Donald C. Story, and Jeffrey S. Steeves, eds., *Political Leadership and Representation in Canada* (Toronto: University of Toronto Press, 2007).

11. Tony L. Hill, *Canadian Politics: Riding by Riding* (Minnesota: Prospect Park Press, 2002), p. 22.

12. Steven Chase, Erin Anderssen. and Bill Curry, "Stimulus Spending Favours Tory Ridings," *The Globe and Mail*, October 21, 2009, available at http://www.theglobe-andmail.com/news/politics/stimulus-program-favours-tory-ridings/article1333239/. Accessed August 17, 2011.

13. David A. Good, "Minority Government: Politics, Planning, and the Public Service" (paper prepared for the "Governing Without a Majority: What Consequences in Westminster Systems?" conference, Université de Montréal, November 12, 2010, p. 9), available at http://www.criteres.umontreal.ca/pdf/D.Good-presentation.pdf. For an opposing view see Paul E.J. Thomas, "Measuring the Effectiveness of a Minority Parliament," *Canadian Parliamentary Review* (Spring 2007), pp. 22–31.

14. Don Martin, "Tories have Book on Political Wrangling," *National Post*, May 17, 2007, available at http://www.canada.com/nationalpost/news/story.html?id=16b42ac1-56a5-429c-a013-d9464dce3de1&tk=0. Accessed August 17, 2011.

15. Government of Canada, Report of the Standing Committee on Procedure and House Affairs, "Question of Privilege Relating to the Failure of the Government to Fully Provide the Documents as Ordered by the House" (Ottawa: House of Commons, 2011), p. 18.

16. Hodgson, "The Impact of Minority Government on the Senior Civil Servant," p. 233.

17. Good, "Minority Government."

18. Good, "Minority Government," p. 1.

19. John C. Courtney, "Prime Ministerial Character: An Examination of Mackenzie King's Political Leadership," *Canadian Journal of Political Science* 9, no. 1 (March 1976), p. 98.

20. Conservative Party of Canada, "Here for Canada: Stephen Harper's Low-Tax Plan for Jobs and Economic Growth," April 2011, available at http://www.conservative.ca/media/ConservativePlatform2011_ENs.pdf. Accessed August 17, 2011.

21. Aucoin, Smith, and Dinsdale, *Responsible Government*, p. 58.

22. Peter Regenstreif, *The Appeal of Majority Government* (Toronto: Longmans, 1965).

23. Hodgson, "The Impact of Minority Government on the Senior Civil Servant."

24. Russell, *Two Cheers for Minority Government.*

25. Jeffrey Simpson, *The Friendly Dictatorship* (Toronto: McClelland & Stewart, 2001).

26. White, *Cabinets and First Ministers.*

27. Eugene Forsey, "The Problem of 'Minority' Government in Canada," *Canadian Journal of Economics and Political Science* 30 (1964), pp. 1–11; and Howard Cody, "Minority Government in Canada: The Stephen Harper Experience," *American Review of Canadian Studies* 38 (2008), pp. 27–42.

✗ **NO**

The Case for an Effective Minority Government

ANNA ESSELMENT

The Westminster-style parliamentary system can result in numerous types of governments. In Canada, we are most familiar with majority governments. This is where an election results in one party winning over 50 percent of the seats in the House of Commons (at least 155 of 308). As a result, and with new fixed election dates in Canada, the governing party can control the parliamentary agenda with relative ease for the ensuing four years. When this does not occur, the party with the most seats (but not a majority) may be asked to form the government as a minority. A minority government may govern as a single party on an issue-by-issue basis, or with the declared (but informal) support of another smaller party. A more formal coalition could also result, with a larger and smaller party joining forces to govern, or by a collection of smaller parties banding together to hold the confidence of Parliament.

The predominant wisdom in Canada is that minority governments are unstable, ineffective, and temporary, often laden by partisan rancour and the constant threat of an impending election. When we examine minority/coalition governments both abroad and at home, however, we see that minority governments are not by their nature weak; in fact, a minority situation can be quite effective through its tendency to encourage consensus building, to give a role to smaller parties, to increase the power of individual Members of Parliament (MPs), and to strengthen parliamentary institutions such as committees.

MINORITIES AND COALITIONS ARE NOT RARE

In most other countries that use the Westminster model, it is majority governments that are elusive—electoral outcomes elsewhere tend to result in "hung" Parliaments that demand political parties form either a minority government or engage in coalition building to put together a governing entity capable of securing the confidence of the House of Commons.[1] This occurs quite regularly in countries that have some form of proportional representation in their electoral systems, such as Australia, New Zealand, Germany, and Denmark. More recently, the May 2010 general election in the United Kingdom, which, like Canada, follows the single-member plurality (SMP) system of electing representatives, resulted in a Parliament in which no party had won the majority of seats. For a number of days following the election, the three main political parties—Labour, Conservatives, and Liberal Democrats—negotiated which two among them would be capable of

---

Anna Esselment, "The Case for Effective Minority Government." © Nelson Education Ltd., 2011.

putting together a working coalition. Ultimately the Conservative and Liberal Democrat Parties agreed to form a government together.

In Canada, majority governments have tended to be the norm, although we are not unfamiliar with minority governments. To date there have been thirteen minority governments in Canada. Mackenzie King's first minority government lasted almost four years (1921–1925), the traditional tenure for a majority Parliament. The shortest was led by Conservative Arthur Meighan in 1926, which only held government for two and a half months. On average, the duration of minority governments in this country is almost two years.[2] This is a lesser timeframe than the three to four year terms of parliamentary democracies with the most minority governments (Denmark, Norway, Spain, and Sweden), but it suggests that minorities in Canada are not inherently short lived when compared with others around the world.[3]

PRODUCTIVE MINORITIES AND PARLIAMENTARY CONSENSUS BUILDING

Considering that minority governments are not "extreme" cases in the history of Canadian parliaments, we must examine whether or not they can be as effective as majority governments. One measure of effectiveness is the productivity of government. In other words, is a party leading a minority government able to achieve its agenda? Peter Russell has noted that, save for three administrations, minority parliaments in Canada have been quite effective in passing legislation that has benefited Canadians.[4] For good reason, some observers focus primarily on the achievements of Lester Pearson's two minority governments in the 1960s as the best examples. Under his leadership, the Parliament of Canada set up a national medicare program, the Canada and Quebec Pension Plans, the new Canadian flag, Royal Commissions on the Status of Women and on Bilingualism and Biculturalism, and it refused to send troops to Vietnam.[5] However, the so-called "glory years" should not be confined to Pearson's time as Prime Minister. John Diefenbaker's minority government in 1957 was able, among other things, to increase old age pensions, expand unemployment insurance benefits (as it was then called), provide money to help farmers, cut taxes for low-income families and small businesses, and establish a Royal Commission on Energy.[6] Pierre Trudeau's 1972 minority also cut personal income tax, instituted higher pensions and family allowances, and removed the federal sales tax on children's clothing and shoes.[7] In Paul Martin's time as Prime Minister, he laid the foundation for a national child care program (albeit later rescinded by Stephen Harper's minority government), and in Stephen Harper's first minority, Conservatives cut the GST, reshaped the child care agenda, introduced tougher crime legislation, and imposed a new Accountability Act overseeing conduct within government—in total, his government passed 65 of the 125 bills introduced in Parliament.[8] Clearly minority governments can also be productive governments.[9]

Furthermore, many of these achievements were the result of consensus building within Parliament. Unlike under a majority government, there is no guarantee that a proposed piece of legislation will pass through Parliament. The decree of the Prime Minister and a whipped vote of cabinet and caucus members alone cannot ensure successful passage through the Commons because the government does not have enough votes. Consequently, there is a much greater need to consult with other parties about certain items that are important to the governing party's agenda in order to secure agreement for their success. This requires communication, deliberation, negotiation and, ultimately, Parliamentary consensus on bills with one or more opposition parties. Pierre Trudeau was able to work well with David Lewis, the leader of the NDP, on much of the government's agenda from 1972 to 1974.[10] Paul Martin's 2005 budget included many items requested by the NDP in order to garner that party's support. New funding for housing, seniors, and the unemployed were a result of close cooperation between the Liberals and the NDP. Likewise, the 2008 decision to extend Canada's combat role in Afghanistan and the 2010 decision to continue a "military training" effort in that country was a result of a bipartisan effort that included Bob Rae, the Liberal Foreign Affairs critic at the time, heading a special Commons committee to study the issue. Greater cooperation also informed the contents of the 2009 budget where the Conservatives sought to provide a more palatable response to the global economic crisis and agreed to provide economic updates to Parliament.[11] Seeking a consensus lends greater legitimacy to government decision making since it is the result of true *parliamentary* consultation rather than the decision taking of one person (the prime minister) or party. Considering that the popular vote for the governing party in 2004, 2006, and 2008 did not exceed 38 percent,[12] we see that minority parliaments must take into account the positions of other parties and, by extension, the views of many more Canadians.

GREATER ROLES FOR SMALLER PARTIES

Given the SMP electoral system and Canada's inherent regionalism, there have developed a number of smaller parties at the federal level that may win parliamentary seats but which have little hope of winning government (the NDP and Bloc Québécois come readily to mind). Minority governments provide a way for smaller parties to have more influence without requiring them to shed their identities.[13] Majority governments can ignore smaller parties altogether, and a coalition government between a larger and smaller party often entails the junior partner signing on to a governing agenda that tends to favour the policy inclinations of the larger party. This can have the effect both of diluting the identity of the smaller party and possibly alienating its voter base that may resist being enveloped by a stronger party. In contrast, minority parliaments increase the chances of non-governing parties' bills successfully passing into legislation because of multiparty cooperation and support. Furthermore, the ability to select which bills to support on a more ad hoc basis, or for a certain length of time in Parliament, gives smaller parties influence on those particular issues since the governing party is always seeking support and thus is more amenable to changes that will secure agreement. The 1985–87 legislative alliance between the Ontario Liberals and the NDP is a good case in point. The Ontario Progressive Conservatives had only won a minority government after the 1985 election. The Premier, Frank Miller, tried to lead a government but soon resigned once it became known that the Liberals and NDP had forged an accord that would allow the Liberals to govern, as a minority, for two years with NDP support. No NDP members were brought into cabinet, and the NDP remained the third party in the Legislative Assembly. However, many NDP policies were included in the accord and implemented over the ensuing two years.

We see this greater role for smaller parties at the federal level as well. Mackenzie King worked with the Progressives and, as mentioned earlier, Pierre Trudeau's minority relied on the NDP for support. Paul Martin also worked with the NDP, while Stephen Harper was able to obtain support, at different times, from all three opposition parties throughout his two minority administrations. Giving a stronger role and influence to smaller parties, without asking them to abandon long-standing principles or policies, is unique to minority governments. As with consensus decision making, this enhances the representative role of Parliament. Canadians who voted for parties *other* than the one forming government have increased influence over the decisions of government. This is rarely the case in majority governments where the smaller parties are just that: small players, relegated to the opposition benches with few, if any, opportunities to provide meaningful input into government decision making.

GREATER ROLES FOR INDIVIDUAL MPS

The role of the individual Member of Parliament can be enhanced by a minority parliament. A good indication is the number of Private Members' Bills (PMB) passed. A PMB is introduced by MPs who are not cabinet ministers. They can address any matter, but must not involve the raising or spending of public money unless pre-approved by a cabinet member. It is difficult to pass a PMB, since many tabled by opposition members do not often correspond with the government's policy agenda. Only 235 PMBs have been given Royal Assent since 1910, although many more have been introduced into the legislative process.[14] PMBs do have a better chance of success in a minority Parliament because an MP can cooperate with and/or cajole members of other opposition parties (and occasionally government members) to support his or her initiative. During the combined seven years of minority government under Paul Martin and Stephen Harper (2004–2011), twenty-nine PMBs were passed by Parliament. During the eleven years of majority rule under Prime Minister Jean Chrétien (1993–2004), only twenty-seven PMBs were passed by Parliament.[15]

An individual MP's power is augmented in other ways as well. One is simply that every vote truly does count—the government cannot pass its legislative agenda without the support of some members of the opposition benches. In order to avoid an election for which they may be ill-prepared, some opposition parties have a more open policy about whether their members can vote for government-initiated bills. Having to court these votes "requires a government to consult with MPs in advance to ensure their support and possibly to make changes to policies in order to accommodate their specific interests."[16]

Similarly, in order to increase its seat count, individual opposition MPs may be covertly courted by the governing party to cross the floor. MPs may be persuaded with promises of a cabinet post or other attractive positions within government.[17] Two recent examples are former Conservative MP Belinda Stronach, who joined the Liberals in May 2005 and saved the government from losing a vote of non-confidence, and David Emerson, who crossed from the Liberals to the Conservatives after the 2006 election and resumed the cabinet post he had held under the previous Liberal administration. Targeting and inducing individual members to prominent positions within the government occurs less often in a majority situation.

STRENGTHENING COMMITTEES

The House of Commons has a number of committees that serve to assist in the review of proposed legislation. In a majority Parliament most members of committees are from the government caucus. Consequently, members of the opposition parties do not have much influence over the amendment process and, at the end of the committee stage, bills tend to remain in the same form as they arrived. In a minority government, however, opposition MPs have the upper hand in committees. Debate on the bill is thus more meaningful, proposed amendments more successful, and, arguably, the government is truly held to account.[18] One example of this is Bill C-10, introduced by the Harper government in May 2006, which proposed mandatory minimum sentences for firearms offences. The opposition parties were against the high minimums imposed by the bill and the non-government members of the Standing Committee on Justice and Human Rights made significant amendments that removed what they viewed as the harsher elements of the proposed legislation.[19] While Bill C-10 was later incorporated into an omnibus bill entitled "Tackling Violent Crime" that passed in the House in February 2008, the government proceeded in this manner *because* of the power of the Justice committee to influence the content of its individual crime bills. Combining bills into one larger piece of legislation demonstrates that a government frustrated with committees "bogging down" the process can grind committee work to a halt, as Stephen Harper did in 2008.[20] Learning to compromise at the committee stage is a feature of minority government to which all parties must become accustomed.

HOW TO IMPROVE A MINORITY GOVERNMENT

To this point we have seen that minority governments can be very effective. They can improve consensus building in Parliament, they provide a greater role for smaller parties, the role of the individual MP is enhanced, and they can strengthen certain parliamentary institutions such as committees. Many of these character-istics of minority government are what some scholars desire in their calls for the "reform" of Parliament. At the same time, it is clear that there are ways to improve a minority government in Canada and the following section will outline some possible ideas.

First, we can no longer view minorities as exceptions to the majority rule. Minority government outcomes are distinct possibilities in democracies using par-liamentary systems. While the demise of the Bloc Québécois in the 2011 general election may result in a return to majority governments for the next couple of Parliaments, Canadian politics is always surprising and Quebeckers' experiment with the NDP may be fleeting. The party could lose seats to the Liberals or Con-servatives in the next election or, if nationalism swells again at the provincial level, a resurgent Bloc Québécois or similar Quebec-only party may lead to further minority governments at the federal level. This could also occur if westerners become disenchanted with the Conservative Party, and a new regionally based party in B.C. or the Prairies takes root. Furthermore, while Canadians may not yet realize that minority government can also mean stable, effective government, they continue to embrace electoral reform in order to improve representation in Parliament. A recent poll suggested that 58 percent of Canadians are willing to open up the Constitution in order to bring about changes to the single-member plurality system by which the percentage of seats won by each party is roughly equivalent or proportional to its percentage of the vote.[21] As noted in other coun-tries with proportionality built into their electoral systems, minority and coalition governments become the new reality in governance and that expectation by the public can contribute to the stability of minority governments.[22] Should similar changes be made in Canada, we must be prepared to accept the same.

Second, how the media views and reports on politics during a minority govern-ment must evolve. Because the longevity of government is not guaranteed as it is in a majority, the media focuses solely on clashes between parties and leaders and, by extension, the prospect of the government's demise, instead of the issues and instances of parliamentary cooperation and consensus. Horse-race journalism is certainly a prominent feature of political reporting everywhere, but it can paint an inaccurate picture of parliamentary instability. There will be debate in the Commons, there will be tough questions posed to the prime minister and govern-ment of the day, there will be a degree of political posturing among the members, but none of this implies the implosion of the government and the dissolution of Parliament to make way for new elections. Unless on conventional confidence matters or those motions and legislation explicitly declared as such, bills that fail to be passed by the House should not be portrayed by the media as major defeats for the government. A minority government will suffer more legislative hardships in the Commons than a majority government, but this is simply a characteristic of such a Parliament. Arguably, the media's constant preoccupation with the next election likely fuels election fatigue among Canadians that would not exist otherwise if the perception of minority government as a permanent feature of Westminster systems was an accepted axiom.

Third, and as an extension of the first two points, Canadian political culture must shift to be more accepting of minority governments. As argued above, they can be both stable and effective and are not an "aberration" in Westminster systems. If we consider that Canada's electoral system is predisposed to produce majority governments, the appearance of minority parliaments (especially three in a row) must be for a reason. Canadians of late have been wary of handing over a strong mandate to any one party; "Work together!" seems to be our message to our politicians. In fact, it could be argued that Canadians have shifted to embrace minority government and it is our representatives who must be more accepting and adapt to Parliaments that require greater power-sharing practices, not resist it.[23] Tom Flanagan has suggested that this may entail

> fewer 'bolt from the blue' announcements of new government policies, [m]ore quiet meetings among leaders or their delegates, [g]overnment invitations to opposition parties to contribute to drafting legislation, [and] [a]mendments moved in good faith, not just to obstruct.[24]

Embracing such practices is clearly out of the comfort zone for many of our representatives, particularly those who have extensive experience as members in a majority government and who would prefer to fight in numerous elections until such a Parliament is produced. However, as wisely noted by Eugene Forsey:

> [P]oliticians…have no right to inflict on us the conspicuous waste of a series of general elections just because we elect a Parliament that does not suit them. It is our Parliament, not theirs. They are our servants, not our masters.[25]

Successfully shifting political cultural in Parliament and thus improving a minority government will involve not only greater power-sharing practices, but also a lessening of control over messaging and "permanent campaigning" by all parties, but particularly by the party in power. It is no secret that the Office of the Prime Minister (PMO) under Stephen Harper has tight control over government messaging. Only a few ministers are permitted to speak to the media, civil servants must have press releases or announcements "approved" by the PMO, and early in his tenure as prime minister, Harper implemented a "list" system regarding questions from the press gallery so that he could avoid being ambushed by reporters' questions.[26] Many of these tactics are part of the "permanent campaign"[27] practised by many parties in power. It is certainly important to parties in a minority government since the possibility of being thrown back into an election is greater than those enjoying a majority. In the permanent campaign, politicians and their close advisers consult often with trusted pollsters and strategists to ensure that action taken in government is viewed positively by their supporters and potential supporters. Every move is tactical and geared toward ensuring success at the polls during the next election. In other words, the campaign does not end when the votes are counted—it continues in office in order to prepare for the *next* election, whenever that might be. This explains why having control over the "message" is critical and the steps taken to do so (by silencing Members of Parliament, for example) are to ensure that no dilution or detraction from that message occurs. The advent of the permanent campaign is a result, among other things, of the professionalization of elections, the growing and diversified electorate, and access to sophisticated polling information that gives a party a more accurate snapshot of how segments of the public think about certain issues. While the permanent campaign can permeate majority governments as well, it has less of an impact given the almost guaranteed four-year lifespan of the government. If Canadians in general, and politicians in particular, can increasingly view minority governments as part of the political system, the need for control over the message by the PMO may be alleviated and improve the prospects for minority government.

A fifth, but no means final, change to improve minority government would be a clear understanding of the constitutional rules of parliamentary government. Peter Russell has made a compelling case for the codification of our unwritten conventions;[28] this would clarify the role and powers of the Crown that oversee our parliamentary democracy and arm Canadians with the knowledge of how governments are formed and dissolved. This would also go a long way to debunk the "myths" that the prime minister is directly elected, that *only* an election can determine which party will form the government, and that it is a "coup" for smaller parties in a minority Parliament to suggest forming a coalition to hold the confidence of Parliament. The 2008 constitutional crisis (whereby the recently elected Conservative minority government was at risk of losing power to a proposed formal coalition of the Liberal and NDP parties with BQ legislative support) was a crisis only insofar as there was a general lack of understanding by the politicians[29] and the public about the constitutional conventions that guide parliamentary democracy. As Russell notes:

> At the present time, it appears that there is neither agreement among our political leaders on what these conventions are nor understanding by the majority of politically engaged citizens of what they mean…[t]he lack of political consensus on fundamental principles of our constitution poses a serious threat to the stability of our parliamentary democracy. It means that the principle players in our constitutional politics do not agree on the fundamental rules of the game.[30]

New Zealand has pressed forward with just such a task and its Cabinet Manual[31] outlines in detail the roles and responsibilities of different players (including the

Governor-General, Ministers, and Cabinet) and on "situations" such as elections, transitions, and government formation. A similar undertaking here, made publicly accessible, would assist Canadians in their understandings of our political system and clear up what has to be viewed as the murkier waters of a minority Parliament.

IS A MAJORITY GOVERNMENT REALLY THAT GREAT?

While minority governments are often more stable and effective than we may admit, majority governments have a four-year term during which the party in power can get through its policy agenda more easily. The implication is that a majority government is better equipped for long-term policy planning than a minority government. This is not necessarily true; at most, a majority government is better at four-year planning (the time until the next election must be fought). There are obvious exceptions to this argument: Brian Mulroney helped ensure a steady revenue stream with the implementation of the GST and that Canada would be competitive with American markets by passing the North American Free Trade Agreement. But there are similar examples under minority regimes: Lester Pearson's administration, for instance, implemented national medicare and a pension for all Canadians. In short, long-term policy visions cannot be compartmentalized into "majority" or "minority" categories; they are more likely the result of particular leaders and issues.

Second, minority governments have often been accused of raising the level of partisan attacks in the Commons and seizing opportunities to belittle the opposition or government. Let's be clear—parliamentary government is "party" government. Partisanship is a characteristic of our system and unlikely to fade in any Parliament, be it majority or minority. Moreover, political opportunism is not the sole purview of minority governments. One only need be reminded of the 2000 general election, called early by Liberal Prime Minister Jean Chrétien for the primary reason of demoralizing and undermining the newly formed Canadian Alliance party and its leader Stockwell Day. Merely months after Day had been elected as head of the party, and just weeks after entering the House of Commons, Chrétien and the Liberals asked for a dissolution of Parliament and a subsequent election. While newcomer Day was able to increase the number of parliamentary seats in the House, he certainly did not perform as well as his supporters had hoped. Not surprisingly, Chrétien and the Liberals were able to win enough seats for another majority.

Third, while Marland in this volume correctly distinguishes between a super and functioning majority, he dismisses too easily the phenomenon of a "false" majority. A false majority occurs when the governing party wins a majority of parliamentary seats but fails to win more than 50 percent of the popular vote.[32] Of the forty-one Parliaments in Canada's history, fourteen have been "false majorities"; there have been no true majorities (where the majority of seats and over 50 percent of the popular vote coincide) since 1968. In 1997, for example, Jean Chrétien and the Liberal

Party won a majority government with only 39 percent of the popular vote! This means that over 60 percent of citizens who voted in that election selected a party *other* than the Liberals to represent them. Regionalism and the SMP electoral system have certainly led to these types of outcomes—that point is readily conceded. But the larger implications of false majorities on the representative function of Parliament, and the representation needs of Canadians, are ones that must be seriously considered. Despite the apparent "stability" of majority governments, citizens have become increasingly disengaged with the political and electoral process partly because they lack true representation in Parliament.[33] Minority governments enhance the representative function of Parliament and, by extension, the ability of political parties to represent Canadians across the country.

Fourth, where minority parliaments strengthen the influence of smaller parties, increase the power of individual MPs, and render more meaningful the work done in committees, majority governments can have the opposite effect. Opposition parties are unable to influence the government's agenda when the party in power has a majority. There is little need for consensus decision making, negotiation, or cooperation. Private members' bills from the smaller parties have little chance of success. The majority party also controls the committees and thus the ability of opposition members to contribute to the law-making process with amendments to legislation is substantially reduced. In a way, opposition parties are truly relegated to their "opposing" function and have fewer avenues of keeping the government to account.

Finally, a majority government does not alleviate the overarching role of the PMO. While control over the message may be more tightly regulated in a minority government, the power of the Prime Minister's Office and the excesses of majority government are likely to remain. Donald Savoie has effectively detailed the concentration of power in the "centre" of government (the PMO, PCO, Finance Department and Treasury Board)[34] and the suspicion is that Canada's "friendly dictator"—Prime Minister Harper—will reverse "parliamentary government," arguably enjoyed since 2004, back into "prime-ministerial" government:

> When the same handful of political leaders directs government and controls parliament, these trends are particularly unfriendly to the democratic capacity of parliamentary government....Minority government is no cure-all, but it has the great merit of providing a better prospect of resisting these trends and strengthening the democratic capacity of parliamentary government. As Eugene Forsey put it, "A government without a clear majority is likely to stop, look and listen."[35]

CONCLUSION

This side of the debate has argued that minority government is neither rare nor an aberration of the Westminster system of government. It can increase government accountability, parliamentary representation, the role of smaller parties and individual

MPs, and strengthen committees. Minority government can also be quite stable and effective. The challenge for Canadians and their representatives is to accept that minority parliaments may occur more often and to embrace the advantages they bring. While we have now returned to majority rule under Stephen Harper and the Conservatives, the "excesses" of a majority government that could return over the next four years may serve to remind us that minority parliaments aren't so bad after all.

NOTES

1. A 1990 study found that, between 1945 and 1987, only 13 percent of Western European and Commonwealth parliamentary democracies were single-party majority governments. The rest were either minorities or coalition governments. See Karre Strom, *Minority Government and Majority Rule* (Cambridge: Cambridge University Press, 1990), p. 65.

2. This includes Stephen Harper's 2008–2011 minority government. See Peter H. Russell, *Two Cheers for Minority Government* (Toronto: Emond Montgomery, 2008).

3. Ibid.

4. Ibid.

5. Martha Hall Findlay. "The Potential in a Minority Government," *Policy Options* (October 2010), pp. 54–55.

6. Peter C. Newman, *Renegade in Power* (Toronto: McClelland and Stewart, 1973), pp. 64–65.

7. Richard Gwyn, *The Northern Magus* (Toronto: McClelland and Stewart, 1980), pp. 149–150.

8. CBC News, "The 39th Parliament: A Dysfunctional or Productive Session?" September 9, 2008, available at http://cbc.ca/news/canadavotes/issuesanalysis/sheppard-legislativetally.html. Accessed May 17, 2011.

9. See also Paul E.J. Thomas, "Measuring the Effectiveness of a Minority Parliament," *Canadian Parliamentary Review* 30, no. 1 (2007), pp. 22–31.

10. Gwyn, *The Northern Magus*, pp. 149–150.

11. CBC News, "Ignatieff Puts Tories 'On Probation' with Budget Demand," January 28, 2009, available at http://www.cbc.ca/news/canada/story/2009/01/28/ignatieff-decision.html. Accessed June 2, 2011.

12. Elections Canada, *Elections*, available at http://www.elections.ca/content.aspx?section=ele&lang=e. Accessed June 18, 2011.

13. Joaquin Artes and Antonio Bustos, "Electoral Promises and Minority Governments: An Empirical Study," *European Journal of Political Research* 47, no. 3 (2008), pp. 307–333; and Mark Chalmers, "Canada's Dysfunctional Minority Parliament," *Making Minority Government Work* (Institute for Government UK, December 2009), p. 31.

14. Library of Parliament, "Private Members' Public Bills Passed by Parliament: 1910 to Date," available at http://www.parl.gc.ca/Parlinfo/Compilations/HouseOfCommons/legislation/privatememberspublicbills.aspx. Accessed June 21, 2011.

15. Ibid. Paul Martin was prime minister of the Liberal majority government for a few months in 2004.

16. Chalmers, "Canada's Dysfunctional Minority Parliament," p. 32.

17. Ibid.

18. Thomas, "Measuring the Effectiveness of a Minority Parliament," pp. 24–25.

19. Parliament of Canada, "Bill C-10: An Act to Amend the Criminal Code," June 6, 2007, available at http://www.parl.gc.ca/About/Parliament/LegislativeSummaries/bills_ls.as p?lang=E&ls=c10&Parl=39&Ses=1&source=library_prb. Accessed July 5, 2011.

20. Don Martin, "Tories have Book on Political Wrangling," *National Post*, May 17, 2007, available at http://www.nationalpost.com/news/story.html?id=16b42ac1-56a5-429c-a013-d9464dce3de1&k=0. Accessed July 5, 2011.

21. Canadian Press, "Are Canadians Over Their Constitutional Phobias?" *CBC News Online*, May 27, 2011, available at http://www.cbc.ca/news/politics/story/2011/05/27/pol-constitution-poll.html. Accessed June 21, 2011.

22. Howard Cody, "Minority Government in Canada: The Stephen Harper Experience," *American Review of Canadian Studies* 38, no. 1 (2008), pp. 28–29.

23. Tom Flanagan, "A Canadian Approach to Power-Sharing," *Policy Options* (September 2010), pp. 32–36.

24. Flanagan, "A Canadian Approach to Power-Sharing," p. 36.

25. Eugene Forsey, "The Problem of 'Minority' Government in Canada," *The Canadian Journal of Economics and Political Science* 30, no. 1 (1964), p. 6.

26. Lawrence Martin, *Harperland: The Politics of Control* (Toronto: Viking Canada, 2010).

27. Sidney Blumenthal, *The Permanent Campaign: Inside the World of Elite Political Operatives* (Boston: Beacon Press, 1980).

28. Peter H. Russell, "Learning to Live with Minority Governments," in Peter H. Russell and Lorne Sossin, eds., *Parliamentary Democracy in Crisis* (Toronto: University of Toronto Press, 2009), pp. 136–149.

29. Some may argue a deliberate misguidance of the public on the issue.

30. Russell, "Learning to Live with Minority Governments," p. 148.

31. Cabinet Office, Department of Prime Minister and Cabinet, *Cabinet Manual*, (Wellington: Government of New Zealand, 2008).

32. Russell, *Two Cheers for Minority Government*, pp. 8–9.

33. Elisabeth Gidengil et al., *Citizens* (Vancouver: UBC Press, 2004).

34. Donald J. Savoie, *Governing from the Centre: The Concentration of Power in Canadian Politics* (Toronto: University of Toronto Press, 1999).

35. Russell, *Two Cheers for Minority Government*, pp. 101–102.

POSTSCRIPT

Alex Marland develops a solid case for majority government. This is done partly by showing not so much what is good about legislative majorities but what is bad about legislative minorities. The latter do seem to get in the way of rational planning and do seem prone to spending money foolishly to ensure support for one party or the other. Marland also reveals that majority governments typically escape these failings of minority governments and allow parties in power to act productively and rationally. But on reading Marland's effort one sometimes gets the feeling that he (along with other Canadians) wishes to take the politics out of politics. The shenanigans and game playing some see in a minority government might be viewed by others as an opening up of a political system that too often is closed and unreceptive. Politics, at least the democratic variety, is messy, so anything that adds to this quality should not be rejected out of hand. Marland also appears to think that productive government can only be synonymous with majority government, but some challenge this claim. From some scholarly viewpoints, the Harper minority governments, for example, did more than nothing.

Anna Esselment also presents a convincing case for her side of the debate. She puts to rest the notion that minority governments amount to irregularities in the body politic—they are clearly not. Esselment also gently leads us through the arguments for a minority government and then offers sound suggestions to make this type of government work even better. She then ends with a query about whether majorities are really as wonderful as people claim them to be (and supplies the expected answer). All nicely done, but we do have a query or two for Esselment. She likes the consensus-based process for policymaking in minority governments, but one wonders if this process nullifies the bold initiatives that are more likely to be the brainchild of a single party (or a few within a party) than the result of a group representing the various parties. Esselment is rightly impressed with the more democratic nature of minority governments, but even she realizes that sometimes the politicking can go too far. One of her solutions to this blemish is the reform of the electoral system, but it is not clear that Canadians are ready for such a reform. Polls may say they are indeed ready, but other indicators say differently (voters clobbered a proposal for proportional representation in the 2007 Ontario election). So we are back to a minority government that can sometimes resemble children playing in a sandbox.

To participate in this debate, a student first needs an understanding of parliamentary government. This can be acquired by reading the relevant chapters of a good introduction to Canadian politics—for example, Heather MacIvor, *Parameters of Power: Canada's Political Institutions,* 5th ed. (Toronto: Nelson Education, 2010). A more thorough treatment can be gained in the student edition of Peter Hogg's *Constitutional Law of Canada, 2010* (Toronto: Thomson Carswell, 2010). The next step is to appreciate more directly the place of majority and minority government in the parliamentary system, and for this one should go to Jennifer Smith, "Canada's Minority Parliament," in James Bickerton and Alain-G. Gagnon, eds., *Canadian Politics*, 5th ed. (Toronto: University of Toronto Press, 2009).

Now we are ready to tackle the literature on the merits of majority and minority governments. The best place to start is Peter H. Russell, *Two Cheers for Minority Government: The Evolution of Canadian Parliamentary Democracy* (Toronto: Emond Montgomery, 2008). The title reveals that the author has a decided preference in this debate, but the volume still offers a good analysis of majority and minority governments. Other relevant readings are Howard Cody, "Minority Government in Canada: The Stephen Harper Experience," *American Review of Canadian Studies* 38, no. 1 (2008), and Paul E.J. Thomas, "Measuring the Effectiveness of a Minority Parliament," *Canadian Parliamentary Review* 30, no. 1 (2007). A study with an international flavour is Joaquin Artes and Antonio Bustos, "Electoral Promises and Minority Governments: An Empirical Study," *European Journal of Political Research* 47, no. 3 (2008).

As both articles in this debate note, minority governments can lead to a lot of manoeuvring, some of which can have major implications for the governing of a country. In late 2008, the newly elected minority government of Stephen Harper faced a situation that appeared fatal to its existence, and the prime minister took actions that startled many Canadians. For readings on this relevant event, see Peter H. Russell and Lorne Sossin, eds., *Parliamentary Democracy in Crisis* (Toronto: University of Toronto Press, 2009), and Peter H. Russell et al., eds. *Essential Readings in Canadian Government and Politics* (Toronto: Emond Montgomery, 2010), chs. 21 (Tom Flanagan) and 22 (various authors).

Is the Prime Minister Too Powerful?

✔ **YES**
HUGH MELLON, "Coming to Terms with Political Realities:
Exploring the Breadth of Prime-Ministerial Power"

✘ **NO**
PAUL BARKER, "Limits on the Power of the Prime Minister"

Students of Canadian politics appreciate that the prime minister is at the centre of political life in Canada. As leader of the national government, the prime minister determines the priorities that set the public agenda. The prime minister is also able to make appointments to important positions, and acts to represent Canada on the world stage. Perhaps the greatest indicator of the power and influence of the first minister is his or her sheer prominence. Canadians might be hard-pressed to name the provincial premiers or the chief justice of the Supreme Court of Canada, but few, if any, would experience the same problem with the prime minister.

There is thus little debate about the significance of the prime minister in Canadian politics. What might be debatable, however, is whether the prime minister dominates to the point that he threatens the healthy functioning of democracy in Canada. There are some who believe, strongly, that such is the case. Canada does not really have parliamentary government, they say, but in fact has what might be called "prime-ministerial" government. According to this perspective, the prime minister encounters few constraints on the exercise of his powers. All the typical powers associated with the prime minister—determining appointments, setting the overall direction of the country, representing Canada's interests in foreign dealings—are exercised with very little opposition. The Latin phrase *primus inter pares* ("first among equals") was once used to describe the prime minister's status: the prime minister was powerful (*primus*), but he faced individuals or challengers who were not merely his subordinates but his equals (*pares*) in some respects. Now, it is argued, the prime minister has no equals—he is *primus*, without any qualification.

Any proposition is only as strong as the supporting evidence. A look at Canadian political life does suggest some backing for the thesis of a prime-ministerial government. The prime minister appears able to pass bills into law with little difficulty. He or she also decides who shall sit in cabinet and who shall hold the senior positions in the judiciary and the public service. The prime minister is front-and-centre in the media's coverage of Canadian politics; indeed, he or she might be considered a celebrity or a superstar. The fact that Canadians look instantly to the prime minister in times of trouble also speaks to his or her primacy. When the great recession of 2008 began, most Canadians turned to the prime minister for guidance on how the country should respond.

The question, however, is whether all this is enough to confirm the prime-ministerial government thesis. The corroborating evidence, to be sure, is impressive, but is it sufficiently impressive to allow us to conclude that Canada is a country with a leader who faces few limits to his or her power? Some answer no. How, for example, can one ignore the influence of provincial premiers? Canadians may find it difficult to name political leaders in the provinces, but there is little doubt that premiers can frustrate prime-ministerial ambitions. Similarly, members of the prime minister's own government, the cabinet ministers, can make matters difficult for the prime minister. One day the prime minister appears invincible, the next day quite vulnerable. Such is the life of any celebrity.

In the readings, Hugh Mellon, a professor at King's University College at the University of Western Ontario, contends that the prime minister has an undue degree of power. Paul Barker, one of the editors of *Crosscurrents*, argues that supporters of the thesis of prime-ministerial government exaggerate the power open to the prime minister.

YES

Coming to Terms with Political Realities: Exploring the Breadth of Prime-Ministerial Power

HUGH MELLON

From Confederation in 1867 until 2011, a period of 144 years, only twenty-two individuals have served as Canada's prime minister. In one of the world's longest, consistently democratic political systems, fewer than two dozen individuals have held this position. The small number becomes even more striking when you realize that numerous occupants held the office for only a short time and that only a handful of skilled politicians occupied this esteemed position for significant periods of time. John A. Macdonald served from 1867 until 1873 and then from 1878 until his death in 1891, while Laurier was prime minister from 1896 to 1911. Diefenbaker (1957–1963) won two minority governments plus a huge majority in 1958. Borden (1911–1920), St. Laurent (1948–1957), and Mulroney (1984–1993) each won two national elections while Pierre Trudeau held the post from 1968 to 1979 and then from 1980 to 1984, and Jean Chrétien (1993–2003) won three successive majorities. Stephen Harper (2006 onward) won two minority governments and then triumphed with a majority victory in 2011. Yet even these achievements are humbled by William Lyon Mackenzie King, who endured over two decades as prime minister (1921–1926, 1926–1930, and 1935–1948). In short, these ten individuals held the position for well over 80 percent of the time Canada has existed as a self-governing nation. This is a remarkable statistic, one that should give rise to reflection upon the position of prime minister and the autonomy and authority that accompany it.

Even if we are prepared to accept that these individuals were superior political candidates and/or leaders (admittedly a contentious hypothesis), it is sobering to contemplate the limited number of occupants of this powerful position. What happens when so much power is confined for substantial periods to a limited number of individuals? Can we hold governments accountable when we have so few individuals with firsthand experience? Do prime ministers truly represent a popular mandate, or are they the political beneficiaries of an elite system marked by disciplined parties and declining public participation in voting? Bear in mind that voter turnout in the last four Canadian federal elections has ranged between 58 and 65 percent, and in the 2011 Ontario provincial election, was below 50 percent, hardly evidence of mass public participation. Are there institutional and political limits sufficient to regulate the behaviour and occasional excesses of Canada's prime ministers? Taken together, these questions and concerns lead to fears that prime ministers are able to consolidate an excess of power, a situation fraught with significant potential dangers. The argument to be made here is that the limitations provided by the political system upon their power are woefully inadequate, and that this reality should concern all those interested in the state of Canada's democratic experience.

When preparing this argument, it was fascinating to take a moment to glance at the Government of Canada website devoted to the prime minister. Readers are urged to do the same, for the self-presentation of the office is enlightening. On October 16, 2007, the day of a Throne Speech and the convening of Parliament, the site was replete with assertions that the prime minister was taking dramatic action on major issues. The prime minister, Stephen Harper, was accorded credit for commissioning a panel to report on Canada's participation in the Afghanistan conflict, announcing a crackdown on drug crimes, promoting a "bolstering" of Arctic sovereignty, and sorting out matters relating to the Atlantic Accord with the premier of Nova Scotia. Repeating this informal test when updating this chapter on June 27, 2011, one finds similar indications of prime-ministerial primacy in national life. There is reference to the prime minister unveiling the arrangements for an upcoming royal tour, as well as his observance of the national day of remembrance for victims of terrorism. Clicking upon the prime ministerial prompt brings further evidence of prime-ministerial leadership supplemented by a designated prime-ministerial photo of the day and the awarding of the "Prime Minister's Volunteer Awards." The accompanying visuals accentuate the prime minister's visibility. Browsers are given the impression of a powerful, overarching prime minister who is leading the action on issues across the board. The combined message is one of assertive action and central direction.

This impressionistic approach to the topic is intriguing but not conclusive, so therefore let us move to making the case for the excesses of prime-ministerial power. Those looking to test the extent of this power have different avenues available to them. What will be attempted here is to examine in turn those sources often cited as offering countervailing influences or checks upon that power in order to show their individual and collective weaknesses as sources of restraint. If each of these sources of control are found wanting, then this consolidates the argument of overreaching prime-ministerial ambition and power. Each of the presumed checks is not without some influence, but as a control upon prime-ministerial determination, they have noteworthy limitations, and while they may on occasion serve as a major check, this is likely more the exception; their ongoing strength should not always be assumed. The sources of restraint to be considered are (1) cabinet and the leading members of the prime minister's political party; (2) public opinion and the constitutional requirement of periodic elections; (3) Parliament and its institutionalized opposition and features such as Question Period; (4) the media; and (5) the workings of Canadian federalism. But first a few words upon the role and constitutional authority of the prime minister are in order.

Those wishing to engage in the debate over prime-ministerial power will find a significant and growing literature on the role and authority of the Canadian prime minister. Notable works include Donald J. Savoie's *Power: Where Is It?* and his *Governing from the Centre*,[1] Jeffrey Simpson's *The Friendly Dictatorship*,[2] and the various prime-ministerial memoirs and autobiographies. In fact, as this essay goes to print, there are two new memoirs hot off the press: Brian Mulroney's *Memoirs: 1939–1993*[3] and Jean Chrétien's *My Years as Prime Minister*.[4] Those looking for a biographical treatment, on the other hand, might try Lawrence Martin's two-volume life of Chrétien (with the prime-ministerial portion covered in volume two, *Iron Man: The Defiant Reign of Jean Chrétien*) or his study of the Stephen Harper government, *Harperland: The Politics of Control*.[5] These and other related works merit examination in light of the debate presented here.

PRIME MINISTERS AND THEIR AUTHORITY

Prime ministers govern formally upon the basis of their ability to lead a ministry capable of retaining majority support in the elected House of Commons. This role is the product of British traditions and constitutional conventions, for, as Peter Hogg reminds us, the *British North America Act*, which ushered in Confederation in 1867, makes no formal reference to the position. Hogg states, "[T]here is no mention of the Prime Minister, or of the cabinet, or of the dependence of the cabinet on the support of a majority in the House of Commons: the composition of the actual executive authority and its relationship to the legislative authority were left in the form of unwritten conventions—as in the United Kingdom."[6] From these beginnings has sprung an office possessing wide-ranging and influential political tools. Parliamentary arrangements fuse power while disciplined political parties make control easier. As a result, the prime minister can oversee both executive authority and legislative deliberations. Today the office wields tremendous control, leading Jeffrey Simpson, a senior Ottawa observer, to conclude, "The Canadian prime minister is more powerful within this system than any democratically elected leader in other advanced industrial countries."[7] American separation of powers and the lesser degree of discipline among British political parties offer stronger restraints than those encountered by a Canadian prime minister.

Prime ministers possess an impressive political arsenal. One highly significant tool is the power to make a multitude of senior governmental and public service appointments both at home and abroad. Among the many prime-ministerial appointees are cabinet members, ambassadors, parliamentary secretaries, the Governor General, senators, and Crown corporation executives. Earlier reference was made to Prime Minister Harper's website and the announcement of an advisory panel of elite Canadians to advise on the Canadian involvement in Afghanistan. The website makes clear that this is a prime-ministerial announcement, and there is a link to a visual in which Harper is seen announcing the panel's creation.

When you take this power in its totality, its potential is obvious. Those wishing to get ahead will soon realize whose opinion will determine their possibilities. Party workers dreaming of a Senate appointment or cabinet advancement likewise know where their appointment will come from. Also note that there are fewer restraints upon the appointment power than are found in the U.S. congressional system, in which various key appointments need ratification by another branch of government.

The prime minister exercises parliamentary leadership and directs the flow of events, aided by cabinet and the whip's office. In practice, attention and clout gravitate to the prime minister and his or her centrality to Question Period, media coverage, and debate. What is more, remember that the upper house in the bicameral legislative arrangement, the Senate, is appointed by the prime minister. The house, crafted to offer "sober second thought" coupled with regional representation, is composed of prime-ministerial appointees. Opportunities for conflicts of interest are immediately evident.

Prime ministers have in the past also possessed the power to set the dates for elections, which allows them to capitalize upon the movement of polls or to catch the opposition unprepared. This power may be constrained by the movement to fixed elections at the federal level proposed by the Harper government. Whatever the case regarding fixed or flexible election dates, there is an imbalance in resources between a calculating prime minister and those in opposition.

Prime ministers chair cabinet, which may often entail further strategic advantages, such as the authority to alter cabinet membership, the power to set items on or off a particular agenda, and the ability to offer support or roadblocks to particular ministers. Prime ministers have the authority to appoint senior officials and bureaucrats throughout the government. This comes with ongoing authority to monitor their performance should an issue or political pressures warrant it. These powers are important for several reasons. One is the obvious asymmetrical relationship born of having chosen an individual for a post while retaining the ability to elevate or discipline that person over time. A second is the likelihood of a line of communication from the prime minister through the officials allowing the prime minister to bypass a cabinet minister or ministers. In an environment in which knowledge is power, the availability of multiple information sources is a significant asset. A third reason is the use of appointments and job appraisals to solidify the ranks of loyalists and serve the interests of partisanship and the leader. Political office involves the use of teams of advisors and loyalists, and patronage is one of the most often selected lubricants for the inner workings of this dynamic team and coalition building.

Opposition parties often score points over the presumed excesses of prime-ministerial appointments, but the advantages of the appointment power and back-channels of information are considerable. Jean Chrétien, for example, was one more prime minister who had donned the mantle of outraged defender of the public interest while in opposition. Appointments made by the Mulroney government were scrutinized and frequently challenged. Yet, upon election to the prime ministership, the self-same Chrétien found himself less interested in reform. In their study of the first Chrétien government (1993–1997) Greenspon and Wilson-Smith offer this description of the Chrétien attitude:

> He intended to exercise the prerogatives of the office. "It is better that I make the appointments and be accountable for them," others remembered him saying, "than someone else makes them and I be accountable."[8]

Advisors and bureaucratic aides for the prime minister are built into the institutional order. In the carrying out of his or her role as national leader and voice of the country on the international and domestic stages, the prime minister is aided by central agencies and the top levels of staff at the national office of his or her respective political party. Two central agencies, the Prime Minister's Office (PMO) and the Privy Council Office (PCO), are well connected to the prime minister's political or bureaucratic needs for information, contacts, supporting documents, and advice. Meanwhile, the link to his or her political party allows control over campaign planning, national opinion polling, and candidate selection. Leaders attempting to recruit high-profile candidates can often assure them of an easy ride to a desirable riding nomination. Taken together, the prime minister has access to tremendous supports and avenues for influence. This facilitates prime-ministerial direction over important issues such as national unity and federal–provincial relations. Donald Savoie, a long-time student of government and bureaucracy, reports that with regard to this policy field, "briefing material prepared by the PCO for new ministers makes it clear that 'the Prime Minister has direct responsibility for the conduct of federal–provincial relations.'"[9]

By virtue of their position and the practices of modern communications, prime ministers both deliver government messages and oversee the crafting of communications planning. Whether it be through appearances at vital symbolic events (e.g., Remembrance Day commemorations), leaders' election campaign debates, government websites, or media settings such as the year-end fireside chat, prime ministers are at the centre of coverage. Government media strategies often reinforce the centrality of the prime minister. For example, it was Prime Minister Paul Martin himself who appeared in a highly publicized media address in the spring of 2005 to defend the Liberal Party from allegations arising from corruption within government advertising expenditures. When the government of Brian Mulroney announced its intention to "explore" the possibility of Canada–U.S. free trade, media preparation included a personal call from Mulroney to U.S. President Ronald Reagan and a major prime-ministerial address to the House of Commons.[10]

As with the overtures made to the U.S. leadership about free trade, prime ministers are generally the dominant voice of Canada internationally. They attend highly visible gatherings such as meetings of the G7 or G8, the group composed of the leaders of the richest countries. They also publicly identify themselves with major foreign initiatives. Like his predecessors, Stephen Harper has been the primary Canadian figure at senior international events. Take, for example, Harper's visit to Germany in June 2007, where he participated in talks with both the president and the prime minister of France; the Canada–European Union Summit; and the gathering of the G8, which brought Harper into contact with the political leaders of Germany, the U.S., Great Britain, France, Japan, Italy, and Russia, as well as providing him with introductions to significant German business leaders. He was thereby able to present skepticism about the Kyoto Accord as the official national position at a time when support for greater environmental protection was strongly urged among the general Canadian populace.[11]

The breadth of the responsibilities and power available to prime ministers gives them a commanding role in the machinery of government and the broad political landscape. They have a paramount influence over major government appointments; parliamentary debate and questioning; major policy directions in key fields such as federal–provincial relations, foreign policy, and other government priorities; media coverage and campaign strategizing; and the leadership of their political party. Their judgment is supplemented by the advice and support of two major central agencies, pollsters, and leading strategists in their own political party. They chair cabinet meetings and set its composition and agendas. This is tangible power supported by senior civil servants, cabinet colleagues, and media advisors. If we are serious about controlling or at least constraining prime-ministerial power, we need to devote increased attention to this task, for at the moment, the leading candidates for restraining the political executive are limited, sporadic, and occasionally unpredictable in their impact.

CABINET AND THE LEADING MEMBERS OF THE PRIME MINISTER'S POLITICAL PARTY

Stephen Harper became Canada's prime minister upon the election of January 23, 2006; his new cabinet, which included a high-profile defector from the opposition Liberals, was subsequently unveiled in early February with great fanfare. Yet this new team and its specific ministerial assignments were not to remain in place for long. Within little more than a year and a half, this heralded cabinet was altered by two ministerial shuffles. In January 2007, a shuffle affecting such major departments as Environment, the Treasury Board, Justice, and Citizenship and Immigration took place. Later, in August 2007, a second major upheaval occurred, and those responsible for the high-priority fields of Foreign Affairs, Indian Affairs and Northern Development, Industry, Defence, Heritage, and Agriculture were shifted into other roles. Learning a new portfolio, with its attendant responsibilities and multimillion-dollar expenditures, is a Herculean task. Once appointed, the new minister is badgered by the press and client groups seeking audiences and signs of policy direction. Periodic shuffles force new responsibilities on those already endeavouring to master other cabinet assignments and their associated policy challenges and weighty briefing books.

Amid the shuffles, Prime Minister Harper, the cabinet designer, remained firmly in place at the centre. Donald Savoie explains the strength of the prime minister's position this way:

> Ministers…know full well that they sit in Cabinet only because one person wants them to be there—the prime minister. The prime minister may well be reluctant to swing the axe, but no one knows for certain if or when he will do it.[12]

The power to assign positions permits the elevation of favourites, the demotion of discontents, and the stymieing of the plans of ambitious underlings. Although cabinet selections need to reflect important political cleavages such as region, gender, party factions, and language, do not underestimate the clout arising from the authority to design cabinets and to favour the loyal and supportive.

Prime ministers enter the office with the upper hand over fellow party members. Winning a majority is a tonic for party morale—the leader is a champion. Winning a minority is a disappointment but not necessarily a death sentence. Political parties are often patient with leaders who have been reduced to minority status. Pierre Trudeau successfully endured the humiliation of 1972, and Paul Martin was given another chance after the reduced Liberal numbers in 2004. Prime ministers who win only a minority government typically pledge that they have learned a lesson, that the voters have spoken, and that next time their efforts will produce a parliamentary majority. Meanwhile, minority governments are often in a vulnerable position, and efforts are made within the party to mute expressions of disloyalty to the leader. This should not be surprising, since the potential successor to replace the prime minister is likely to be found in cabinet, and thus his or her approval rating is bound up with that of the government he or she serves.

Note, however, that there is no intention here of speaking of a similar relationship between opposition leaders and their internal party rivals. Past experience, as in the relations between Joe Clark and Brian Mulroney (1980–1984) and between John Turner and Jean Chrétien (1984–1990), indicates that without the lubricant of patronage and power, the party leader is far more vulnerable. Hence, the prime minister likely has better job security than the leaders of the opposition parties.

The condition of contemporary Canadian political parties makes them weak as guardians of ongoing accountability. Many of us may have an image rooted in history of mass parties in which there is an integrated organization with a dedicated membership who form a sort of institutional family with memory and well-worn conventions. This may no longer be a suitable vision. Sid Noel offers an insightful reexamination of parties in his essay "Leaders' Entourages, Parties, and Patronage,"[13] which encourages us to reassess what we expect of parties. In the past, parties were major vehicles for fundraising, member attachment, and campaign preparation.

Much has changed, though. Federal campaign reforms have provided public funding for parties. (Note, though that current Prime Minister Harper has indicated the likely reduction and/or termination of these funds, it is difficult at this point to speculate on what will ensue.) Campaigns are often leader-driven media efforts organized around a centrally set theme and schedule. Citizen attachment to politics appears to be waning, as turnout at the last two federal elections was only in the high 50s/low 60s percent level, and a sampling of recent provincial elections in Ontario (2011), Newfoundland (2007), and Nova Scotia (2006) offers little evidence of voter enthusiasm. Even the 2007 Quebec election, which featured debate over sovereignty and national unity, had a turnout percentage only in the low 70s. Party efforts to allow the signing up of new members during leadership selection seem to produce only temporary votes for preferred candidates rather than ongoing life-blood. There are ample reasons for concern about the vitality of Canadian parties.

Noel suggests that we instead think about parties as vehicles taken over for periods by ambitious and well-heeled individuals backed by professional entourages personally loyal to them. The party label becomes more of a brand than a historic family that has shared a history together.

> Though actual titles may vary, the inner circle of a typical entourage consists of a chief fundraiser, a chief organizer or campaign director, a communications director (media adviser), one or two senior strategists, a personal aide ("gatekeeper"), a chief media spokesperson or "spinner" (if this role is not filled by the communications director), an opinion pollster, an advertising director, and possibly a spouse.[14]

These and other professionals directly linked to the leader sustain the leader and drive the political party's national presentation. Who then has the status within the party to restrain the prime minister? Those who suggest that cabinet and its particular political party will serve as controls on prime-ministerial influence and decisions have a difficult case to make. Meanwhile, the political party organizational trends delineated by Noel show little sign of abating.

Before exploring the impact of public opinion on elections, it is important to confront head-on the case of the intra-party feud within the Chrétien government involving the challenge from Paul Martin. Some might imagine that the resulting upheaval and change in leadership upends the argument made here. The conventional narrative is that Martin served dutifully as finance minister between 1993 and 2002, helping to fight the deficit and control government finances. Over time, he chafed under the wear and tear of subservience to an individual whom he had challenged in the 1990 Liberal leadership race. Chrétien, for his part, grew tired of Martin's ambition and the machinations of his loyalists. Their overt jockeying for position and strategizing for the future replacement of "yesterday's man" with the political and economic wizard whose cabinet work was yielding annual fiscal surpluses was incessant. Especially galling to Chrétien was a meeting in Toronto's Regal Constellation Hotel in 2000 that was explained by Martin allies as a quiet gathering of Liberals interested in renewal, at which only some of the attendees were operatives in the service of Martin's cause. Intense press coverage and speculation nonetheless ensued. Chrétien responded by staying on and calling an election for late November, which produced a third majority government for the prime minister. Pressure for change continued apace, though, and in 2002 Chrétien finally replaced Martin in cabinet while also acknowledging that the time until his own upcoming departure from office was limited. A leadership vote was subsequently held in late 2003, and Martin won with over 90 percent of the votes.

But what is the lesson of this fandango of bitterness, intrigue, and media headlines? Is it that the cabinet and the prime minister's political party can, in a timely and effective manner, regularly hold a prime minister accountable for his or her performance? No, it is, rather, that a prime minister, even one who distrusts grand gestures and bold initiatives, can survive for years in office aided by a coterie of loyalists and that change is exhausting, long, and debilitating. Lawrence Martin, the noted biographer of Chrétien, put it this way:

> For those who thought of public service as an altruistic or ennobling pursuit, the endless power struggle between Chrétien and his finance minister was distressingly juvenile. Chrétien had made the public interest such a personal game that he chose to let a meeting of opponents in a hotel room become his ostensible reason for staying in power for four more years.[15]

If there is a moral to this story, perhaps it is that the struggle for leadership within a political party is an awkward, time-consuming, and often embarrassing display of ambition and rivalry. This conclusion is reminiscent in various ways of the struggles during the death throes of the Diefenbaker government during its minority period of 1962–1963.[16] Cabinet members' or other senior party figures' questioning of the party leader is a blunt and cumbersome tool for controlling the prime minister's performance for a number of reasons. One of the most important of these is that the prime minister has to continue to govern while sorting out the party struggle. Many may understandably join the prime minister in labelling the challenge(s) unseemly and counterproductive. The second key reason is that challenging a leader requires a credible alternative party figure willing to engage in the face-off. Announcing such an intention automatically sets the contender apart. Having thrown his or her hat into the ring, it is unlikely that this person could ever regain the trust of many party loyalists. The third major weakness of this check on prime-ministerial power is that it can cause paralysis within the governing party rather than improved accountability and attentiveness.

PUBLIC OPINION AND ELECTIONS

Are elections effective vehicles for the enforcement and maintenance of prime-ministerial accountability? At a basic level, an election offers potential for either changing or maintaining a particular government, but there are practical limits to its use. Power does periodically change hands, as in the federal elections of 1993 (Chrétien Liberals unseated Kim Campbell Progressive Conservatives and win a majority) and 2006 (Harper Conservatives won minority over Martin Liberals). What is more, Canadian elections are generally useful for fulfilling certain other political functions. Pammett regards them as being good at recruiting candidates and potential leaders, and offering political "parties opportunities to revive and re-establish their organizations."[17] Yet there is more to the story. Canadian elections don't securely foster citizen interest and belief in the political system. Voter turnout is mired in a string of sub-par levels. In the seven most recent federal elections—1993, 1997, 2000, 2004, 2006, 2008, and 2011—turnout as a percentage of eligible voters was only in the 60s with the exception of 2008 when it dipped into the high 50s (Elections Canada website). If a winning party's share of the votes ranges from the high 30s to the low/mid 40s, a common occurrence, and only roughly 65 percent of those eligible actually vote, this is hardly strong democratic control. Little wonder that Pammett points to those who feel it an advantage that elites are given opportunities to fashion plans without mass scrutiny.[18] Not surprisingly, he also points out the purposeful vagueness of party campaign appeals and the ease with which parties jettison inconvenient pledges. Party election platforms have an uncertain shelf life once a government has been elected—hardly an effective constraint upon government action.

Elections are about the making of a government in the sense that, after an election, the Governor General reviews the results and asks the leaders of the party with the most elected members, or most visible support within the legislature, to form a government. This is a fundamentally important task, but let us not exaggerate its impact on the power and influence of a prime minister in the conduct of his or her office. Elections are sporadic and much can happen between them. In the past, prime ministers possessed the power to set the dates for elections, which could allow them to capitalize upon the movement of polls or to capture the opposition unprepared. There is currently debate within various Canadian jurisdictions about moving to fixed election dates as in the United States. This may help constrain one aspect of prime-ministerial discretion. It remains to be seen whether it will produce increased accountability, though. Fixed dates of four or five years apart, for example, still leave a long period between elections.

Election campaigns rely upon citizen participation and involvement, but as already noted, there is reason to worry on this front, given the low levels of voter turnout and public interest. Coupled with this lack of popular interest is the resulting opportunity for elites and active interest groups to marshal their resources and influence in support of favoured causes. With regard to the free trade election of 1988, for example, Brian Mulroney's *Memoirs* makes clear his recognition of the value of business support as a counter to the anti–free trade campaign of the Liberals and NDP: "The Canadian business community, led by Tom D'Aquino and the Business Council on National Issues, rallied vigorously in support of free trade. During the election campaign, business leaders spoke out bluntly and purchased ads in favour of the trade agreement. Their support was unprecedented and effective."[19] And in the 1988 election, the Mulroney Progressive Conservatives were returned with a sizable parliamentary contingent of 169 of 295 seats and 43 percent of the popular vote. More than half of voters marked ballots for parties officially opposed to the primary agenda item of the sitting prime minister, yet free trade became a reality.

PARLIAMENT

Our examination now turns to the traditional understanding that Parliament serves as a representative forum wherein governments are judged and regularly called to account through vehicles such as the regular Question Period, the rigours of open debate, and the challenge of maintaining confidence among a collection of active and probing legislators. Assumptions of active and probing debate underestimate the disciplined character of Canadian political parties, which almost always stays on script. Question Period and debate are more often about reciting prepared positions and looking for catch phrases suitable for news coverage than about uncovering underlying realities or scrutinizing administrative detail. Votes are overwhelmingly cast upon party lines. Coordinated party strategy is thus more often a defining feature than an active restraint upon prime-ministerial behaviour.

Prime ministers choose cabinets and lead the parliamentary charge, but it should also be acknowledged that their power depends upon the skillful handling of caucus. Leaders must maintain support through those periods when their government's fortunes appear to be waning. Styles vary, but good team building allows a prime minister great leeway. According to Lawrence Martin, "Mulroney was known for his soothing strokes, Trudeau was a study in patience, Mackenzie King was famous for his incisive summations."[20] Their attentiveness paid off, as each enjoyed a career of striking duration and achievement.

Those across the aisle from the ruling party suffer from several key limitations in the parliamentary fray. First of all, the single-member electoral system used at the federal and provincial levels historically militates against opposition parties that do not have a major regional base, such as the Bloc Québécois.[21] Take the just-mentioned 1988 federal election. The Liberals and NDP together obtained over 51 percent of the votes cast but received only 126 of the 295 seats. For an added example, note the 1997 federal election, in which the Jean Chrétien federal Liberals managed 155 of 301 seats with less than 39 percent of the votes cast. More recently, in the 2011 election, Stephen Harper and the Conservatives took 167 of 308 seats with only 39.6 percent of the votes cast. Voter turnout for this election was only about 61 percent.

A second deficiency is the striking imbalance of resources available to a government as compared to the parliamentary opposition. Being in power means having command of the bureaucracy and enjoying the resulting perks. Prime ministers can direct the preparation of briefing material, can strategize about when to release favourable or damaging information, as well as solicit alternative proposals from staff, with the cost being borne out of government revenues. Governments also engage in active public opinion polling, thus offering the prime minister and his or her cabinet up-to-date insights into the public mood. These opportunities are more pronounced in a parliamentary setting where parliamentarians are often relatively inexperienced. In his 1997 book, *Mr. Smith Goes to Ottawa: Life in the House of Commons*, Docherty refers to this situation and laments instances in which government benches featured more veteran talent than their parliamentary rivals or caucus colleagues: "Simply put, it is difficult for both government backbenchers and opposition members to keep cabinet accountable when they lack the experience and parliamentary savvy of members of the executive."[22]

It must be acknowledged that there are features of parliamentary life that serve to highlight government behaviour and raise questions requiring serious responses. A good example of this was the work done by the Auditor General's office to uncover the details of the sponsorship scandal that plagued the Chrétien and Martin governments.[23] Offices such as those of the Auditor General, the Commissioner of Official Languages, and the Privacy Commissioner have significant powers. These control mechanisms play a valuable role, yet their impact is more often than not momentary, and parliamentary skirmishing overshadows their reports replete with analysis and administrative concerns.

The tests of stamina and commitment provided by the daily grind of Question Period and debate are not without importance. Prime ministers must have a diverse skill set and be accomplished performers as well as administrators. Yet, the question at issue here is not whether the job is easy but, rather, whether there are sufficient controls upon prime-ministerial power. Party discipline, public inattention, and the imbalance of cabinet and opposition resources provide reasons to doubt that there are adequate restraints given the public money and critical issues at stake.

MEDIA

There is always room to make the argument that the media, armed with their rights of free expression and opportunities for investigation, are a source of restraint upon prime-ministerial ambition. Certainly stories critical of the government can be aired, but the deeper, more complicated questions are (1) how much of a government's actions are going to be scrutinized; (2) to what degree Canadians are vigilant about following and working to understand news coverage; and (3) whether politicians are becoming more skilled in massaging press coverage and spinning messages favourable to their cause, thereby gaining an advantage over the press. There is reason to speculate that the answers to each of these will lead us to question further the effectiveness of the media's performance as a check on power.

As to the question of breadth of coverage, there is a limit to how much the media, no matter how vigilant, can be aware of. The Canadian government is a multibillion-dollar enterprise with branch offices (embassies, office buildings, and services) spread out nationally and internationally. How much of this can we reasonably expect the media to cover? At what point will budgets, audience ratings, and entertainment pressures outweigh the coverage of all that governments do? Note that what is being argued here is that the media operate under certain kinds of limitations and work to serve an audience that itself has time and attention pressures. Is it realistic to imagine that the media have resources for news coverage sufficient to oversee the full range of prime-ministerial power?

The second fundamental question is about the vigilance of the audience to (1) demand this kind of detailed coverage and (2) to watch and act upon them. If the media are to act as a check on power that can be regularly depended upon, then there is an implied understanding that the citizens will patronize them. Television ratings, bestseller lists, and so forth do not suggest that expanded news coverage is necessarily prevailing. Instead, it may be an option more appealing in civics classes than in the real world of media ratings and commercial broadcasting. Open-line shows airing aggressive comments supplied voluntarily by opinionated members of the general public may be entertaining, but how worried about such opinions is a prime minister in faraway Ottawa and a couple of years away from an election?

The final question under this heading relates to the balance of power between busy journalists covering a multitude of breaking stories and the expanding ranks of media advisers, spin doctors, and pollsters servicing prime ministers. Governments take great care in choreographing public events with desired story lines. Note, for example, the Harper government's institution of a "Message Event Proposal" system that enables "the increasingly powerful Prime Minister's Office to vet requests for public events across the federal government."[24] Political advisers have grown more adroit in defining media strategies and prescribing visuals that charm the eye but perhaps do little more. Election campaigns seem to be caught up in image management. In the words of Paul Nesbitt-Larking in his well-known Canadian media text, "Winning elections seems to depend more and more on the control of image and style."[25] Thus, with the influence of media gurus shaping the presentation strategies of political leaders, there may well be reason to be cautious in judging the impact of the press in its implicit struggle between the investigation into, and acceptance of, prime-ministerial messages.

THE WORKINGS OF CANADIAN FEDERALISM

A further check upon prime-ministerial ambition may be found in the restraint provided by the division of powers and the existence of assertive and sizable provincial governments. Strong executive power at both the federal and provincial levels has produced a political system in which first ministers' meetings and intergovernmental agreements are important sources of policy decisions. Herman Bakvis, for example, asserts that "while power may be highly centralized in the hands of the prime minister, the same holds true for provincial premiers. In other words, prime ministerial power and ambition can be easily checked by strong resistance from some of the larger provinces."[26] Executive federalism and competing federal and provincial agendas are thus offered as sources of meaningful restraint.

While important as an argument, there is still something troubling about offering the closed and secretive world of intergovernmental bargaining as a constraint upon the actions of prime ministers. Instead of providing comfort that interested citizens might be able to monitor their federal leaders' initiatives, this would seem to intensify the concerns that drive the argument provided by this essay. Many governmental access-to-information regulations offer matters of federal–provincial negotiation as an exception. Which Canadians outside of elite circles had access to the high-stakes negotiations that produced the Constitution Act of 1982, the Meech Lake Accord, the Charlottetown Accord? The restraint offered by federal–provincial confrontation is at best a minimal sort. Advocates of this control assume that provinces and their self-interested political agendas offer more than simply the countervailing force of another competing executive or set of executives. Surely this is a limited type of counter force to underlying democratic fears of overall executive dominance.

Federal and provincial governments have a complex political relationship wherein competing claims are voiced and debated. Attention to the division of powers and to provincial reactions may on many occasion serve to limit federal government proposals. Yet, it is also true that despite having limited jurisdiction in various social policy fields such as health and higher education, the federal government has been able to shape events through the power to spend or to withhold spending, or to re-shape patterns of federal–provincial interactions. What recourse was available to Ontario, Alberta, and British Columbia when the Mulroney government limited the growth in their Canada Assistance Plan transfers in the early 1990s? What recourse was available to provinces when the early budgets of the Chrétien government cut back on transfers and added to provincial expenditure burdens? Federalism and strong provincial governments are a restraint, but do not overlook or underestimate the strength of the federal government position.

CONCLUSION

The prime minister has several sources of significant power, and the political system has inadequate safeguards to combat the excesses of this power. Prime ministers have major advantages in inter-party competition. Elections, meanwhile, are sporadic, and parliamentary life is seemingly more defined by party discipline and the divide between ins and outs than by a collective appraisal of detailed policy and budgetary plans. At the same time, the press contributes to improved accountability, but there are noteworthy limitations to its impact. Governments are huge entities, and only a selection of events can be reported since audience and budgetary pressures constrain coverage. Prime ministers, meanwhile, are supported by a growing circle of advisors, pollsters, and spin doctors that help protect their position. Constraining power is not an easy task. Considering ways to improve the actual track record on this front is an important topic for future debate.

Only a very few Canadians have ever achieved the prime-ministerial pinnacle. Perhaps one of the reasons for the limited number is the imbalance between restraints upon power and the reinforcements of that power. There is a struggle between the exercise of real power by a relatively small number of ambitious and skilled politicians and the efforts of other political actors to keep that power in check—a struggle that warrants vigilance.

NOTES

1. Donald J. Savoie, *Power: Where Is It?* (Montreal and Kingston: McGill-Queen's University Press, 2010) and *Governing from the Centre: The Concentration of Power in Canadian Politics* (Toronto: University of Toronto Press, 1999).

2. Jeffrey Simpson, *The Friendly Dictatorship* (Toronto: McClelland and Stewart, 2001).

3. Brian Mulroney, *Memoirs: 1939–1993* (Toronto: Douglas Gibson Books, 2007).

4. Jean Chrétien, *My Years as Prime Minister* (Toronto: Knopf Canada, 2007).

5. Martin Lawrence, *Iron Man: The Defiant Reign of Jean Chrétien* (Toronto: Penguin, 2003) and *Harperland: The Politics of Control* (Toronto: Viking, 2010).

6. Peter Hogg, *Constitutional Law in Canada*, student ed. (Toronto: Carswell, 2001), p. 1.2.

7. Jeffrey Simpson, *The Friendly Dictatorship*, p. 4.

8. Edward Greenspon and Anthony Wilson-Smith, *Double Vision: The Inside Story of the Liberals in Power* (Toronto: Doubleday Canada, 1996), p. 220.

9. Donald Savoie, "Power at the Apex: Executive Dominance," in James Bickerton and Alain-G. Gagnon, eds., *Canadian Politics*, 4th ed. (Peterborough, ON: Broadview, 2004), p. 146.

10. Mulroney, *Memoirs*, pp. 394–397.

11. CBC News, "Harper Lands in Germany as G8 Summit Approaches," June 4, 2007, available at http://www.cbc.ca/canada/story/2007/06/03/harper-summit.html?ref=rss. Accessed November 9, 2007.

12. Savoie, *Governing from the Centre*, p. 91.

13. Sid Noel, "Leaders' Entourages, Parties and Patronage" in Alain-G. Gagnon and Brian Tanguay, eds., *Canadian Parties in Transition*, 3rd ed. (Peterborough, ON: Broadview, 2007), pp. 197–213.

14. Ibid., p. 206.

15. Lawrence, *Iron Man*, p. 431.

16. Denis Smith, *Tory Rogue: The Life and Legend of John Diefenbaker* (Toronto: Macfarlane Walter & Ross, 1995).

17. Jon H. Pammett, "Elections," in Michael and Glen Williams, eds., *Canadian Politics in the 21st Century*, 7th ed. (Toronto: Nelson, 2008), p. 164.

18. Ibid., p. 165.

19. Mulroney, *Memoirs*, p. 633.

20. Lawrence, *Iron Man*, p. 373.

21. David Docherty, *Legislatures* (Vancouver: UBC Press, 2005), pp. 125–126.

22. David Docherty, *Mr. Smith Goes to Ottawa: Life in the House of Commons* (Vancouver: UBC Press, 1997), p. 9.

23. Office of the Auditor General of Canada, "Chapter 3–The Sponsorship Program," *2003 November Report of the Auditor General of Canada* (Ottawa, 2003), available at http://www.oag-bvg.gc.ca/internet/English/parl_oag_200311_03_e_12925.html. Accessed August 14, 2011.

24. CBC News, "PMO Holds Grip on Message Control: Records," June 7, 2010, available at http://www.cbc.ca/news/politics/story/2010/06/07/pmo-message-event-proposals. html. Accessed August 15, 2011.

25. Paul Nesbitt-Larking, *Politics, Society, and the Media*, 2nd ed. (Peterborough, ON: Broadview, 2007), p. 146.

26. Herman Bakvis, "Prime Minister and Cabinet in Canada. An Autocracy in Need of Reform," *Journal of Canadian Studies* 15, no. 4 (2001), p. 68.

✗ NO
Limits on the Power of the Prime Minister
PAUL BARKER

Many close observers of Canadian politics believe that political power in Canada resides largely with the prime minister and his small group of close advisers. Those who make this argument are careful to admit that the prime minister comes up against some limits, but at the same time they describe Canada as "a kind of monarchy" that is "mandated by democracy."[1] The source of the prime minister's great influence, they say, lies in his access to so many "levers of power."[2] He leads the governing party, controls cabinet and its members, commands the attention of the media, sets the overall direction of the country, and much more. Also important, highly qualified officials located in the central agencies—"superbureaucrats"—help the prime minister control all relevant matters.[3] There are some who reject the notion that government in Canada amounts to "prime-ministerial government."[4] But such sentiments receive little attention. According to a popular text in Canadian politics, "[m]ost observers agree that Cabinet government has been transformed into a system of prime-ministerial government...."[5] And other reputable sources also diligently outline the case that the prime minister's powers of influence dwarf those of others in the political process.[6]

The belief that the prime minister wields a great deal of power has some merit. The nature of parliamentary government is to situate power in the hands of the political executive, so we expect the prime minister to be influential. But to suggest that this forms the basis of a kind of monarchical democracy goes too far. Though many specific criticisms of the thesis of prime-ministerial government may be made, there are basically two problems with it. One is that it fails to note sufficiently that the prime minister faces some formidable players in the political process. The prime minister is simply not that powerful. There are forces both inside and outside government that can challenge the leader of the governing party. The other problem relates to the conception of competition. The theory of prime-ministerial government assumes that competition for power is viable only when it is patently obvious or present. But prime ministers can be challenged simply by the threat of a new competitive force. The prime minister operates in a world of "virtual competition," in which the challenges sometimes appear as only potentialities. The lack of a corporeal presence matters little, because the prime minister acts as if the challenges are real. The key implication here is that there is indeed competition in Canadian politics—more so than suggested by a counting of the observable competitors—and that Canada is not nearly as vulnerable to the effects of concentrated power as suggested by those who see the influence of only the prime minister.

INSIDE GOVERNMENT

The idea of an almost domineering prime minister certainly exaggerates the power the prime minister commands outside the formal structures of government, and it can be argued that it is an exaggeration also of the power commanded inside government. Let us begin with the latter. Donald J. Savoie writes that "[it] is hardly possible to overemphasize the fact that the Canadian prime minister has no outer limits defining his political authority within the government."[7] In fact, one can overemphasize the influence of the prime minister. Outer limits exist, and one has to look only at the relations between prime ministers and their ministers to see this point. Take, for instance, former prime minister Jean Chrétien and his then finance minister, Paul Martin. According to Mr. Chrétien himself, the finance minister had a great deal of leeway in the making of fiscal policy. "I am not going to tell my finance minister what to do," said Mr. Chrétien.[8] And this has been the tradition at the federal level: the finance minister runs the budgetary process. Of course, this is not to say that the prime minister is shut out of this important process—the national leader can never ignore the economic health of the nation. The fact remains, however, that the finance minister is a powerful player in Canadian politics. Even in the heavily prime-ministerial government of Stephen Harper, events suggest that the finance minister sometimes goes his own way—and gets his way.[9]

There are instances of other ministers taking actions that reveal the limits of prime-ministerial power. Allan Rock, a federal Minister of Health in the Chrétien government, wanted to raise the profile of the federal government in the Canadian health care system. The health minister outlined a "new plan for health care"[10] that would indeed give a greater role to Ottawa but also held out the possibility of major disruptions in relations between the federal government and the provinces. Many assumed, though, that the latter would be acceptable because it was thought that the prime minister had given his consent to the initiative. But the prime minister had done no such thing. A minister had announced a major policy initiative with serious implications for federal–provincial relations—without the prime minister's agreement.[11]

In the government of Paul Martin, signs of conflict between the first minister and elected members of his party became clear. Initially, Prime Minister Martin appeared to look favourably on a decision that would see Canada work with the United States to develop a ballistic missile defence system for North America. But dissent in the party helped produce a contrary decision. The prime minister also faced resistance from Liberal Members of Parliament (MPs) who disagreed with his government's support of legislation favouring same-sex marriage. The weakness of Mr. Martin was in part made possible because backbenchers realized that the prime minister was, most of the time, in a minority situation and needed their support. A majority situation might, of course, easily quash these differences. But the fact is that minority governments are part of parliamentary government, and they serve to lessen the power of the first minister.

The experience so far of the governments of Stephen Harper, at first glance, reveals a prime minister more than able to control his ministers. Reports disclose a number of actions that support this perception. Prime Minister Harper prefers a "hub and spoke" management style, which means that Mr. Harper—as the hub—is able to more easily keep track of the ministers, who are the individual spokes.[12] As with all governments, ministers in the Harper government received "mandate" letters outlining their priorities and what was expected of them, but these letters were much more precise and specific than the usual ones.[13] The Prime Minister's Office (PMO), an agency tied tightly to the prime minister, has assumed much more power and used this influence to carefully prescribe and monitor ministerial statements and interactions with the media and other players in the political process. Yet, even with these developments, cabinet members have managed at times to act in ways contrary to the wishes of the first minister. Harper's minister for intergovernmental affairs publicly disassociated himself from the government's important support of Quebec as "a nation within a united Canada." Other ministers have rebelled against the interventions of the PMO and refused to agree to significant government positions on important issues.[14] More generally, it has to be remembered that the precarious position of minority governments sometimes causes the prime minister to assume a much more controlling posture, a position also made necessary in the case of the Harper government by the relative inexperience of the cabinet. With a new majority Conservative government, it will be interesting to see whether controls are relaxed and pave the way for more differences between the prime minister and his ministers.

Ministerial ambition (combined with backbencher support) can sometimes do more than limit prime ministerial power—it can also fatally weaken the head of the government. At the turn of the century, many in the Liberal Party expected Mr. Chrétien to leave office soon and open the way for a leadership race; he had already governed for two full terms, and he was getting older. But the prime minister, upset by attempts within his own party to oust him, surprised many with his actions. He contested a third election in late 2000—and won—and suggested at a minimum that he would complete his third term as leader of the country. The prime minister's actions, especially his speculations on his own future, infuriated both party members and Liberal MPs who wished to see Mr. Martin become prime minister, and they began to call for Mr. Chrétien to step down. For a time, the prime minister resisted, but it was all to no avail. Mr. Martin had made great efforts to gain support of Liberal MPs who failed to make it into cabinet or who were ignored by the prime minister and his advisers in the Prime Minister's Office.

The finance minister also had in place an impressive organization dedicated to making him the prime minister. In August 2002, Jean Chrétien announced he would leave office in early 2004, and, by late 2003, he was gone.[15]

For some, the demise of Mr. Chrétien was a product of special circumstances and hardly a sign of inherent prime-ministerial weakness. The former prime minister had been confronted by a minister determined to succeed him and a large group of returning MPs who received nothing from a prime minister unable to give them much. Mr. Chrétien also had no real organization in place to confront his competition—he was too busy running the government and uncertain about continuing beyond his third mandate.[16] All this may be true. But it is also true that a prime minister had been *effectively* pushed aside, an unexpected event in the life of an individual who has many levers of power at his behest. A former senior official in the PMO and respected observer of government gives his read of the demise of Mr. Chrétien:

> …Savoie's 1999 metaphor of an all powerful love-like prime minister casting bolts of electricity into the system would have to be recast in 2003 as Jean Chrétien has been sent into retirement after losing control first of his party, then of his caucus. The events of the past year prove that Canada does not have a dictatorship, friendly or otherwise.[17]

There is another component of the prime-ministerial thesis that weakens under examination. As part of his attempt to ensure his powerful position, the prime minister (with his advisers) aims to keep his ministers out of trouble so that he "can get things done in areas that matter a great deal."[18] But the prime minister fails in this regard; he is not sufficiently powerful to accomplish this purpose. In these situations, ministers are not acting against the prime minister's wishes. Rather, they are merely being ministers, carrying out their mandates, and in so doing they run into difficulties. One has only to look at the Harper government for confirmation of this point. In 2008, the country learned that the federal Minister of Foreign Affairs had left some confidential papers at the house of his girlfriend. It also turned out that the girlfriend had had intimate relations with a figure connected to the Montreal crime world and had been married to a senior member of the Hell's Angels. The minister lost his job. In 2010, Helena Guergis resigned her position in the federal cabinet following allegations that she, among other things, allegedly permitted her office to be used by her husband to carry out private business. A subsequent investigation found no substance to the claims against the minister, but the damage had been done. Also in 2010, the minister of International Cooperation misled the House of Commons on matters relating to her department—in other words, she failed to tell the truth. Unlike in the preceding two cases, the minister survived the fallout from the action, but she had injured the Harper government.[19] There are other instances in the Harper government—and preceding ones—that could be detailed, but these are sufficient to reveal the limits of prime-ministerial power.

On balance, it seems that the prime minister cannot really control his individual ministers. At times, they will pursue agendas that are inconsistent with the prime minister's actions. As Herman Bakvis says, "one can...find examples of ministers carving out their own sphere of influence and taking initiatives."[20] The odd minister may also try to unseat the prime minister—and succeed. At other times, ministers will seek to please the prime minister, but the nature of the job—the power and responsibilities—will land ministers in trouble no matter what the prime minister and his central-agency officials attempt to do. Moreover, it is not just the individual ministers who can constrain the prime minister. The collective ministerial or cabinet decision-making system operates to disperse power. For proponents of the prime-ministerial government thesis, the cabinet system works largely to the advantage of the prime minister. In cabinet, he purportedly sets the agenda, controls the dissemination of information, and makes the final decision (and sometimes he fails to bring his decision to cabinet's attention). But this, too, overstates the case. Most prime ministers realize, sooner or later, that this is a recipe for prime-ministerial overload and that government functions well only when ministers run their own departments. Consequently, the cabinet system reflects the power of ministers. According to one study of the Chrétien years, the prime minister's "preference [was] to keep out of the hair of his ministers except in the most unusual circumstances."[21] The Privy Council Office (PCO), one of the most important advisory bodies to the prime minister, comes to a similar conclusion. "The tone of government may be set by the Prime Minister and the cabinet," reads a PCO document, "but most of the policies of the government flow from the exercise of the individual responsibilities of ministers."[22] Even in the Harper government, where there are hints of a more centralized cabinet system, official reports insist on a collegial cabinet decision-making system relying on the initiatives of individual ministers.[23]

Government consists of more than just the executive branch. There are the legislature and the judiciary. The functioning of these two branches also contests the notion of an imperial prime minister. Admittedly, the legislature provides less of a challenge for the prime minister than the other two branches. Nevertheless, it can provide a test for the prime minister, and indeed the first minister under pressure can take actions to strengthen this part of government. Former prime minister Paul Martin, for instance, made a commitment to a number of changes that would strengthen the legislature.[24] Under his plan, party discipline in the House of Commons would be loosened and parliamentary standing committees would be granted more influence. Private members' bills would receive closer consideration, and the ethics commissioner would report to Parliament (and not to the prime minister). A proposal that has already had some effect allows parliamentary committees some say in the appointment of Supreme Court justices. Not surprisingly, the current prime minister, when in his minority situation, also felt the influence of the House of Commons, so much so that one of his senior advisers charged that the opposition parties had effectively—and unconstitutionally—become the de facto government.[25]

As for the judiciary, the advent of the Charter of Rights and Freedoms has made the courts a much more important player in Canadian politics. Some downplay the impact of the courts' interpretation of the Charter on other political actors, including the prime minister. But others suggest that the courts, with their interpretation of the Charter, have altered the distribution of power in Canada.[26] Even when decisions that may favour the prime minister are rendered, the transfer of power is taking place because it is the courts that are exercising authority, not the government leader. The prime minister also sometimes fails in an attempt to use the courts to the government's advantage. The Martin government referred its same-sex marriage legislation to the Supreme Court of Canada partly in the hope that the court would find the traditional definition of marriage inconsistent with the Charter of Rights and Freedoms. With this ruling, the prime minister could avoid the politically damaging task of acting against those who still believed in the traditional definition. But the highest court refused to address this issue and simply said that the new legislation outlining a new definition of same-sex marriage was acceptable without saying whether the old definition was unacceptable. The prime minister himself would thus have to apply the deathblow to a definition of marriage still supported by a large part of the electorate. The adjudication of non-Charter issues can also reveal the power of the courts. In 1998, the Supreme Court of Canada laid out the rules that would govern the secession of Quebec from Canada. Though the opinion of the court is non-binding, it has effectively determined how this country might come to an end. Arguably, the most important decision affecting Canada was not made by the most important individual in Canadian politics; it was made by others.

OUTSIDE GOVERNMENT

Proponents of prime-ministerial government claim that their theory applies only to developments *within* government. The fact that the provinces or the media may limit the power of the first minister is irrelevant because the theory of prime-ministerial government does not extend outside the halls of government. Yet, these outside forces are sometimes used to demonstrate the power of the prime minister. The media, for instance, allegedly turn the first minister almost into a celebrity, which adds to the influence of the office of the prime minister. Similarly, globalization—another external force—also seemingly plays into the hands of the prime minister because it increasingly requires national leaders to make important decisions. Accordingly, it appears that these outside forces ought to be considered when attempting to assess the power of the prime minister. When this is done, it can be seen that they represent a double-edged sword for the prime minister. The media can place the prime minister in the spotlight and make the leader of the government appear well beyond others in the political process, but the media can also hurt the prime minister in at least two related ways. The media practise what some call "gotcha journalism," which is an attempt to highlight the gaffes and mistakes of political leaders.[27] Mr. Chrétien was often the target of this kind of journalism, and Mr. Martin also experienced at times a rough ride from the media. Prime Minister Harper has endeavoured to anticipate the influence of the media by restricting their access to ministers and forcing reporters to accept an arrangement whereby the PMO can select who shall ask questions at press conferences. These and other actions—which include calling on the RCMP to eject journalists from a hotel in which Conservative MPs were meeting—suggest a prime minister able to get the upper hand on the media.[28] This is a plausible interpretation, but another is that the Harper offensive against the press reveals the power of the media and the sheer desperation governments feel in their interactions with the fourth estate. The media can also use their investigative resources to force an issue onto the political agenda that can hurt the prime minister. The media made much of Mr. Chrétien's attempt to convince a government agency to provide financial assistance to a business concern in the former prime minister's riding. They also played an important role in making the problems with a government sponsorship program into a scandal. As for the current prime minister, he has so far escaped any full-blown media investigations, but his government's policy on Afghanistan has attracted a great deal of media interest, as has his allegedly Caesar-like style of leading.[29]

Globalization is another external force that may limit the power of the prime minister. *Globalization* has many meanings and definitions, but basically it focuses on how worldwide forces, especially economic ones, are eroding national boundaries. At present, the nation-state is the primary organizing principle of world politics; however, globalization works to supplant this principle and insert a new one that emphasizes the clout of *supra*national institutions (political and otherwise). In these circumstances, leaders of nation-states, including the prime minister of Canada, should see their power reduced. And in fact there is evidence of weakened leaders as they accept the dictates of international trade agreements and new tax regimes that demand a common playing field upon which the world's multinational corporations can play.

Proponents of the prime-ministerial government thesis are, however, unconvinced by this kind of analysis. Savoie, for one, says that leaders still maintain great power in a global world because "[t]he designers of the new order in many ways will have to be national politicians and national public services."[30] But this participation of national leaders may be short-lived; they might turn out to be their own gravediggers. Also, those believing in leaders' continued preeminence may be guilty of confusing globalization with "internationalization."[31] The latter refers to the heightened interaction between nation-states, a development that strengthens nation-states and their leaders. But globalization is different; its functioning does not really depend on national leaders getting together and making decisions. Globalization seeks to bypass nation-states because it sees them as an obstacle. It is of interest to note that the original proponent of the prime-ministerial government thesis in the Canadian context now admits that the "power that any Canadian prime minister is able to exercise has been leeching away."[32] According to Denis Smith, the prime minister can hardly stand up to the relentless effects of multinational corporations, free trade agreements, and the worldwide financial markets. In plain terms, globalization greatly curbs the influence of the prime minister.

The provinces represent another force outside the national government that reduces the power of the prime minister. In fact, it may be argued that the provinces are more deserving of attention than other forces outside government because they effectively are *within* government at the national level. As many students of Canadian federalism have argued, there are few policy matters that fail to involve both orders of government.[33] One order thus constitutes an extension of the other and vice versa. Another way to see the possible uniqueness of the provinces in the theory of prime-ministerial government is to compare the parliamentary system with the presidential one. Those who see the prime minister as being too powerful point to the separation of powers in the American political system and how this arrangement limits the president. They then note that the absence of such an arrangement in Canada strengthens the prime minister. But the supporters of the theory of prime-ministerial government fail to finish the story. Government in Canada may not be divided *within* government, but it is divided *between* governments. The operation of the federal principle in Canada (unlike that in the U.S.) gives Canada its own version of the separation of powers. To exclude the provinces in a consideration of the power of the prime minister is to fail to appreciate the full operation of government in Canada. As Richard Simeon and Elaine Willis suggest, the nature of federalism in Canada almost appears as the natural attempt of any democracy to find ways to ensure that power is never too concentrated:

> In Canada, the closest parallel to divided government is found not in relations between executive and legislative but in federalism itself. Much of the imagery surrounding divided government in the United States is replicated in analyses of federal–provincial relations in Canada. Just as an assertive Congress challenges the president, so do assertive provinces challenge Ottawa.[34]

When one does consider the provinces and their impact on the prime minister, the restraining effect of the provinces can be seen quite clearly. The provinces have constitutional authority over important matters, and they represent strong regional interests that can clash with the overall national interest. The sheer size and wealth of some provinces also play a part in relations between the provinces and the prime minister. Recent developments reveal the difficulties the provinces pose for the first minister. Over the past decade, Mr. Chrétien, Mr. Martin, and even a reluctant Mr. Harper (who respects provincial jurisdiction more than his predecessors) have attempted to establish a role for Ottawa in health care. In these efforts, they have admittedly succeeded in attaching some stipulations to the use of additional financial assistance from the federal government. But the fact remains that the provinces still largely control the shaping and formulating of health policy. Even more recently, Prime Minister Harper sought to make adjustments to a federal–provincial fiscal arrangement that makes available federal financial support to less well-off provinces. Some provinces accepted the change, but one province condemned it and urged all of its residents (and Canadians) to vote against Mr. Harper, while another launched a constitutional challenge.

Contemporary events are not the only relevant pieces of evidence when considering federal–provincial relations and the power of the prime minister. The history of federalism, at least since the end of the Second World War, is the history of declining federal power. "The prominent characterizing feature of the evolution of the Canadian federation in the postwar period," write Robin Boadway and Frank Flatters, "is the gradual but persistent decentralization of fiscal responsibilities from the federal government to the provinces (and their municipalities)."[35] Recently, as reflected in its efforts to affect health care, the federal government has sought to reverse this trend, to give the national interest—and the prime minister—greater prominence in important areas of public policy.[36] But the trend seems too strong. The money and power have shifted from the federal government to the provinces. The prime minister leads a government that must contend with the reality that it exists in one of the world's most decentralized federal states. The implication of this for the thesis of prime-ministerial government should be clear: the prime minister may not have a United States Congress to deal with, but he or she does have the provinces.

VIRTUAL COMPETITION

In a well-received book on Canadian politics, Donald J. Savoie writes that prime ministers "have in their hands all the important levers of power." But a few paragraphs later, he also writes that "one of the main preoccupations of the most senior officials in government is to protect the prime minister."[37] The power of the prime minister is evidently combined with a rather precarious hold on office, a state of affairs that seems distinctly odd. Surely a powerful prime minister is free of constant concern for his or her very survival, yet the reality appears otherwise. Even Mr. Chrétien himself admitted his vulnerability: "It's a survival game played under the glare of light. If you don't learn that, you're quickly finished."[38] The prime minister supposedly governs with few checks; nevertheless, he or she participates in a game of survival in which *all* participants risk fatal blows.

Part of the explanation for this puzzling state of affairs has already been provided. There are constraints on the prime minister's power. The prime minister needs to worry about his or her situation because he or she faces challengers. But the near desperate situation of the prime minister suggests that something more is at work. The prime minister does countenance challengers whom all can see—cabinet ministers, the provinces, the media, the opposition. However, the prime minister also contends with threats to his or her position, which amount to competitive forces that are not so evident—a kind of "virtual competition." Normally, we associate competition with entities that are clearly present, but competition can also come in the form of possibilities and potentialities. The result is an individual or organization that possesses a near-monopoly situation but that feels itself to be under siege. In the world of business, this phenomenon is recognized. Powerful companies dominate sectors of the private market, but their chief executive officers admit that they are almost terrified by competition.[39] The traditional conception of competition demands the existence of clear competitors who force the more powerful actors to adjust their behaviour accordingly, but another conception sees competition in ghostly threats with very imaginable and lethal outcomes.

With this latter notion of competition, the anxiety experienced by the prime minister and his advisers becomes more understandable. The prime minister feels himself to be in a game of survival because he *is* in a game of survival: "The press want to get you. The opposition want to get you. Even some of the bureaucrats want to get you."[40] On the surface, these sentiments of Mr. Chrétien seem mere hyperbole—there are challenges to a prime minister's power, but not to this extent. But perhaps the former prime minister knows better, for he appreciates the possibilities of disaster in his environment. Take, for instance, the opposition. Normally the House of Commons attracts little attention in discussions of the prime minister's power; party discipline reduces the legislature to a bit player in Canadian politics. But a misstep in Parliament, perhaps during Question Period, can damage the prime minister. That is why his senior advisers spend so much time preparing him and cabinet members for their session in the House of Commons. Of course, this is not to say that Parliament rivals the prime minister, but it is to say that members of Parliament have the capacity to ruin a prime minister. Much like a company that can be undermined overnight by a new invention, the prime minister can find himself in serious trouble with a careless response to a question or an insensitive appreciation of a parliamentary matter.

Perhaps even more unsettling in politics (and business) are the threats from the truly unforeseen entities. A prime minister can try to defend himself from the dangers posed by the House of Commons and other well-known elements in the political process. More difficult is a defence against something that essentially emerges from nowhere—a new charismatic leader, a past indiscretion coming to light, a debilitating court decision. In such a world, anything does become possible and prime-ministerial vigilance turns into a practical obsession with challenges to the government.

The important consequence of virtual competition is that the Canadian political process is much less susceptible to the evils of concentrated power than commonly thought. Again, experience in the private sector is instructive. There are well-known companies with positions of incredible influence and wealth who do not act like entities with a near monopoly of the market. Under monopoly conditions, the expectation is that prices will rise, quality will decline, and innovation will disappear. However, this fails to transpire with these companies. Instead, prices fall, quality rises, and innovation takes place.[41] With the appropriate adjustments, the same phenomenon can be seen in political life. Under prime-ministerial government, we should experience high costs, bad public policy, insensitive politicians, and few fresh approaches to societal problems. Some may claim that Canada has all of these, but this would be an exaggeration of the true situation. There are a number of indicators of good government in Canada, a reality that clashes with the predictions of prime-ministerial government. Canada has social policies that are admired around the world, it sometimes serves a useful purpose in foreign affairs, and the United Nations annually places Canada either at the top of or near the top of the list of the world's best nations in which to live. These outcomes hardly seem consistent with the evils of concentrated power.

CONCLUSION

There is no argument with the claim that Canada's prime minister has substantial influence and that he is the most powerful player in Canadian politics. The objections arise when the claim extends to the notion that the first minister has no real challengers. The thesis of prime-ministerial government suggests that the distance between the prime minister and the other players in the Canadian political process in terms of power is great. The reality, however, is that the gap is not substantial and that it can be bridged. Both inside and outside government, there are entities that can remind the prime minister that politics is a game of survival for all players. Inside government can be found ambitious cabinet ministers, disgruntled backbenchers, and newly empowered judges; outside government are the media, premiers, provinces, and a world that pays less and less attention to national leaders. To be fair to those who subscribe to the theory of prime-ministerial government, the challenges that emanate from within and from without government are not equally forbidding. The proponents of prime-ministerial government focus on power relations inside government, and one is certainly on more solid ground when trying to argue for the presence of a prime minister without equals inside government than when endeavouring to do the same in relation to matters outside government. But even inside government the prime minister must be on guard. Moreover, there are always the threats inherent in the world of virtual competition. Many survey the Canadian political process and see very little for the prime minister to worry about, but they do not see what the prime minister sees.

Ultimately, the belief in the all-powerful prime minister founders because it is at odds with the reality of Canada. This country has its problems; nevertheless, it is recognized as a functioning democracy with public policies that stand up well against those of other nations. Unless one believes in benevolent dictatorships, good public policy cannot generally be said to coexist with a political system in which much of the political power lies with one person and his advisers.[42] Canada's national leader is powerful, but not to the point where power turns into a corrupting force. Fortunately, the competitive pressures in Canadian politics are simply too great for us to have reached this point.

NOTES

1. Donald J. Savoie, "The King of the Commons," *Time*, May 3, 1999, p. 64.

2. Donald J. Savoie, *Governing from the Centre: The Concentration of Power in Canadian Politics* (Toronto: University of Toronto Press, 1999), p. 72.

3. Colin Campbell and George Szablowski, *The Superbureaucrats* (Toronto: Macmillan, 1979).

4. Keith Archer et al., *Parameters of Power: Canada's Political Institutions*, 3rd ed. (Toronto: ITP Nelson, 2002), p. 241.

5. Rand Dyck, *Canadian Politics: Critical Approaches*, 6th ed. (Scarborough: Thomson Nelson, 2011), p. 554. Bolding has been removed.

6. See, for example, Donald Savoie, "First Ministers, Cabinet, and the Public Service," in John C. Courtney and David E. Smith, eds., *The Oxford Handbook of Canadian Politics* (Toronto: Oxford University Press, 2010).

7. Savoie, *Governing from the Centre*, p. 108.

8. Edward Greenspon and Anthony Wilson-Smith, *Double Vision: The Inside Story of the Liberals in Power* (Toronto: Doubleday Canada, 1996), p. 163.

9. Lawrence Martin, *Harperland: The Politics of Control* (Toronto: Viking Canada, 2010), p. 175; and Paul Wells and John Geddes, "Why You Don't Know about Stephen Harper," *Maclean's*, February 7, 2010, pp. 24–25.

10. Robert Fife and Giles Gherson, "Rock Proposes New National Health Plan," *National Post*, January 27, 2000, pp. A1, A11.

11. Anne McIlroy, "Rock's Grand Plan Was News to the PM," *The Globe and Mail*, March 4, 2000, p. A3.

12. Brian Laghi, "Discipline, Control Mark PM's Management Style," *The Globe and Mail*, April 8, 2006, pp. A1, A4.

13. John Ivison, "With a Fistful of Power," *National Post*, September 1, 2007, p. A6.

14. Ian Brown, "In Harper's Regime, Big Daddy Knows Best," *The Globe and Mail*, May 13, 2006, p. F6; Brian Laghi and Jane Taber, "Offshore Deal a Crucial Test for

MacKay," *The Globe and Mail*, June 13, 2007, p. A12. One might also cite the case of Bill Casey, a Conservative backbencher who failed to support his party's budget and was subsequently ejected from the caucus of the Conservative Party.

15. For more on this, see Susan Delacourt, *Juggernaut: Paul Martin's Campaign for Chrétien's Crown* (Toronto: McClelland and Stewart, 2003).

16. For a picture of the complexity of Chrétien's situation, see Eddie Goldenberg, *The Way It Works: Inside Ottawa* (Toronto: Douglas Gibson Books, 2006), ch. 22; and the former prime minister's memoirs, Jean Chretien, *My Years as Prime Minister* (Toronto: Knopf, 2007), ch. 14.

17. Thomas Axworthy, "Our Public Service Malady: A Diagnosis," *The Globe and Mail*, September 27, 2003, p. D4. (In this article, Axworthy is reviewing a new book by Savoie: *Donald J. Savoie, Breaking the Bargain: Public Servants, Ministers, and Parliament* [Toronto: University of Toronto Press, 2003].)

18. Savoie, *Governing from the Centre*, p. 336.

19. John Geddes, "The Bev Oda Affair and the Tories Scandal-Management Strategy," *Maclean's*, February 28, 2011.

20. Herman Bakvis, "Prime Minister and Cabinet in Canada: An Autocracy in Need of Reform?" *Journal of Canadian Studies* 35, no. 4 (Winter 2001), p. 65.

21. Greenspon and Wilson-Smith, *Double Vision*, p. 35.

22. Privy Council Office, *Responsibility in the Constitution* (Ottawa: Minister of Supply and Services, 1993), p. 62.

23. Government of Canada, *Accountable Government: A Guide for Ministers and Secretaries of State, 2011* (Ottawa: Her Majesty the Queen in Right of Canada, 2011), p. 37.

24. For a discussion of these changes, see Peter Aucoin and Lori Turnbull, "The Democratic Deficit: Paul Martin and Parliamentary Government," *Canadian Public Administration* 46, no. 4 (2003).

25. Tom Flanagan, "Liberal Tactics Amount to Constitutional Back-seat Driving," *The Globe and Mail*, February 20, 2007, p. A19.

26. See the debate between Peter H. Russell and F.L. Morton in Mark Charlton and Paul Barker, eds., *Crosscurrents: Contemporary Political Issues,* 3rd ed. (Scarborough: ITP Nelson, 1998), Issue 14.

27. George Bain, *Gotcha! How the Media Distort the News* (Toronto: Key Porter Books, 1994).

28. Christopher Dornan, "The Cool on the Hill," *The Globe and Mail*, October 20, 2007, p. F3. For an update on Harper government and the media, see Martin, *Harperland*, ch. 7.

29. See, for example, John Ivison, "With a Fistful of Power," p. A6; and Lawrence Martin, "A Prime Minister at the Top of His Imperious Game," *The Globe and Mail*, October 22, 2007, p. A15.

30. Savoie, *Governing from the Centre*, p. 107.

31. See Jan Aart Scholte, "The Globalization of World Politics," in John Baylis and Steve Smith, eds., *The Globalization of World Politics: An Introduction to International Relations* (New York: Oxford University Press, 1997).

32. Denis Smith, "Is the Prime Minister Too Powerful?–Yes" in Mark Charlton and Paul Barker, eds., *Crosscurrents: Contemporary Political Issues,* 2nd ed. (Scarborough: Nelson Canada, 1994), p. 159.

33. See, for example, Richard Simeon, "The Federal–Provincial Decision Making Process," in *Ontario Economic Council, Issues and Alternatives–1977: Intergovernmental Relations* (Toronto: Ontario Economic Council, 1977), p. 26.

34. Richard Simeon and Elaine Willis, "Democracy and Performance: Governance in Canada and the United States," in Keith Banting, George Hoberg, and Richard Simeon, eds., *Degrees of Freedom: Canada and the United States in a Changing World* (Montreal and Kingston: McGill-Queen's University Press, 1997), p. 171.

35. Robin Boadway and Frank Flatters, "Fiscal Federalism: Is the System in Crisis?" in Keith G. Banting, Douglas M. Brown, and Thomas J. Courchene, eds., *The Future of Fiscal Federalism* (Kingston: School of Policy Studies et al., 1994), p. 137.

36. Gerard Boismenu and Peter Graefe, "The New Federal Tool Belt: Attempts to Rebuild Social Policy Leadership," in *Canadian Public Policy* 30, no. 1 (2004), pp. 71–89.

37. Savoie, *Governing from the Centre*, pp. 72–73.

38. Ibid., p. 313.

39. Robert J. Samuelson, "The Gates of Power," *The New Republic*, April 23, 2001, p. 31.

40. Savoie, *Governing from the Centre*, p. 313.

41. Samuelson, "The Gates of Power."

42. One might also believe in a "friendly dictatorship." See Jeffrey Simpson, *The Friendly Dictatorship* (Toronto: McClelland & Stewart, 2001).

POSTSCRIPT_____

In his article, Mellon employs a useful approach to making his case. He documents the arsenal of powers available to the prime minister—the powers are truly impressive—and then makes short work of any possible obstacles that might block the path of the first minister. Yet, there are a few openings for those who wish to think differently. Take, for example, the case of former prime minister Jean Chrétien. Mellon himself seemingly admits that Chrétien left office in part because the fates were aligned against him—more concretely, his former finance minister, Paul Martin, and much of his party wanted him gone. Surely, this is evidence that weakens claims of an all-powerful prime minister. Mellon might also be guilty of downplaying the capacity of the media to seriously damage any government and its leader. It is true, as Mellon writes, that the press can cover only so much of government; he is also correct when he says that governments spend increasingly more time managing journalists. But the media need not be expansive in its coverage to hurt a prime minister, and, as Barker says, efforts to curtail the press have the quality of desperation and last resort.

In his article, Paul Barker points out additional problems with the thesis of prime-ministerial government. Ministers can challenge the prime minister—without necessarily facing dismissal—and forces outside government aside from the media can reduce the influence of the prime minister. But Barker, too, may be guilty of exaggeration—he may, in other words, underestimate the true power of the prime minister. He is impressed with how ministers are able to challenge the prime minister, but it looks as if he has ignored the fact that most of these challenges end with the prime minister getting his or her way. As for the prime minister failing to keep the ministers out of trouble, this may be seen as amounting to very little. Finally, Barker might better appreciate that the prime minister has assumed increasing control over the years. The depiction of Prime Minister Harper in Lawrence Martin's recent book *Harperland* suggests the unbelievable: namely, a government leader in reach of full control.

To begin an analysis of the power of the prime minister, the interested student first needs to understand the system of parliamentary government and the prime minister's formal role in it. For this, one might consult Peter Aucoin, "Prime Minister and Cabinet," in James Bickerton and Alain-G. Gagnon, eds., *Canadian Politics,* 3rd ed. (Peterborough: Broadview Press, 1999) or Michael Whittington, "The Prime Minister, Cabinet, and the Executive," in Michael Whittington and Glen Williams, eds., *Canadian Politics in the 21st Century*, 6th ed. (Scarborough: Thomson Nelson, 2004). Jeffrey Simpson's book *The Friendly Dictatorship* (Toronto: McClelland & Stewart, 2001) can then be read for an engaging discussion of the thesis of prime-ministerial government. A more recent journalistic account of the power of the prime minister is Lawrence Martin, *Harperland: The Politics of Control* (Toronto: Viking Canada, 2010).

With these readings completed, the student is ready to tackle the work of Donald Savoie, who is most responsible for the focus on prime-ministerial power: Donald J. Savoie, "The Rise of Court Government in Canada," *Canadian Journal of Political Science* 32, no. 4 (December 1999); Donald J. Savoie, *Governing from the Centre: The Concentration of Power in Canadian Politics* (Toronto: University of Toronto Press, 1999); and Donald J. Savoie, *Court Government and the Collapse of Accountability in Canada and the United Kingdom* (Toronto: University of Toronto Press, 2008). For a shorter presentation of Savoie's position, see Donald J. Savoie, "Power at the Apex: Executive Dominance," in James Bickerton and Alain-G. Gagnon, eds., *Canadian Politics,* 4th ed. (Peterborough: Broadview Press, 2004), or Donald J. Savoie, "The Federal Government: Revisiting Court Government in Canada," in Luc Bernier, Keith Brownsey, and Michael Howlett, eds., *Executive Styles in Canada: Cabinet Structures and Leadership Practices in Canadian Government* (Toronto: University of Toronto Press, 2005). Savoie has recently published an update on his views concerning the power of the prime minister: Donald J. Savoie, *Power: Where Is It?* (Montreal & Kingston: McGill-Queen's University Press, 2010), ch. 6. This is a must-read piece.

To appreciate the genesis of this discussion in Canada, one should read Thomas A. Hockin, ed., *Apex of Power: The Prime Minister and Political Leadership in Canada,* 2nd ed. (Scarborough: Prentice-Hall, 1977). The belief that the position of prime minister has become almost too powerful is not limited to those who examine Canadian politics. Other parliamentary democracies may also be operating under prime-ministerial government. For more on this, see Patrick Weller, *First among Equals: Prime Ministers in Westminster Systems* (London: George Allen & Irwin, 1985). Weller has also produced a consideration of cabinet government and the prime minister in Patrick Weller, "Cabinet Government: An Elusive Ideal?" *Public Administration* 81, no. 4 (2003).

Proponents of prime-ministerial power are not without their critics. A critical examination of their position can be found in Herman Bakvis, "Prime Minister and Cabinet in Canada: An Autocracy in Need of Reform?" *Journal of Canadian Studies* 35, no. 4 (Winter 2001). The article addresses directly the analysis of Savoie and others who subscribe to the theory of prime-ministerial government, and he provides as well a useful bibliography on the topic of prime-ministerial power. For an account of the fall of former prime minister Jean Chrétien, one might read Susan Delacourt, *Juggernaut: Paul Martin's Campaign for Chrétien's Crown* (Toronto: McClelland and Stewart, 2003). But on this subject students should also consult the relevant chapters of the memoirs of former prime minister Jean Chretien and his close adviser, Eddie Goldenberg: *Jean Chretien, My Years as Prime Minister* (Toronto: Knopf, 2007), and Eddie Goldenberg, *The Way It Works: Inside Ottawa* (Toronto: McClelland and Stewart, 2006). Prime ministers in other countries also experienced difficult (and limiting) times, including former prime minister Tony Blair of Great Britain. For more on Blair, one might read Jonathan Powell, *The New Machiavelli: How to Wield Power in the Modern World* (London: The Bodley Head, 2010). Powell, who was Blair's chief of staff, pours cold water all over the thesis of prime-ministerial government.

Finally, a study uses experts to compare the power of prime ministers in various countries. The experts have determined that Canada has the most powerful prime ministers. Need anything more be said? See Eoin O'Malley, "The Power of Prime Ministers: Results of an Expert Survey," *International Political Science Review* 28, no. 1 (2007).

Is a Mixed-Member Proportional Electoral System in Canada's Interest?

✔ **YES**
JOHN L. HIEMSTRA AND HAROLD J. JANSEN, "Getting What You Vote For"

✗ **NO**
NELSON WISEMAN, "Unintended Consequences of Proportional Representation"

Canadian elections produce curious results. Take the recent federal election. In an article on the election, political scientists at Simon Fraser University noted a few "oddities." The Conservative Party won 20 percent more seats in Ontario even though their popular vote in Ontario grew only five percentage points—39.2 percent to 44.4 percent. In Quebec, nearly one in four of the voters sided with the Bloc Québécois, but only one in twenty of the seats went to the party (four out of seventy-five). The New Democratic Party (NDP) did very well in the election, but it, too, was hit with weird outcomes. Its share of the vote in Manitoba increased over the previous election, yet, it won only half the seats that it did in the previous election. Even more strange, they received a third of the vote in Saskatchewan but no elected members. For this last result, the scientists at Simon Fraser observed, somewhat facetiously, that "[t]he NDP set a record of sorts for 21st century elections." If these oddities were limited to the 2011 election, they would be of little consequence. But these oddities pop up all the time. In some elections, the winning party secures nearly all of the seats with a percentage of the vote that fails to reach 60 percent; in others, the winners do secure all the seats with barely 60 percent of the vote. This propensity to give parties more than they seemingly deserve means the opposite also happens: political parties receive less than they deserve. The NDP performed surprisingly well in the 2011 federal election, winning a little over 30 percent of the seats with about the same percentage of votes, but in the 2004 election it was a different story—they won 16 percent of the vote, but only 6 percent of the seats.

On viewing these outcomes, one might be tempted to conclude that the Canadian electoral process had simply got the math wrong. Surely, the percentage of seats won should roughly reflect the percentage of votes won. But that is not how elections work in Canada. Instead, the electoral system divides the country into constituencies or districts and then declares the one who receives the most votes as the winner in each constituency. With these rules, a party may win many seats by small margins, producing the resulting disjunction between the distribution of seats and votes. In the Canadian electoral system, there is no reward for coming second, third, or any place other than first. Only the candidate with the greatest number of votes gets to sit in legislative assemblies.

Of course, an explanation is not a defence. For some, the single-member plurality (SMP) system, the name commonly given to Canada's election system, is unacceptable. The system plainly distorts the preferences of voters; it gives some parties too many seats and others too few. In a democracy, it might be argued that an electoral system should strive to represent the true wishes of the people. But this fails to occur in Canada. Accordingly, various types of proportional representation (PR) electoral systems have been proposed to establish a greater equality between the percentage of votes and percentage of seats won. One type of PR system has become especially popular: this is the mixed-member proportional (MMP) system. Under MMP, some seats are still selected through the old system—the winner is the candidate with the most votes in the district—but others are selected or appointed from party lists to ensure that in the end the percentage of seats is proportional to the percentage of votes. Basically, the number of seats won through the SMP method are adjusted through the party lists to provide for greater fairness in the electoral system. One of the attractions of MMP is that it soothes the concerns of those who feel that we are moving too fast with electoral reform. MMP manages to mix the old with the new, a seemingly acceptable arrangement.

But many still remain uncomfortable with MMP and PR in general. Some feel this way because they fear that the reforms inevitably lead to weak coalition governments, while others believe that proportional representation produces elected officials without any constituency responsibilities. Arguably, a more important concern is the inability of PR systems to work well with the possibility of the cycling of majorities in government. Research has shown that voting can lead to one majority being easily trumped by another. PR proponents claim that their system will more accurately reflect the will of the people, but the fact is that there is no one majority that registers the wishes of the electorate—there are many. In light of the inherent instability of government actions, it might be preferable to have an electoral system that allows voters to more easily identify elected officials responsible for the offerings of government. If so, MMP and other versions of PR become unattractive because of their tendency to produce multiparty coalitions. Alternatively, the single-member plurality system looks ideal because it usually elects single-party majority governments. In coalition governments, the existence of many policymakers makes it easier to escape responsibility; in majority governments, the presence of only one party enhances efforts directed at ensuring accountability.

In the past few years, three provinces have held referenda on electoral reform. Two asked the citizenry whether MMP should be introduced, and a third held two referendums on the viability of another type of electoral system. The fact that in three of the referendums a majority of the voters rejected change while the fourth failed to meet the required level of support suggests that Canadians find proposed changes to the way we elect politicians wanting. It is unlikely this issue will disappear soon, however, for perceptions of the failings of the single-member system are too widespread. Plus, academic scholars continue to write on the issue and diligent public interest groups such as Fair Vote Canada (www.fairvote.ca) ensure that the issue remains topical.

In the debate, John Hiemstra, Harold Jansen, and Nelson Wiseman wrangle over the merits of introducing a system of MMP in Canada. Hiemstra is a professor of political science at King's University College in Edmonton, while Jansen teaches at the University of Lethbridge. Nelson Wiseman is a professor of political science at the University of Toronto. A point of clarification: as evident from Wiseman's essay, the Canadian system is sometimes called "first past the post."

✔ **YES**
Getting What You Vote For
JOHN L. HIEMSTRA AND HAROLD J. JANSEN

Some critics say Canada should keep the plurality electoral system because it "works." Who in their right mind would oppose something that works? But how can Canadians know whether an electoral system truly works within our larger political system? We argue that Canadians need to identify all of the relevant normative criteria we want our electoral system to achieve, and then empirically test whether the current plurality system, or a new MMP electoral system, best achieves these values. The literature on electoral systems produces the following list of key values: certainly electoral systems must produce *stable* and *effective* governments. But, the results of elections must also be *fair* for all voters. All voters should be *represented* in the one elected political chamber in Canada, the House of Commons, that votes on legislation affecting us all. The power of every vote cast in an election should be *equal* to all others. Electoral systems should enable citizens to hold governments *accountable* for their actions. The electoral system should *justly accommodate* all sectors of the national political community in ways that encourages national unity. In our essay, we argue that the current plurality electoral system does not "work" because it empirically fails to achieve many of these key values in practice. Adopting an MMP system, on the other hand, would truly "work" because it simultaneously embeds all of these important values in the electoral system that produces the political officials who run Canadian politics.

This essay argues that the plurality method for electing Members of Parliament (MPs) to the House of Commons should be replaced with a system of proportional representation (PR). There are many variants of PR in use around the world, but the one we advocate for Canada is a mixed-member proportional (MMP) electoral system. MMP would make every vote count, enhance national unity, give an accurate reflection of the political opinions of Canadians in the House, and strengthen MPs' sense of obligation to the voters. This essay draws on national and provincial examples to make this case, since both levels currently use the plurality electoral system.

A MODEST REFORM

In Canadian federal elections, we use the current single-member plurality electoral system to decide who will be our representatives in the House of Commons. The country is divided into 308 single-member districts, each of which elects one MP to the House. The winner in each district is decided by the plurality formula.

Simply put, the candidate in a riding who wins more votes than the other candidates—even if the total number of votes is less than 50 percent—is the winner and takes the seat as MP in the House of Commons.[1]

Adopting MMP would require only modest reforms to our current system; it could be implemented by a simple act of Parliament and without a constitutional amendment. The number of federal MPs per province is determined by several factors, of which population is the most important. Under the plurality system, the provinces are carved into geographical electoral districts, with one MP elected in each district. Under MMP, this would continue to happen, but only half of the MPs allocated to each province would represent single-member districts as they do now. The other half would be chosen from each party's lists in such a way as to ensure that each party's representation in Parliament matched its share of the popular vote in that province.

In Alberta, for example, under the plurality formula used in the 2011 national election, the Conservative Party won all but one of Alberta's twenty-eight seats, with the other going to the NDP. If Alberta voters got what they individually voted for, the outcome would have been much different: nineteen Conservative seats, five NDP seats, three Liberal seats, and one Green seat. It's hard to disagree that this would be a fair and equitable outcome. But can we practically achieve this outcome? Adopting an MMP electoral system is a modest reform that would virtually guarantee this outcome.

If the election had been held under MMP,[2] fourteen MPs would have been elected in single-member districts. The Conservatives would likely have won thirteen of those seats and the NDP would likely have won the other. The remaining fourteen MPs for Alberta would not represent specific districts but would be chosen from each of the parties' lists in such a way that their overall number in Alberta's Parliament accurately reflected their share of the vote. The Conservatives' 65 percent of the vote would have entitled them to nineteen of the overall twenty-eight Alberta MPs, so six MPs from the Conservative list would have been added to the thirteen MPs elected in single-member districts, bringing their total to nineteen. The NDP's share of the vote would have entitled them to five seats; they would receive four list seats to add to the one elected under the plurality system. None of the other parties would have won any seats in single-member districts, but their share of the overall vote would have entitled them to some list seats—the Liberals would have been awarded three, and the Green Party, one seat. In this way, MMP would ensure each party earned the number of seats to which it was entitled.[3]

Although the MMP way of calculating the number of seats each party would receive is more complicated than under the plurality system, casting a vote in a federal election under MMP would be straightforward. Voters would vote twice: once for the candidate they want to represent their particular district in the House of Commons and a second vote for the party list they prefer. The local candidate they support may even be from a different party. Voters in countries around the world seem to have no trouble using MMP, so there is little reason to expect Canadians would either.

There are many variations in how MMP systems have been implemented throughout the world. But the increased popularity of MMP reflects an emerging consensus that MMP systems offer the "best of both worlds."[4] Voters continue to have an individual MP who is "theirs" and can deal with local problems they are having with government, which is a distinct advantage of the plurality system. At the same time, however, voters benefit from having their political ideas reflected accurately in our national deliberative chamber, the House of Commons. Clearly, this is the major advantage of proportional representation; an MMP system would ensure that voters consistently get what they actually voted for.

MAKING EVERY VOTE COUNT

As a democratic state, all Canadians should have a say in composing the House of Commons, since it deliberates on and approves the laws that govern us all. Sadly, Canada's plurality electoral system repeatedly fails to deliver just and equitable representation when it allows the "winner to take all."

An electoral system is unjust when it fails to give each vote its due. And what are voters due? The answer is clearly "representation." Surely all Canadian voters have a right to be represented in the one and only chamber that is elected. Our plurality electoral system is frequently unjust. In the 2011 federal election, for example, more than 60 percent of voters supported parties other than the Conservative Party, yet they were represented in the House of Commons by less than half of the members of Parliament. In 2011, fully 49.6 percent of voters cast votes for candidates who did not get elected. Thus, they ended up being represented by MPs they did not vote for and a party they did not support. The plurality system effectively disenfranchised nearly half of the voters in the 2011 election.[5]

The injustice done by the plurality electoral formula is illustrated even better by the results of two provincial elections. In the 2001 British Columbia provincial election, Gordon Campbell's Liberal Party won 97 percent of the seats (seventy-seven out of seventy-nine) with only 58 percent of the vote. That left the 21 percent of voters who supported the NDP with only two seats, and the 21 percent who supported other parties with none. In the 2007 provincial election, Prince Edward Island's Liberals won almost 53 percent of the vote, but took 85 percent of the seats. An even more dramatic case of injustice happened in the 1987 New Brunswick election where the plurality system gave every seat to one party. Frank McKenna's Liberal Party won 100 percent of the seats with 60 percent of the popular vote. This left the other 40 percent of the voters unrepresented by the parties they supported. Besides misrepresenting the views of voters, the single-member plurality system in these cases returned very small oppositions, making it difficult for legislatures to hold the government accountable, the traditional function of oppositions in our British-style parliamentary system. These are not isolated cases, either. In the words of one of Canada's leading scholars of political parties and elections, lopsided provincial election results are the "dirty little secret" of provincial politics.[6]

The other serious defect in the plurality electoral system is its inequity; that is, it often makes your vote count for less than others. For example, in the 2011 federal election, 518,736 voters in Manitoba and Saskatchewan voted Conservative and elected twenty-four MPs. In Quebec, the plurality system rewarded the 627,650 people who voted Conservative with only seven MPs. It took more than 100,000 votes to elect a Conservative MP in Quebec, while in the Prairies, it took just over 20,000 votes to do so. An even more extreme inequity occurred in the 2000 federal election, when 1,051,209 voters in Ontario supported the Canadian Alliance party, but the plurality system gave it only two seats in that province. In British Columbia, on the other hand, the plurality system rewarded the 797,518 Canadian Alliance voters with twenty-seven seats. In other words, it took fewer than 30,000 B.C. Alliance voters to elect an MP, while in Ontario, it took over half a million to do so.

Plurality is a "winner takes all" system that almost always over-rewards the winning party. In contrast, MMP is widely recognized as more just and equitable in that it accurately translates the percentage of the vote each party wins into a proportionate percentage of seats in the House of Commons. MMP would greatly reduce the injustice and inequity experienced by voters under the plurality system. In short, MMP would give you what you vote for, which is reason enough to adopt it in Canada.

MMP AND GOVERNMENT EFFECTIVENESS

Proportional representation systems such as MMP are almost always acknowledged as the fairest electoral systems.[7] Yet some still reject any kind of PR for Canada because they fear it would make the government ineffective. They argue that the plurality method produces stable and effective majority governments out of minority electoral returns, while MMP would produce unstable and ineffective minority governments. While stability and effectiveness are important values, Canadians should not have to choose between these values and justice and equity when designing an electoral system. Fortunately, the experiences of other countries show that PR electoral systems can do both, offering both improved representation and effective government. It is easy to selectively present a specific example of a country where either a proportional or plurality electoral system has worked well or not well. The most valuable evidence, however, comes from studies that systematically incorporate the experience of multiple countries. Arend Lijphart, a noted expert on electoral systems, did just this in a comparative study of established democracies and found that countries using PR maintain public order and manage the economy as well as countries that use majoritarian electoral systems, such as plurality.[8]

Besides this comparative evidence, we can look at Canada's experience with minority governments. Canada has had effective government since well before Confederation. Yet there does not seem to be any connection between this effectiveness and the plurality electoral system's ability to produce majority governments. In fact, the plurality system produced eight minority governments from the seventeen elections since 1962, which is not exactly a stellar record.[9] In spite of these minority governments, Canada's governments have generally been effective. In his seminal study of Canada's Parliament, C.E.S. Franks concludes that "there is no evidence that minority parliaments are less efficient than majorities."[10]

It is true that minority governments have tended to fall more quickly than majority governments in Canada. It is critical to understand that this is due less to the inherent instability of minority governments than to the perverse incentive the plurality system gives to some parties to seek an early collapse of minority governments. Large parties know that a small shift in the vote toward their party will often be magnified into a large increase in seats and thus a majority government for them. The Conservative government proved this in 2011, when they went from a minority government to a majority. Although the Conservative share of seats in the House of Commons jumped 8 percent, going from 46 percent in 2008 to 54 percent in 2011, their share of the vote increased only by about 2 percent, from 37.7 percent to 39.6 percent.

If Canada adopted MMP, minority and coalition governments would undoubtedly be even more common than has been the case historically. But we have already seen that the frequent minority governments under the plurality system do not render the government ineffective. Nor is it the case that coalition governments are automatically weak or unstable. In PR systems such as MMP, political parties normally win a steady percentage of the vote in each election. Since forcing an election under MMP would likely not dramatically alter party strengths in Parliament, this electoral system strongly encourages parties to work for just policy compromises within Parliament. Thus, coalition governments under MMP would be able to "get things done" for Canada. The big improvement that coalitions under an MMP system deliver is that they get things done while involving a majority of the MPs who truly represent more than a majority of Canadians. PR gets rid of artificial majority governments that make decisions on important issues such as health care reform or climate change with the support of less than half of the voters.

Critics also suggest that PR causes unstable governments by promoting too many small parties. Under plurality, however, Canada has already produced many small parties, a contradiction of "Duverger's law," which asserts that a plurality electoral system tends to produce a two-party system. This diversity of smaller parties should not be denied, however, since it reflects the real political views of Canadians. Even so, in most provinces except Ontario and Quebec, the province-wide lists required by MMP would elect relatively few MPs. To earn a seat in the

House of Commons from these party lists, a party would still require a significant proportion of the vote. Thus the system would still discourage splinter parties.

In sum, Canada has remained stable even though the plurality system has produced repeated minority governments and has encouraged destabilizing regional parties. The reason for this is Canada's strong, democratic, and tolerant political culture. Adopting MMP would not suddenly change this. Nor would MMP transform Canada into an unstable regime such as pre–Second World War Weimar Germany.[11] Canada's strong, democratic political culture has kept and will continue to keep our system stable. Canada with MMP would more likely resemble modern Germany, which has used MMP for over five decades and remains eminently stable and unified.[12]

MMP CAN INCREASE NATIONAL UNITY

Some critics also argue that MMP would weaken national unity. They charge that it would magnify divisions between regions and between English and French cultures. They claim that, although the plurality electoral system has treated this diversity unfairly, at least this system has kept our country stable and united. The facts show, however, that quirks in plurality actually serve to worsen these divisions in Canada.

One way the plurality system undermines national unity is by "rewarding" small, regionally concentrated parties. Canadian history is full of examples of small, regional parties that have won substantial representation in Parliament. Parties such as the Progressives, Social Credit, the Creditistes, and the Reform Party have flourished under a plurality electoral system by being able to translate a relatively small number of votes into a relatively large share of the seats. Particularly troublesome is the tendency of plurality to reward regionally concentrated parties that, in some cases, have promoted separatism or a sectional view of Canada. The plurality system has multiplied their negative impact by rewarding them with far more seats than their electoral support warrants. In the 2008 federal election, for example, the separatist Bloc Québécois (BQ) won 65 percent of the seats in Quebec with the support of only 38 percent of Quebec voters. This also occurred in Quebec provincial elections, where the plurality system has allowed the separatist Parti Québécois to form four majority governments even though the party has never won a majority of the votes. In 1998, the PQ won a majority government (76 out of 125 seats) with 42.9 percent of the vote, but the provincial Liberal Party won the support of more Quebec voters, with 43.6 percent of the vote.

Another way the plurality electoral system weakens national unity is by robbing seats from small, nationally oriented parties with supporters dispersed across the country. For example, the NDP is a national party with a social democratic vision for the whole country, with some support in all regions of the country. Yet, under the plurality system, it always receives fewer seats in the House of

Commons than its support would justify. In the 2006 federal election, for example, the NDP earned only twenty-nine seats (9.4 percent) in the House of Commons, even though the party earned 17.5 percent of the vote across the country. Even more shocking is that a million more Canadians voted for the NDP than supported the BQ, but the NDP won twenty-two fewer seats. Under MMP in the 2006 election, the NDP would have won fifty-five seats (from every province in Canada except P.E.I.), a fair reflection of its national support. Unfortunately, the plurality system hurts small parties with support dispersed across the regions, even when they try to appeal to all Canadians, wherever they might live.

The plurality system also weakens national unity by over-rewarding large parties in regions where they have strong support while under-rewarding them where their support is weak. Thus, Canada often lacks truly national parties in the House. When large parties win the majority of the seats in one region and few in another region, the party caucus discussions will tend to be dominated by the larger group, thereby perpetuating and worsening divisions in Canada. In the 1980 federal election, for example, the Liberal Party formed the government but did not win a single seat in British Columbia, Alberta, or Saskatchewan, although it won over 20 percent of the vote in these provinces. Meanwhile, it won seventy-four of seventy-five seats, or 99 percent of the seats, in Quebec with 68 percent of the popular vote. In 2011, more people voted for the Conservative Party in Quebec than in Manitoba and Saskatchewan combined, but the plurality system's distortions gave the Conservatives twenty-four seats in Manitoba and Saskatchewan, but only seven in Quebec. While the Conservatives are undoubtedly strongest in the West, the electoral system does not reflect the depth of their support in Quebec and Eastern Canada. One of the biggest stories on election night was the New Democratic Party's historic breakthrough in Quebec, but this breakthrough was partly a product of the electoral system. Although the NDP took 43 percent of the vote there, the plurality system translated this into over three-quarters of the seats in Quebec. Put another way, only about 36 percent of all the votes cast for the NDP in 2011 were cast in Quebec, but Quebec MPs make up 57 percent of the NDP's parliamentary caucus. This flaw leads voters to develop a regionally skewed perception of the parties' support, in this case overestimating the NDP's support in Quebec, and underestimating the Conservatives' appeal in the same province. It also handicaps the governing and opposition parties' ability to include regional viewpoints in their caucus discussions. In fact, plurality gives parties an incentive to favour regions where they might receive large electoral payoffs, while ignoring other regions.

The weaknesses of the plurality system, Alan Cairns concludes, make Canada's electoral system "divisive and detrimental to national unity."[13] MMP is a better way to handle Canada's regional divisions, since it gives seats to national parties in direct proportion to the percentage of popular votes they win in the election. Since every vote counts in MMP, parties have a strong incentive to take a national viewpoint on issues and to search for votes in all regions. While MMP allows voters to develop and support regional parties, it does not unfairly reward those parties. It also encourages the growth of parties that will integrate the regions of Canada.[14]

THE PLURALITY SYSTEM PRODUCES FALSE MAJORITY GOVERNMENTS

Another claim for the plurality electoral system is that it allows voters to select a government at the same time as they elect their representatives. Indeed, forming a cabinet is largely routine in Canada's parliamentary system, where the party winning the most seats usually forms the government. But it is an illusion to suggest that voters purposefully or automatically select a government. In fact, the majority of Canadians have not been involved in selecting most of Canada's governments. Since the Second World War, only two of our national governments have been formed by a party that won a majority of the popular vote in an election (1958 and 1984).[15] Over time, the plurality system is producing governments with a majority of seats but resting on the support of an increasingly small proportion of the electorate.[16]

In practice, the plurality system routinely allows a minority of voters to select the majority of the seats, and thus determine the government. This problem with plurality is closely related to Canada's multiparty system. In the 1997 federal election, when five major parties contested the election, the plurality system translated the Liberals' 38.5 percent of the vote into a majority government. These results were not an anomaly; such distortions occur repeatedly in federal and provincial elections. The fact that there are four parties in Parliament isn't an accident; it reflects the diversity of political visions in Canada's political culture. This reality must be reflected in our foremost representative and debating legislative chamber.

The plurality electoral system also allows a small shift in the vote to determine who will form the next government. In the 1979 election, Joe Clark's Conservatives were supported by 36 percent of Canadians and took 48 percent of the seats to form a minority government. The Liberals gathered 40 percent of the vote and took only 40 percent of the seats. Nine months later, in the 1980 election, the Liberals increased their share of the vote by only 4 percent but now won a clear majority government with 52 percent of the seats. And in the following election of 1984, a shift of 17 percent of the vote to the Mulroney-led Tories allowed the Progressive Conservatives to increase their seats by 38 percent, from 37 percent to 75 percent of the seats. Defenders of the plurality electoral system often cite this property of the plurality system as a desirable feature. They argue that the sensitivity of the plurality system to small shifts in the popular vote allow voters to defeat governments. Is it really fair and appropriate to give the power to determine who will or will not form a government to a tiny minority of voters?

Furthermore, this mechanism works very inconsistently under plurality. While a shift in the popular vote may cause a change of government, just as often, it does not. The actual seat totals depend on a number of factors, including the regional distribution of the vote, the number of political parties, and the division of the vote between these parties. The relationship between seats and votes under the plurality system is not a smooth line on a graph; it is far more random than that. Should governments be determined by chance factors?

Two sequential provincial elections in British Columbia pointedly illustrate this type of chancy outcome in the formation of governments under plurality. The NDP failed to form the government in 1986 when its 42.6 percent of the vote translated into 31.9 percent of the seats. In the 1991 election, however, NDP popular support dropped to 41 percent of the vote, yet it took 68 percent of the seats and formed the new government. Sometimes, in fact, plurality allows a party to win more seats and form the government with fewer votes than the main opposition party. In the 1979 federal election, for example, the Conservatives formed a minority government when they won 36 percent of the vote and 136 seats, while the Liberals won 40 percent of the vote and only 114 seats. This "wrong winner" phenomenon is even more common in provincial elections, most recently in the 2006 New Brunswick election, when the Liberals won a majority government despite the fact that more voters supported the Progressive Conservative Party. Had then PC Premier Bernard Lord followed the recommendation of his Commission on Legislative Democracy and implemented an MMP system, he might still have been premier.

Selecting a government through the plurality electoral system has the further side effect of producing an unfair public perception of the parties' strengths. A month after the 1988 federal election, nobody remembered that the Tories won 57 percent of the seats with only 43 percent of the vote. The public is constantly reminded of the percentage of seats a party won, but not the percentage of the vote it won. A month after the 2011 election, everyone referred to the "Harper majority government," forgetting he received only 39.6 percent of Canadian votes.

The plurality system is often associated with a two-party political system. The diversity and complexity of Canadian society, however, has meant that Canada has developed many political parties. It is a mistake to think that we can solve the problems created by the plurality system by wishing the country had a two-party system rather than reforming the electoral system itself to reflect the reality of Canadian society. We must accept that Canadians have deeply held political views and choose different parties to express these views. An electoral system should not artificially constrict these views. Political parties ought to play the critical role of providing an integrated set of principles around which they harmonize the many diverse and sometimes conflicting policies into a coherent platform. This would give voters a real choice. The truly democratic response to these voter differences is to amend our electoral system so that it responds to the diversity of beliefs and actions of Canadians, and not to force the current system to produce the number of parties critics want. The real challenge is to allow the deeply held political views of Canadians to be properly, safely, and fairly expressed and accommodated in politics. People with different ethnic, religious, or ideological views often arrive at, or endorse, a particular policy for their own distinct reasons. An MMP system will give no viewpoint a hegemonic grip on the system; rather it will force all parties to discuss their real differences as a means of arriving at mutually acceptable policies. The end result is that governments elected by proportional representation tend to reflect the preferred policies of citizens much better than do those elected by the plurality system.[17]

Since MMP would make the House of Commons accurately reflect the opinions and views of Canadians, it would be better to shift the duty of forming governments away from "chance" and to our MPs. This would give the majority of voters a stronger say in the creation of government. It would place the task of forming governments in the hands of our MPs who currently hold the power of dissolving governments. This conforms with and develops Canada's parliamentary theory.

THE PLURALITY SYSTEM WEAKENS REPRESENTATIVE DEMOCRACY

Indeed, MMP would give voters a greater say over all aspects of their MPs' actions, since it obliges MPs to represent their supporting voters. What we see in Canada today is that the plurality electoral system is weakening representative democracy. Representative democracy was created in response to the historically increasing number of citizens entitled to be involved in politics but who lacked the time or energy to study political issues and devise fitting solutions. Most Canadians expect their representatives to engage actively in policymaking for them. Even so, plurality fails to give representatives a clear mandate from the voters and fails to enable voters to hold MPs responsible for their actions. Instead, the plurality system is increasingly encouraging Canadians to weaken or even bypass representative democracy. The weakening of the relationship between voters and representatives occurs because plurality requires politicians and parties to compromise too early in the process. Before an election, politicians are forced to develop lowest common denominator policies that will appeal to a plurality of voters in each riding. For example, some voters believe the state should strongly intervene to protect the environment, while others believe market forces will correct environmental problems. In response to this spectrum of opinions, most political parties develop a compromised platform that homogenizes the environmental views of Canadians. While this is done to attract the wide range of voters necessary to win a plurality of votes in a single district, it tends to homogenize the resulting MPs' views, and thus undermines wide-ranging debate about environmental policy in the House of Commons.

Early compromises on policy produce pragmatic, look-alike parties. Election campaigns increasingly focus on party leaders and image, and downplay principles, policy platforms, and the teams of politicians behind the leaders. Pragmatic parties make principled discussion rare in the House of Commons and foreclose the opportunity for accommodation between principled party platforms. Consequently, voters seldom know what their MPs and parties stand for and find it difficult to hold them accountable. At the same time, MPs do not receive clear mandates from voters. In these and other respects, plurality weakens the relationship between voters and representatives.

Increasingly, voters are turning away from these indistinct parties. Many are abandoning the electoral process altogether, as Canada's decreasing levels of voter turnout indicate.[18] Some are turning to interest groups for better representation. Political parties are responding to this challenge to their representative role by merely becoming brokers for interest groups. Other voters are pushing reforms such as recall, referenda, and initiative, which bypass representative democracy.[19] Thus, the dynamic set in motion by plurality actually encourages voters to bypass their representatives, a process that is undermining the very essence of our representative democratic system.

IMPROVING THE QUALITY OF REPRESENTATION

In opposition to plurality, an MMP electoral system would strengthen Canada's political system by encouraging a new dynamic. MMP encourages strong political parties, but would also encourage them to define how they are distinct from the others in order to attract votes. To compete effectively, parties would need to develop clearer principles and to define their policy platforms. This would allow political parties to become vehicles for voters to give mandates to MPs and also to hold them accountable between elections. MPs would clearly feel more obliged to act in accordance with the principles and policies that they agreed to with supporters. This would include serving the individual voters according to these principles, if the parties want to maintain electoral support. MPs with a sense of obligation to voters would be a clear advance over the current plurality system that limits voters to rubber-stamping or jettisoning representatives at election time.

One common criticism of MMP systems is that they create "two classes" of MPs, namely, those elected in single-member districts and party list MPs. The argument is that those MPs who represent single-member districts have different responsibilities than those who are elected from party lists. The evidence from Germany, the country with the longest experience with MMP, suggests that such concerns are misplaced. The German experience has been that party list MPs do get involved in constituency work, often focusing on single-member districts where their party lost. There is also little evidence in the German case to suggest that party list MPs are more likely to be cabinet ministers than MPs elected by plurality.[20]

Again, PR has been superior to the plurality electoral system in bringing minority parties into legislatures. Although we can point to specific exceptions in both proportional and plurality electoral systems, the overall evidence from other countries shows that PR improves the quality of representation in various ways. It has also increased the parliamentary representation of women, ethnic groups, and cultural minorities.[21] Significantly, PR has done so without extensive affirmative action programs. PR has also allowed parties to improve the overall quality of individual MPs on their lists. PR also allows citizens to be free to join the political party of their choice and to decide whether their party's MPs will be "trustees" who will independently deliberate on issues; "delegates" who mechanically reflect their views; "mirrors" that reflect their gender, age, ethnic, or other characteristics; or defenders of their party's interests and positions.[22] If "party bosses" dominate under MMP, it will be the fault of those who create parties that tolerate them and of the voters who support them. When this has proven to be a significant problem, many countries have developed systems that allow voters to change the order of the names on the list, thus removing some of the control party officials have over who gets elected.

MMP allows parties and governments to be as good or as flawed as the people they represent. It leaves the public free to decide which groups or principles or approaches it wants represented by creating parties to reflect these concerns. MMP ultimately leaves the voters to decide which parties they want to be represented by in the House of Commons. For example, if 7 percent of Canadians support the Green Party's approach to environmental issues, MMP will give it 7 percent of the seats, no more and no less.

CONCLUSION

Democratic principles are the foundation upon which political life in Canada rests. The plurality and MMP electoral systems are structures through which Canadians can exercise their democratic choices. But structures are not neutral. They reflect values that the people in a society want the system to advance and thus encourage citizens to act in a certain way. The dominant value of our current plurality system is stability—which it is supposed to achieve by translating a minority of votes into a majority government. In spite of the plurality electoral system, however, Canada has frequently produced minority governments. The plurality system also produces electoral outcomes that aggravate and intensify Canada's regional divisions. Too many outcomes of the plurality electoral system have been chancy, unfair, and inequitable. Also, plurality has encouraged the growth of pragmatic and brokerage parties that weaken the incentives of MPs to represent their voters. In spite of these problems, Canada remains a stable, democratic political system.

Since Canada is stable in spite of the plurality system, it has ample room to add the values of justice, equity, and representativeness to stability by adopting an MMP electoral system. MMP makes every vote count and produces results that are proportionate to what voters desire. MMP would also best serve Canada's distinctive needs. It would increase Canada's stability by improving regional representation in major parties, while reducing the unjustified strength of small, divisive parties that happen to have regionally concentrated support.

The biggest asset of MMP, however, is that it enhances representative democracy by encouraging MPs and parties to develop a clearer profile on principles and policies. Voters will have a better idea of the mandate they are giving to MPs and thus be able to hold MPs accountable for their principles, policies, and political actions. An MMP electoral system should be adopted in Canada since it is the fairest and most effective way to fix Canada's real democratic deficit.

NOTES

1. Only 40 percent of MPs elected in 2006 won their seats with a majority of the vote in their constituencies. In fact, one MP won a seat with the support of fewer than a third of the voters in his constituency. This is not unusual: in 2004, only 44 percent of MPs won their seats with a majority of the vote.

2. We are assuming that half of the seats would be allocated in single-member districts, and the other half would be allocated from party lists for the entire province. We are also assuming that voters would support the same party with their list vote as they supported in single-member districts.

3. See David M. Farrell, *Electoral Systems: A Comparative Introduction* (New York: Palgrave, 2001), pp. 97–111, for more details on how MMP works in Germany. See the Law Commission of Canada, *Voting Counts: Electoral Reform in Canada* (Ottawa: Law Commission of Canada, 2004), pp. 83–125, for a detailed discussion on how MMP might be implemented in Canada.

4. Matthew Soberg Shugart, "'Extreme' Electoral Systems and the Appeal of the Mixed-Member Alternative," in Matthew Soberg Shugart and Martin P. Wattenberg, eds., *Mixed-Member Electoral Systems: The Best of Both Worlds* (Oxford: Oxford University Press, 2001), pp. 25–51.

5. This is not an unusual result; in 2004, a majority of Canadian voters (50.2 percent) voted for a candidate in their riding who did not win.

6. R. Ken Carty, "Doing Democracy Differently: Has Electoral Reform Finally Arrived?" (speech delivered at the Timlin Lecture, March 1, 2004, University of Saskatchewan).

7. Andrew Reynolds and Ben Reilly, *The International IDEA Handbook of Electoral System Design* (Stockholm: International Institute for Democracy and Electoral Assistance, 1997), p. 62.

8. Arend Lijphart, "Democracies: Forms, Performance, and Constitutional Engineering," *European Journal of Political Research* 25 (1994), pp. 1–17; see also Arend Lijphart, *Patterns of Democracy: Government Forms and Performance in Thirty-Six Countries* (New Haven: Yale University Press, 1999), chs. 15 and 16.

9. The plurality system not only fails to produce regular majority governments but frequently fails to produce the strong oppositions needed to effectively run a parliamentary system. See Alan C. Cairns, "The Electoral System and Party System in Canada, 1921–1965," *Canadian Journal of Political Science* 1 (1968), pp. 55–80.

10. C.E.S. Franks, *The Parliament of Canada* (Toronto: University of Toronto Press, 1987), p. 50.

11. Enid Lakeman reports that if Weimar Germany had used plurality, the Nazis would likely have won all the seats; cited in Michael Lind, "A Radical Plan to Change American Politics," *The Atlantic Monthly* 270, no. 2 (August 1992), pp. 73–83.

12. In a review of the research on this question, Louis Massicotte, "Changing the Canadian Electoral System," *Choices* 7, no. 1 (February 2001), p. 21, states that claims of PR undermining democracy have been "discredited." Massicotte's study is updated in Paul Howe, Richard Johnston, and Andre Blais, eds., *Strengthening Canadian Democracy* (Montreal IRPP, 2005).

13. Cairns, "The Electoral System and Party System in Canada," p. 92.

14. Harold J. Jansen and Alan Siaroff, "Regionalism and Party Systems: Evaluating Proposals to Reform Canada's Electoral System," in Henry Milner, ed., *Steps toward Making Every Vote Count* (Peterborough: Broadview, 2004), pp. 43–64, conclude that MMP would be among the best choices to prevent exacerbating regional conflicts.

15. Richard Katz, "Electoral Reform Is Not as Simple as It Appears," in Henry Milner, ed., *Making Every Vote Count* (Peterborough: Broadview, 1999), p. 101, points out that if rejected ballots are included in the vote totals for the 1984 election, then even the Mulroney government did not have the support of a majority of voters, leaving only one government that had the support of a majority of the electorate.

16. Richard Johnston, "Canadian Elections at the Millennium," *Choices* 6, no. 6 (September 2000). Updated version of article can be found in Howe, Johnston, and Blais eds., *Strengthening Canadian Democracy*.

17. G. Bingham Powell, Jr., *Elections as Instruments of Democracy: Majoritarian and Proportional Visions* (New Haven: Yale University Press, 2000), ch. 9.

18. Although there are certainly multiple causes for voter turnout levels, most comparative analyses find that proportional representation systems are associated with higher turnout. See Pippa Norris, *Electoral Engineering: Voting Rules and Political Behaviour* (Cambridge: Cambridge University Press, 2004), ch. 7.

19. See Nick Loenen, *Citizenship and Democracy: A Case for Proportional Representation* (Toronto: Dundurn, 1997), ch. 5, for a comparison of PR with these other reforms.

20. Louis Massicotte, *Á la recherche d'un mode de scrutin mixte compensatoire*. Document de travail, Québec, Secrétariat à la réforme des institutions démocratiques, Décembre 2004, ch. 8. Available online at http://www.institutions-democratiques. gouv.qc.ca/publications/mode_scrutin_rapport.pdf. Accessed August 20, 2011.

21. Norris, *Electoral Engineering,* ch. 8, demonstrates that PR enhances the representation of women. The effect for ethnic minorities is more complex. The plurality system represents minorities well if they are geographically concentrated, but has a harder time when minorities are dispersed. See Norris, *Electoral Engineering,* ch. 9.

22. Several conflicting definitions of representation confuse this debate; see Hanna Fenichel Pitkin, *The Concept of Representation* (Los Angeles: University of California Press, 1967).

✗ NO
Unintended Consequences of Proportional Representation
NELSON WISEMAN

One can only be a skeptical agonistic in predicting the consequences of adopting proportional representation. Once implemented, however, it will difficult to undo. The Burkean dictum, "If it is not necessary to change, it is necessary not to change," is the philosophic conservative argument against embracing proportional representation (PR). In this view, opposition to PR is based on the wisdom of historical experience. Some defenders of the status quo consider the devil they know preferable to the one they do not. Cynics intone that PR will not change much. Power, they claim, will be even more concentrated in the hands of party leaders and their entourage of apparatchiks because the commonly proposed variant of PR for Canada, mixed-member proportional (MMP), will likely leave the designation of the candidates elected by PR to party elites.

Stable countries seldom make radical institutional changes. They do not jump on bandwagons that cater willy-nilly to their era's temperament. Canada's fundamental political principles have been shaped without the use of PR. This means that its potential adoption ought to be considered thoughtfully and cautiously. PR may have deleterious implications for the operation of other elements of Canada's institutional infrastructure. PR proponents generally ignore or gloss over them.

SIGNIFICANCE OF ELECTORAL SYSTEMS

The success or failure of polities has relatively little to do with their electoral systems. Canada, in comparative perspective, has not fared poorly with its current first-past-the-post (FPTP), or single-member plurality (SMP), electoral system. Canada belongs to an elite group of states, making up only 13 percent of the world's population, categorized as "full democracies."[1] Some states that sport PR are flawed or flailing democracies. Some are authoritarian. They suffer a "democratic deficit"—the appealing but trite term often pinned on Canada's political condition.

Canada's policy outputs and quality of life are the envy of many in states with PR. Immigrants are not deterred from coming to Canada because of its allegedly democratically deficient electoral system. Canadians, in turn, are not drawn to relocate to states such as Latvia, Bolivia, and Iraq because their PR systems are irresistible democratic beacons. People in those states "know" less about what they are going to get in government policy and performance with their PR electoral systems than Canadians do with FPTP.

Nelson Wiseman, "Unintended Consequences of Proportional Representation." © Nelson Education Ltd., 1994, 2008.

Political scientists are in the vanguard of PR's boosters. They consider themselves experts in institutional design. Most political scientists who weighed in on the Meech Lake and Charlottetown Accords favoured those debacles too.[2] The Accords, products of a hyperventilated constitutional reform industry, depleted the capital of the politicians who sponsored them and proved disintegrative for the polity. This has not, however, chastened many of the same political scientists from pursuing a re-engineered electoral system via PR. Historians have been less sanguine about both mega-constitutional tampering and sweeping reforms of the electoral system. They have a better appreciation of the established institutions that have served Canadians well.

FPTP ought not to be judged solely by how precisely votes are converted into party seats. This is too narrow a gauge. What must also be weighed are geography, sociology, and history. Certainly, many states with PR have fared well. They have stable governments, progressive public policies, and honest public administration. PR's partisans are quick to cite states such as Germany and New Zealand. Other states with PR, however, have done poorly.

The United Kingdom and the United States are vibrant democracies. They informed the adoption of Canada's FPTP system. India went from being a British colony, like Canada, to becoming the world's largest democracy, and managed to do so with FPTP. FPTP is a very old institution, but that is an insufficient rationale for its dispatch. Marriage, the family, monarchy, and the church are old institutions too, yet they are not dismissed as outmoded. More vital to a state's welfare than its electoral system are its political cultural underpinnings. This refers to the health and vigour of its civil society, the independence and probity of the judiciary, media freedoms, transparency and accountability in public administration, informed dialogue and debate in the formulation of public policies, and the unfettered competition of political ideas. On these scores, any democratic audit of Canada must regard its electoral system as a sidebar. The term "democracy" is too readily bandied about in debates about the electoral system. Democracy has a kaleidoscopic quality that includes but profoundly transcends its electoral rules.

There are complex ramifications to any change in an electoral system. Change does not occur in an institutional vacuum. With PR, Canadians will still have their parliamentary system, their federal–provincial fandangos, and their beloved Charter of Rights. Canadians may be unhappy with their parliamentarians, but they want to keep their parliamentary system. That system arose in the context of two loosely knit parties, government and a "loyal" opposition ready to take the reins of office if the government faltered. Canadian parliamentary practice evolved with new parties being accommodated within the FPTP system. Party discipline has increased dramatically and many lament this, but PR will reinforce and not reverse it. PR elections, if international experience is any guide, will also lead to the further proliferation of parliamentary parties.[3] This will likely accentuate popular frustration with Parliament.

Most Canadians are unaware that alternatives to the single-member plurality system are not alien to Canada's history. Public appetite for electoral reform was greater a century ago than it is today. In the 1920s, when the Progressives were in full flight as the second-largest federal party, they agitated for PR. Parliament debated its merits and rejected it in a free vote.[4] As the Progressives and their causes quickly lost altitude, nothing came of the PR idea federally. Manitoba and Alberta adopted new electoral regimes that produced more proportionality but that did not render them more democratic in terms of converting public opinion into public policy.

Manitoba used the Hare system of PR—with its single transferable ballot—between the early 1920s and late 1950s to elect MLAs in Winnipeg, which formed one large multi-member constituency.[5] In Manitoba's rural single-member ridings, the alternative or transferable ballot was used. In both cases, voters marked their ballots preferentially (1, 2, 3, and so on if they wished). The victor in rural ridings was declared only after securing 50 percent of the first and subsequently transferred ballots, while Winnipeg candidates required a vote total determined by a formula that divided the number of votes cast by the number of seats. Most of the elections led to coalition governments, but the Co-operative Commonwealth Federation leader who joined one of them came to call it a "fool arrangement,"[6] a nightmare for his party. Most provinces have had multi-member constituencies at some time in their histories, and some adopted a religious denominational basis of representation. These were sometimes legally mandated (as in Newfoundland) and other times (as in Prince Edward Island and New Brunswick) they were governed by customs—unwritten but well understood rules. British Columbia used the alternative vote in the 1950s. It also used dual-member constituencies that only disappeared in 1991.

Proponents of PR argue that the appearance of more parliamentary parties may be neutral because PR eliminates strategic voting. Voters can opt for their preferred party rather than feeling they ought to plump for the lesser of evils, which is what many do under FPTP when they calculate that their party has little chance of success in their riding. A proliferation of parties, however, may also have drawbacks. It may lead to governmental deadlock or produce a government whose agenda results in voters not getting what they thought they had voted for. PR will also further weaken an MP's discretion. Those elected on party lists, as in the MMP system, will be beholden to their party and not to riding constituents since they will not be representing any constituency beyond their party.

DISAPPOINTMENTS OF PR

PR proponents often talk of it as a tonic for citizen alienation, cynicism, low voter turnout, and overbearing, unresponsive government. Claims that link the electoral system to pathologies of citizen disengagement—low voter turnout and low levels of citizen efficacy and trust in government—are dubious. Governments produced by PR are not necessarily more sensitive and responsive to public opinion or more adaptable to changing circumstances and public needs than are governments produced by FPTP. Notwithstanding their MMP system, German political analysts are no less preoccupied with *verdrossenheit*, or voter disillusionment, than their Canadian peers. In the past few decades, voter turnout has decreased across the Western industrialized world.[7] Canada is no exception. In New Zealand, which had a voter turnout of 89 percent using FPTP in 1984, voter turnout in the first election with MMP in 1996 declined to "probably the lowest voting turnout of any twentieth-century" election in the country's history.[8]

There are better indicators of a citizenry's contentment with its electoral system than voter turnout. Like about thirty other states, Italy uses PR, and it had compulsory voting from 1945 to 1993.[9] The efficaciousness of its electoral system therefore could not be measured by voter turnout. Other indicators, however, pointed to the Italian public's discontent with PR. In 1991, Italians voted in a referendum to modify their electoral system so that 75 percent of MPs would be elected by FPTP. They wanted more of what PR proponents allege is the undemocratic, unfair FPTP system. Their referendum victory did not bear fruit, though, as politicians finessed it and, in Italy's 2006 election, eighteen parties elected MPs. Seven parties won thirty or more seats each. In a 2007 reprise of public discontent with PR, more than 800,000 Italians signed a petition to try to force another referendum that would reduce the number of smaller parties by greater use of FPTP. They wanted "to move Italy away from decades of political instability."[10]

Paradoxically, low voter turnout may signify satisfaction or justifiable apathy with the state of political affairs. It may reflect the public's sense that it does not much matter who gets elected, that the ship of state is stable or that its trajectory is impervious to change and that the quality of one's life and material well-being are secure or unaffected by whomever holds government's reins. High voter turnout may reflect societal angst, as it did in Quebec's emotionally charged and divisive sovereignty referendum in 1995. It was an astronomical 94 percent, but families, coworkers, and others with long-standing cordial relations found the passions unleashed by the referendum tore asunder their amicable bonds. That is one reason why there has been little appetite for another referendum.

Expecting that PR would produce a more consensual, accountable, and transparent politics, New Zealanders voted in favour of an MMP system in a referendum. They saw PR as a way of holding politicians to their promises. They realized that there would be more proportionality in their parliament's composition, but they did not appreciate the critical importance of the party vote, rather than the constituency vote, in determining the government's ultimate complexion. After New Zealand's first MMP election, party leaders disappeared behind closed doors for eight weeks, hammered out party alignments, and horse-traded cabinet portfolios. The small New Zealand First party, which had campaigned on getting rid of the National Party government and its fiscally conservative policies, turned around and threw its lot in with it. This is not what those voting for the upstart party expected. Public opinion judged the new style of politics reprehensible. In the aftermath of the first MMP election, politicians—who had been cool to PR—embraced it while the public turned against it. Polls showed that voters would have overwhelmingly rejected MMP in another referendum.[11] New Zealanders' hopes for a less adversarial, more cooperative politics were dashed. They expected that the denial of a majority for any one party would be positive, but they found to their chagrin that coalition cabinets behaved like the old single-party majority ones did. The same is likely to happen in Canada.

One rationale for PR is that it will make Parliament more of a social mirror of society. Proponents foresee more women and minorities placed high on the party lists used in the MMP system so that parliamentary faces will be more diverse. That did occur in New Zealand where women's representation rose from 21 to 29 percent. There is no guarantee, however, that it will happen: Israel's 2006 election returned only 17 women (or 14 percent) to its Knesset, a lower percentage than that in Canada's 2006 election (21 percent) and Ontario's 2007 election (27 percent). Furthermore, the rationale for greater representation of politically disadvantaged groups overlooks where power actually resides in a parliamentary system—with the cabinet and not with the more representative party caucuses. Again, the New Zealand case is instructive: more women than ever appeared in Parliament after the first MMP election, but fewer women, only one, appeared in a cabinet of twenty, a "power reversal" for New Zealand's female MPs.[12] In contrast, women constituted 21 percent of Canada's 1997 post-election cabinet.

There is something troubling about engineering group representation by using PR. It is divisive of a common citizenship. The notion that only a woman, an Aboriginal, or a member of a visible minority can represent members of those groups is pernicious because it categorizes citizens in ways that may not be their primary or preferred political identification. It tells men or non-Aboriginals, for example, that a woman or an Aboriginal may be an unworthy representative of their interests. This view of representation detracts from a cardinal democratic principle: respect for an individual's unmediated choice of who ought to represent him or her. It tells individuals that their gender or the colour of their skin or their Aboriginal status is more important than who they want to represent them.

The Latvian and Belgian experiences are also instructive for Canadians pondering the alleged virtues of MMP. Latvia's population is less than the City of Toronto's, and its size is roughly comparable to the Greater Toronto Area. Latvia's president until recently was a Cold War émigré to Canada. A distinguished graduate of the University of Toronto and McGill University, she served as vice president of the Science Council of Canada and was admitted as an Officer of the National Order of Quebec. Immensely popular in her native land, Vaira Vīķe-Freiberga was drafted to become its president in the post-Soviet era and was twice elected to the post. During her tenure, she wistfully recalled the simplicity of Canada's electoral system and compared it to the daunting challenge she faced in trying to get the leaders of Latvia's eleven parties in the Saeima (Parliament) to construct a stable government.[13] Latvia's experience is a reminder of the potential proliferation of parties and its consequences even in small states. In Belgium, negotiations over forming a government were still ongoing nearly a year after the country's 2010 election.

The proposed MMP system that Ontarians rejected in 2007 by a margin of 63 percent to 37 percent set a bar of 3 percent for a party to gain representation. In Israel's 2006 election, with the bar set at 2 percent, thirty-one parties competed, and twelve won seats. Compare Canada to small states such as Latvia and Israel. When one considers Canada's vastness, its regional and cultural fault lines, and the uneven distribution of its natural resource endowments and economic wealth, the chances are heightened for more parties and for more regionally and cultur-ally divisive ones. In small states, regional parties are not a concern. In Canada— as the Progressives in the 1920s and the Reform Party and the Bloc Québécois in the 1990s demonstrated—an appetite for regional parties exists and they have, by definition, voraciously narrow agendas. These are not broad-based national par-ties representing a cross-section of socioeconomic interests and groups.

A virtue of FPTP is that it encourages "big tent" or brokerage parties. A party hoping to gain power must strive to incorporate, accommodate, cater to, and express the interests of a medley of groups and regions. Such parties—a mélange of people from different regions and strata of society—fulfill a nationally inte-grative role. They endeavour to be the representational social mirrors that many MMP proponents eagerly demand of the electoral system. Perversely, MMP could contribute to ghettoizing and dividing groups in the cause of representing them. Senior citizens, for example, concerned that their issues are overlooked, would have an incentive to withdraw from a large inclusive party such as the Liberals, Conservatives, or the New Democratic Party (NDP) and could be encouraged to form, for example, their own Pensioners Party. This occurred in Israel. and when the 2006 election dust settled, the Pensioners Party played a major role in the cabinet's construction and in the discussion of the issue of war and peace, something about which its election platform said nothing. Similarly, Aboriginals, women, or religious minorities may be dissuaded from participation in parties that are broad-based nationally and programmatically. MMP encourages them to hive themselves off and use a new party, constructed on the limited identities of its supporters, to extract concessions for narrow self-serving interests with less pressure to compromise than exists under the present system. The creation of a Toronto Party, insistent on full-blown provincial status for the city, would not contribute to national or provincial unity. If successful, it would be devastating for Ontario's hinterlands; they are dependent on fiscal transfers for social pro-grams and infrastructure made possible by their being part of a larger, wealthier provincial state.

In constructing coalition governments in a multiparty context, the smallest party to the coalition may exert disproportionate influence in determining the fate and policy thrust of the government. Conversely, a party that consistently wins a significant plurality of votes in elections could be kept from participating in government indefinitely. Small single-issue parties could consistently wield more power than the largest, but sidelined, party. Another possibility is a grand coalition of the two largest parties, as occurred in Germany after its 2005 election. Whatever configuration of parties forms the government, it will not be what voters voted for or thought they were going to get. Proportionality in the legislature will likely not translate into proportional influence in government. Coalition governments constructed under MMP—such as one where the largest party teams up with a fourth-place finisher—will give that small party disproportionate influence compared to the second- and third-largest parties.

A threshold of 5 percent of votes as a condition for parliamentary representation, as in New Zealand and Germany, may be thought of as an effective rampart against regional and other culturally divisive parties. The representational bar in Canada, however, whatever the percentage threshold, will be set provincially rather than for the country as a whole.[14] That is, if a party wins 30 percent of Albertans' votes, it will get 30 percent (or at least nine) of the province's current twenty-eight seats in parliament. The three most westerly and resource-rich provinces could throw up a Western Rights Party even more potent than the Reform Party. A British Columbia First Party dedicated to pursuing nothing but B.C.'s interests is conceivable. Such parties will not contribute to national unity and coherent national policymaking. Some in the East will be sure to make a case for an Atlantic Party. Although the four Atlantic provinces account for only 10 percent of the seats in the House of Commons, just a few seats—ten or eleven, which is a third of the Atlantic seats—could propel such a narrowly focused party into a king-maker role in a fragmented Parliament. Imagine a proliferation of provincial and other parties—the Family Coalition Party, the Marijuana Party, the Libertarian Party, the Party of People with Disabilities, and so forth—and consider their influence in the making and breaking of coalition governments. With MMP providing incentives for the formation of such parties, the effect on Canadian unity of the current somewhat unbalanced regional caucuses will appear piddling in comparison.

PUSH FOR PR

Proponents agitate for PR even as public opinion appears disconnected from the issue. In the past decade, five provinces and Parliament have toyed with electoral reform. Prince Edward Island's voters, like Ontario's, when given a chance to weigh in on MMP, turned it down decisively (64 percent said no) in a 2005 referendum. When one considers that turnouts in FPTP elections in P.E.I. have consistently been over 80 percent, public detachment from the electoral reform issue is revealed in the turnout for the referendum: a paltry 35 percent. In Ontario, a poll conducted before its 2007 referendum found that only 28 percent were familiar with the MMP proposal, and the Conservative leader reported that, in all his travelling around the province, only three people raised the issue.[15] In the Ontario referendum, 138,000 fewer valid votes were cast than in the FPTP election that took place concurrently.[16]

Like the constitutional reform misadventures of earlier days, the pursuit of PR is an elite pleasure industry of political scientists, political junkies, and smaller parties such as the Greens and the NDP who have an interest in it. The Ontario referendum won majority backing in only 5 of the province's 107 constituencies, and 4 of those were won by the NDP. Paradoxically, the NDP, which has never secured a percentage of federal parliamentary seats commensurate with its share of the popular vote, may ultimately be a casualty of the MMP system it seeks. Its self-styled coalition of unionists, feminists, environmentalists, gays and lesbians, people of colour, and others may well fracture.

A majority of British Columbia's voters, 57 percent, opted for the single transferable vote (STV) in their 2005 referendum on electoral reform, but that proved insufficient because the B.C. government had set a bar of 60 percent approval for its adoption. One reason support for electoral system change was greater in B.C. in 2005 than in Ontario was that the quirkiness of the FPTP system had been displayed in three consecutive B.C. elections. In 1991, the NDP won power even while its popularity dipped below levels it had attained when it lost in the 1970s and 1980s. Then, in 1996, the NDP was reelected to another majority although the Liberals won more votes. In 2001, when the Liberals swept to power on an impressive 57 percent of the vote, they won a lopsided seventy-seven (or 97 percent) of the seventy-nine seats.

In Ontario's 2003 election, in contrast, the Liberals formed a government with a healthy but more modest majority after capturing a decisive 46.5 percent of the vote. The Ontario result was historically consistent with past results, and the election of a Liberal majority government was not publicly perceived as "stolen," which is admittedly a potentially unseemly upshot of FPTP. Ontario produced a mix of governments—three parties won majority governments over the course of three elections in the span of eight years between 1987 and 1995. While no party captured a majority of the votes, the results in each election reflected a popular consensus for change in favour of the party that prevailed. In B.C., the appetite for electoral reform dampened dramatically after the FPTP system proved less capricious in the 2005 provincial election; the Liberals, with 46 percent of the vote won forty-six seats, and the NDP, with 42 percent, won thirty-three seats. Consequently, in a second referendum on STV in 2009, fewer than 39 percent of B.C. voters opted for changing the electoral system, a sharp contrast to the majority that had supported the idea just four years earlier.

The three provincial governments conducting the referenda did not tell voters that they would set a 60 percent bar when they originally promised a referendum. We may only speculate on why they set it so high. Most politicians, particularly those from the large parties, prefer the status quo. FPTP holds out a better prospect for them to wield majority power. In Manitoba, Saskatchewan, and Nova Scotia, where the NDP is a major party, it has not pursued PR, in contrast to the federal and Ontario NDP, which are minor parties. Politicians from large parties tend not to publicize their preference for FPTP because that could alienate some voters. Nevertheless, they may promise a referendum on the issue because they perceive that the public will appreciate the idea that its will counts, and the public may reward the party that gives it a direct voice in the matter. That is what happened in New Zealand. To capitalize on this belief, in both the B.C. and Ontario cases, the referenda were held by the governing party at the same time as the general election. In Ontario, the Conservatives declared that they were opposed to MMP only on the eve of the referendum, after public opinion surveys made it clear that it would fail.[17]

Both the B.C. and Ontario governments encouraged those favouring PR by opening the issue, but the governments themselves would not speak in favour of it and insisted that they were neutral. Both provinces used a Citizens' Assembly (CA) to consider and propose, if the Assembly so decided, an alternative electoral system. The Citizens' Assemblies were exercises in deliberative democracy, a supplement to representative democracy. Political scientists and others expert in electoral systems educated the Citizens' Assemblies in the various forms and outcomes of PR and FPTP systems. Then, the CA members, meeting on weekends, opted for PR over the FPTP status quo. In Ontario's case, they chose the MMP form of PR by a vote of ninety-four to eight. The ultimate upshot, the referendum's results, demonstrated that the Assembly's members were whistling in the wind: barely more than a third of their fellow citizens embraced their proposal at the ballot box.

The Citizens' Assemblies' members did not reflect their citizen peers' views. Nor was the CA as representative of the public as the government claimed. Unlike a legal jury, randomly selected with service mandatory, only citizens interested in serving on the Assembly could be chosen. In B.C. and Ontario, the CAs were constructed to reflect gender balance. With each constituency permitted one representative, this meant that no men were eligible to represent half of the constituencies and no women the other half. Notwithstanding the gender balance, the Ontario Assembly was not a representative demographic mirror of the public. One Assembly member observed that a third of the members were retirees. Also unrepresentative of their communities were those who appeared at the twenty-nine meetings in seventeen cities. "In some cases the public were homogeneous–e.g., a large group from an old age home."[18] Public interest was also low; attendance ranged from seven in Dryden to about two hundred in Toronto, a city of well over two million.

The CAs' recommendations in both B.C. and Ontario to jettison FPTP were predictable. Those making oral and written submissions to Ontario's CA were not representative of Ontarians' public opinion. Self-selected, they were overwhelmingly in favour of PR with 692 of the 986 submissions offering "pro" comments and only 78 (or 8 percent) tendering "con" comments. A repeated theme in the submissions was that PR would produce a more demographically representative legislature. Women and visible minorities' underrepresentation in political institutions was depicted as systemic discrimination. It is noteworthy, then, that of all the comments submitted to the CA, only 21 percent were by women, a lower percentage than the percentage of women in Ontario's legislature. This suggested that women were less interested than men in the Assembly's work but the Assembly, given its gender composition, could not be accused of systemic discrimination.

CONFRONTING THE OTHER SIDE

John Hiemstra and Harold Jansen offer a number of rationales for discarding FPTP and adopting PR. They project positive scenarios with MMP. They note that one of the main arguments for FPTP is that it offers good prospects for stable government because a plurality of votes for a party usually translates into a majority of seats. As they accurately observe, Canada has nonetheless frequently had minority governments. Indeed, an oddity of the Jean Chrétien years was that—with five parties elected to produce a pizza parliament in 1993, 1997, and 2000—a majority government emerged at all. The 2004, 2006, and 2008 elections, with only four parliamentary parties, yielded the more logical outcome—a minority government. If the current four parliamentary parties survive, and even if new ones do not appear, FPTP majority governments composed exclusively of members from a single party are less likely in the future.

Canada's minority as well as majority governments have provided relative political stability by international standards. The greatest threats to Canadian unity, paradoxically, have come during periods of majority government, as during the Meech Lake imbroglio, the Charlottetown Accord, and Quebec's sovereignty referendums and when all the parties (except for the Bloc Québécois) sided with the government.

Hiemstra and Jansen contend that FPTP aggravates and intensifies regional divisions because it produces regionally lopsided caucuses. Certainly, the success of the Chrétien Liberals in capturing 98 of Ontario's 99 seats in 1993 and then 101 and 100 of the province's 103 seats in the 1997 and 2000 elections respectively demonstrated lopsidedness. The Liberals won those contests with bare majorities of between 51 and 53 percent of Ontarians' votes. The dramatic overrepresentation of Liberals in Ontario was twinned with their substantial underrepresentation in the West. Conversely, the Reform/Alliance Party with the support of between 24 and 26 percent of Ontario's voters in that same trio of elections did not win more than 2 seats in 2000 and was shut out in 1997. Such outcomes are unusual, produced by what proved to be but a temporary fissure on the political right with Reform/Alliance and the Progressives Conservatives competing for the same pool of voters to the Liberals' benefit. The 2004, 2006, and 2008 elections produced more typical and less severe distortions after the right reunited. In Ontario in 2006, the Liberals won 52 percent of the seats with 40 percent of the votes, the Conservatives won 39 percent of the seats with 35 percent of the votes, and the NDP won 12 percent of the seats with their 19 percent of votes.

Neither the lopsided results of the elections in the 1990s nor the more balanced results of more recent elections affected national unity. It is the premiers and the provinces, rather than the federal caucuses that vote along predictable party lines, that are the pivotal players in national unity debates. The impact on national unity of the mathematical asymmetry between seats and votes produced by FPTP pales in comparison to the impact on unity that would happen if unabashedly selfish regional parties were to emerge and take root. MMP would likely unleash them.

Hiemstra and Jansen blithely and naively assume that, with MMP, the existing parties would continue to secure levels of popular support across the country similar to those of the past. What would change positively, from their perspective, is that the existing party caucuses would more accurately reflect those parties' differing levels of regional support. This, however, would almost certainly not occur because the existing party system would most likely fracture, given the incentive MMP provides for regional and narrow single-issue parties. Such parties would likely fracture one or more of the established broadly based parties. By definition, single-issue parties lack an overarching policy agenda and a "big tent" mentality that strives to incorporate people from different backgrounds, interests, and regions. Canada's diversities and social heterogeneity would fuel these new parties. Such parties would not foster what Canadians share in common. They would highlight non-ideological divisions among Canadians rather than economic class divisions, such as the gaps between the rich and poor wherever they live in Canada. Broadly based parties and platforms will compete with and give way to narrow special-interest parties. A virtue of the existing system is that it encourages parties to broker, within themselves, Canada's regional and social diversities.

CONCLUSION

FPTP has served Canada well in comparative perspective. To replace it with MMP would contribute to endangering national unity. MMP could produce governments with policies tailored to single-interest parties that capture very low percentages of the vote. Their handfuls of seats could disproportionately determine the government's complexion and direction. The MMP solution to the shortcomings of FPTP may prove worse than the problem. Adopting MMP is akin to buying a pig in a poke.

NOTES

1. Laza Kekic, "The Economist Intelligence Unit's Index of Democracy," 2007, pp. 3 and 6, available at http://www.economist.com/media/pdf/DEMOCRACY_INDEX_2007_v3.pdf. Accessed August 20, 2011.

2. Alan C. Cairns, "Political Science, Ethnicity and the Canadian Constitution," in David P. Shugarman and Reg Whitaker, eds., *Federalism and Political Community: Essays in Honour of Donald Smiley* (Peterborough: Broadview, 1989), p. 117.

3. André Blais and Ken Carty, "The Psychological Impact of Electoral Laws: Measuring Duverger's Elusive Factor," *British Journal of Political Science* 21 (1991), pp. 79–93.

4. Denis Pilon, "Explaining Voting System Reform in Canada, 1874 to 1960," *Journal of Canadian Studies* 40, no. 3 (Fall 2006), p. 147.

5. *Revised Statutes of Manitoba, 1940*, I, ch. 57. For analysis of the results, see Nelson Wiseman and K.W. Taylor, "Ethnic vs. Class Voting: The Case of Winnipeg, 1945," *Canadian Journal of Political Science* 7, no. 2 (June 1974), pp. 314–328.

6. *Winnipeg Free Press*, Sept. 17, 1949.

7. S. Pharr, R. Putman, and R. Dalton, "Trouble in the Advanced Democracies." *Journal of Democracy* 11, no. 2 (2000), pp. 5–25.

8. Jack Vowles, "Offsetting the PR Effect? Party Mobilization and Turnout Decline in New Zealand, 1996–99," *Party Politics* 8, no. 5 (2002), p. 587.

9. International Institute for Democracy and Electoral Assistance (Stockholm, Sweden) http://www.idea.int/vt/compulsory_voting.cfm. Accessed August 20. 2011.

10. "Italian Election Petition Earns 800,000 Signatures," *The Globe and Mail*, July 25, 2007.

11. Thérèse Arsenau, "Ideas," CBC radio program, February 9, 1998.

12. Thérèse Arsenau, "Electing Representative Legislatures: Lessons from New Zealand," in Henry Milner, ed., *Making Every Vote Count: Reassessing Canada's Electoral System* (Peterborough: Broadview, 1999), p. 140.

13. Interview with Joe Schlesinger, "Foreign Assignment," CBC-TV program, February 21, 2004.

14. *Constitution Act, 1985 (Representation)*, Statutes of Canada, 1986, c. 8, Part I.

15. Robert Benzie, "Reform's on the Ballot: Now If They Only Cared," *The Toronto Star*, September 1, 2007.

16. Elections Ontario, available at http://www3.elections.on.ca/internetapp/realtimereferendum.aspx?lang=en-ca&gf73=0&contestid=2&channel_id={923146e7-4d81-42a8-99f0-e61f5ab50387}&lang=en, and http://www3.elections.on.ca/internetapp/realtimehome.aspx?lang=en&channel_id={923146e7-4d81-42a8-99f0-e61f5ab50387}&lang=en. Accessed October 21, 2007.

17. Robert Benzie, "Reject MMP, Conservatives Tell Voters," *The Toronto Star*, October 9, 2007.

18. Citizens Assembly Blog, "Update on the Consultation Phase of the Ontario Citizens' Assembly," March 3, 2007.

POSTSCRIPT

The two articles present some good arguments, but they also leave some questions unanswered. John Hiemstra and Harold Jansen nicely reveal the benefits of a mixed-member proportional (MMP) system, but one wonders whether they understate the possible costs of such a system. Coalition governments, an inevitable result of MMP in Canada, may produce policies whose coherence is lacking. The benefit of single-member plurality (SMP) is that a single voice typically determines policy, but the multiple voices in MMP may produce government outputs that endeavour to satisfy the demands of the varied parties in government. Hiemstra and Jansen are little worried with the prospect of two types of MPs under MMP. However, it seems possible that those unattached to a constituency may find themselves a little lost, especially in light of the fact that constituency work makes up the bulk of the activity of most elected representatives. The two authors also applaud MMP because of its ability to ensure appropriate representation in government. But again one wonders. The presence of coalition governments will produce power arrangements in government that fail to reflect the distribution of the vote in the legislature. A minor party, with little of the popular vote, may team up with a more powerful party to secure its aims in exchange for support. In other words, there is no guarantee that the distribution of the popular vote will be recorded in the actions of government. MMP addresses concerns of representation in the legislative branch, but may have little effect on the distribution of support in the most powerful branch in parliamentary government—namely the executive branch.

Wiseman makes a number of good points, the most important of these arguably being the failure of some to realize that a rough equating of the quality of democracy with a nation's electoral system is foolish. But it is also true that Wiseman's effort is not invulnerable to criticism. Canada may indeed be more attractive than other countries with PR, but this does not mean that Canada should eschew any serious consideration of electoral reform—successful nations can always become more successful. Wiseman is critical of the attempt of MMP to make formal political life more representative of society, but the fact that women, for instance, typically represent about one-fifth of elected representatives can be unsettling. Finally, Wiseman may also be charged with failing to assuage or ease feelings that the existing electoral system in Canada is simply unfair. There may indeed be problems with MMP—nothing is ever perfect—but at least it seeks to ensure that the parties and their supporters get what they deserve.

Students wishing to pursue the subject of electoral reform might begin with Heather MacIvor's short overview of electoral reform in Heather MacIvor, "A Brief Introduction to Electoral Reform," in Henry Milner, ed., *Making Every Vote Count: Reassessing Canada's Electoral System* (Peterborough: Broadview

Press, 1999). Another useful introduction to elections and electoral reforms is John Courtney, *Elections* (Vancouver: UBC Press, 2004), ch. 6. The next task is to dive into the detailed analyses of the first-past-the-post system and its main competitors. Here, students might start with J. Paul Johnston and Harvey E. Pasis, eds., *Representation and Electoral Systems: Canadian Perspectives* (Scarborough: Prentice-Hall, 1990). This text contains many of the classic articles on electoral reform in Canada, including the seminal article by Alan C. Cairns and the response to his article by J.A.A. Lovink. Other examinations of electoral reform (such as MMP) include Henry Milner, ed., *Making Every Vote Count: Reassessing Canada's Electoral System* (Peterborough: Broadview Press, 1999); Henry Milner, "The Case for Proportional Representation," in Hugh Thorburn and Alan Whitehorn, eds., *Party Politics in Canada*, 8th ed. (Scarborough: Prentice-Hall, 2001); Louis Massicotte, *Changing the Canadian Electoral System* (Montreal: Institute for Research on Public Policy, February 2001); and the entire July–August 2001 issue of *Policy Options*. A rigorous analysis of electoral reform and MMP can also be found in Law Commission of Canada, *Voting Counts: Electoral Reform in Canada* (Ottawa: Law Reform Commission, 2004). For those who wish to see how the electoral system has shaped the history of elections in Canada, the book to consult is Lawrence Leduc et al., eds. *Dynasties and Interludes: Past and Present in Canadian Electoral Politics* (Toronto: Dundurn Press, 2010)

The issue of electoral reform is not merely a matter of concern for academics. Provincial governments in Canada have been looking long and hard at this issue, and some have held referendums on the matter. For more on developments in the provinces, students should see Harold J. Jansen, "Making the Impossible Possible: Electoral Reform and Canada's Provinces," in Thomas M.J. Bateman and Rick Myers, eds., *Braving the New World: Readings in Contemporary Politics*, 4th ed. (Scarborough: Nelson, 2008). As for reports on the referendums, the following are relevant: Laura B. Stephenson and Brian Tanguay, *Ontario Referendum on Proportional Representation: Why Citizens Said No* (Montreal: IRPP, 2009), and Mark E. Warren and Hilary Pearse, *Designing Deliberative Democracy: the British Columbia Citizens' Assembly* (New York: Cambridge University Press, 2008).

The experience of other countries with the plurality system and proportional representation is relevant to the discussion of electoral reform in Canada. On this topic, the following might be consulted: Michael Dummett, *Principles of Electoral Reform* (Oxford: Oxford University Press, 1997), Matthew Soberg Shugart and Martin P. Wattenberg, ed., *Mixed-Member Electoral Systems: The Best of Both Worlds?* (Oxford: Oxford University Press, 2001), and Andre Blais, *To Keep or to Change First Past the Post? The Politics of Electoral Reform* (New York: Oxford University Press, 2008). Also, special attention may be given to Arend Lijphart,

"Democracies: Forms, Performance, and Constitutional Engineering," *European Journal of Political Research* 25 (1994), pp. 1–17. What makes this article so central to the debate is that it denies that one must concede a decline in the effectiveness of government in order to introduce PR. For more on Lijphart's work, students might want to consult Arend Lijphart, *Patterns of Democracy: Government Forms and Performance in Thirty-Six Countries* (New Haven and London: Yale University Press, 1999), chs. 15–16.

Should the Court Challenges Program Be Reinstated?

✔ **YES**
A. WAYNE MACKAY, DANIEL MCGRUDER, AND KENNETH JENNINGS, "Why the Government Was Wrong to Cancel the Court Challenges Program"

✘ **NO**
TASHA KHEIRIDDIN, "Why the Government Was Right to Cancel the Court Challenges Program"

Few government programs with such modest budgets have generated as much controversy as the Court Challenges Program. When the Conservative minority government of Stephen Harper eliminated the program in 2006, the announcement caused dramatically different reactions. Some lauded the government's courage in cutting a program that had benefitted a small number of very vocal special interest groups. Others decried the move as both a major setback in the promotion of equality in Canada and a negative reflection on Canada's international status as a promoter of human rights. At the heart of this debate have been important differences in how justice is conceived and how to ensure that the equality provisions of the Charter of Rights and Freedoms are met.

The roots of the Court Challenges Program go back to the Liberal government of Pierre Trudeau in 1977. The government of Quebec had passed the controversial Bill 101, which was intended to strengthen the protection of the French language in the province while curtailing the usage of English. Rather than challenging the provisions of the bill directly, the Trudeau government chose an indirect approach by establishing the Court Challenges Program. This provided funding to minority language groups so they could challenge provincial laws that threatened the guarantee of minority language rights under the *Constitution Act, 1867*. In order to appear balanced, in the first three years, the program funded three cases defending English language rights in Quebec and three cases defending French language rights in Saskatchewan and Manitoba. When the Charter of Rights and Freedoms was adopted in 1982, the mandate of the Court Challenges Program was expanded to allow challenges to government policies under the language provisions of the new Charter.

When the equality provisions of section 15 of the Charter came fully into effect in 1985, there was growing pressure on the government to expand the range of challenges that could be funded by the program beyond linguistic rights. A special parliamentary committee examining the issue of equality rights noted that, within a very short period of time, a significant number of cases had been launched by individuals against various government departments and agencies. However, the committee expressed concern that "the imbalance in financial, technical and human resources between the opposing parties constitutes a serious impediment to those who might wish to claim the benefit of section 15, thus reducing the effectiveness of resorting to the courts as a means of obtaining redress" (*Equality for All: Report of the Parliamentary Committee on Equality Rights,* Ottawa: House of Commons, 1985, p. 133). The committee feared that the equality provisions of the Charter would be without real substance if disadvantaged or marginalized groups within Canadian society were not provided with the resources to mount real challenges to government policies.

As a result, the Conservative government of Brian Mulroney expanded the program, opening the door to funding of court challenges based on sections 15 (equality), 27 (multiculturalism), or 26 (sexual equality) of the Charter. In 1989, the program was renewed with a five-year budget of $12 million and moved to the Human Rights Centre at the University of Ottawa in order to make the management of the program and the selection of groups and cases funded more at arm's length from the government.

Despite these changes, the Conservative government had a change of heart in 1992. While Minister of Justice, Kim Campbell terminated the program, justifying the move as part of a series of cost-cutting measures the government was implementing. The decision invoked widespread criticism and became an issue in the run-up to the 1993 election. In response to growing pressures, all federal parties went on record stating that they would reinstate the program if elected to office. When the Liberal government of Jean Chrétien came to power in 1994, the Court Challenges Program was reinstated with an annual funding of $2.7 million. Although funding was provided by the federal government through the Department of Canadian Heritage, the program itself was re-created as an independent national nonprofit organization. Its supporters hoped that this arrangement would make it more difficult to cut the program in the future. During the Chrétien years, the Court Challenges Program funded a number of significant challenges under the equality provisions of the Charter, especially in the area of women's rights.

However, changing political tides suddenly placed the Court Challenges Program in doubt when the Conservative minority government came to power in 2006. One of the program's harshest critics, Ian Brodie, was now part of the new government's inner circle, serving as chief of staff to Stephen Harper. Thus, it came as no surprise to many observers when the new government announced that it was eliminating all funding to the Court Challenges Program in its first government budget, effectively killing the program.

Critics of the program hailed the Conservative decision, arguing that the move was long overdue. Others expressed alarm that the cut was a major setback for human rights in Canada and represented a shift away from fundamental Canadian values of equality. This debate is taken up in the two readings that follow. Law professor Wayne MacKay and law students Daniel McGruder and Kenneth Jennings argue that it was a fundamental mistake to cancel the program. They argue that this has made justice and real equality less accessible for many poor and marginalized Canadians. In contrast, writer Tasha Kheiriddin argues that the Harper government made the right decision. She believes that the decision brought a justifiable end to an ideologically driven program that had too long favoured a few special interest groups, while excluding others whose views were less popular.

✔ **YES**

Why the Government Was Wrong to Cancel the Court Challenges Program

A. WAYNE MACKAY, DANIEL MCGRUDER, AND KENNETH JENNINGS

In cancelling the Court Challenges Program in September 2006, the federal government, headed by Stephen Harper, made justice less accessible for many disadvantaged Canadians and thereby struck a blow against equality—one of Canada's core values. This was not a cost-saving reduction but, rather, a statement of policy and ideology that should alarm Canadians. To its credit, the government did admit that it was attacking the program on its merits and not just to save money. There were even some statements that the liberated funds would be used in other more effective ways. The truth of that claim remains to be proven. What is clear is that Canada has lost a valuable and effective program that helped to make the promises of equality in the Charter of Rights a reality for more people. The program was not perfect, but its elimination is radical surgery that is not justifiable. We would go so far as to assert that the program cancellation significantly detracts from one of Canada's core values—the pursuit of a more egalitarian society.

SUPPORTING CANADA'S CORE VALUES OF JUSTICE AND EQUALITY

It was American founding father Alexander Hamilton who said, "The first duty of society is justice." It was this kind of thinking that animated the late prime minister Pierre Trudeau's pursuit of a "just society"—a society in which governments are actively involved in promoting the welfare of all of its citizens. In a society as privileged as Canada, it is sometimes easy to take for granted the promise of justice for all citizens of our country. However, these freedoms are usually hard-won, and come at a price. We should be proud to live in a country that cherishes fundamental freedoms for all its people, and we should be proud to live in a society where our legal and political systems strive for justice and fairness. Accordingly, we should be saddened at the cancellation by the current federal government of the Court Challenges Program (CCP), which allowed some of Canada's most disenfranchised citizens to pursue justice in our courts.

The Court Challenges Program, created in 1978, provided funds to support test cases of national significance to dispute and clarify the constitutional rights of Canadians. The Court Challenges Program is not a big program (its funding being a miniscule fraction of the federal budget), but it is an important one, both substantively and symbolically. To realize this, one need only consider the question, what does it say about a government that it is willing to help fund citizens in challenging its own laws? We think it says positive, not negative, things about the country and those who govern it.

The cancellation of the CCP, though minor in budgetary terms, represents a significant loss for all Canadians. It is a subtraction from the human rights of every citizen. Fundamentally, this is a question of access to justice. When we enshrine constitutional rights, we should be able to expect that if Canadians believe the government is violating their rights, they can challenge that infringement. But if citizens or other residents, due to financial constraints, cannot enforce respect for their rights by having their day in court, then our constitutional democracy is a hollow shell, and the rights enshrined in the Canadian Charter of Rights and Freedoms are thereby diminished.

Commitment to the protection of Charter rights for disadvantaged individuals and groups is one of Canada's core values. As the Supreme Court of Canada indicated in the *Quebec Secession Reference* (1998), this is true both before and after 1982. If we wish to continue to enjoy these rights, and maintain our place as a leader in human rights on the world stage, it is the duty of every Canadian to call for the reinstatement of the Court Challenges Program.

THE COURT CHALLENGES PROGRAM—BENEFITS OF JUSTICE AND FAIRNESS

The Canadian Constitution establishes important constitutional rights, including the rights of everyone to equality before and under the law, and to equal protection and benefit of the law without discrimination. However, these rights are empty unless the individuals and groups they are designed to protect can exercise and enforce them. Since the Charter was adopted twenty-five years ago, successive federal governments have recognized that they have the responsibility to ensure that disadvantaged minorities have funding to take Charter cases to the courts. The Court Challenges Program, by providing modest contributions to the cost of important test cases dealing with language and equality rights, has made constitutional rights more accessible to all Canadians. Without the Court Challenges Program, Canada's constitutional rights are real only for the wealthy—this is unfair, and it does not comply with the rule of law, which is also a fundamental principle of Canadian society and our Constitution, as recognized in the *Quebec Secession Reference* and in other judicial and political venues, as well as in the preamble to the Charter of Rights.

Since its inception, the Court Challenges Program has funded numerous court challenges that have helped to give meaning to the Canadian Charter of Rights and Freedoms for many Canadians who would otherwise have been unable to assert their constitutional rights. This is achieved through partially funding the court costs of select, needy Canadian individuals or groups who are allegedly being disadvantaged through laws passed by the Canadian government.

The Court Challenges Program has advanced the constitutional rights enshrined in the Charter. An example of this is the CCP-funded case of *Canadian Newspapers Co. v. Canada (Attorney General),* in which a victim of a sexual assault was at risk of having her name published in a newspaper. Relying on the funding of groups through the Court Challenges Program, the victim successfully defeated the threat of disclosure and confirmed the right to privacy for future victims. Other cases, such as *Egan v. Canada* have furthered the doctrine of substantive equality in Canadian society. This particular case brought about the recognition of sexual orientation as a ground of discrimination.

The real contribution of the Court Challenges Program stems from just these sorts of cases, which demonstrate the CCP's facilitation of substantive equality. Unlike formal equality, which overlooks personal differences, substantive equality is concerned with the impact of the law on different groups of individuals. Substantive equality requires that there be equal impacts on persons affected by a law, while formal equality insists that all people be treated identically. The fundamental problem with formal equality is that people are not identical—to treat them identically is actually to treat them unequally, based on the inherent disadvantages that an individual or group faces. Thus, justice requires that in order to value people equally, we must sometimes treat them differently. The challenge is to know when to take account of differences, but both judges and academics now provide guidance to facilitate this difficult task.

The case of *Eldridge* (as mentioned on the CCP website) provides a good context in which to illustrate the benefits of substantive equality. In that case, a number of deaf patients challenged the British Columbia medicare system for failing to ensure that sign language interpreters were available for medical appointments and procedures. The formal equality approach would see no problem here, since every patient that comes into a hospital is getting the same medical services delivered without the aid of interpreters. However, the substantive equality mode of analysis adopted by the Supreme Court recognizes that the impact of not having interpreters adversely affects deaf people. Without interpreters, deaf patients cannot adequately communicate with doctors and medical personnel, and are more likely to be improperly diagnosed and receive inferior treatment. By virtue of their disability, deaf people did not receive the full and equal benefit of the British Columbia medicare system. The substantive equality approach ensured that the deaf minority were able to access the same level of care as that enjoyed by the hearing majority, by providing interpreters for the deaf in hospitals.

A substantive approach to equality recognizes that patterns of disadvantage and oppression exist in society and requires that lawmakers and government officials take these systemic factors into account when drafting laws and formulating policies.[1] One of Canada's fundamental values is the rule of law: the principle that no one is above the law. Law only mirrors justice when it is based on fundamental principles that are known and applicable to all. By doing away with the Court Challenges Program, the federal government has weakened the rule of law by limiting access to an essential enforcement mechanism—the court challenge. By so doing, it has in effect placed itself and its actions "above the law" in the sense that the great majority of Canadians cannot afford to challenge the laws and policies of the government, as is their constitutional right. In a democracy, we demand that our politicians and lawmakers be accountable to the polity. The Court Challenges Program, by funding citizens in challenging their laws and policies, was a shining example of the government's commitment of accountability to all its constituents, particularly those minorities whose views are not always reflected in a majoritarian democracy.

Canada has long been recognized as an international leader in human rights and a beacon of hope to the disenfranchised and the oppressed on the larger world stage. By cancelling the Court Challenges Program, the government has not only tarnished its international human rights record and reputation but also shrunk from its role as an exemplar of freedom and hope. As recently as May 2006, Stephen Harper's Conservative government appeared before a United Nations committee in Geneva to defend its commitment to human rights in Canada, citing the Court Challenges Program as evidence of this commitment. As stated by the government, "[t]his uniquely Canadian program has been successful in supporting a number of important court cases that have had direct impacts on the implementation of linguistic and equality rights in Canada." Canada vouched to remain a society that values transparency and equal access to basic human rights and benefits of the law. The cancellation of this program flies in the face of the government's public position on human rights and its commitment to the protection of the Charter rights of disadvantaged individuals and groups. To be an effective world leader, Canada must walk the talk and lead by example.

CRITIQUES OF THE PROGRAM—CHALLENGING THE CHALLENGER

It has been said that the Court Challenges Program, while once an important part of the Canadian justice system, is no longer needed. After twenty-five years, critics say, how can there still be any novel challenges left to fund? This criticism shows disrespect to all Canadian residents who may need protection of their equality rights, including women, Aboriginal peoples, people with disabilities, members of racialized minorities, immigrants, refugees, lesbians and gay men, children, and seniors. The government itself has publicly stated that there remain dimensions of the constitutional provisions currently covered by the CCP that still require clarification. The CCP has a proven track record of facilitating the realization of the promise of justice enshrined in the Charter for these sometimes disadvantaged groups. Even if the annual numbers of cases funded by the CCP are fewer, ensuring that this promise remains real and accessible to all Canadians should be just as important now as it was in the early years of the Charter.

The Court Challenges Program has been attacked on the charge that it is not accountable. This is not a sustainable objection. The CCP has an established track record as an effective and accountable institution that promotes access to justice. It provided quarterly reports on its activities to the government and published an annual report with statistics on the number and types of cases that it had funded. The annual report and public documents were available on the CCP's website. On several occasions, independent evaluators have furnished the program with high praise, most recently in 2003–2004. The only information that the CCP does not divulge for the purposes of public and government oversight is information legally restricted by solicitor–client privilege. In this way, the CCP has remained accountable while protecting its beneficiaries and their personal information.

But what of these beneficiaries? The Court Challenges Program has been the subject of two criticisms in this regard. Critics of the CCP dislike some of the cases that it has supported: cases related to same-sex marriage, voting rights for prisoners, and *Criminal Code* provisions regarding hitting children. The fact that some individuals and groups do not agree with some of the test cases funded by the Program is no reason to cancel it. No one among us is likely to agree with every single test case that appears. But it is important to let such cases proceed on their merits to the courts to be decided on the basis of our Constitution and our laws. The point of a constitutional human rights regime is to ensure that diverse claims, perspectives, and life experiences are respected and taken into account in the design of laws and policies. The equality guarantees and the language rights in the Constitution were designed to help minorities, whose views and needs may not always be respected by governments, to be heard on issues that affect them. Cancelling the Court Challenges Program mutes their voices further, and makes Canada a less open and tolerant society.

In a similar vein, critics have pointed out that the program is too selective in whom it represents. But the CCP only has limited funds for important test cases. Therefore, it stands to reason that these limited resources go to those who need them most—those whose cases are the most promising, and those whose rights have been the most seriously infringed. Considering that the CCP issues a full report on every case it funds, thus alleviating the accountability issue, this criticism actually indicates the need for further funding, not cancellation, as some opponents of the program would like.

CONCLUSION—OUR VISION FOR CANADIAN SOCIETY

Fyodor Dostoyevsky once intimated that a society must be judged by how it treats its weakest members. In the final analysis, then, an assessment of the Court Challenges Program turns on what sort of vision we have for Canadian society. Are we willing to relegate our weakest and most vulnerable citizens to second class constitutional status? Or should we give them the means and encouragement to pursue the elusive promises of the Canadian Charter of Rights? The Court Challenges Program, while not perfect, was certainly a step in the right direction. Those who need to point out the imperfections in our laws in order that they may live on equal footing with others deserve to be heard. By cancelling the Court Challenges Program, the government has made it more difficult for those on the margins of Canadian society to be heard. The role of governments should be to reduce economic barriers to the exercise of our constitutional rights; not to increase the height of those barriers. Canada has been rightly applauded for its record on human rights at home and abroad, and we hope that this rather mean-spirited cancellation of the Court Challenges Program is not a sign of a policy shift with more surprises yet to come.

NOTE

1. The first part of this sentence is paraphrased from the CCP website, http://www.ccppcj.ca/e/rights/rights-charter.shtml.

✖ **NO**

Why the Government Was Right to Cancel the Court Challenges Program

TASHA KHEIRIDDIN

In the words of the late, great American economist Milton Friedman, "Nothing is so permanent as a temporary government program." By targeting groups with specific characteristics—such as sex, race, disability, or income bracket—government programs create political constituencies, and in a democracy, constituencies vote. Whenever the state terminates a program, it inevitably generates howls of protest from the affected group, which claims that its "rights"—usually code for "financial benefits"—have been taken away. The pressure exerted by interest groups is frequently so strong that governments back down and maintain the programs, especially when faced with the prospect of an imminent election.

That is why the Conservative government exhibited remarkable courage last fall when it cancelled a spate of ineffective and outdated initiatives. It put an end to the One-Tonne Challenge (an environmental program which gave comedian Rick Mercer considerable airtime but did little to improve the environment), closed 12 Status of Women offices (instead of paying bureaucrats to keep the lights on, the government decided the money would be better spent by women working in their communities) and terminated the Court Challenges Program (an initiative which funded legal challenges to government legislation, led mostly by interest groups).

It is on this last program that we focus our attention, because the decision to end it represents more than just sensible policy, but a potential turning of the page in Canadian politics. Even if the concept of the CCP was defensible when the Charter of Rights and Freedoms was new, few can say that 25 years later, the Charter needs testing at the taxpayer's expense. In an interview in 2005, excerpted in *Rescuing Canada's Right,* former federal justice minister John Crosbie, who renewed funding for the CCP 20 years earlier, agreed that the time for the program "is long past. . . . If the civil rights advocates want to, let them pay for their own challenges."

In that same interview Crosbie also made a more disturbing comment. He affirmed that the Progressive Conservative government renewed the CCP in 1985 because of "political correctness. If we had discontinued the program we would have received very bad publicity . . . reinforcing our image as not being 'with it' on social issues." And therein lies the most compelling reason to cancel the CCP. The program survived all these years not on its merits as a program, but as part of a larger agenda of left liberal special interest politics.

How did this agenda come about, and how did the CCP fit into it? For the answer, we must cast our eyes back to 1968, when newly elected prime minister

---

Tasha Kheiriddin, "Why the Government Was Right to Cancel the Court Challenges Program" *Political Opinion Magazine*, Feb. 2007. Copyright © Institute for Research on Public Policy, 2007.

Pierre Elliott Trudeau began shaping what he called the Just Society. His project was profoundly interventionist, seeking to use the power of government to "correct" social inequalities, whether of means, status or rights. It would ultimately culminate in the entrenchment of equality rights in the Charter some 13 years later.

In Trudeau's first term in office, however, his strategy was more subversive. It involved using the state's resources to fund external actors, chiefly special interest groups, to lobby in favour of the type of interventionist policies he wanted to implement. These lobbying efforts mobilized the public and created the impression of widespread support for his government's initiatives. The funds were disbursed mainly through the Citizenship Branch of the Secretary of State, which journalist Sandra Gwyn, writing for *Saturday Night* magazine in 1972, colourfully described as "a freespending *animateur sociale.* . . . Massive grants went out to militant native groups, tenants' associations and other putative aliens of the 1970s."

At the same time, in response to the rise of separatism in Quebec, Trudeau sought to dilute the tension between Canada's two solitudes by implementing state-funded multiculturalism. Former civil servant Bernard Ostry, who headed the Citizenship Branch at the time, confirmed that "millions of dollars were made available to the branch to ensure justice and fairness to every ethnic group that wished to preserve and celebrate its cultural heritage."

Trudeau also brought in official bilingualism, in part to reassure French Canadians outside Quebec and Anglophones inside that province that their language rights would be protected. Between 1970 and 1982 official language minority groups received $76 million in funding from the federal government; not surprisingly, during that time the number of these groups doubled, to 370. Sociologist Leslie Pal, in his seminal work *Interests of State,* chronicled how the federal cabinet authorized a new "Social Action Program" to "animate" French-Canadian minorities in "desired directions." This support was then extended to women's groups, ethnic groups, native and youth groups as well.

The CCP formed part of this state-supported interest group strategy. Trudeau initially set up the CCP in 1978 to sponsor minority language law challenges, in particular to Quebec's Bill 101. Between 1978 and 1982 it funded six cases, three in Quebec and three in Manitoba and Saskatchewan, with a total annual budget of $200,000. But with the equality provision of the Charter, section 15, coming into force in 1985, interest groups began demanding direct government funding of minority rights litigation of all kinds, not just linguistic.

Trudeau had departed the political scene, but as Crosbie pointed out, the new Progressive Conservative government wanted to be seen as "with it" on social issues. Crosbie also claimed, in a 2001 interview with Ian Brodie (now chief of staff to Prime Minister Stephen Harper), that the Tories wanted to promote a progressive agenda without creating new entitlement programs. An expanded CCP was seen to fill that need, and in 1985 the program's budget was increased to $9 million over five years.

In his book *Friends of the Court,* Brodie reported that, by 1989, 15 percent of that budget was being used for "community outreach" to encourage litigation and in some cases even create new interest groups. Furthermore the program was spending $1,421 per application on "public information," more than 10 times what it spent deciding which application to fund. Yet when the CCP came up for renewal again in 1989, the Progressive Conservatives increased its budget to $12 million over five years, and outsourced its management to the Human Rights Centre of the University of Ottawa.

What did taxpayers get for their money? In its first decade, the CCP funded equality rights challenges by a variety of groups, including LEAF (the Women's Legal Education and Action Fund), the Charter Committee on Poverty Issues, Equality for Gays and Lesbians Everywhere (EGALE), the Canadian Prisoners' Rights Network, the Canadian Committee on Refugees and the Equality Rights Committee of the Canadian Ethnocultural Council. Of the 24 equality rights judgments the Supreme Court handed down between 1984 and 1993, 9 had a party or intervenor that was funded by the CCP, and most of these were successful.

While these groups battled for different causes, they all had one thing in common: they sought to advance the doctrine of substantive equality. Unlike formal equality, which requires that the law treat all persons equally, substantive equality posits that to treat people equally, the law must actually treat some people differently. This "different but equal treatment" is said to compensate for discrimination suffered as a result of belonging to a "disadvantaged group," such as women, Aboriginal people, immigrants, gays and lesbians, etc.

The CCP was instrumental in advancing the concept of substantive equality through its funding of two LEAF-led cases, *Andrews v. Law Society of British Columbia* and *Schacter v. Canada.* Ironically, in both cases the plaintiffs were white males. In *Andrews,* a British lawyer argued that the B.C. Law Society's refusal to admit him because he wasn't a Canadian citizen was discriminatory; being a "non-citizen" made him part of a disadvantaged group. In *Schacter,* an adoptive father sought the same paternity leave benefits as a natural father, claiming that adoptive parents should be treated the same as parents with biological children.

In both cases, the plaintiffs were successful, entrenching the doctrine of substantive equality in Canadian jurisprudence. The cases also advanced what is known as "political disadvantage theory," which advocates that minority groups whose interests are excluded from the executive or legislative branches of government can resort to the courts to defend those interests. It implies an ever-growing range of "discrete and insular minorities," to quote former Canadian Supreme Court Justice Bertha Wilson in *Andrews.* These minorities may not have been envisaged by the framers of the Charter, but if they are analogous to other minorities that do enjoy protection, the argument goes, they should be given the same rights. This line of reasoning led to the establishment of the "reading-in" doctrine in *Schacter,* which established that courts could read in (i.e., rewrite) Charter provisions to protect this growing list of disadvantaged minorities. Possibly the most controversial use of this doctrine was to later read in sexual orientation as a prohibited ground of discrimination under section 15, as analogous to race, sex, religion or age.

By funding these types of cases, the CCP had a profound impact on the courts' interpretation of section 15. The *Andrews* decision laid the foundation for more successful challenges down the road involving freedom of speech, abortion, gay rights, prisoners' voting rights and pornography. Politically speaking, in most of these cases, the causes advanced were "progressive" or of a left-liberal persuasion. They furthered Trudeau's Just Society project, with the state as social engineer, constantly deploying its power and resources to accommodate differences and "correct" inequalities.

Not surprisingly, whether a litigant received funding from the CCP depended on where he or she stood on the political spectrum. In *The Charter Revolution and the Court Party,* authors Ted Morton and Rainer Knopff concluded, "The CCP has been a funding bonanza for LEAF and other equality seeking groups on the left." In some cases, CCP grants appear to have had little to do with financial need and much to do with connections and ideology. For example, in the late 1980s, Toronto lawyer Beth Symes received a CCP grant to challenge the fact that she couldn't deduct the expenses for her nanny. At the time, Symes was a practising lawyer and was one of the founders of LEAF.

Litigants who were not bent on advancing the doctrine of substantive equality or other left-liberal views were not as warmly received by the CCP. Morton and Knopff reported, "Nonfeminist groups such as REAL Women and Kids First saw their applications for litigation funding either ignored or rejected." A group of Native elders in British Columbia who wished to challenge the constitutionality of the Nisga'a agreement were refused funding as well; their lawyer, John Weston, ended up setting up an autonomous foundation to fund their case. In 1992, as part of a general package of restraint measures, the Progressive Conservative government terminated the CCP. The outcry was immediate. Interest groups, together with powerful supporters including Supreme Court Justice Wilson and Max Yalden, Chief Commissioner of the Canadian Human Rights Commission, lobbied for the CCP's reinstatement and made it an election issue in the 1993 federal campaign. Liberal leader Jean Chrétien vowed to reestablish the program, and Prime Minister Kim Campbell softened her position and promised to create a new Charter Law Development Fund. A year after sweeping to power in 1993, the Liberals inaugurated a new CCP with annual funding of $2.75 million. After 1997, according to Brodie, the beneficiaries of the CCP were also given a direct role in the management of the program.

Overall, the effect of the CCP has been to privilege some litigants over others, and advance those litigants' particular view of equality in the courts. It has helped further a statist political agenda by institutionalizing it in the form of government-sponsored interest group litigation. The 2006 decision to scrap the

CCP is thus justifiable and long overdue. It is completely inappropriate for government to favour one side of the debate on the Charter by funding it to the exclusion of other voices. While groups should be able to use all the levers at their disposal, including the courts, to make their case for social change, no group has the right to do so at taxpayers' expense.

Worse yet, by entrenching substantive equality as a doctrine in our courts, CCP-funded cases have perversely made it an advantage to be disadvantaged. As long as one remains a member of a disadvantaged group, one is entitled to use the resources of the state to improve one's position. Instead of encouraging individuals to advance themselves on their merits, this type of politics fractures society into rent-seeking groups, which look to the state to correct perceived inequalities. This increases people's dependence on government, and expands the power of the state in the life of the citizen. The result is not a more equal society, just one with a different set of rules as to how you get ahead: who can best curry favour with bureaucrats doling out government grants, who has the better lawyer to assert their "disadvantaged group" status, who has the better lobbyist to pressure the state to do its bidding.

In sum, if the government rigs the game to give some a greater say in the legal debate, it is not furthering equality—it is just creating a new inequality. For all these reasons, Canadians are better off without the CCP, and the government should hold firm in its decision to cancel the program.

POSTSCRIPT

Both critics and supporters of the Court Challenges Program acknowledge that the Charter of Rights and Freedoms is not a self-enforcing document. Without judicial review and litigation, the Charter would have little effective impact. Thus, supporters of the Court Challenges Program argue that government funding of litigation is not to be feared but to be seen as a healthy antidote to some of the weaknesses of democracy. Such programs give voice to those individuals and causes that might otherwise not be heard and therefore contribute to the achievement of a more substantive form of equality within society. For an argument along these lines, see Gregory Hein, "Interest Group Litigation and Canadian Democracy," *Choices,* 6(2) (March 2000), pp. 3–31.

However, critics of the Court Challenges Program do not see it necessarily as a sign of a healthy democracy. Ian Brodie has argued that the Court Challenges Program was more of a sign of an "embedded state" in which the distinction between "public" and "private" break down. By deciding who to fund, the government can often choose to favour those groups that reflect its own agenda while denying funding to those that do not. For a more extensive treatment of Brodie's concerns about the Court Challenges program, see Ian Brodie, "Interest Group Litigation and the Embedded State: Canada's Court Challenges Program," *Canadian Journal of Political Science,* XXXIV, no. 2 (June 2000), pp. 357–376, and Ian Brodie, "The Court Challenges Program," *Fraser Forum* (October 2002), pp. 15–16. Further criticisms of the Court Challenges Program can be found in Barry Cooper, "Some Implications of the Embedded State in Canada," in Alain Cairns, Philip Resnick, and Gerald Kernerman, eds., *Insiders and Outsiders: Alan Cairns and the Reshaping of Canadian Citizenship* (Vancouver: University of British Columbia Press, 2005), and Robert I. Martin, *Most Dangerous Branch: How the Supreme Court Has Undermined Our Law and Our Democracy,* (Montreal and Kingston: McGill-Queen's University Press, 2003).

An important element in the defence of the Court Challenges Program, as reflected in the second reading in this issue, is the concept of "substantive equality." According to this concept, implementation of the goal of equality is not achieved simply through the neutral application of formal rules of law. A focus on formal legal equality may result in outcomes that are unbalanced and unfair. Therefore, for the concept of equality to have real substance, it is necessary for the law and public policies to take into account the different social and political situations of specific groups. Supporters claim that the Court Challenges Program does this by assisting those who may not have adequate resources to challenge discriminatory laws. Without such assistance, genuine or "substantive" equality will not be achieved. For a discussion of the importance of this concept to the development of the women's rights movement in Canada, including the role of the Court Challenges Program, see chapter two, "The Path to Substantive Equality," in Christopher Manfredi, *Feminist*

Activism in the Supreme Court: Legal Mobilization and the Women's Legal Education and Action Fund (Vancouver: University of British Columbia Press, 2000). This study is of particular interest since the Women's Legal Education and Action Fund (LEAF) has been one of the principal beneficiaries of the Court Challenges Program. For further discussion of the problems that arise when people have differential access to the justice system, see Lynn Smith, "Have the Equality Rights Made Any Difference?" in Philip Bryden, Steve Davis, and John Russell, eds., *Protecting Rights and Freedoms: Essays on the Charter's Place in Canada's Political, Legal, and Intellectual Life* (Toronto: University of Toronto Press, 1994).

For further material in defence of the Court Challenges Program, see Kathleen Ruff, "Final Appear," *Canadian Forum,* 17 (June 1992), p. 14 and the websites "Save Court Challenges" at http://www.fafia-afai.org/en/node/365 and "Save the Court Challenges Program of Canada" at http://www.savecourtchallenges.ca. The official website of the Court Challenges Program is http://www.ccppcj.ca.

Is Ethnic Diversity an Inherent Cause of Conflict?

✔ **YES**

BARBARA HARFF AND TED ROBERT GURR, *Ethnic Conflict in World Politics* (Boulder: Westview Press, 2004): 1–17

✘ **NO**

JOHN MUELLER, "The Banality of 'Ethnic War,'" *International Security*, 25, no. 1 (Summer 2000): 42–70

In the wake of the Cold War, the dissolution of former communist regimes and the decline of ideological polarization gave way to the emergence of ethnic divisions as important political identifiers in many parts of the world. The eruption of conflict in the former Yugoslavia was the first in a series of very serious internal struggles that arose in the 1990s. In the developing world, a number of similarly vicious civil wars likewise stole the headlines. Ethnic divisions led to the separation of Eritrea from Ethiopia. In the wake of the 1991 Gulf War, Kurdish nationalists set up a functionally independent authority in northern Iraq. In Somalia, the state dissolved into factional and clan-based fighting. Elsewhere, the resurgence of ethnic awareness in the politics similarly seemed to suggest that Cold War proxies and ideological conflicts would give way instead to conflicts based on deep-seated identities. One particularly influential scholar of ethnic awareness, Benedict Anderson, argued that nationalism was a more persistent cultural form than ideological conflicts, that nations formed "imagined communities" which reinforced political boundaries as overriding cognitive tropes.

The largely unforeseen descent of Rwanda into civil conflict and genocide in mid-1994 brought particular attention to the relevance of ethnic conflict in the developing world. When Rwandan President Habyarimana's plane was shot down over the capital city of Kigali on April 9, 1994, the incident sparked a well-organized frenzy of violence aimed at eliminating an entire ethnic group: the minority Tutsi population of Rwanda. Over the ensuing 100 days, an estimated 800 000 Rwandans, from both the Tutsi minority and the Hutu majority, were killed in one of the most egregious acts of genocide in world history. In the midst of the fighting, the small United Nations–mandated peacekeeping force, the United Nations Assistance Mission in Rwanda (UNAMIR), was dismantled and reduced to a minimal detachment, unable to intervene as it was forced to bear witness to an orgy of killing. The genocide came to an end with the victory of rebel forces in July 1994 but refugee flows and contagion effects were felt in neighbouring Congo and elsewhere for several years afterward. The incident led to widespread concern over the inaction of the international community to respond to a human tragedy.

In the wake of the Rwandan genocide, many called for increased attention to ethnic tensions in the developing world. One common assertion was that the United Nations was not fully informed of the facts on the ground in Rwanda in the run-up to the conflict. UNAMIR had been poorly briefed on the political situation in Rwanda and the events unfolding in Rwanda took some time to be fully understood by outside observers. A large group of scholars led the call for systematic documentation of pending ethnic conflicts and minorities at risk of targeting for ethnic cleansing or genocide. The widespread view that a stronger United Nations intervention might well have contained the genocide motivated many to call for a more pre-emptive strategy for dealing with potential ethnic conflicts, and in many ways motivated a more active intervention in the case of Kosovo (1998–99).

The events of September 11, 2001 and ensuing US interventions in Afghanistan and Iraq, as well as the general subsiding of major ethnically based conflicts throughout the developing world, have diverted attention away from internal ethnic discord. Nonetheless, ethnic divisions continue to motivate widespread conflict in several areas. Despite promising signs of the renunciation of hostilities between the Northern Arab–dominated government of Sudan and Southern-based African rebels, war has persisted and worsened between the government and the black Africans of Darfur. Afghanistan has likewise descended into a civil conflict that could boil down to an ethnic divide between the majority Pashtun and minority populations. Elsewhere, long-running ethnic and religious rivalries threaten internal conflict or loom beneath the surface in many states, such as Burma, Nigeria, Lebanon, and Sri Lanka. Initial nationalist resistance to the American invasion and occupation of Iraq in 2003 has likewise devolved into a civil conflict pitting the large populations of Kurds, Arab Sunni, and Arab Shi'i against one another.

However widespread the phenomenon of ethnic conflict appears, scholars are by no means united in their assessment of the concept. Some point to the deep-seated and persistent nature of ethnic awareness as a particularly salient feature of division in developing societies, prone to prompt civil conflict. Others argue that ethnic awareness is little more than a convenient tool used by entrepreneurial leaders and local criminals for their own ends. In the first essay, Barbara Harff and Ted Robert Gurr, two scholars who have taken a central role in identifying the factors behind ethnic conflict, make the case for its persistence in developing areas. In the second essay, John Mueller argues instead that ethnic conflict is overstated, that in fact most ethnic conflicts, such as the genocide in Rwanda, are reflective not of widespread hatreds endemic to one ethnic group or another but of the ambitious and self-aggrandizing behaviour of small groups of criminals and thugs.

✔ **YES**
Ethnic Conflict in World Politics
BARBARA HARFF AND TED ROBERT GURR

Protracted conflicts over the rights and demands of ethnic and religious groups have caused more misery and loss of human life than has any other type of local, regional and international conflict since the end of World War II. They are also the source of most of the world's refugees. In 2002 about two-thirds of the world's 15 million international refugees were fleeing from ethnopolitical conflict and repression. At least twice as many others have been internally displaced by force and famine. At the beginning of the new millennium millions of people in impoverished countries are in need of assistance, hundreds of thousands of desperate emigrants from conflict-ridden states are knocking at the doors of Western countries, and, to make things worse, donor fatigue among rich states threatens to perpetuate inequalities and misery.

Ethnopolitcal conflicts are here to stay. Figure 1 shows that the number of countries with major ethnic wars increased steadily from a handful in the early 1950s to thirty-one countries in the early 1990s. We also know that between the

FIGURE 1

NUMBERS AND PROPORTIONS OF COUNTRIES WITH MAJOR ETHNIC WARS, 1946–2001

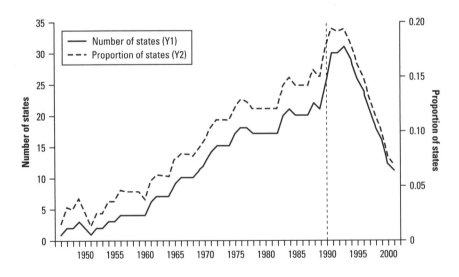

Barbara Harff and Ted Robert Gurr, *Ethnic Conflict in World Politics*, Boulder: Westview Press, 2004, 1–17. Reproduced with permission of Perseus Book Group.

mid-1950s and 1990 the magnitude of all ethnopolitical conflicts increased nearly fourfold—an astonishing increase in light of what was hoped for in the aftermath of World War II.

The Holocaust should have enlightened us about what ethnic and religious hatred can do when used by unscrupulous leaders armed with exclusionary ideologies. Many people hoped that with the end of colonialism we could look forward to a better world in which nation-states would guarantee and protect the basic freedoms of their peoples. When the United Nations came into existence, were we wrong to believe that a new world order would emerge, one in which minimum standards of global justice would be observed and violators punished? Is it still possible that a civil society will emerge in which citizens eschew narrow ethnic interests in favor of global issues?

Instead we have witnessed more genocides and mass slaughters, an increase in ethnic consciousness leading to deadly ethnic conflicts, and religious fanaticism justifying the killing of innocent civilians in faraway lands. Some progress has been made to check ethnic wars since the mid-1990s, but we badly need more innovative ideas about how to fight the scourges that plague mankind. To top it off, the international political will to act has been waning in the wake of Somalia, Bosnia, Rwanda, Liberia, Burundi, the Democratic Republic of Congo, and other conflicts that need international attention. There is also the risk that, in the aftermath of the September 11 terrorist attacks on the World Trade Center in New York, the Western "war on terrorism" will divert international attention away from enduring problems.

[...]

DEFINING AND MAPPING THE WORLD OF ETHNIC GROUPS

Ethnic groups, like the Kurds, Miskitos of Central America, and the Turks in Germany are "psychological communities" whose members share a persisting sense of common interest and identity that is based on some combination of shared historical experience and valued cultural traits—beliefs, language, ways of life, a common homeland. They are often called **identity groups**. A few, like the Koreans and the Icelanders, have their own internationally recognized state or states. Most, however, do not have such recognition, and they must protect their identity and interests within existing states.

Some religious groups resemble ethnic groups insofar as they have a strong sense of identity based on culture, belief, and a shared history of discrimination. Examples are Jews and the various sects of Shi'i Islam. Politically active religious groups, such as offshoots of the Muslim Brotherhood, are motivated by grievances similar to ethnic groups.

Many ethnic groups coexist amicably with others within the boundaries of established states. The Swedish minority in Finland, for example, has its own cultural and local political institutions, which are guaranteed by a 1921 international agreement between Sweden and Finland. For eighty years the Swedish minority has had no serious disputes with the Finnish people or government. Since the 1960s the Netherlands has welcomed many immigrants from the Third World with relatively little of the social tension or **discrimination** aimed at immigrants in Britain, France, and Germany. Even in these tolerant countries the explosive growth of asylum seekers has led to some antiforeign political movements and xenophobic attacks.

If peaceful relations prevail among peoples for a long time, their separate identities may eventually weaken. For example, the Irish-Americans were a distinctive minority in mid-nineteenth-century North America because of their immigrant origins, their concentration in poor neighborhoods and low-status occupations, and the deep-rooted prejudice most Anglo-Americans had toward them. After a century of upward mobility and political incorporation, the Irish descent has little political or economic significance in Canada or the United States, although many Irish-Americans still honor their cultural origins.

The ethnic groups whose status is of greatest concern in international politics today are those that are the targets of discrimination and that have organized to take political action to promote or defend their interests. A recent study, directed by the second author, surveys politically active national peoples and ethnic minorities throughout the world. As of 2001, the project has identified and profile 275 sizable groups that have been targets of discrimination or are organized for political assertiveness or both.[1] Most larger countries have at least one such ethnic group, and in a few countries like South Africa and Bolivia, they comprise half of more of the population. Taken together the groups involve more than 1 billion people, or a sixth of the world's population. Figure 2 shows how these groups were distributed among the regions of the world in 2001. When the Soviet Union dissolved into fifteen independent republics at the end of 1991, the political demands of **ethnonationalists** like the Latvians, Ukrainians, and Armenians were met. Since then, however, at least thirty additional ethnic groups in the new republics have made new political demands.

The Minorities at Risk survey shows that about 80 percent of the politically active ethnic groups in the 1990s were disadvantaged because of historical or contemporary discrimination. Forty percent of these groups (111 out of 275) surveyed face discriminatory policies and practices harmful to their material well-being. For example, almost all indigenous peoples in the Americas have high infant mortality rates due in part to limited pre- and post-natal health care; Tamil youth in Sri Lanka have long been discriminated against by university admission policies that favor the majority Sinhalese. The survey also identified 135 minorities subjected to contemporary political discrimination. For example, Turkish governments have repeatedly banned and restricted political parties that sought to represent Kurdish interests; in Brazil people of African descent make up more than 40 percent of the country's population but hold less than 5 percent of seats in the national congress. Cultural restrictions also have been imposed on at least

FIGURE 2
POLITICALLY ACTIVE ETHNIC GROUPS BY REGION, 2001

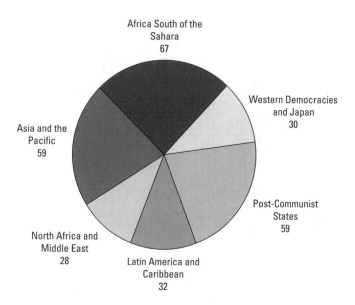

116 minorities. Muslim girls attending French secondary schools have been expelled for wearing head scarves; principals of Hungarian-language schools in Slovakia have been dismissed for not speaking Slovak at Hungarian teachers' meetings. Such restrictions may seem petty but symbolically their effects can be a painful and enduring reminder that the dominant society disvalues a minority's culture.

Ethnic groups that are treated unequally resent and usually attempt to improve their condition. Three-quarters of the groups in the survey were politically active in the 1990s. They did not necessarily use violence, however. On the contrary, most ethnic groups with a political agenda use the strategies and tactics of interest groups and social movements, especially if they live in democratic states. Figure 3 shows the highest level of political action among minorities in 1995. One-quarter were politically inactive (some of them had a history of intense activism), half were mobilizing for or carrying out political action, and only one-quarter used violent strategies of small-scale rebellion (including terrorism) or large-scale rebellion. The latter include the most serious and enduring of all conflicts within states, including ethnic wars between Hutus and Tutsis in Burundi and Rwanda, civil wars by southerners in Sudan and Muslim Kashmiris in India, and wars of independence by Kurds in Turkey and Iraq and by Palestinians in Gaza and the West Bank.

FIGURE 3

STRATEGIES OF POLITICAL ACTION USED BY ETHNOPOLITICAL MINORITIES IN 1995

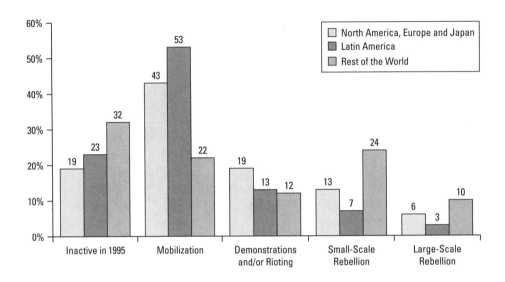

Figure 13.3 also shows the relative frequency of different kinds of political action among world regions. The highest level of mobilization in 1995 was in Latin America—mainly among indigenous peoples. Ethnic rebellions were uncommon in Europe and the Americas and when they did occur were mainly terrorist campaigns. Rebellions were much more numerous in Africa, Asia, and the Middle East. [...]

STATES OR PEOPLES?

Historically, ethnic groups, nations, states, empires, and other forms of large-scale social organization—for example, Islam and Christendom—have coexisted, but since the seventeenth century the dominant form of social organization has been the **state system**—the organization of the world's people into a system of independent and territorial states, some of which controlled overseas colonial empires.

Despite attempts to change the existing world order by insisting that the state was obsolete, as Marxists proclaimed, the state remains the key actor in international relations. Key, because the state at the very minimum controls the principle means of coercion. Ethnic groups rarely are equal in terms of power, legitimacy, or economic resources. But it is wrong to suggest that the state is a single monolithic enterprise. Instead, we may want to think of the state as a recognized territorial entity in flux. It is one thing to think of England as an established state since the Middle Ages, yet Germany in something like its present form has existed only since 1870. The new states that emerged in the Middle East, Asia, and Africa following the demise of empires were often just creations of the former colonizers, endowed with neither historical nor cultural continuity, nor boundaries that recognized the living space of ethnic groups. Thus for example, we have states such as Burundi and Rwanda in both of which a Tutsi minority rules a Hutu majority, which led to major conflicts and postindependence genocidal killings in both countries.

Some would argue that certain states should have no independent existence, either because the notion of territory was not part of their people's culture or because they would be better off within the boundaries of established states. Indeed, one could ask how viable, necessary, or rational is the division of the Arabian peninsula into many sheikdoms, some of which have emerged as independent states only since the 1960s. But, what are the alternatives? In tribal communities, local loyalties were very well developed, but rarely extended beyond the narrow boundaries of family or clan, thus leaving local communities at the mercy of would-be conquerors and usurpers. Necessity may have been the force that unified some warring tribes, laws and coercion are the means that have kept them together.

[...]

On the one side, states act independently of their constituent parts, such as peoples and institutions. After all, we talk about the economic viability or capabilities of states, not of the people who reside within the state. Today most states control capital through either public ownership or state-owned enterprises. But some theorists will see the state as passive, reacting mainly to pressures emanating from society. Though scholars disagree on the extent of cooperation and conflict between the state and society, it is still a fact that the state is a legally recognized sovereign entity in international law, endowed with rights and obligations vis-à-vis other states, groups, and its own citizens. Whatever the reasons that give birth to specific states, the nation-state is today the primary actor in international relations. It is the state that defines, provides, and controls the public good, through regulation and institutions. It is the state that enforces the rules through coercion and punishment.

Let us apply some of these arguments to the historical situation of the Kurds, whose situation is symptomatic of many other **ethnonationalists**. After the demise of the Ottoman Empire following World War I, they were the largest ethnic group within the former empire without a state of their own. Instead, Kurds came to live within five other states, the largest segment of them now citizens of the new Republic of Turkey. Ever since, the Turkish government has tried through incentives, coercion, discrimination, and punishment to undermine Kurdish ethnic consciousness, hoping to deter any attempts to secede. Here the state has become omnipotent, using all means at its disposal to subdue Kurdish national aspirations.

An essential question is whether or not a people have rights to a territory on which they resided for many centuries. International law today recognizes that it is inadmissible to acquire territory by waging an aggressive war, but the reality is somewhat different. International law, often invoked but seldom enforced, was used to bolster the legality of the Gulf War in 1990, ostensibly to free Kuwait from the Iraqi occupation, as well as U.S. intervention in Panama and Vietnam. Israel, invoking its defensive posture in the 1967 war, holds on to territory inhabited by Palestinians for centuries. The Abkhaz in Georgia have technically won an independence war, but are not recognized by the international community of nation-states. What does this mean for the rights of groups vis-à-vis states? It means that sometimes group rights are recognized by individual states and the international community and sometimes, depending on various power constellations, they are not. However, international law can provide the justification or the means to establish claims to specific territory. Let us look briefly at the state as arbiter, problem-solving agent, or restrictor or denier of the rights of collectivities.

Indeed, few states are able to unite a multitude of **ethnies** into a harmonious unit. Although long-established liberal democracies probably are more successful than autocracies in doing so, problems persist. Recall the situation of African-Americans prior to the Civil Rights movement and current issues ranging from outright discrimination to disenfranchisement. Consider that Native Americans are a people organized into a number of self-governing segments or "nations" within the greater American nation yet are economically and politically dependent on the United States.

One of the more heretical thoughts that comes to mind is whether the institutionalized state has a future, given the many ethnic groups that clamor for independence. The answer has to be yes, because what is it that these ethnic groups demand? They seek the right to govern their own territory, which they hope will become a sovereign, internationally recognized state. What this suggests is that the current international system may fragment into hundreds of mini-states unless ethnic demands can be satisfied within existing states. In fact more than a dozen ethnic wars were settled in the 1990s by granting autonomy to ethnonationalists within existing states. Successful settlements like these depend on the political system. Democracies are better able to accommodate ethnic demands than autocracies. But it is also true that in newly emerging democracies, ethnic demands may exceed the capacity of state structures, thus leading to failure of existing states.

The ascendance and expansion of the state system has meant that states are parties to most deadly conflicts: wars between states, civil wars within states, and **genocides** and political mass murders by states. But here we find a different phenomenon at work. States wage war, but people decide to make war. Here the collective can triumph over state structures. The collective will as exemplified by prevailing ideologies and political movements within the state system have dramatically influenced ethnic conflict. In the 1920s and 1930s, anti-Semitic doctrines in Germany and other European countries promoted ethnic polarization. They competed with Communist doctrine in the Soviet Union, which emphasized the common interests of all Soviet peoples and minimized the significance of ethnic and nationalist identities. In the 1940s and 1950s anti-colonialism emerged as a major form of resistance against European domination in Asia and Africa. With the help of liberation ideologies, nationalists were able to unite diverse ethnic groups in their efforts to replace colonial rule by European powers with their own independent states. And they succeeded beyond what was expected. By the early 1960s almost all European-ruled colonial territories had gained independence and become members of the state system. But the success came at a cost as tribal and ethnic consciousness soon re-emerged in a number of states. Congo immediately after its independence from Belgium in 1970 and Nigeria a decade later experienced major ethnic wars. More recently we have seen a new kind of resistance to the state system that has affected every world region except Latin America: It is an accelerating wave of self-determination movements.

But there are other trends. At times throughout the twentieth century, ethnic peoples have coalesced across boundaries to join in common causes—for example, by joining pan-Islamic, **pan-Arab**, and **indigenous peoples'** movements. In the Arab world such movements have been short-lived and have been characterized by constantly shifting coalitions. Despite paying lip service to equality of economic status, a shared religion, and the brotherhood of a common ancestry, Arabs have continued to fight fellow Arabs.

But rarely has a common ethnic or religious background been sufficient to cause peoples to subordinate the interests of states to a greater transnational identity or cause, even a limited one. This is especially true for peoples of countries with long-established boundaries who have developed identities beyond their immediate tribes and clans.

At present we witness two competing trends in human organization. At one extreme, we see a reemergence of xenophobia in long-established countries—for example, the increase in exclusive ethnic identity that motivates antiforeign excesses in Germany, France, and Great Britain. No less extreme are movements that demand ethnic purity in formerly heterogeneous federations, such as Serbian nationalism in the former Yugoslavia. At the other end of the continuum are oppressive leaders who defend existing boundaries at all costs, despite historically justified claims by national peoples, such as Palestinians in the Middle East and Kurds in Iraq, for internal autonomy or independence. Ironically, the new elites of former Asian and African colonies share with Saddam Hussein a willingness to fight to maintain existing boundaries and states, despite arbitrarily drawn borders that accommodated European interests but ignored demographic and cultural realities.

The End of the Cold War

The Cold War between the Soviet bloc and the U.S.-led Western alliance created, for better or worse, a sense of stability among most of the world population. Policymakers' calculations concerning conflict outcomes could be made with greater confidence in a more rigidly ordered world. The dissolution of the global system from a loose, bipolar world into an ethnically fragmented multipolar system left in its wake a greater sense of insecurity among the leaders of the established states. This is what U.S. President Bill Clinton alluded to when he told a journalist, "I even made a crack the other day ... 'Gosh, I miss the Cold War.'" How does one deal with hostile warlords in Somalia and respond to ethnic and nationalist unrest in the Soviet successor states? Finding a workable framework for this new era and defining the role of the United States, Clinton added, "could take years."[2] By the end of Clinton administration, no clear framework or consistent set of policies had emerged, though the administration had shifted toward more proactive engagement.

But events do not wait for policymakers to devise new frameworks. With the collapse of Soviet hegemony at the end of the Cold War, the citizens of the former Soviet Union and Eastern Europe were freed to act upon communal rivalries with a vengeance. The demise of communism in the former Soviet Union left a political and ideological vacuum that is only gradually being filled. It was ideology that bound historically hostile peoples together; now old rivalries have reemerged, and neighbors have again become antagonists fighting for power, status, and control of adjacent territories. Communist citizens' place in society was predictable, and their economic welfare was guaranteed at a basic level. Communism in its ideal form also instilled a sense of collective responsibility and solidarity that over came more parochial identities. The transformation of socialist societies into predatory capitalist societies has led to a sense of alienation and isolation and an increased emphasis on narrow group interests and self-interests. This increased sense of isolation has been circumvented by a heightened ethnic awareness and, in some states, a growth in intolerance toward members of other groups.

A decade after the end of the Cold War, the ethnic landscape of post-socialist states is remarkably diverse. The Russian Federation has been widely and justly criticized for fighting a dirty war against rebels in the breakaway republic of Chechnya. But during the 1990s it also successfully negotiated autonomy agreements with Tatarstan, Bashkiria, and some forty other regions of the Russian Federation, thus defusing a number of potentially violent conflicts. A new sense of common interest and identity is being built among most of the peoples of Russia. In East Central Europe, the civil wars that broke up the Yugoslav Federation contrast sharply with Czechoslovakia where ethnic conflict between the Czech and Slovak republics ended peacefully in a "velvet divorce" in 1993. Nationalist governments in Romania and Slovakia cracked down on the restive Hungarian minorities in the early 1990s, but the nationalists were ousted in democratic elections in the late 1990s and Hungarian politicians joined new coalition governments. And the new democratic government of Bulgaria, whose Communist regime had perse-cuted the country's large Turkish Muslim minority, granted the Turks full cultural, economic, and political rights. The Roma (gypsies) are a worrisome exception to these trends toward ethnic tolerance. They are disliked and discriminated against throughout Europe, East, and West.

CONTEMPORARY EXAMPLES OF ETHNOPOLITICAL CONFLICT

Since the 1960s increasing numbers of ethnic groups have begun to demand more rights and recognition, demands that are now recognized as the major source of domestic and international conflict in the post–Cold War world. The protagonists in the most intense ethnic conflicts want to establish their **autonomy** or indepen-dence, as is the case with many Kurds. Other ethnic conflicts arise from efforts by subordinate groups to improve their status within the existing boundaries of a state rather than to secede from it. For example, most black South Africans wanted—and gained—majority control of state power. Turkish and other recent immigrants to Germany worried about their security, seek greater economic opportunities, and hope to become citizens. Native peoples in the Americas want to protect what is left of their traditional lands and cultures from the corrosive influences of modern society. Here we consider some implications of both kinds of ethnic conflict.

The **civil wars** accompanying the dissolution of Yugoslavia into five new states show that subject people's demands for autonomy often escalate into warfare. After Slovenia, Croatia, and Bosnia declared independence in summer 1991, Serbia—the dominant partner in the old Yugoslavian Federation—tried to reestab-lish its **hegemony** by promoting uprisings by Serbian **minorities** in the latter two states. These Serbs justified their actions by recounting Croat atrocities against Serbs during World War II. They devised brutal and often deadly policies called **ethnic cleansing,** which involved the murder or forced removal of Croatians, Bosnian Muslims, and other minorities from areas in which Serbs lived and prompted hundreds of thousands of refugees to flee to surrounding countries. In Serbia proper the government and local activists severely restricted the activities of Albanian and Hungarian minorities.

One of the longest modern civil wars was waged by the people of the Ethiopian provinces of Eritrea, who supported a war of independence that lasted from the early 1960s until 1991. The Eritrean nationalists received some diplomatic and military support from Middle Eastern states such as Egypt, whereas in the first decade of conflict the imperial Ethiopian government relied heavily on military assistance from the United States. Even the military-led **revolution** that overthrew Emperor Haile Selassie in 1974 did not end ethnic conflict. Instead, the new Marxist military leaders of Ethiopia sought and received support from the Soviet Union to enable them to continue the war against Eritrea. By the end of the 1970s many other ethnic groups in Ethiopia were stimulated into rebellion by the Eritreans, Tigreans, Oromo, and others that culminated in the rebels' triumphal capture of the Ethiopian capital, Addis Ababa, in May 1991.

Unlike the situation in Yugoslavia, there was no serious international effort to check the Ethiopian civil war. No major power recognized Eritrea as an independent state; international organizations regarded the conflict as an internal matter, and there was no media-inspired publicity of atrocities that might have prompted greater action. Only when famine threatened the region did the Ethiopian government allow humanitarian assistance but then prevented distribution of the aid in rebel-held areas.

Following thirty years of warfare, the moderate policies of the new revolutionary government allowed for a peaceful reconciliation. The government made and kept a commitment to hold referendums in 1993 to set up autonomous regional governments or, in the case of Eritrea, to allow full independence. The Eritrean referendum in April 1993 resulted in a 99.8 percent vote in favor of independence. Eritrean independence was accepted by the Ethiopian government, and the new state immediately received diplomatic recognition from the United States and many other countries.

But new sources of ethnic tension soon cropped up. Some Eritreans living in the Ethiopian capital were forced to leave the country, with retaliatory threats by Eritreans to expel Ethiopians. Political and economic tensions escalated until May 1998, when the two countries began a deadly two-year war over some scraps of disputed territory. The Eritrea-Ethiopia conflict, like that between Muslims and Hindus in the Indian subcontinent, shows that separation is not a perfect solution for ethnic tensions because it may lead to future conflicts within and between states.

[...]

Enduring Conflicts, Changing International Responses

We cannot entirely blame the explosion of ethnic conflict in the early 1990s on the end of the Cold War. Figure 13.1 shows clearly that the extent of conflicts worldwide between ethnic groups and states increased steadily from 1950 to 1989, before the Cold War ended. Thus we need to identify other factors that contributed to that explosion. We begin with three Third World examples, which may offer some clues to why some ethnic conflicts were neither affected by nor indirect by-products of Cold War confrontations.

In the 1970s the newly independent African states of Uganda and Equatorial Guinea experienced intense ethnopolitical conflict that had little relationship to the tensions produced by the Cold War. Dictators Macias Nguma of Equatorial Guinea (1968–1979) and Idi Amin of Uganda (1971–1979) each sought to consolidate power by killing thousands of their ethnic and political rivals. These horrifying events elicited no substantive response from the United Nations and few condemnations from individual states. Amin and Macias were virtually free to kill people they defined as enemies, in part because their countries were of little consequence to either the United States or the Soviet Union.

The third case was Rwanda, in which during a genocide in 1994 800,000 to 1 million Tutsis and moderate Hutus perished. When Tutsi exiles of the Rwandan Patriotic Front launched a major invasion from bases in Uganda in 1993, Hutu armies and militias responded with counterattacks. Intermittent negotiations led to the Arusha Accords, but the mobilization of Hutu militias continued. In neighboring Burundi, massacres following a 1993 coup led to a massive exodus of some 342,000 refugees to Rwanda. Militant Rwandan Hutus sought to undermine the Arusha Accords. They probably arranged the downing of the aircraft that carried the presidents of Rwanda and Burundi, Juvenal Habyarimana and Cyprien Ntaryamira, back from peace talks in Tanzania on April 6, 1994. This signaled the beginning of a killing spree in which Belgian peacekeepers and the moderate Rwandan prime minister, Agathe Uwilingiyimana, were among the first to die. Ethnic Tutsis were the primary targets. In the next 100 days, some 800,000 people were killed by marauding Hutu militias, encouraged by their leadership and hate propaganda. In July 1994, Tutsi rebels seized the capital, declared victory, and named a Hutu president. At the end of July Tanzania recognized the new government and Western powers promised aid. But killings continued in Hutu-dominated refugee camps in Zaire.

What these three cases show is that despite warnings of impending disasters, especially in Rwanda, Western powers had little or no interest in intervening. UN peacekeepers in Rwanda were poorly armed and few in number, and their mandate was to remain impartial.

Could more have been done? [...] We believe the international community has an obligation to protect the rights of minorities, beginning with protecting the most basic rights to life and security. For example, and from our point of view, the civil wars and ethnic killings in the breakaway states of former Yugoslavia could have been preempted by early and active international mediation that would have led to guaranteed independence and security for all newly emerging states in the region and to commitments from all parties to protect the rights of each state's ethnic peoples. But the international community is only gradually acquiring the legal principles, political will, and foresight to respond effectively to such conflicts.

In the three cases described above, the consequences of colonialism were a major impediment to decisive action. Colonial subjects in Africa and Asia had few rights, and many ethnic groups were trapped within artificial boundaries imposed by the departing colonial power. Faced with challenges from peoples of different cultures and kinships, most leaders of newly independent Third World countries opted to accept existing boundaries, insisting on absolute sovereignty and the inviolability of territorial borders. This insistence on the right to conduct internal affairs without outside interference gave unscrupulous dictators like Macias and Amin freedom to commit atrocities against their subjects in the name of "nation building." In Rwanda and Burundi, French favoritism, U.S. disinterest, and the UN's self-imposed limited mandate conspired to allow unscrupulous leaders to exploit ethnic tensions.

If the United Nations and the superpowers were indifferent to ethnic conflict and mass murder in peripheral states of the Third World, could regional organizations have responded? Many such deadly episodes occurred in the member states of the Organization of African Unity (OAU, founded in 1963) and the Organization of the Islamic Conference (which represents all states that have significant Muslim populations). But these organizations have usually been politically divided and have had few resources; thus, they have seldom responded to ethnic warfare and severe human rights violations in member states. The OAU, for example, was limited by its charter to mediating conflicts between African states, not within them. In 1981 and 1982, the OAU made its first effort at active peacekeeping when it sent a multinational force to help de-escalate a civil war between communal rivals in Chad; the effort was largely a failure. Partisan support for Rwandan rebels by Uganda did little to defuse the situation. After the Arusha Accords, the OAU verbally condemned international inaction, but had little more to offer than postconflict negotiations.

The impotence of Third World regional organizations combined with the reluctance of the superpowers during the Cold War era to interfere in the internal affairs of states that had little impact on global competition virtually ensured that most ethnic conflicts would remain domestic affairs, even if they led to gross violations of human rights. However, and despite Rwanda, we think that since 1991 the United Nations and the last remaining superpower, the United States, have taken more vigorous action against human rights violators and aggressive states.

[...]

The expanded role of the United States is illustrated by the dispatch of U.S. troops returning from the Gulf War to assist flood victims in Bangladesh in April and May 1991 and by the U.S.-led mobilization of reluctant states to intervene militarily in Iraq during the 1991 Gulf War in a renewed spirit of collective responsibility.

[...]

Regional organizations in the Third World are also taking a more active role in response to internal conflicts. Their leaders are involved in drafting and arguing for extensions to the human rights conventions that would allow for some exceptions to the rule of nonintervention. In the early 1990s, for example, the OAU established a new mechanism for conflict resolution and prevention that, in effect, redefined the OAU doctrine of noninterference in the affairs of member states. The OAU now monitors elections, makes periodic assessments of emerging conflict situations, and sends envoys to countries in which serious crises are brewing. For example in early 1993 the OAU sent a sixty-man observer mission to Rwanda to monitor a cease-fire between rival Hutu and Tutsi armies, but it had neither political nor military clout.

Nongovernmental organizations (NGOs) such as Amnesty International, Human Rights Watch, and the International Crisis Group also play a role by calling attention to ethnic conflict and repression. Activists have lobbied their respective governments and the United Nations to take active roles in supporting humanitarian efforts, have denounced various interventions, and have reported human rights violations to international agencies.

CONCLUSION

We have shown that the "explosion" of ethnopolitical conflicts at the end of the Cold War was, in fact, a continuation of a trend that began as early as the 1960s. It is a manifestation of the enduring tension between states that want to consolidate and expand their power and ethnic groups that want to defend and promote their collective identity and interests. The breakup of the USSR and power shifts elsewhere within the state system have opened up opportunities for ethnic groups to pursue their interests. Coincidentally, the CNN-led explosion of global news coverage has increased public awareness of the human dimensions of these conflicts and thus has contributed to pressures on policymakers to take constructive action.

Recent developments send encouraging signals to those who are concerned about checking the rise of ethnopolitcal conflict and human rights abuses such as ethnic cleansing. For the first time since World War II, the United Nations has begun to realize the vision of its founders: New leadership in the UN, notably Boutros Boutros-Ghali, past secretary general, and Kofi Annan, the current secretary general, have tried to change the role of the UN from reactive to proactive in its role as peacekeeper, intervener, arbiter, and mediator in communal and regional conflicts. A consensus is emerging that the United Nations should establish minimum standards of global security through collective decision making. Of course, the UN's ability to work for world security is directly dependent upon its ability to influence the outcome of emerging ethnic or nationalistic conflicts. However, the continuing caution apparent among most member states over enhancing UN military capabilities signals those who stir up ethnic hatred that they may face a minor roadblock, rather than a major obstacle.

[...]

NOTES

1. The study is detailed in Ted Robert Gurr, *Peoples Versus States: Minorities at Risk in the New Century* (Washington, DC: U.S. Institute of Peace Press, 2000). Current information can be accessed on the project's website, www.cidcm.umd.edu/inscr/mar or, alternatively, www.minoritiesatrisk.com. Five rules were used for identifying groups to be included in the study: (1) Only countries with populations greater than 500,000 were analyzed; (2) only groups that numbered 100,000 or exceeded 1 percent of the population of a country were included; (3) ethnic groups that live in several adjoining countries were counted separately within each country; (4) divisions within an ethnic group within a country were not counted separately—for example, Native Americans in the United States were analyzed as one group, not as three hundred plus separate tribes; (5) twenty-five minorities with political or economic advantages were included [...].

2. Quoted in "Clinton Seeks Foreign Policy Bearings in Post Cold War Fog," *Washington Post*, October 17, 1993, p. A28.

✗ NO
The Banality of "Ethnic War"
JOHN MUELLER

On December 7, 1941, as it is commonly put, "the Japanese" attacked Pearl Harbor. No one of course takes this expression literally to suggest that the entire population of Japan, or even a major portion of it, directly participated in the assault. Rather it is understood to mean that some of Japan's military forces, ordered into action by Japan's government and perhaps supported to varying degrees by the Japanese population, launched the attack. In discussions of ethnic war, by contrast, such distinctions are often missing. When we say "the Serbs" and "the Croats" are engaged in ethnic war, the implication frequently is that those two groups have descended into a sort of Hobbesian war of all against all and neighbor against neighbor.

In this article I assess the violence that took place in the former Yugoslavia and in Rwanda in the 1990s and argue that the whole concept of "ethnic warfare" may be severely misguided. Specifically, insofar as it is taken to imply a war of all against all and neighbor against neighbor—a condition in which pretty much everyone in one ethnic group becomes the ardent, dedicated, and murderous enemy of everyone in another group—ethnic war essentially does not exist. I argue instead that ethnic warfare more closely resembles nonethnic warfare, because it is waged by small groups of combatants, groups that purport to fight and kill in the name of some larger entity. Often, in fact, "ethnic war" is substantially a condition in which a mass of essentially mild, ordinary people can unwillingly and in considerable bewilderment come under the vicious and arbitrary control of small groups of armed thugs.

[...]

Because the violence in Yugoslavia and Rwanda was carried out chiefly by small, ill-disciplined, and essentially cowardly bands of thugs and bullies, policing the situation would probably have been fairly easy for almost any organized, disciplined, and sizable army. An extreme aversion to casualties and a misguided assumption that the conflicts stemmed from immutable ethnic hatreds, however, made international military intervention essentially impossible until the violence appeared to have run its course.[1]

ETHNIC WARFARE IN CROATIA AND BOSNIA

Two explanations are commonly given for the wars in the former Yugoslavia. One is that elemental and ancient ethnic hatreds had only temporarily and superficially been kept in check by communism and that with its demise, murderous nationalism erupted. This perspective has been developed most famously and influentially by

John Mueller, "The Banality of 'Ethnic War'", *International Security*, 25: 1(Summer, 2000), pp. 42≠70. © 2000 by the President and Fellows of Harvard College and the Massachusetts Institute of Technology.

Robert Kaplan, who described the Balkans as "a region of pure memory" where "each individual sensation and memory affects the grand movement of clashing peoples," and where the processes of history and memory were "kept on hold" by communism for forty-five years, "thereby creating a kind of multiplier effect for violence."[2] The other explanation holds that the violence was a reaction to continuous nationalist propaganda spewed out by politicians and the media, particularly on Serbian television, that played on old fears and hatreds. As a Belgrade journalist put it to an American audience, "You must imagine a United States with every little television station everywhere taking exactly the same editorial line—a line dictated by David Duke. You too would have war in five years."[3]

The Shallowness of Militant Nationalism in Yugoslavia

Actually, support for militant nationalism in Yugoslavia was not all that deep even at the time of its maximum notice and effect in the early 1990s. The rise of some militant nationalists in elections during that period stemmed less from their wide appeal and more from their ability to manipulate the system and from the disarray of their opposition. In their key victories in 1990, Franjo Tudjman's nationalists in Croatia massively outspent the poorly organized opposition, using funds contributed by well-heeled militants in the Croatian diaspora—particularly in North America. And their success was vastly exaggerated by an electoral system, foolishly designed by the outgoing communists, that handed Tudjman's party 69 percent of the seats with only 42 percent of the vote. In the same election, less than a quarter of the Serbs in Croatia voted for their nationalist party. The same sort of distortions, though to a lesser degree, took place in the elections in Bosnia. In early elections in Serbia, Slobodan Milošević controlled the media and essentially bought the vote by illegally using public funds—hardly a sign of enormous public appeal, and an act that was foolhardy as well because it greatly accelerated the breakup of the country Moreover, like Tudjman's party, Milošević's party was comparatively well organized and widely based and had an enormous advantage under the election rules. Although it garnered less than half the vote, it gained 78 percent of the seats. Milošević's fortunes were further enhanced because Kosovo Albanians boycotted the election, allowing his party to win that area.[4]

A poll conducted throughout Yugoslavia in the summer and autumn of 1990, even as nationalists were apparently triumphing in elections, more accurately indicates the state of opinion after centuries of supposed ethnic hatreds and after years of nationalist propaganda. The question, "Do you agree that every (Yugoslav) nation should have a national state of its own?" elicited the following responses: completely agree, 16 percent; agree to some extent, 7 percent; undecided, 10 percent; do not agree in part, 6 percent; and do not agree at all, 61 percent.[5]

At times, particularly in Serbia during the rise of Milošević, militant nationalists were able to orchestrate huge public demonstrations, which have often been taken to suggest their popular appeal. But in general it is unwise to take large, noisy crowds, which clearly are heavily self-selected, as representing public opinion more generally.[6] Moreover, much of the crowd behavior in Yugoslavia in the early 1990s was manipulated—Milošević's party often paid mobs with free food, transportation, and liquor.[7] And if crowd behavior is to be taken as indicative of wider attitudes, it should be pointed out that even the poorly organized opposition was able to mount massive demonstrations in 1991 and 1992 in Zagreb, Belgrade, and Sarajevo.[8]

Finally, the casual notion that each ethnic or national group in Yugoslavia (or indeed anywhere) is united by deep bonds of affection is substantially flawed. Serbs in Serbia have expressed little affection for the desperate and often rough rural Serbs who have fled to their country from war-torn Croatia and Bosnia.[9] Indeed, as Christopher Bennett argues, in profound contrast with Kaplan, after World War II the "great divide within Yugoslav society was increasingly that between rural and urban communities, not that between peoples."[10]

Armed Thugs and the Banality of "Ethnic Warfare" in Yugoslavia

The violence that erupted in Yugoslavia principally derived not from a frenzy of nationalism—whether ancient or newly inspired—but rather from the actions of recently empowered and unpoliced thugs. Politicians may have started the wars, and they may have whipped up a fair amount of hatred. But the effective murderous core of the wars were not hordes composed of ordinary citizens ripped loose from their repression or incited into violence against their neighbors. Rather the politicians found it necessary to recruit thugs and hooligans for the job.

Significantly, the Serbian (or Yugoslav) army substantially disintegrated early in the hostilities. There may well have been hatreds, and there surely was propaganda. But when ordinary Serb soldiers were given an opportunity to express these presumed proclivities or to act in response to the ingenious televised imprecations in government-sanctioned violence, they professed they did not know why they were fighting and often mutinied or deserted en masse.[11] Meanwhile, back in Serbia young men reacted mainly by determined draft-dodging. Some 150,000 or more quickly emigrated or went underground. In one city, only two of the 2,000–3,000 "volunteers" expected in a call-up showed up, and in several towns there were virtual mutinies against conscription. Overall, only 50 percent of Serbian reservists and only 15 percent in Belgrade obeyed orders to report for duty.[12]

Because Serbs from Serbia proper were unwilling to fight outside their own republic, Belgrade had to reshape its approach to the wars in Croatia and Bosnia in major ways. As a Serbian general put it, modification of Belgrade's military plans was made necessary by "the lack of success in mobilisation and the desertion rate."[13] Part of the solution involved arming the locals, particularly in Serb areas of Croatia and Bosnia.[14] But in general the fighting quality of the militaries, especially initially, was very poor: There was a lack of discipline, ineffective command and control, and, especially in the case of the Serbs, a reluctance to take casualties. Such deficiencies, as Steven Burg and Paul Shoup observe, "led all sides to rely on irregulars and special units."[15]

[...]

As Warren Zimmermann observes, "the dregs of society—embezzlers, thugs, even professional killers—rose from the slime to become freedom fighters and national heroes." Robert Block notes that "gangsters, outlaws, and criminals have had a special place in the war in the former Yugoslavia. Their skills in organizing people and their ruthlessness made them natural choices for Balkan rabble-rousers looking for men to defend cities or serve as nationalist shock troops." And David Rieff points out that "one of the earliest, deepest, and most pervasive effects of the fighting" was "to turn the social pyramid on its head.... Simple boys from the countryside and tough kids from the towns found that their guns made them the ones who could start amassing the Deutschemarks and the privileges, sexual and otherwise."[16]

There was also Rambo-like affectation: Each fighter dressed as if "he had been cast as a thug by a movie director," observes Block. Indeed, one Serbian para-military unit called itself "the Rambos" and went around in webbed masks and black gloves with black ribbons fetchingly tied around their foreheads.[17] Naser Orić, a muscular and charismatic former bodyguard who became the Muslim warlord of Srebrenica, and, until 1995, its protector, liked to wear leather jackets, designer sunglasses, and thick gold chains. Members of the Muslim paramilitary group the "Black Swans," which sometimes served as the bodyguard for Bosnia's president when he ventured outside Sarajevo, wore a round patch depicting a black swan having intercourse with a supine woman.[18]

Thus, as Susan Woodward notes, "paramilitary gangs, foreign mercenaries, and convicted criminals roamed the territory under ever less civil control." And "war crimes," observes Norman Cigar, were their "primary military mission."[19] Vladan Vasilijević, an expert on organized crime, says that most of the well-documented atrocities in Bosnia were committed by men with long criminal records. And a United Nations (UN) commission notes a "strong correlation" between paramili-tary activity and reports of killing of civilians, rape, torture, destruction of prop-erty, looting, detention facilities, and mass graves.[20]

[...]

A COMPARISON: RWANDA

I have stressed the importance of vicious and opportunistic, but often substantially nonideological, criminals and criminal-like elements in the development of the wars in Croatia and Bosnia. This approach seems much sounder than ones that seek to explain the wars as conflicts in which murderous communal rage, exploding from pent-up ancient hatreds or the cynical manipulation of malevolent, short-sighted politicians, induces a Hobbesian conflict of all against all and neighbor against neighbor. There are doubtless instances, however, in which the Hobbesian vision comes closer to being realized. The 1994 genocide inflicted by ethnic Hutus against Tutsis in Rwanda may be a case in point. Closer examination, however, suggests a number of similarities with the wars in Croatia and Bosnia.

Much of the writing about the genocide, in which some 500,000 to 800,000 perished in a matter of weeks—mostly by being hacked to death with machetes or hoes—gives the impression that the conflict was one of all against all, friends against friends, neighbors against neighbors, even Cain against Abel. Friends and neighbors (and even brothers perhaps) did kill each other, but it seems that by far the greatest damage, as in Croatia and Bosnia, resulted from the rampages of murderous thugs.

Far from a spontaneous eruption, the basic elements of the genocidal process had been planned for years by Hutu extremists who were substantially in charge of the ruling party, the government bureaucracy, and the police.[21] Throughout the country Hutus and Hutu police were urged—or ordered—to engage in the killing, and many do seem to have responded enthusiastically. Joining was the Presidential Guard, numbering 700–1,500 men, and the Hutu army, which consisted of some 50,000 men, most of them hastily recruited in the previous few years from landless peasants, the urban unemployed, and foreign drifters who had chiefly signed up not for ideological reasons, but rather for the guaranteed food and drink (each man was entitled to two bottles of beer a day, a luxury by Rwandan standards) and for the opportunity to loot, because pay was low and irregular.[22]

Finally, there was the Interahamwe, militia bands that had been created and trained by Hutu extremists. As Philip Gourevitch points out, the Interahamwe had its genesis in soccer fan clubs, and it recruited jobless young men who were "wasting in idleness and its attendant resentments," and who tended to see the genocide as a "carnival romp."[23] Moreover, their ranks were expanded by hordes of opportunists once the genocide began. Gérard Prunier notes that a "social aspect of the killings has often been overlooked": As soon as the killing groups "went into action, they drew around them a cloud of even poorer people, a *lumpenproletariat* of street boys, rag-pickers, car-washers, and homeless unemployed. For these people the genocide was the best thing that could ever happen to them. They had the blessings of a form of authority to take revenge on socially powerful people as long as these were on the wrong side of the political fence. They could steal, they could kill with minimum justification, they could rape, and they could get drunk for free. This was wonderful. The political aims pursued by the masters of this dark carnival were quite beyond their scope. They just went along."[24] "Drunken militia bands," notes Gourevitch, "fortified with assorted drugs from ransacked pharmacies, were bused from massacre to massacre."[25] There were about 1,700 "professional Interahamwe" who received training and uniforms, and thousands or tens of thousands joined up (sometimes under coercion) after the genocide began.[26]

As in Yugoslavia, criminals were released from jail to participate in the destruction,[27] and the prospect for enrichment by looting was vastly escalated during the genocide and was used as a specific incentive by the leaders—many of whom were happy to take booty as well.[28] The killers were fully willing to murder fellow Hutus suspected of not being loyal to the cause, and they often forced other Hutus, on pain of instant death, to join the killings.[29] Others participated by manning roadblocks or by pointing out local Tutsis to the marauding *genocidaires*. "I didn't have a choice," one cooperating priest pointed out, "It was necessary to appear pro-militia. If I had had a different attitude, we would all have disappeared."[30]

Many Hutus, however, did hide and protect Tutsi neighbors and sometimes strangers despite the pressure, and despite the fact that the punishment for such behavior could be instant, brutal death.[31] The number of Hutus who did so probably was as high as the number who, under pressure from the often drunken and always-murderous *genocidaires,* indicated where some Tutsis might reside or be hiding.[32] Most of the others, it appears, simply withdrew whether in approval or disapproval of the cataclysm surrounding them: "We closed the door and tried not to hear," said one.[33]

Although an extensive study by Human Rights Watch ventures no direct estimates, it does suggest at various points that the killers numbered in the "tens of thousands."[34] A study by African Rights in London amasses a detailed listing of those in the Hutu elite who directed the genocide and comes up with 600 or 700 names.[35] As indicated earlier, the Presidential Guard comprised some 700–1,500, the army perhaps 50,000, and the Interahamwe militias another 50,000. A year after defeating the genocidal regime, Tutsi forces had 33,000 people incarcerated under suspicion of participating in the genocide—a figure that later rose to at least 125,000.[36]

It may be reasonable to suggest from all this that there were some 50,000 hardcore killers. This would easily be enough to have accomplished the genocide: If each of these people killed one person a week for the course of the 100-day holocaust, more than 700,000 would have perished. This number would represent some 2 percent of the male Hutu population over the age of thirteen. That is, 98 percent of the male Hutu population older than thirteen was not in this group.

It is possible that 200,000 participated in the massacres, though this is likely to be a rather high figure that would include people who, under pressure from the hard-core *genocidaires,* did nothing more than point out where local Tutsi lived or simply manned roadblocks under orders. This would still represent less than 9 percent of the Hutu male population over the age of thirteen. (Though by all accounts very much outnumbered by men and boys, women and girls did join in the genocide. In addition, boys younger than thirteen also often participated.[37] If these groups are added to the base, the percentages would be much lower.)

In some sense, of course, these are astoundingly high figures. In a normal year, by comparison, the proportion of males older than thirteen who committed murder in Rwanda was probably something like 1 in 2,000. Nonetheless, a situation in which more than 90 percent of the over-thirteen male Hutu population did not participate in killings hardly seems to justify the notion that the situation was one of all against all or neighbor against neighbor. As in Croatia and Bosnia, the chief dynamic of the depredations seems to have been furnished by marauding bands of violent, opportunistic, and often drunken thugs.

CONCLUSIONS

This analysis of the experiences in the former Yugoslavia and Rwanda suggests that ethnicity is important in "ethnic wars" more as an ordering device than as an impelling force; that the violence would probably have been fairly easy to police; that the wars did not necessarily derive from the ethnic peculiarities of those regions; and that the wars were by no means inevitable. In addition, some of the wars' key dynamics may have considerable applicability to other violent conflicts.

Ethnicity Is Important Only as an Ordering Device

Michael Ignatieff compares the conditions that prevailed in the former Yugoslavia to a Hobbesian state of nature.[38] But the experience in Yugoslavia and in Rwanda calls this image into question. People did not descend into the war of "every man against every man" that Hobbes so vividly depicted and so ardently abhorred. What happened in Croatia, Bosnia, and Rwanda did resemble a Hobbesian state of nature, but it came about not because people generally gave into murderous enmity, but because they came under the arbitrary control of armed thugs. Ethnicity proved essentially to be simply the characteristic around which the perpetrators and the politicians who recruited and encouraged them happened to array themselves. It was important as an ordering device or principle, not as a crucial motivating force.

[...]

International Policing Could Probably Have Been Effective

Hobbes's greatest mischief comes from his solution to the problem he invents. He assumes that *every* person is, at base, "radically insecure, mistrustful of other men, and afraid for his life." Therefore the only way out of the mess is for everyone permanently to surrender to an authoritarian ruler, one who primarily values glory and stability over doctrinal orthodoxy or ideological purity, and one who will maintain the necessary force to keep all people from once again giving in to their natural proclivities for isolation, hostility, and insensitivity to the rights of others.[39]

But the experience in the former Yugoslav and Rwanda suggests that this monumental—perhaps even impossible—task is hardly required. Most people most of the time do not have much difficulty getting along and creating useful rules and patterns of conduct that allow them to coexist peacefully.[40] Police may be needed, even necessary, to maintain order, but they need not normally be numerous. Nor does their control need to be Leviathan-like, because they mainly need simply to protect the many from the few, rather than everyone from everyone else as Hobbes would have it.

It follows that policing the situation in Yugoslavia and in Rwanda would not have been the major challenge often anticipated. Essentially, the intimidating, opportunistic thugs were successful mainly because they were the biggest bullies on the block. But, like most bullies (and sadists and torturers), they substantially lacked organization, discipline, coherent tactics or strategy, deep motivation, broad popular support, ideological commitment, and essentially, courage.[41] Consequently, if confronted by a military force with these qualities, their most likely reaction would be to flee. And, to a considerable degree, this seems to be what happened both in Yugoslavia and in Rwanda.

[...]

As in Yugoslavia, the marauders in Rwanda were put down fairly easily when confronted with a reasonably coherent military force. Several thousand refugees were saved in a Kigali stadium because the United Nations Assistance Mission to Rwanda, which Prunier characterizes as "the powerless UN 'military' force," simply forbade the murder squads entry. And when the Tutsis eventually were able to get their comparatively capable army into the country, they had to battle for the capital city, but took over the rest of the country with a minimum of fighting. For the most part, Hutu authorities, like their counterparts in the former Yugoslavia, simply ordered their forces to flee when confronted with military force.[42]

[...]

What Happened in Yugoslavia and Rwanda Could Happen Anywhere

If my assessment is essentially correct, it suggests that what happened in Yugoslavia and Rwanda is not unique, but could happen just about anywhere. The Serbian writer Aleksandar Tisma has gloomily concluded from his country's tragedy that "there are civilized people and less civilized people. Here in the Balkans, people don't belong to the civilized but to the less civilized."[43] But the wars in Yugoslavia did not break out because the peoples there are "less civilized." When criminals and sadists are given free rein, they can easily debase the conditions of life.

And thugs are everywhere—at least in small numbers—and only small numbers are necessary if the conditions are ripe. England may seem rather tranquil and well ordered in many respects, but it is also the home of some of the world's most notorious soccer hooligans. Canada often seems to be a nation of eminently reasonable people, but that is not the conclusion one would draw from watching a hockey game. Denmark may today remind people mainly of Hans Christian Andersen and little mermaids, but it once was the home of world-class marauders, and it seems unlikely that that propensity has been fully bred out of the race in the intervening centuries.[44] Moreover, as various studies have suggested, it is often possible to get ordinary people to participate in acts of considerable cruelty when they are placed, voluntarily or involuntarily, in a supportive environment—ideological or ethnic hatred is by no means necessary for this capacity to emerge.[45] Under the right conditions, thugs can rise to a dominant role, others can lend a hand or withdraw into terrified isolation or studied indifference, and any place can degenerate into a Bosnia or a Rwanda.

What Happened in Yugoslavia and Rwanda Was Not Inevitable

The catastrophes that engulfed Bosnia, Croatia, and Rwanda did not have to happen. They emerged not out of inevitable historic necessities, but were instigated and orchestrated by designing politicians and local extremists who, however, often did not know how to control the violent processes they had set into motion.

Yahya Sadowski finds that cultural strife is found about as much in developed countries as in poorer ones, but that such strife is less likely to turn violent in prosperous societies. From this he concludes that economic advancement tends to reduce cultural violence.[46] But it seems, rather, that the actions of leading politicians and police organizations are most important in keeping ethnic and cultural conflict from leading to major violence. Prosperous societies do seem to do better in this regard than poorer ones (which in fact is probably one of the reasons for their comparative prosperity). Prosperity may therefore be beneficial if it helps to develop competent governments and police forces, but wealth itself is not the key operative factor. Thus it is entirely possible to imagine Bosnian-like chaos in prosperous Quebec or Northern Ireland if the Canadian or British authorities had attempted to deal with cultural conflicts by encouraging murderous rampage rather than through patient policing and political accommodation.

On the other hand, because of sound political policies, ethnic violence has been avoided in Bulgaria and Romania even though those countries are hardly more developed than Serbia or Bosnia. And the experience in Macedonia, where political leaders have sought calm accommodation, suggests that the disasters in the more prosperous areas of the former Yugoslavia, far from being inevitable, could almost certainly have been avoided if politicians and police had behaved more sensibly.[47]

[...]

In the end, the basic operation—and the fundamental banality—of much ethnic violence is neatly summed up in a Bosnian expression: "Teško narodu kad pametni ucute, budale progovore, a fukare se obogate." That is, "It is difficult for the people when the smart keep quiet, fools speak out, and thugs get rich."[48] The mistaken—even racist—notion that an entire ethnic group is devotedly out to destroy another ethnic group can in such cases shatter any ability to perceive nuance and variety, and it can be taken to suggest that efforts to foster elite accommodation are essentially irrelevant and therefore bound to prove futile. Further, the all-against-all image can discourage policing because it implies that the entire ethnic group—rather than just a small, opportunistic, and often cowardly subgroup—must be brought under control.

NOTES

1. I am concerned here with ethnic violence and warfare—a condition in which combatants arrayed along ethnic lines seek to kill each other—not particularly with ethnic hatreds. It is important to distinguish common, knee-jerk, and sometimes hateful ethnic slurs—no matter how unpleasant and politically incorrect their expression may often be—from prejudice that is expressed in violence. As James D. Fearon and David U. Laitin have pointed out, ethnic violence is actually exceedingly rare when one considers how many Archie Bunkers there are in the world and how many opportunities there are for it to occur. Fearon and Laitin, "Explaining Interethnic Cooperation," *American Political Science Review,* Vol. 90, No. 4 (December 1996), pp. 716–717. Some analysts argue that "conflicts among nations and ethnic groups are escalating." Samuel P. Huntington, "Why International Primacy Matters," *International Security*, Vol. 17, No. 4 (Spring 1993), p. 71. Others believe "there is a virtual epidemic of armed civil or intranational conflict." See David A. Hamburg, *Preventing Contemporary Intergroup Violence* (New York: Carnegie Corporation of New York, 1993). But such wars and conflicts did not increase in number or intensity in the 1990s. See Yahya Sadowski, *The Myth of Global Chaos* (Washington, D.C.: Brookings, 1998); Ernest J. Wilson and Ted Robert Gurr, "Fewer Nations Are Making War," *Los Angeles Times,* August 22, 1999. p. M2; Steven R. David, "Internal War: Causes and Cures," *World Politics,* Vol. 49, No. 4 (July 1997), pp. 552-576; and James D. Fearon and David D. Laitin, "Weak States, Rough Terrain, and Large Scale Ethnic Violence since 1945," paper presented at the annual meeting of the American Political Science Association, Atlanta, Georgia, September 25, 1999. Rather, what is new is that some of these wars and conflicts have taken place in Europe, an area that had previously been free from substantial civil warfare for nearly half a century. However, militant nationalism—whether violent or not—may well already have had its day in Central and Eastern Europe. Hypernationalists (and even some that are not so hyper), who sometimes appeared threateningly formidable at the polls in the early 1990s, have been reduced in elections in many places to the point of extinguishment.

2. Robert D. Kaplan, "A Reader's Guide to the Balkans," *New York Times Book Review,* April 18, 1993, pp. 1, 30–32. See also Robert D. Kaplan, "History's Cauldron," *Atlantic Monthly,* June 1991, pp. 93–104; and Kaplan, *Balkan Ghosts: A Journey through History* (New York: St. Martin's, 1993). For Kaplan's more recent doomsaying, now focused also on Africa, see his "The Coming Anarchy," *Atlantic,* February 1994, pp. 44–76. For a devastating critique of the argument, see Noel Malcolm, "Seeing Ghosts," *National Interest,* Summer 1993, pp. 83–88. See also V.P. Gagnon, Jr., "Ethnic Nationalism and International Conflict: The Case of Serbia," *International Security,* Vol. 19, No. 3 (Winter 1994/95). pp. 133–134; Russell Hardin, *One for All: The Logic of Group Conflict* (Princeton, N.J.: Princeton University Press, 1995), chap. 6; Sadowski, *Myth of Global Chaos;* and Brian Hall, "Rebecca West's War," *New Yorker,* April 15. 1996, p. 83. For Kaplan's more recent reflections, see his "Reading Too Much into a Book," *New York Times,* June 13, 1999, pp. 4–17.

3. Quoted in Noel Malcolm, *Bosnia: A Short History* (New York: New York University Press, 1994), p. 252. On this argument, see, for example, Christopher Bennett, *Yugoslavia's Bloody Collapse* (New York: New York University Press, 1995), pp. viii, 10, 242; Warren Zimmermann, *Origins of a Catastrophe: Yugoslavia and Its Destroyers* (New York: Times Books, 1996), pp. 120–122; Christopher Cviić, "A Culture of Humiliation," *National Interest,* Summer 1993, p. 82; Jack Snyder and Karen

Ballentine, "Nationalism and the Marketplace of Ideas," *International Security,* Vol. 21, No. 2 (Fall 1996), pp. 25–30; Michael Ignatieff, "The Balkan Tragedy," *New York Review of Books,* May 13, 1993, p. 3; Noel Malcolm, "The Roots of Bosnian Horror Lie Not So Deep," *New York Times,* October 19, 1998; Tim Judah, *The Serbs: History, Myth, and the Destruction of Yugoslavia* (New Haven, Conn.: Yale University Press, 1997), pp. 285, 309; and Peter Maass, *Love Thy Neighbor: A Story of War* (New York: Vintage, 1996), p. 227.

4. On Tudjman's spending, see Susan L. Woodward, *Balkan Tragedy: Chaos and Dissolution after the Cold War* (Washington, D.C.: Brookings, 1995), pp. 119, 229; Bennett, *Yugoslavia's Bloody Collapse,* p. 199; Lenard J. Cohen, *Broken Bonds: Yugoslavia's Disintegration and Balkan Politics in Transition,* 2d ed. (Boulder, Colo.: Westview, 1995), p. 95; Marcus Tanner, *Croatia: A Nation Forged in War* (New Haven, Conn.: Yale University Press, 1997), p. 222; and David Binder, "Gojko Susak, Defense Minister of Croatia Is Dead at 53," *New York Times,* May 5, 1998, p. A25. On Tudjman's electoral success, see Bennett, *Yugoslavia's Bloody Collapse,* p. 127; Woodward, *Balkan Tragedy,* pp. 117–119; Laura Silber and Allan Little, *Yugoslavia: Death of a Nation* (New York: Penguin, 1997), p. 90; and Cohen, *Broken Bonds,* pp. 99–100. On the Serb vote in Croatia, see Gagnon, "Ethnic Nationalism and International Conflict," p. 155; and Bennett, *Yugoslavia's Bloody Collapse,* p. 127. Somewhat similarly, a large portion of those Serbs in Bosnia who lived outside areas controlled by Serb nationalists voted with the Muslims for independence from Serbia in a 1992 referendum; see Gagnon, "Ethnic Nationalism and International Conflict," p. 63. On Bosnia, see Steven L. Burg and Paul S. Shoup, *The War in Bosnia-Herzegovina: Ethnic Conflict and International Intervention* (Armonk, N.Y.: M.E. Sharpe, 1999), pp. 50–51, 57. On Serbia, see Gagnon, "Ethnic Nationalism and International Conflict," p. 154; Bennett, *Yugoslavia's Bloody Collapse,* p. 121; Brian Hall, *The Impossible Country: A Journey through the Last Days of Yugoslavia* (New York: Penguin, 1994), p. 48; Woodward, *Balkan Tragedy,* pp. 130, 448–449; Mladjan Dinkic, *The Economics of Destruction* (Belgrade: Video Nedeljnik, 1995), pp. 30, 61–66; see also Judah, *The Serbs,* p. 260. On vote percentages, see Cohen, *Broken Bonds,* p. 158. On the Albanian vote, see Woodward, *Balkan Tragedy,* p. 121.

5. Laslo Sekelj, *Yugoslavia: The Process of Disintegration* (Highland Lakes, N.J.: Atlantic Research and Publications, 1992), p. 277.

6. Thus, because anti-Vietnam War demonstrators in the 1960s in the United States were predominantly young, most commentators came to hold that young people were more opposed to the war than older people; yet poll data clearly show the opposite to have been the case. John Mueller, *War, Presidents, and Public Opinion* (New York: Wiley, 1973), pp. 136–140.

7. Bennett, *Yugoslavia's Bloody Collapse,* p. 98.

8. On Zagreb, see "Yugoslavia: Death of a Nation," Discovery Channel, 1995. On Belgrade, see Gagnon, "Ethnic Nationalism and International Conflict," pp. 157–158; Silber and Little, *Yugoslavia,* chap. 9; Judah, *The Serbs,* p. 174; and Chuck Sudetic, *Blood and Vengeance: One Family's Story of the War in Bosnia* (New York: W.W. Norton, 1998), p. 85. On Sarajevo, see Judah, *The Serbs,* p. 211; and Robert J. Donia and John V.A. Fine, Jr., *Bosnia and Hercegovina: A Tradition Betrayed* (New York: Columbia University Press, 1994), p. 1.

9. Christine Spolar, "Lesser Serbs in Greater Serbia: Refugees of Croatia Fighting Find Little Welcome from Fellow Serbs," *Washington Post,* May 15, 1995, p. A36; Woodward, *Balkan Tragedy,* p. 364; Stephen Kinzer, "Yugoslavia Deports Refugee Serbs to Fight for Rebels in Bosnia and Croatia," *New York Times,* July 6, 1995, p. A6; and Roger Cohen, *Hearts Grown Brutal: Sagas of Sarajevo* (New York: Random House, 1998), p. 296.

10. Bennett, *Yugoslavia's Bloody Collapse,* p. 63. See also Woodward, *Balkan Tragedy,* pp. 238, 241; Ignatieff, "Balkan Tragedy," p. 4; John R. Bowen, "The Myth of Global Ethnic Conflict," *Journal of Democracy,* Vol. 7, No. 4 (October 1996), pp. 3–14; and Sadowski, *Myth of Global Chaos,* pp. 78–80. Interestingly, in his discussion of the Bosnian war, Peter Maass observes that "to a surprising extent, this was a war of poor rural Serbs against wealthier urban Muslims, a Deliverance scenario." Maass, *Love Thy Neighbor,* p. 159. Donia and Fine note that it was the "relatively uneducated armed hillsmen, with a hostility toward urban culture and the state institutions (including taxes) that go with it" who proved "susceptible to Serbian chauvinist propaganda," "allowed themselves to be recruited into Serb paramilitary units," and formed a significant portion of those shelling Bosnia's cities. Donia and Fine, *Bosnia and Hercegovina,* p. 28. See also Fearon and Laitin, "Weak States, Rough Terrain."

11. Norman Cigar, "The Serbo-Croatian War, 1991: Political and Military Dimensions," *Journal of Strategic Studies,* Vol. 16, No. 3 (September 1993), pp. 317–319; Woodward, *Balkan Tragedy,* p. 238; Bennett, *Yugoslavia's Bloody Collapse,* p. 167; Ed Vulliamy, *Seasons in Hell: Understanding Bosnia's War* (New York: Simon and Schuster, 1994), p. 19; Miloš Vasić, "The Yugoslav Army and the Post-Yugoslav Armies," in David A. Dyker and Ivan Vejvoda, eds., *Yugoslavia and After: A Study in Fragmentation, Despair, and Rebirth* (London: Longman, 1996), p. 128; Burg and Shoup, *War in Bosnia-Herzegovina,* p. 51; Gagnon, "Ethnic Nationalism and International Conflict," p. 162; Silber and Little, *Yugoslavia,* p. 177; Tanner, *Croatia,* p. 269; and Judah, *The Serbs,* pp. 185, 189.

12. Jasminka Udovicki and Stojan Cerovic, "The People's Mass Murderer," *Village Voice,* November 7, 1995, p. 27; Stipe Sikavica, "The Collapse of Tito's Army," in Jasminka Udovićki and James Ridgeway, eds., *Yugoslavia's Ethnic Nightmare* (New York: Lawrence Hill, 1995), p. 138; Cigar, "Serbo-Croatian War," p. 315; Tanner, *Croatia,* p. 270; Judah, *The Serbs,* p. 185; and Burg and Shoup, *War in Bosnia-Herzegovina,* p. 51. See also Silber and Little, *Yugoslavia,* p. 177; and Gagnon, "Ethnic Nationalism and International Conflict," p. 162. See also Silber and Little, *Yugoslavia,* p. 177. In all communist countries, certainly including Yugoslavia, people were determinedly subject to decades of communist propaganda in the media. Yet, as history has shown, many—probably most—failed in the end to be convinced by it. If media promotion could guarantee lasting impact, all Yugoslavs would today be worshiping Tito, and all Americans would be driving Edsels. For a discussion, see John Mueller, *Policy and Opinion in the Gulf War* (Chicago: University of Chicago Press, 1994), pp. 129–136. Warren Zimmerman observes, "My most difficult task has been to convey the conviction that all Yugoslavs weren't the bloodthirsty extremists so ubiquitously visible in Western news accounts. Most of the people my wife and I met in six years of living in Yugoslavia were peaceful and decent, without a trace of the hostility on which nationalism feeds.... What amazed me was how many Yugoslavs resisted the incessant racist propaganda." Zimmerman, *Origins of a Catastrophe,* p. xi; see also pp. 209–210.

13. Tanner, *Croatia,* p. 269. See also United Nations Commission of Experts, *Final Report of the United Nations Commission of Experts Established Pursuant to Security Council*

Resolution 780 (1992), Annex III. A Special Forces, ed. M. Cherif Bassiouni, December 28, 1994, par. 29.

14. Burg and Shoup, *War in Bosnia-Herzegovina,* p. 130; and Judah, *The Serbs,* pp. 170–172, 192–195.

15. Burg and Shoup, *War in Bosnia-Herzegovina,* p. 137. There were at least eighty-three of these groups operating in Croatia and Bosnia: fifty-six Serb, thirteen Croat, and fourteen Muslim, with 36,000–66,000 members. See UN Experts, *Final Report,* par. 14.

16. Zimmermann, *Origins of a Catastrophe,* p. 152. Block, "Killers," p. 9. Rieff, *Slaughterhouse,* p. 130. Reportage by Peter Maass is peppered with such phrases as "drunken hillbillies," "death and thuggery," "they don't wear normal uniforms, they don't have many teeth," "the trigger fingers belonged to drunks," "the Bosnians might be the underdogs, but most of their frontline soldiers were crooks," "bullies," massive oaf," foul-smelling warlord," "mouthing the words, 'Bang, you're dead,' through rotten teeth," "an unshaven soldier would point his gun at a desired item and grunt," "only drunks and bandits ventured outside," "goons with guns," "Serb soldiers or thugs—and the difference is hard to tell." See Maass, *Love Thy Neighbor,* pp. 6, 7, 16, 30, 42, 48, 61, 69, 77, 79, 80, 85. Reporter Ed Vulliamy describes them as "boozy at their best, wild and sadistic at their worst" or as "toothless goons" with "inflammable breath." See Vulliamy, *Seasons in Hell,* pp. 19, 46.

17. Block, "Killers"; UN Experts, *Final Report,* par. 291; and Cohen, *Hearts Grown Brutal,* p. 126.

18. Burg and Shoup, *War in Bosnia-Herzegovina,* p. 137; and UN Experts, *Final Report,* at par. 142.

19. Woodward, *Balkan Tragedy,* pp. 254, 356, 485; and Cigar, "Serbo-Croatian War," p. 323. See also Mischa Glenny, *The Fall of Yugoslavia: The Third Balkan War* (New York: Penguin, 1993), p. 185; Chuck Sudetic, "A 'Wild East' Revival in Serbian-Held Croatia," *New York Times,* September 21, 1992, p. A6; Cheryl Benard, "Bosnia: Was It Inevitable?" in Zalmay M. Khalilzad, ed., *Lessons from Bosnia* (Santa Monica, Calif.: RAND Corporation, 1993), pp. 18–25; Vulliamy, *Seasons in Hell,* pp. 307–316; and Bob Stewart, *Broken Lives: A Personal View of the Bosnian Conflict* (London: HarperCollins, 1994), pp. 318–319. See also Rieff, *Slaughterhouse,* p. 83; Ignatieff, *Warrior's Honor,* p. 131; and Sikavica, "Collapse of Tito's Army," p. 138. Vulliamy quotes Reuters reporter Andrej Gustinčić: "Gangs of gun-toting Serbs rule Foča, turning the once quiet town into a nightmare landscape of burning streets and houses.... Some are members of paramilitary groups from Serbia, self-proclaimed crusaders against Islam and defenders of the Serbian nation, others are wild-eyed local men, hostile towards strangers and happy to have driven out their Muslim neighbors. No one seems to be in command, and ill-disciplined and bad-tempered gunmen stop and detain people at will." See Vulliamy, *Seasons in Hell,* pp. 90–91. Many of the "wild-eyed local men," according to another report, were local criminals who "donned uniforms and took part enthusiastically in the subsequent looting." See Julian Borger, "Friends or Foes?" *Guardian Weekly,* January 19, 1997, p. 23. Similarly, the town of Bosanski Novi was ruled by five roaming Serbian armed groups, the most brutal of which was a well-known local mafia known as the "Spare Ribs" that had donned uniforms. See Judah, *The Serbs,* p. 227.

20. On Vasilijevic, see Firestone, "Serb Lawmaker Is Called Vicious Killer." UN Experts, *Final Report,* par. 21.

21. Gérard Prunier, *Rwanda Crisis: History of a Genocide* (New York: Columbia University Press, 1995), p. 169; and African Rights, *Rwanda: Death, Despair, and Defiance,* rev. ed. (London: African Rights, 1995), pp. 51–52.

22. Prunier, *Rwanda Crisis,* pp. 113, 242–243; and African Rights, *Rwanda,* pp. 49, 65.

23. Philip Gourevitch, *We Wish to Inform You That Tomorrow We Will Be Killed with Our Families: Stories from Rwanda* (New York: Farrar, Straus and Giroux, 1998), p. 93.

24. Prunier, *Rwanda Crisis,* pp. 231–232. See also Allison Des Forges, *"Leave None to Tell the Story": Genocide in Rwanda* (New York: Human Rights Watch, 1999), pp. 11, 261.

25. Gourevitch, *We Wish to Inform You,* p. 115.

26. African Rights, *Rwanda,* pp. 55, 61–62, 114.

27. Gourevitch, *We Wish to Inform You,* p. 242.

28. African Rights, *Rwanda,* pp. 55, 61–62, 114.

29. Prunier, *Rwanda Crisis,* p. 247; African Rights, *Rwanda,* chap. 14; and Gourevitch, *We Wish to Inform You,* pp. 307, 309.

30. Prunier, *Rwanda Crisis,* pp. 253–254; and Gourevitch, *We Wish to Inform You,* p. 136.

31. African Rights, *Rwanda,* pp. 1017–1022.

32. Prunier, *Rwanda Crisis,* p. 253; and Des Forges, *"Leave None to Tell the Story,"* pp. 11, 260–262.

33. Des Forges, *"Leave None to Tell the Story,"* p. 262.

34. Ibid., pp. 2, 16, 260, 262.

35. African Rights, *Rwanda.*

36. Gourevitch, *We Wish to Inform You,* p. 242.

37. Bill Keller, "In Mozambique and Other Lands, Children Fight the Wars," *New York Times,* November 9, 1994, p. A14.

38. Ignatieff, "Balkan Tragedy."

39. Robert P. Kraynak, *History and Modernity in the Thought of Thomas Hobbes* (Ithaca, N.Y.: Cornell University Press, 1990), pp. 165, 176, 179.

40. On this issue, see Bruce L. Benson, "The Spontaneous Evolution of Commercial Law," in Daniel B. Klein, ed., *Reputation: Studies in the Voluntary Elicitation of Good Conduct* (Ann Arbor: University of Michigan Press, 1997), pp. 165–189; Robert C. Ellickson, *Order without Law: How Neighbors Settle Disputes* (Cambridge, Mass.: Harvard University Press, 1991); and John Mueller, *Capitalism, Democracy, and Ralph's Pretty Good Grocery* (Princeton, N.J.: Princeton University Press, 1999), chap. 4.

41. Judah observes of Bosnian Serb General Ratko Mladić that "his war was a coward's war. He fought few pitched battles but managed to drive hundreds of thousands of unarmed people out of their homes," and he also questions Mladić's mental stability. Judah, *The Serbs,* pp. 230–231. On this latter issue, see also Robert Block, "The Madness of General Mladic," *New York Review of Books,* October 5, 1995, pp. 7–9; and Jane Perlez, "A Grim Turn for 2 Embattled Serb Leaders," *New York Times,* December 15, 1995, p. Al.

42. Prunier, *Rwanda Crisis,* pp. 254, 268, 377; Gourevitch, *We Wish to Inform You,* pp. 156–157; and Alan J. Kuperman, "Rwanda in Retrospect," *Foreign Affairs,* Vol. 79, No. 1 (January-February 2000), pp. 94–118.

43. Quoted in Jane Perlez, "Balkan Voice of Reason and Despair," *New York Times,* August 14, 1997, p. B1.

44. On the murderous rivalries of motorcycle gangs in tranquil Denmark, see Stephen Kinzer, "Biker Wars in the Land of 'The Little Mermaid,'" *New York Times,* May 6, 1996, p. A4. In this case, however, the thugs are taken to be an aberrant "social pathology" and they are not held to be typical of the entire national spirit as so often happens in Kaplanesque discussions of the Balkans.

45. Stanley Milgram, *Obedience to Authority: An Experimental View* (New York: Harper and Row, 1975); Philip C. Zimbardo, Craig Haney, Curtis Banks, and David Jaffe, "The Mind Is a Formidable Jailer," *New York Times Magazine,* April 8, 1973. pp. 38ff; Christopher R. Browning, *Ordinary Men: Reserve Police Battalion 101 and the Final Solution in Poland* (New York: HarperCollins, 1998); and Fred E. Katz, *Ordinary People and Extraordinary Evil: A Report on the Beguilings of Evil* (Albany: State University of New York Press, 1993).

46. Sadowski, *Myth of Global Chaos,* pp. 174–176.

47. In 1991 Robert Kaplan declared that "Macedonia is once again poised to erupt. Never in half a century has there been so much anger in Macedonia, as its people wake up from a Communist imposed sleep.... Unable to stand on its own, like its more populous and historically grounded neighbor Serbia, Macedonia could implode under the pressures of Albanian nationalism from the west and Bulgarian nationalism from the east. And this is to say nothing of the pressures of Greek nationalism from the south.... The various popular convulsions in the Balkans are inexorably converging on Macedonia.... It is a tragic yet fascinating development. Rarely has the very process of history been so transparent and cyclical." Kaplan, "History's Cauldron," p. 104. See also his "Ground Zero: Macedonia: The Real Battleground," *New Republic,* August 2, 1993, p. 15. Inspired by such wisdom, applications of the now-popular notion of "preventative diplomacy" would have concentrated on exactly the wrong place in the early 1990s. On Bulgaria, see Venelin I. Ganev, "Bulgaria's Symphony of Hope," *Journal of Democracy,* Vol. 8, No. 4 (October 1997), pp. 125–139. On Romania (and also Slovakia), see Robert H. Linden, "Putting on Their Sunday Best: Romania, Hungary, and the Puzzle of Peace," *International Studies Quarterly,* Vol. 44, No. 1 (March 2000), pp. 121–145.

48. Cohen, *Hearts Grown Brutal,* p. 297.

POSTSCRIPT

No matter the causes behind so-called ethnic wars, there is good reason to be concerned that civil conflicts of this sort appear to be on the upswing. The persistence of unresolved colonial-era grievances and artificial borders will continue to cause problems of internal legitimacy and cohesion in many developing states. Continuing violence in Darfur, Iraq, and elsewhere pits rival groups against one another in bloody conflicts that claim staggering numbers of lives. What is more, public cynicism, the relative dysfunction of the United Nations Security Council, and the reticence of the United States and its allies to intervene in these civil conflicts since the invasion of Iraq hinder any attempts to bring an end through armed interventions or diplomacy.

However, the diagnosis of the causes of ethnic strife is certainly an important consideration in thinking through possible solutions to the problem. If ethnic awareness is a deep-seated and significant cause of civil conflict, then it is likely advisable to accept ethnic diversity as a given and promote power-sharing, federalism, and in extreme cases partition as a solution. If mere criminality and individual manipulation of ethnic awareness is the real culprit, then institutions of global justice such as the criminal tribunals held for Yugoslavia and Rwanda, the Special Court for Sierra Leone, or the International Criminal Court (or some form of alternative justice mechanism such as truth commissions) seem to be the more logical choice.

Can Trade Liberalization Benefit Both Rich and Poor?

✔ **YES**
GARY HUFBAUER, "Free Trade," *The National Interest* 95 (May/June 2008): 15–18

✘ **NO**
JOSEPH E. STIGLITZ, "Fair Trade," *The National Interest* 95 (May/June 2008): 19–24

There is little doubt that the globalization of the world's economy is taking place at an extraordinarily rapid pace. World merchandise exports have expanded at an average annual rate of approximately 6 percent since 1950, compared with a 4.5 percent rate in world output. In 1913, the entire flow of goods in world trade totalled only U.S. $20 billion. In contrast, today's international trade in goods and services stands at about U.S. $6 trillion a year. Foreign direct investment (FDI) has been growing at an even faster pace than trade. During recent decades, FDI has been reported to have expanded by 27 percent per year, representing an average growth of U.S. $205 billion a year. Today, there are more than 2000 large multinational corporations (operating in six or more countries) and well over 8000 smaller ones. Together, these 10 000 multinationals are estimated to control over 90 000 subsidiaries.

At the same time, technology has been undergoing a similar process of globalization. Miniaturization and computerization have speeded up communications and transportation times while reducing costs. Rapid developments in communications, when combined with the globalization of financial markets, have led to a sharp increase in the movement of capital. Together, these developments have helped propel an expansion of the global economy, which is not limited by traditional geographical constraints. Factors such as geography and climate no longer give a particular region a comparative advantage.

For some observers, the rapid pace of economic globalization is a welcome trend. The lowering of economic barriers, greater openness to competitive market forces, and the reduction of artificial market restraints are seen as promoting higher economic growth and prosperity. Consumers have access to cheaper, more diverse, and more advanced products. Expansion of trade and investment generates jobs. At the same time, globalization is said to generate positive political dividends. States that adjust to the changing market are able to generate higher rates of economic growth and technological innovation. They have more resources to deploy in the international arena to both promote and defend their interests. Countries that are linked by economic ties and have a mutual interest in promoting economic growth are more likely to seek stable, peaceful, and cooperative ties with other states. Similarly, firms and workers with a stake in trade advancement and economic growth are more likely to be supportive of active and constructive foreign policies that are aimed at maintaining these benefits. Edward Mansfield, in *Power, Trade, and War* (Princeton, N.J.: Princeton University Press, 1994), suggests that the data clearly support the contention that trade and peace are closely related—higher levels of freer trade are usually associated with lower levels of international hostility and antagonism.

Despite this optimistic picture, economic globalization clearly has its downside. An increasingly liberalized economic world imposes severe adjustment burdens on certain segments of workers and firms. The distribution of wealth, both within and between states, has become more unequal. Exposure to the uncertainties and insecurities of foreign competition has led to demands for protectionist measures and the abandonment of multilateral cooperation. Critics are concerned that unfettered global competition creates overwhelming pressures to abandon domestic social policies, environmental regulations, and human-rights protections.

Such concerns have in turn given rise to a growing backlash against globalization itself. Globalization for many people, it is argued, has become a "race to the bottom." At the heart of globalization is growing poverty and inequality, which can be reversed only if the forces of globalization themselves are curtailed. As the massive demonstrations at several international summits have shown, anti-globalization movements have grown significantly in recent years.

The following essays discuss the implications of globalization and trade liberalization. In the first essay, Gary Hufbauer argues that trade liberalization benefits both developed and developing countries. His essay was written during the primaries leading up to the November 2008 U.S. presidential election. In the debates between Hillary Clinton and Barack Obama, the candidates focused on the negative impact that free trade was having on workers in the "rust belt" states. Hufbauer rejects these concerns, arguing that citizens in both wealthy industrialized countries and poorer developing countries ultimately benefit from the expansion of trade liberalization. In contrast, Joseph Stiglitz discusses the negative costs associated with trade liberalization as it has been practised by countries like the United States. He focuses on trade reforms that he argues would promote fair trade, for both rich and poor countries, rather than free trade.

✔ **YES**
Free Trade
GARY HUFBAUER

Free trade can benefit everyone—the developed and developing world. In large part because of open markets, the global economy is experiencing its greatest half century. In fact, free trade has increased American household income by lowering costs of products, increasing wages and making more-efficient American companies. And even though open markets may come with costs, the gains of globalization exceed them five times over. So, this means when there are burdens to be borne at home, Congress can well afford to help spread the benefits as workers transition. And if done right, free trade benefits the developing world, too, helping bring states out of poverty, allowing them to bargain on equal terms with far-larger countries and potentially stemming state failure.

Yet, the Democrats have splattered their primaries with nonsense about a "time-out" from trade agreements and "opting out" of the North American Free Trade Agreement (NAFTA). As president, neither Senator Hillary Clinton (D-NY) nor Senator Barack Obama (D-IL) could indulge such foolishness. The purpose of their catchy phrases, as everyone knows, is to snare convention delegates, not make policy. But enthusiastic supporters will call their candidate to account if he or she reaches the Oval Office.

Throughout the history of the world trading system—which is to say since the end of the Second World War—the twin objectives of U.S. commercial policy have been to foster economic prosperity and promote U.S. political alliances. These objectives will not vanish when a new president enters the White House in January 2009.

"Opting out" of NAFTA is the sort of ludicrous suggestion that can only surface on the campaign trail. Trade between the United States and its NAFTA partners represented almost 30 percent of total U.S. trade with the world in 2007. U.S. exports to Canada and Mexico totaled $378 billion in 2007, and some of this trade would be jeopardized—to the consternation of American farmers, industrialists and their congressmen. The United States needs the cooperation of Canada and Mexico on multiple fronts, from energy supplies to missile defense. Retreating from NAFTA would not only imperil relations with close neighbors, it would severely diminish U.S. credibility around the world.

Trade is almost miraculous in its effects. Even before NAFTA, the General Agreement on Tariffs and Trade (GATT—now the World Trade Organization, WTO) was born in Havana in 1947, part of a grand design to ensure European economic recovery. The GATT's role was to slash the protectionist thicket that sprang from

Gary Hufbauer "The Fair Play Debate: Free Trade", *The National Interest*, May/June 2008, pp. 15–18. Copyright © 2008 The National Interest.

the Depression and political divisions in the 1930s. During its first year, the GATT sponsored negotiations among twenty-three countries that led to forty-five thousand tariff concessions, covering 20 percent of world trade. Since then, seven successive "rounds" have reduced barriers on a progressively wider scope of commerce, now including more than 150 countries and reaching 90 percent of trade in the global marketplace. The payoff from GATT far exceeds the wildest expectations of those delegates meeting at Havana over a half century ago. World trade has expanded twenty-seven times between 1950 and 2005 (adjusted for inflation), and the world economy has enjoyed the best fifty years in recorded history.

Opposition to free trade is shortsighted—forgivable perhaps for an unemployed machinist in Ohio, but hardly the stuff of presidential policy. Free trade boosts growth and provides meaningful employment. A serious danger in the decades ahead is cascading violence in regions of low development, countries often characterized by political instability and feeble growth. Collectively, they are home to billions of people. Some of them, like Mexico and Colombia, are fighting drug lords and insurgents. Others, like Pakistan and Afghanistan, are fighting al-Qaeda. These are precisely the countries that will benefit the most from open trade and investment policies. Yet many of these countries have either marginalized themselves by erecting one barrier after another to world commerce or have been marginalized not only by the restrictive practices of the United States, Europe and Japan, but also by their own peers in the developing world.

Thus, for example, Tunisia maintains an import-weighted average tariff wall of 20 percent, which, among other harmful effects, slashes trade with its neighbors in the Middle East and North Africa as well as the rest of the world. In a perfect stroke of trade-policy inequity, the United States collects about the same tariff duties annually (approximately $400 million) from impoverished Cambodia as from wealthy Britain, even though Britain exports more than twenty times as much as Cambodia to American shores each year ($57 billion versus $2.5 billion). An outstanding example of the power of open markets is South Korea, a country that has handsomely prospered. In contrast, North Korea, which has followed a path of isolation, remains mired in poverty.

A country that accedes to the WTO, such as Ukraine is now doing, must first undertake a series of legislative and structural reforms to bring its trade regime up to par with the practice of other WTO members. This process gives the newly admitted states the basis for a stronger economy, thanks to the spillover effects to commercial law, property rights and many other areas. Over past decades, many developing countries have prospered from these disciplines. Once in, the country can join negotiations with other members and bring trade complaints to the WTO's dispute-settlement body. The new inductee becomes a full-fledged member of the WTO "club," with all the attendant rights and privileges. Thus, tiny Antigua won an important case against the mighty United States, and midsized Peru was victorious over the European Union.

Put simply, the World Trade Organization engages countries of all economic sizes and political shapes in a cooperative setting designed to liberalize commerce to their mutual advantage. It is hard to imagine President Obama or President Clinton paying serious attention to naysayers such as Senator Sherrod Brown (D-OH) or Lou Dobbs, who would have the United States turn its back on the most successful piece of economic architecture since 1945.

Furthermore, Democratic and Republican presidents alike have often pushed the free-trade agenda to buttress their foreign-policy objectives. Foreign policy was a core reason why President Harry Truman supported the GATT in the late 1940s in the face of opposition from leading Republicans, notably Senator Robert Taft (R-OH and intellectual godfather of the aforementioned Senator Sherrod Brown). Truman wanted to banish the specter of American isolationism in the Great Depression and forge an enduring transatlantic alliance. More recently, trade agreements have changed the political tenor with partners as varied as our immediate neighbors to the north and south, and China, our potential peer to the east.

Foreign-policy logic has thus informed many of the U.S. trade-policy choices that find expression in free-trade agreements (FTAs), beginning with Israel (1958), then Canada (1989) and Mexico (1994), and more recently Jordan (2000), Chile (2004), Australia (2004), Bahrain (2004), Morocco (2004) and Peru (2007). In each of these cases, the goal was to strengthen political relations as well as boost two-way trade and investment. Likewise, the two FTAs now awaiting congressional ratification with South Korea and Colombia are motivated by hopes of cementing alliances—in Asia where U.S.-Korea military ties are gradually supplanted by economic alliances and in South America where the overarching U.S. priorities are to root out terrorism and drug trafficking and establish a bulwark against Venezuela's Hugo Chávez. But FTAs are not just foreign-policy tools; FTA partners now buy more than 42 percent of total U.S. exports.

Our memories of the vital role played by trade diplomacy during the cold war are now fading. Even as we expand our global commerce, and even when rising exports are offsetting economic weakness at home, public support has slipped— both for the WTO and for other parts of the free-trade agenda. Polls suggest that U.S. popular opinion has swung into opposition; NAFTA and China have become metaphors for all that is supposedly wrong with globalization. But, no other tools of foreign policy—from traditional diplomacy to military operations—have the same change-making potential as trade. When properly implemented, in association with market reforms, free trade can lift the lives of hundreds of millions of people.

Still, economists teach that there is no such thing as a free lunch, and this is just as true of free trade as anything else. Dismantling trade barriers almost always entails adjustment costs as workers and firms change their jobs and products. This applies to the United States just like other countries. Moreover, gains are spread widely across the American population while costs are concentrated on older workers in less-dynamic industries (think clothing and auto parts)—a severe political handicap. But serious analysis shows that gains exceed costs by *at least* five to one. In fact, U.S. gains from globalization are so large that Congress could easily afford to quintuple the size of our meager trade-adjustment programs (now under $1 billion a year), in order to cover far-more impacted workers in manufacturing and service industries with much-better transition assistance.

The important point is that free trade is not some sort of "gift" to foreign countries; it pays off for the United States as well, to the tune of $10,000 annually for each American household. U.S. firms and consumers alike benefit from low prices. U.S. companies and their employees gain new access to markets abroad. More efficient U.S. firms thrive and expand, and in this way, trade creates new and higher-paying jobs for American workers.

In the heated Ohio primary, one of the presidential candidates tossed out bogus numbers about "jobs lost" on account of NAFTA (supposedly a million) and trade agreements in general (supposedly millions). The image evoked by these sound bites—huge annual permanent job losses with no offsetting job gains—has no foundation in economics and can best be attributed to poetic license.

The challenge awaiting the next president, in contrast to the current presidential contestants, is to move forward, not backward. NAFTA will be fifteen years old in January 2009, and improvements based on experience would be a tonic for North American relations. Labor provisions could be given sharper teeth; and the North American partners could pioneer sensible measures to address climate change, energy needs and security concerns. If Senator Obama or Senator Clinton should reach the White House, the NAFTA sound bite should be transformed by political alchemy from "opt out" to "upgrade."

Apart from NAFTA, the next president will be faced with multiple challenges outlined by U.S. Trade Representative Susan Schwab. The most important items on the agenda will be a successful conclusion of the Doha Development Round; the ratification of pending free-trade agreements with, namely, South Korea and Panama; and engaging U.S. partners on issues ranging from currency values to climate change. Some features of life in the White House seldom change, and one of them is the essential role of trade policy in international diplomacy.

✗ NO
Fair Trade
JOSEPH E. STIGLITZ

It has become commonplace for politicians of both political parties to trot out rhetoric about how we need free-but-fair trade. Expanding markets through trade liberalization, it is urged, is a win-win situation. How is it, then, that in spite of assertions that *everyone* benefits from trade, there is so much opposition, in both developed and developing countries? Is it that populists have so misled ordinary citizens that, though they are really better-off, they have come to believe they are doing worse?

Or is it because trade liberalization has, in fact, made many people worse off, in developed and developing countries alike? Not only can low-skilled American workers lose their jobs or be paid less, those in developing countries suffer, too. They end up having to take the short end of the stick time and time again in trade agreements because they have little leverage over the big boys. And the links between trade liberalization and growth are far weaker than liberalization advocates claim.

A closer look at both data and standard economic theory provides further insight into the strength of the opposition to trade liberalization. In most countries around the world, there is growing inequality. In the United States, not only is there a steady uptick in poverty, but median household income has been falling for at least eight years. There are many factors contributing to these changes: technology, weakening of social mores, labor unions and, lest we forget, trade liberalization. More than sixty years ago, prominent economists Paul Samuelson and Wolfgang Stolper explained that trade liberalization in high-income countries would lower wages of unskilled workers. The economists showed that even a movement toward free trade brought wages of unskilled workers around the world closer together, meaning, for example, that America's unskilled workers' pay would fall toward that of India and China. Although their model stems from the mid-twentieth century, some of its assumptions hold even more true today. In particular, globalization has greatly reduced disparities in knowledge and technology between the developed and developing world. Lower-paid workers in the developing world now often have the tools, and increasingly, even the education, to perform the same tasks as their counterparts in developed countries. American workers simply get paid more to do the same task. Quite obviously, this can hurt even the higher-paid skilled American worker.

More generally, *standard* economic theory does not say that everyone will be better-off as a result of trade liberalization, only that the winners *could* compensate the losers. They could take a portion of their gains, give it to the losers and

Joseph Stiglitz "The Fair Play Debate: Fair Trade", *The National Interest*, May/June 2008, pp. 19–24. Copyright © 2008 The National Interest.

everyone could be better-off. But, of course, the winners, which in much of America are the very well-off, haven't compensated the losers; indeed, some have been arguing that to compete in the new world of globalization requires cutbacks in government spending, including programs for the poor. The losers then lose doubly.

These results of traditional economic theory are based on assumptions like perfect information, perfect-risk markets, perfect competition and no innovation. But, of course, we do not live in such a perfect world. Modern economic theory has shown that in the imperfect world in which we live, trade liberalization can actually make *everyone* worse off. For instance, trade liberalization may expose individuals and firms to more risk. In the absence of adequate insurance markets, firms respond by shifting production away from high-return risky activities to safer, but lower-return areas, thereby lowering national income.

Careful studies have found, at best, weak links between trade liberalization and growth. Many studies do show that countries that have increased their levels of trade–China is a good example–have grown faster. But these countries did not liberalize in their earlier stages of development. They promoted exports and restricted imports. And this export promotion worked.

A standard argument for reducing tariffs is that it allows resources, especially labor, to move from lower-productivity sectors into higher-productivity ones. But all too often, it results in moving workers from low-productivity employment into zero-productivity unemployment. For example, workers in Jamaica's dairy industry cannot compete with America's highly subsidized milk exports, so when Jamaica liberalized, opening up its markets to these subsidized imports, its dairies were put out of business. But the dairy workers didn't automatically get reemployed elsewhere. Rather, they simply added to the already-high unemployment rolls. In many countries, where there is high unemployment, there is no need to "release" resources to expand exports. There are a variety of impediments to expanding exports–including internal barriers to trade (such as the absence of infrastructure, which highlights the need for aid-for-trade) and, on an even-more-basic level, the absence of capital. Ironically, under today's rules, trade liberalization may again make matters worse. That is because countries are being forced to open up their markets to foreign banks, which are more interested in lending to multinationals and national monopolies than to local small- and medium-sized businesses, the sources of job creation.

WAXING POLITIC

The case for trade liberalization is far weaker than most economists will admit. Those who are more honest fall back on political arguments: it is not that trade liberalization is such a good thing; it is that protectionism is such a bad thing. Inevitably, it is argued, special interests prevail. But in fact, most successful economies have evolved with at least some protection of new industries at critical stages of their development. In recent work, my colleague from Columbia University, Bruce Greenwald, and I have built on that idea by developing an "infant-economy argument" that looks at how using protection as countries grow can encourage the industrial sector—the sector most amenable to learning and technological progress. The benefits of that support then diffuse throughout the economy. Such policies do not require governments to "pick winners," to identify which particular industries are well suited to the country. These policies are based on a recognition that markets do not always work well, particularly when there are externalities, where actions in one part of the economy affect another. That there are huge spillovers from successful innovation is incontrovertible.

Politicians, of course, are not constrained by economics and economic logic. Even if we see in our model that safeguarding nascent sectors is the best way to support economic growth, trade advocates claim, for instance, that trade creates jobs. But exports create jobs; imports destroy them. If one justified trade liberalization on the basis of job creation, one would have to support export expansion but simultaneously advocate import restrictions—these days, typically through nontariff barriers called dumping and countervailing duties. This is the curious position taken by many politicians who *say* they favor free trade. George W. Bush, for instance, while bandying about terms such as free trade and free markets, imposed steel tariffs at a prohibitive level even against desperately poor and tiny Moldova. This in spite of the fact that Moldova was struggling to make the transition from communism to a market economy. American steel producers could not compete and demanded these kinds of tariffs—they couldn't compete, not because of unfair competition from abroad, but rather because of failed management at home. In this case, eventually the World Trade Organization (WTO) ruled against the United States, and this time, the United States complied.

The important point missed by these politicians—and the economists who serve them ill by using such arguments—is that trade is not about job creation. Maintaining the economy at full employment is the responsibility of monetary and fiscal policies. When they fail—as they have now done once again—unemployment increases, *whatever the trade regime*. In reality, trade is about standards of living. And that raises an important question: whose standards of living, exactly?

DOUBLE STANDARDS

In developing countries, there is another set of arguments against the kind of trade liberalization we have today. The so-called free-trade agreements being pushed by the Bush administration are, of course, not free-trade agreements at all. If they were, they would be a few pages long—with each party agreeing to eliminate its tariffs, nontariff barriers and subsidies. In fact, they go on for hundreds of pages. They are *managed*-trade agreements—typically managed for the special interests in the advanced industrial countries (especially those that make large campaign contributions, like the drug industry). The United States keeps its agricultural subsidies, and developing countries are not allowed to impose countervailing duties. And the agreements typically go well beyond trade, including investment agreements and intellectual-property provisions.

These investment agreements do far more than just protect against expropriation. In a perfect show of how all of this is supporting the developed countries while hurting the developing, they may even give American firms operating overseas protections that American firms operating domestically do not have—such as against loss of profits from new regulations. They represent a step backward in creating a rule of law: disputes are adjudicated in processes that fall far short of the standards that we expect of others, let alone of ourselves. Even worse, the ambiguous provisions can put countries in crisis in an impossible bind. They have given rise to large lawsuits, forcing developing countries to pay out hundreds of millions of dollars. In a particularly egregious example, Indonesia was forced to pay compensation for profits lost when it abrogated an almost-surely corrupt contract that then-President Suharto signed. Even though the abrogation of the agreement took place when Indonesia was falling into crisis and receiving support from the International Monetary Fund, the country was still held responsible for repayment of *anticipated* profits, which were unconscionably large because of the very corruption that many believe contributed to the country's problems in the first place.

In addition, beyond the terms of the investment agreements, the intellectual-property provisions, too, are onerous on developing countries. In fact, the intellectual-property-rights regime that is being foisted on developing countries is not only bad for developing countries; it is not good for American science and not good for global science. What separates developed from less-developed countries is not only a gap in resources but a gap in knowledge. The intellectual-property provisions reduce access to knowledge, making it more difficult to close the knowledge gap. And even beyond their impact on development, the provisions make it more difficult for developing countries to gain access to lifesaving medicines by making it harder for them to obtain generic drugs, which sell for a fraction of the price of the brand-name ones. The poor simply cannot afford brand-name prices. And because they cannot afford these prices, thousands will needlessly die. At the same time, while the drug companies demand these high prices, they spend little on the diseases that afflict the poor. This is hardly surprising: the drug companies focus on profits; one of the problems of being poor is that you have no money—including no money to buy drugs. Meanwhile, the drug companies have been reluctant to compensate the developing countries adequately for the genetic material that they obtain from them that often provides the basis of new drugs; and the intellectual-property regimes almost never provide any protection for developing countries' traditional knowledge, giving rise to worries about biopiracy. The United States, for instance, granted patents for basmati rice (which had been consumed in India for generations), for the healing properties of turmeric and for many uses of neem oil. Had India recognized and enforced these patents, it would have meant, for instance, that every time an Indian had eaten his traditional staple basmati rice, or used turmeric for healing an ailment, he would have had to send a check to the United States in payment of royalties.

Recent bilateral trade agreements are, of course, even worse in many respects than the earlier multilateral ones: how could one expect a developing country to have much bargaining power when negotiating with the United States? As several trade negotiators have told me bluntly, the United States demands, and they either take it or leave it. The United States says, if we make a concession for you, we would have to make it for everyone. In addition, not only does the array of bilateral and regional agreements undermine the multilateral trading system, but it also weakens market economics, as countries must look not for the cheapest inputs, but for the cheapest inputs satisfying the rules of origin. A Mexican apparel firm might be able to produce shirts more cheaply using Chinese buttons, but if he turns to the lowest-cost provider, his shirt will no longer be considered sufficiently "Mexican" to warrant duty-free access to the United States. Thus, the bilateral trade agreements actually impede global trade.

In both the multilateral and bilateral agreements, there has been more of a focus on liberalization and protection of capital than of labor; the asymmetry alters the bargaining power of labor versus capital because firms threaten that if the workers don't accept wage cuts, they will move elsewhere, contributing to the growing inequality around the world.

The cards are stacked against the developing countries in other ways as well. The WTO was a step in the right direction, creating an international rule of law in trade; even an unfair rule of law may be better than no rule of law at all, where the big countries can use their economic muscle without constraints. But the legal process is expensive, and this puts poor countries at a disadvantage. And even when they win, there is little assurance of compliance. Antigua won a big case against the United States, but has no effective way of enforcing its victory. The WTO has ruled that American cotton subsidies are illegal, yet the United States continues to provide them—twenty-five thousand rich American farmers benefit at the expense of millions of very poor people in the developing world. It is America's and Europe's refusal to do anything about their agricultural subsidies, more than anything else, that has stalled the so-called Doha Development Round.

But even in its conception, the Doha Development Round was a development round in name only; it was an attempt by the developed countries to put old wine into new bottles while hoping the developing countries wouldn't notice. But they did. A true development round—a trade regime that would promote development—would look markedly different.[1] It would, for instance, allow freer movement of labor—the global gains from labor-market liberalization are in fact much greater than from the liberalization of capital. It would eliminate agricultural subsidies. It would reduce the nontariff barriers, which have taken on increasing importance as tariff barriers have come down. What the trade ministers from the advanced industrial countries are trying to sell as a development round looks nothing like what a true development round would look like.

TRADE AGREEMENTS AND AMERICA'S NATIONAL INTEREST

The gap between American free-trade rhetoric and the unfair managed-trade reality is easily exploited by the critics of markets and of America. It provides an all-too-easy target. In some countries, America's trade agreements have helped promote democracy: citizens have been so aroused by America's unfair bilateral trade agreements that they have activated civil society, uniting disparate groups to work in unison to protest against the United States. The reason we wanted a trade agreement with Morocco was not because of the importance of our trade relations but because we wanted to build better relations with a moderate Arab country. Yet, by the time the U.S. trade representative put forth his largely nonnegotiable demands, the country had seen its largest street protests in years. If building goodwill was the intent of this and other trade agreements, the effect has been, at least in many cases, just the opposite.

None of this is inevitable. We could easily manage trade liberalization in a way in which there are more winners and fewer losers. But it is not automatic, and it is not easy. We have to devise better ways of safeguarding the losers—we need social protections, not protectionism. To take but one example: America is one of the few advanced industrial countries where there is reliance on employment-related health insurance, and it has, at the same time, a poor unemployment-insurance system. A worker who loses his job, whether as a result of foreign competition or technological change, loses his health insurance; and the paltry sums he gets in unemployment insurance make private purchase unaffordable for most. It is understandable why Americans are worried about losing their jobs as the economy slips into recession. But with most Americans today worse off than they were eight years ago, this recession is beginning even before fully recovering from the last; Americans are seeing their life savings being wiped away by the ever-declining price of housing (their one and only asset). It provides these Americans little comfort to know that someone making more than $100,000 a year, who has just gotten big tax breaks in 2001 and again in 2003, may be better-off as a result of trade liberalization. Vague promises that in the long run they, too, will be better-off provide little comfort—as Keynes quipped, "in the long run we are all dead." The median American male in his thirties has a lower income today than his counterpart thirty years ago. Trade may not have been the only reason for the decline, or even the most important one, but it has been part of the story. Individuals can't do anything about technology;

they can do something about trade. If there are benefits from trade and the winners want to sustain support for trade liberalization, they must be willing to share more of the gains with the losers.

If more developing countries are to benefit more from trade liberalization, we need a fairer trade regime; and if more people are to benefit from trade liberalization, we need to manage trade liberalization better. The United States should move toward a more comprehensive agenda for fairer trade and better-managed trade liberalization.[2] This agenda will ensure that the fruits of trade are shared by both the poor and the rich, in both the developing and developed countries. Without it, we should not be surprised about the backlash we are seeing, both in the United States and abroad.

NOTES

1. In my book with Andrew Charlton, *Fair Trade for All* (Cambridge: Oxford University Press, 2005), we describe in more detail what this regime would look like.

2. I explain this agenda further in my book *Making Globalization Work* (New York: W. W. Norton, 2006).

POSTSCRIPT

The above debate highlights the importance of language and the importance of understanding what is meant by a term. Stiglitz points out that those who often use the term "free trade" are often referring to something that in practice is something different than free trade. Often "free trade agreements," he notes, contain additional barriers to trade rather than meaning a reduction of all barriers to trade. Hence, he advocates instead for what he calls "fair trade."

Fair trade can also have different connotations. Here, Stiglitz discusses changes to the international trading regime that is fairer to all trading partners. The term has also come to refer to a social movement that seeks to establish alternative trade channels by which developing country producers can receive fairer wages for their produce. While still campaigning for changes in the rules and practice of conventional international trade regimes, the fair trade movement focuses on developing trading partnerships with non-governmental organizations or providing certification that a product has been fairly traded. A perspective on this approach to fair trade can be found in Laure Waridel, *Coffee with Pleasure: Just Java and World Trade* (Montreal: Black Rose Books, 2002).

Can Sweatshops and Cheap Labour Benefit the Poor?

✔ **YES**

PAUL KRUGMAN, "In Praise of Cheap Labor," *Slate*, 1997. web.mit.edu/
krugman/www/smokey.html

✘ **NO**

JOHN MILLER, "Why Economists Are Wrong about Sweatshops and the
Antisweatshop Movement," *Challenge*, 46, no. 1 (January/February 2003):
93–122

In 1995, Craig Kielburger, a 12-year-old Canadian boy, read about the tragic story
of Iqbal Masih, a child of the same age who had been murdered in Pakistan. Iqbal
had been sold into child labour by his parents at the age of four. This practice was
common among many poor Pakistani families who, having accumulated debts to
landlords and local merchants, were desperate to find a means of paying them off.
For the next six years, Iqbal worked in deplorable and dangerous conditions, putting in up to 16 hours a day, 6 days a week.

In 1992, Iqbal came into contact with activists working for the Bonded Labor
Liberation Front (BLLF), a human rights organization campaigning against
bonded child labour. Iqbal soon became a spokesperson for the organization,
travelling overseas to tell his story to consumers in Western countries. He
became a symbol for the movement and was awarded the Reebok Human Rights
Youth in Action Award and a future scholarship to an American university.
However, in 1995, at the age of 12, while visiting relatives in a Pakistani village,
Iqbal was murdered, reportedly by those associated with interests in the
Pakistani carpet industry who see the BLLF campaign as a threat. The news of
Iqbal's story catalyzed Craig Kielburger into action, leading him to form his own
award-winning *Free the Children* campaign, aimed at abolishing exploitative
child labour practices throughout the world.

Stories like those of Iqbal have focused attention not only on the problem of
child labour but also on the role of sweatshops and cheap labour practices in the
development of economies throughout the world. Much of this debate has focused
on the practice of retailing multinationals in industrialized countries that turn
to low-wage workers in developing countries as a way of procuring cheap goods.
This allows them to maximize profits while undercutting the prices of competitors.
The term "sweatshop" is often associated with the garment industry, where
companies seek to boost profits by prohibiting collective bargaining and paying

low wages with no benefits. Workers are often forced to work in unsafe conditions and are vulnerable to physical and sexual abuse. Workers in a developing country labour at 16 cents an hour, 12 hours a day, 7 days a week to make a running shoe that sells for $150 in North America, while basketball stars receive multimillion dollar contracts to endorse them.

Critics of such practices see sweatshops as an example of the "race to the bottom" phenomenon that has come to characterize globalization. Big corporations headquartered in industrialized countries seek to escape rigorous labour wage and safety guidelines by looking to factories in countries with more relaxed labour and safety standards. Many developing countries in turn compete for the opportunity to attract these corporations by offering lower labour, safety, and environmental standards than their neighbours. In his book *The Race to the Bottom* (Westview Press, 2000), Alan Tonelson argues that it is often workers in developing countries who are called upon to shoulder the burdens of globalization, while Western multinationals continue to amass profits. Rather that contributing to the development of these countries, corporations supporting these sweatshops simply exploit the poverty and desperation of the poor and vulnerable. As a result, a number of campaigns, including *Free the Children,* have emerged in industrialized countries to publicize the dangers and costs of such cheap labour policies. A growing number of anti-sweatshop organizations have demanded that corporations increase wages, improve safety, observe human rights and environmental standards, and adopt codes of conduct for operating in developing countries. A number of boycott campaigns have been organized against high profile corporations such as Nike, Reebok, and Fruit of the Loom.

While some of these boycotts and public campaigns have been successful, others have not always produced results that are in the best interests of sweatshop workers themselves. In some cases, corporations such as Nike and The Gap simply pulled out of developing countries, leaving the workers out of work and costing the local economies millions of dollars.

Another argument is that this is simply a necessary phase that all countries go through on the road to prosperity. Great Britain and the United States both saw the widespread use of cheap labour and sweatshop conditions in the early phase of their industrialization. As their economies developed and matured, these policies were gradually phased out. For many developing nations, cheap labour is the only commodity that they can offer the industrialized world on a competitive basis. If corporations are not allowed to invest and take advantage of these conditions, labourers in these countries will simply be forced back into agricultural subsistence. It is preferable that these countries go through a transitional period of low wages and poor working conditions in the short run. Once they have been able to build stronger economies, better labour conditions will emerge. The current policies simply mark an important first step toward greater future prosperity.

In the following two essays, we find two quite different takes on the role that cheap labour policies and sweatshops play in the process of development. In the first essay, Paul Krugman, a noted American economist who now teaches at Princeton University, presents his widely read essay, "In Praise of Cheap Labor," which has become somewhat of a classic statement of the pro-sweatshop argument. As his provocative title suggests, Krugman argues that "cheap labour" is really a relative economic concept. What appears as abysmal wages to us may for someone be a vast improvement over even greater poverty in the rural areas. In the second essay, John Miller, an economics professor at Wheaton College and an anti-sweatshop activist himself, provides a critique of the economic assumptions underlying Krugman's argument.

✔ YES
In Praise of Cheap Labor
PAUL KRUGMAN

For many years a huge Manila garbage dump known as Smokey Mountain was a favorite media symbol of Third World poverty. Several thousand men, women, and children lived on that dump—enduring the stench, the flies, and the toxic waste in order to make a living combing the garbage for scrap metal and other recyclables. And they lived there voluntarily, because the $10 or so a squatter family could clear in a day was better than the alternatives.

The squatters are gone now, forcibly removed by Philippine police last year as a cosmetic move in advance of a Pacific Rim summit. But I found myself thinking about Smokey Mountain recently, after reading my latest batch of hate mail.

The occasion was an op-ed piece I had written for the *New York Times,* in which I had pointed out that while wages and working conditions in the new export industries of the Third World are appalling, they are a big improvement over the "previous, less visible rural poverty." I guess I should have expected that this comment would generate letters along the lines of, "Well, if you lose your comfortable position as an American professor you can always find another job—as long as you are 12 years old and willing to work for 40 cents an hour."

Such moral outrage is common among the opponents of globalization—of the transfer of technology and capital from high-wage to low-wage countries and the resulting growth of labor-intensive Third World exports. These critics take it as a given that anyone with a good word for this process is naive or corrupt and, in either case, a de facto agent of global capital in its oppression of workers here and abroad.

But matters are not that simple, and the moral lines are not that clear. In fact, let me make a counter-accusation: The lofty moral tone of the opponents of globalization is possible only because they have chosen not to think their position through. While fat-cat capitalists might benefit from globalization, the biggest beneficiaries are, yes, Third World workers.

After all, global poverty is not something recently invented for the benefit of multinational corporations. Let's turn the clock back to the Third World as it was only two decades ago (and still is, in many countries). In those days, although the rapid economic growth of a handful of small Asian nations had started to attract attention, developing countries like Indonesia or Bangladesh were still mainly what they had always been: exporters of raw materials, importers of manufactures. Inefficient manufacturing sectors served their domestic markets, sheltered behind import quotas, but generated few jobs. Meanwhile, population pressure pushed desperate peasants into cultivating ever more marginal land or seeking a livelihood in any way possible—such as homesteading on a mountain of garbage.

Paul Krugman, "In Praise of Cheap Labor", found at: http://web.mit.edu/krugman/www/smokey.html.

Given this lack of other opportunities, you could hire workers in Jakarta or Manila for a pittance. But in the mid-'70s, cheap labor was not enough to allow a developing country to compete in world markets for manufactured goods. The entrenched advantages of advanced nations—their infrastructure and technical know-how, the vastly larger size of their markets and their proximity to suppliers of key components, their political stability and the subtle-but-crucial social adaptations that are necessary to operate an efficient economy—seemed to outweigh even a tenfold or twentyfold disparity in wage rates.

And then something changed. Some combination of factors that we still don't fully understand—lower tariff barriers, improved telecommunications, cheaper air transport—reduced the disadvantages of producing in developing countries. (Other things being the same, it is still better to produce in the First World—stories of companies that moved production to Mexico or East Asia, then moved back after experiencing the disadvantages of the Third World environment, are common.) In a substantial number of industries, low wages allowed developing countries to break into world markets. And so countries that had previously made a living selling jute or coffee started producing shirts and sneakers instead.

Workers in those shirt and sneaker factories are, inevitably, paid very little and expected to endure terrible working conditions. I say "inevitably" because their employers are not in business for their (or their workers') health; they pay as little as possible, and that minimum is determined by the other opportunities available to workers. And these are still extremely poor countries, where living on a garbage heap is attractive compared with the alternatives.

And yet, wherever the new export industries have grown, there has been measurable improvement in the lives of ordinary people. Partly this is because a growing industry must offer a somewhat higher wage than workers could get elsewhere in order to get them to move. More importantly, however, the growth of manufacturing—and of the penumbra of other jobs that the new export sector creates—has a ripple effect throughout the economy. The pressure on the land becomes less intense, so rural wages rise; the pool of unemployed urban dwellers always anxious for work shrinks, so factories start to compete with each other for workers, and urban wages also begin to rise. Where the process has gone on long enough—say, in South Korea or Taiwan—average wages start to approach what an American teenager can earn at McDonald's. And eventually people are no longer eager to live on garbage dumps. (Smokey Mountain persisted because the Philippines, until recently, did not share in the export-led growth of its neighbors. Jobs that pay better than scavenging are still few and far between.)

The benefits of export-led economic growth to the mass of people in the newly industrializing economies are not a matter of conjecture. A country like Indonesia is still so poor that progress can be measured in terms of how much the average person gets to eat; since 1970, per capita intake has risen from less than 2,100 to more than 2,800 calories a day. A shocking one-third of young children are still malnourished—but in 1975, the fraction was more than half. Similar improvements can be seen throughout the Pacific Rim, and even in places like Bangladesh. These improvements have not taken place because well-meaning people in the West have done anything to help—foreign aid, never large, has lately shrunk to virtually nothing. Nor is it the result of the benign policies of national governments, which are as callous and corrupt as ever. It is the indirect and unintended result of the actions of soulless multinationals and rapacious local entrepreneurs, whose only concern was to take advantage of the profit opportunities offered by cheap labor. It is not an edifying spectacle; but no matter how base the motives of those involved, the result has been to move hundreds of millions of people from abject poverty to something still awful but nonetheless significantly better.

Why, then, the outrage of my correspondents? Why does the image of an Indonesian sewing sneakers for 60 cents an hour evoke so much more feeling than the image of another Indonesian earning the equivalent of 30 cents an hour trying to feed his family on a tiny plot of land—or of a Filipino scavenging on a garbage heap?

The main answer, I think, is a sort of fastidiousness. Unlike the starving subsistence farmer, the women and children in the sneaker factory are working at slave wages *for our benefit*—and this makes us feel unclean. And so there are self-righteous demands for international labor standards: We should not, the opponents of globalization insist, be willing to buy those sneakers and shirts unless the people who make them receive decent wages and work under decent conditions.

This sounds only fair—but is it? Let's think through the consequences.

First of all, even if we could assure the workers in Third World export industries of higher wages and better working conditions, this would do nothing for the peasants, day laborers, scavengers, and so on who make up the bulk of these developing countries' populations. At best, forcing developing countries to adhere to our labor standards would create a privileged labor aristocracy, leaving the poor majority no better off.

And it might not even do that. The advantages of established First World industries are still formidable. The only reason developing countries have been able to compete with those industries is their ability to offer employers cheap labor. Deny them that ability, and you might well deny them the prospect of continuing industrial growth, even reverse the growth that has been achieved. And since export-oriented growth, for all its injustice, has been a huge boon for the workers in those nations, anything that curtails that growth is very much against their interests. A policy of good jobs in principle, but no jobs in practice, might assuage our consciences, but it is no favor to its alleged beneficiaries.

You may say that the wretched of the earth should not be forced to serve as hewers of wood, drawers of water, and sewers of sneakers for the affluent. But is the alternative? Should they be helped with foreign aid? Maybe—although the historical record of regions like southern Italy suggests that such aid has a tendency to promote perpetual dependence. Anyway, there isn't the slightest prospect of significant aid materializing. Should their own governments provide more social justice? Of course—but they won't, or at least not because we tell them to. And as long as you have no realistic alternative to industrialization based on low wages, to oppose it means that you are willing to deny desperately poor people the best chance they have of progress for the sake of what amounts to an aesthetic standard—that is, the fact that you don't like the idea of workers being paid a pittance to supply rich Westerners with fashion items.

In short, my correspondents are not entitled to their self-righteousness. They have no thought the matter through. And when the hopes of hundreds of millions are at stake, thinking things through is not just good intellectual practice. It is a moral duty.

✗ NO
Why Economists Are Wrong about Sweatshops and the Antisweatshop Movement
JOHN MILLER

The student-led antisweatshop movement that took hold on many college campuses during the late 1990s should have pleased economists. Studying the working conditions faced by factory workers across the globe offered powerful lessons about the workings of the world economy, the dimensions of world poverty, and most students' privileged position in that economy.

On top of that, these students were dedicated not just to explaining sweatshop conditions, but also to changing them. They wanted desperately to do something to put a stop to the brutalization and assaults on human dignity suffered by the women and men who made their jeans, t-shirts, or sneakers. On many campuses, student activism succeeded in pressuring college administrators by demanding that clothing bearing their college logo not be made under sweatshop conditions, and, at best, that it be made by workers earning a living wage (Featherstone and United Students Against Sweatshops 2002).

But most mainstream economists were not at all pleased. No, they did not dispute these tales from the factory floor, many of which had been confirmed in the business press (Roberts and Bernstein 2000) and by international agencies (ILO 2000). Rather, mainstream economists rushed to defend the positive role of low-wage factory jobs, the very kind we usually call sweatshops, in economic development and in alleviating poverty.

What is more, these economists were generally dismissive of the student-led antisweatshop movement. [...]

The response of mainstream economists to the antisweatshop movement was hardly surprising. Economists have a penchant for playing the contrarian, and, for the most part, they oppose interventions into market outcomes, even interventions into the labor markets of the developing world.

No matter how predictable, their response was profoundly disappointing. Although it contains elements of truth, what economists have to say about sweatshops misses the mark. That was my conclusion after spending summer and fall of 2000 reading much of what economists and economic journalists had written about sweatshops as I prepared to teach my undergraduate seminar, "Sweatshops and the Global Economy." First, the propositions that mainstream economists rely on to defend sweatshops are misleading, rooted in an exchange perspective that obscures sweatshop oppression. Sweatshop oppression is not defined by labor market exchanges but by the characteristics of a job. Second, policy positions based on these propositions are equally flawed. Economists' claim that market-led economic development, independent of labor and social movements and government regulation, will put an end to sweatshop conditions distorts the historical record. Finally, their assertion that demands for better working conditions in the world-export factories will harm third-world workers and frustrate poverty alleviation is also suspect.

With that said, the challenge issued by mainstream economists to the anti-sweatshop movement remains a formidable one. What economists have to say about the sweatshops has considerable power in the way of persuasion and influence. [...] Often it is their writings that are being distilled in what journalists, government officials, and the general public have to say about sweatshops.

[...]

JUST ENFORCE THE LAW

What to do about sweatshops? That is not a difficult question for most mainstream economists to answer. Just enforce the law, they say (Weidenbaum 1999, 26–28). And avoid other "institutional interventions" that might impair a market-led development that will enhance productivity and thereby raise wages and improve working conditions (Irwin 2002, 214; Sengenberger 1994, 10). By law, they mean local labor law, not some labor standard that ill-informed protesters (or even the International Labor Organization, for that matter) would impose on multinational corporations and their subcontractors in developing economies.

No one in the antisweatshop movement would quarrel with the insistence that the law be obeyed. In fact, several U.S. antisweatshop groups define a sweatshop in legal terms. According to Feminists Against Sweatshops (2002), for instance, sweatshop operators are employers who violate two or more labor laws, from the prohibition of child labor, to health, safety, fire, and building codes, to forced overtime and the minimum wage.

Effective enforcement of local labor law in the developing world, where labor legislation in many countries—on paper, at least—is quite extensive, would surely help to combat sweatshop abuse as well (Portes 1994, 163). For instance, *Made in China,* a report of the National Labor Committee, the leading U.S.-based antisweatshop group, found that subcontractors producing goods for U.S. corporations, including Wal-Mart and Nike, "routinely violate" Chinese labor law. In some of these factories, young women work as long as seventy hours a week and are paid just pennies an hour after pay deductions for board and room, clear violations of China's labor law (Kernaghan 2000). A three-month Business Week investigation of the Chun Si Enterprise Handbag Factory in southern China, which makes Kathie Lee Gifford handbags sold by Wal-Mart stores, confirmed that workers there confronted labor practices that included illegally collected fines, confiscated identity papers, and beatings (Roberts and Bernstein 2000).

But the limitations of this legal prescription for curing sweatshop abuse become obvious when we go to apply it to countries where local labor law, even on paper, does not measure up to the most minimal, internationally agreed-upon labor standards. Take the case of the high-performance economies of Southeast Asia, Indonesia, Malaysia, and Thailand. In those countries, several core labor conventions of the International Labor Organization (ILO) have gone unratified—including the right to organize. Minimum wages are well below the level necessary to lift a family of three above the poverty line, the usual definition of a living wage. And in those countries (as well as China), independent trade union activity is systematically and sometimes brutally suppressed.

[...]

A DEFENSE OF SWEATSHOPS?

The defense of sweatshops offered up by mainstream economists turns on two elegantly simple and ideologically powerful propositions. The first is that workers freely choose to enter these jobs, and the second is that these sweatshop jobs are better than the alternative employments available to them in developing economies. Both propositions have a certain truth to them.

An Exchange Perspective

From the perspective of mainstream economics, every exchange, including the exchange between worker and boss, is freely entered into and only takes place because both parties are made better off. Hiring workers to fill the jobs in the world-export factories is no exception.

Of course, in some cases, workers do not freely enter into sweatshop employment even by the usual standards of wage labor. Sometimes workers are held captive. For example, a 1995 police raid of a fenced-in compound of seven apartments in El Monte, California, found a clandestine garment sweatshop where some seventy-two illegal Thai immigrants were held in virtual captivity as they sewed clothes for brand-name labels (Su 1997, 143). Other times, workers find themselves locked into walled factory compounds surrounded by barbed wire, sometimes required to work fifteen hours a day, seven days a week, subject to physical abuse, and, after fines and charges are deducted from their paycheck, left without the money necessary to repay exorbitant hiring fees. That was the case for the more than 50,000 young female immigrants from China, the Philippines, Bangladesh, and Thailand who were recently discovered in Saipan (part of the Commonwealth of the Northern Mariana Islands, a territory of the United States) working under these near-slavelike conditions as they produced clothing for major American distributors bearing the label "Made in the United States" (ILO 2000).

But in most cases, workers do choose these jobs, if hardly freely or without the coercion of economic necessity. Seen from the exchange perspective of mainstream economics, that choice alone demonstrates that these factory job are neither sweatshops nor exploitative.

Listen to how mainstream economists and their followers make this argument. In response to the National Labor Committee's exposé of conditions in the Honduran factories manufacturing Kathie Lee clothing for Wal-Mart, El Salvadoran economist Lucy Martinez-Mont assured us that "People choose to work in maquila shops of their own free will, because those are the best jobs available to them" (Martinez-Mont 1996, sec. A, p. 14). For economic journalist Nicholas Kristof (1998), the story of Mrs. Tratiwoon, an Indonesian woman, makes the same point. She sustains herself and her son by picking through a garbage dump outside of Jakarta in search of metal scraps to sell. She tells Kristof of her dreams for her three-year-old son as she works. "She wants him to grow up to work in a sweatshop."

Stories such as this one are powerful. The fact that many in the developing world are worse off than workers in the world-export factories is a point that economists supportive of the antisweatshop movement do not deny. For instance, a few years back, economist Arthur MacEwan, my colleague at *Dollars & Sense,* a popular economics magazine, made much the same point. He observed that in a poor country like Indonesia, where women working in agriculture are paid wages one-fifth those of women working in manufacturing, sweatshops do not seem to have a hard time finding workers (MacEwan 1998). And the Scholars Against Sweatshop Labor statement (2001) admits that "Even after allowing for the frequent low wages and poor working conditions in these jobs, they are still generally superior to 'informal' employment in, for example, much of agriculture or urban street vending."

This is not meant to suggest that these exchanges between employers and poor workers with few alternatives are in reality voluntary or that world-export factory jobs are not sweatshops or places of exploitation. Rather, as political philosopher Michael Waltzer argues, these exchanges should be seen as "trades of last resort" or "desperate" exchanges that need to be protected by labor legislation regulating such things as limits on hours, a wage floor, and guaranteed health and safety requirements (Rodrik 1997, 35).

Prevailing Wages and Working Conditions

What mainstream economists say in defense of sweatshops is limited in other ways as well. For instance, an ACIT letter (2000) misstates the argument. The ACIT writes that multinational corporations "commonly pay their workers more on average in comparison to the prevailing market wage for similar workers employed elsewhere in the economy." But, as the SASL authors correctly point out, "While this is true, it does not speak to the situation in which most garments are produced throughout the world—which is by firms subcontracted by multinational corporations, not the

MNCs themselves." The ACIT authors implicitly acknowledge as much, for in the next sentence they write that, "in cases where subcontracting is involved, workers are generally paid no less than the prevailing market wage."

The SASL statement also warns that the ACIT claim that subcontractors pay the prevailing market wage does not by itself make a persuasive case that the world export factories we commonly call sweatshops are anything but that. The SASL authors (2001) emphasize that

> the prevailing market wage is frequently extremely low for garment workers in less developed countries. In addition, the recent university-sponsored studies as well as an October 2000 report by the International Labor Organization consistently find that serious workplace abuses and violations of workers' rights are occurring in the garment industry throughout the world.

The same can be said about other world-export factories. Consider for a minute the working conditions at the Indonesian factories that produce footwear for Reebok, the Stoughton, Massachusetts–based international corporation that "goes to great lengths to portray itself as a conscientious promoter of human rights in the Third World" (Zuckoff 1994). Despite its status as a model employer, working conditions at factories that make Reebok footwear became the focus of the *Boston Globe* 1994 series entitled "Foul Trade" (Zuckoff 1994). The *Globe* tells the story of Yati, a young Indonesian woman in Tangerang, Indonesia. She works sewing bits of leather and lace for tennis shoes sold as Reeboks.

Yati sits at a sewing machine, which is one of sixty in her row. There are forty-six rows on the factory floor. For working sixty-three hours a week, Yati earns not quite $80 a month–just about the price of a pair of Reeboks in the United States. Her hourly pay is less than 32 cents per hour, which exceeds the minimum wage for her region of Indonesia. Yati lives in a nearby ten-by-twelve-foot shack with no furniture. She and her two roommates sleep on the mud and tile floor.

A factory like the one Yati works in is typically owned by an East Asian company. For instance, PT Tong Yang Indonesia, a South Korean–owned factory, pumped out 400,000 pairs of Reeboks a month in 1993. In return, Reebok paid its owner, Tan Chuan Cheng, $10.20 for each pair of shoes and then sold them for $60 or more in the United States. Most of Tan's payment went to purchase materials. Tan told the *Globe* that wages accounted for as little as $1.40 of the cost of a pair of shoes (Zuckoff 1994).

A More Effective Response

As I taught my seminar on sweatshops, I settled on a more effective response to the mainstream economic argument. It is simply this: Their argument is irrelevant for determining if a factory is a sweatshop or if workers are exploited. Sweatshop conditions are defined by the characteristics of a job. If workers are denied the right to organize, suffer unsafe and abusive working conditions, are forced to work over-time, or are paid less than a living wage, then they work in a sweatshop, regardless of how they came to take their jobs or if the alternatives they face are worse yet.

A careful reading of what the mainstream exchange perspective suggests about sweatshop jobs is not they are "good news" for the world's poor but "less bad news" than the usual conditions of work in the agricultural and informal sectors. The oppressive conditions of the work in the world-export factories are not denied by their argument. For instance, ACIT leader Jagdish Bhagwati says sweatshop jobs are a "ticket to slightly less impoverishment" (Goldberg 2001, 30).

[...]

CONFRONTING CRITICS OF THE ANTISWEATSHOP MOVEMENT

Still, none of the above speaks directly to the contention of mainstream economists that imposing "enlightened standards" advocated by the antisweatshop activists onto conditions for employment in the export factories of the developing world will immiserate the very workers the movement intends to help (ACIT 2000).

Core Labor Standards

To begin with, as labor economist Richard Freeman (1994, 80) writes, "Everyone, almost everyone is for some standards" (emphasis in the original). Surely that includes economists who would combat sweatshops by insisting that local labor law be respected. Even their position recognizes that the "voluntary" exchange of labor for wages must be delimited by rules, collectively determined and obeyed by all.

The relevant question is: What are those rules, and are any so basic that they should be applied universally, transcending the normal bounds of sovereignty? For the most part, economists, trained after all as economists and not political philosophers, have little to say on this matter other than to caution that outside of the condemnation of slavery, there is no universal agreement about the appro-priateness of labor standards even when it comes to bonded labor and child labor (Bhagwati 1995, 754; Brown 2001, 94; Irwin 2002, 216).

Nonetheless other economists, even some critical of the antisweatshop movement, are favorably disposed toward international labor standards about safety and health, forced labor, and the right to organize. For instance, Alice Amsden, an economist who opposes establishing wage standards on developing economies, favors the imposition of other labor standards. "The issue," she says, "is not health and safety conditions, the right of workers to be treated like human beings—not to be murdered for organizing unions, for example. These rights are inviolate" (Amsden 1995). At times, even Jagdish Bhagwati has taken a similar position (Bhagwati 2002, 60).

The International Labor Organization, in its 1998 Declaration on Fundamental Principles at Work, took a similar position. The ILO held that each of its 175 members (even if they have not ratified the conventions in question) was obligated "to respect, to promote and to realize" the fundamental rights of "freedom of association and the effective recognition of the right to collective bargaining, the elimination of all forms of forced or compulsory labour, the effective abolition of child labour and the elimination of discrimination in respect of employment and occupation" (2002a).

The empirical evidence of the effect of these core labor standards on economic development is ambiguous. For instance, the Organization for Economic Cooperation and Development (OECD) found that countries that strengthen these core labor standards "can increase economic growth and efficiency" (OECD 2000, 14). International trade economist Jai Mah, on the other hand, found that ratification of the ILO Conventions on freedom of association and on the right to nondiscrimination negatively affected the export performance of developing countries (Mah 1997, 781). And a study conducted by Dani Rodrik, another international trade economist, suggested that low core labor standards enhanced a country's comparative advantage in the production of labor-intensive goods but deterred rather than attracted direct foreign investment (Rodrik 1996, 59).

The Living Wage

Nevertheless, almost all mainstream economists draw the line at labor codes designed to boost wages as opposed to leaving the determination of wages to labor market outcomes. That surely goes for labor codes that call for the payment of a living wage, usually defined as a wage adequate to lift a worker and two dependents out of poverty. The ACIT worries that if multinational corporations are persuaded to increase their wages (and those of their subcontractors) "in response to what the on-going studies by the anti-sweatshop movement may conclude are appropriate wage levels, the net result would be shifts in employments that will worsen the collective welfare of the very workers who are supposed to be helped." (2001). And ACIT leader Bhagwati dismisses the call for multinationals and their subcontractors to pay a living wage as so much first-world protectionism cloaked in the language of "social responsibility" (Bhagwati 2000, 11). As he sees it, students' demand that a "living wage" be paid in developing countries would dull the one competitive advantage enjoyed by these countries, cheap labor.

But, in practice, would a labor standard demanding that multinational corporations and their subcontractors boost their wages beyond the local minimum wage and toward a living wage be a jobs killer? On that point the ACIT letter is silent, as journalists Featherstone and Henwood point out (2001a).

These economists may be short on evidence about the effects of higher wages on the demand for labor by multinational corporations and their subcontractors, but they are long on authority. Their proposition is as simple as this: "Either you believe labor demand curves are downward sloping, or you don't," as a neoclassical colleague said to me. Of course, not to believe that demand curves are negatively sloped would be tantamount to declaring yourself an economic illiterate.

Still, we can ask just how responsive are the hiring decisions of multinational corporations and their subcontractors to higher wages. There is real reason to believe that the right answer is, not very responsive.

Economists Robert Pollin, James Heintz, and Justine Burns recently looked more closely at this question (Pollin et al. 2001). They examined the impact that a 100 percent increase in the pay for apparel workers in Mexico and in the United States would have on costs relative to the retail price those garments sell for in the United States. Their preliminary findings are that doubling the pay of nonsupervisory workers would add just 50 cents to the production costs of a men's casual shirt sold for $32 in the United States, or just 1.6 percent of the retail price. And even if the wage increase were passed on to consumers, which seems likely because retailers in the U.S. garment industry enjoy substantial market power, Pollin et al. argue that the increase in price is well within the amount that recent surveys suggest U.S. consumers are willing to pay to purchase goods produced under "good" working conditions as opposed to sweatshop conditions. (See Elliot and Freeman [2000] for a detailed discussion of survey results.) More generally, using a sample of forty-five countries over the period 1992–97, Pollin et al. found no statistically significant relationship between real wages and employment growth in the apparel industry. Their results suggest that the mainstream economists' claim that improving the quality of jobs in the world export factories (by boosting wages) will reduce the number of jobs is not evident in the data (Pollin et al. 2001).

Even if this counterexample is not convincing, it is important to recall that the demand curve that defines the responsiveness of multinational corporations and their subcontractors to wage increases for factory workers is a theoretical device drawn while holding other economic circumstances constant, including public policy. In reality, those circumstances are neither fixed nor unalterable. In fact, to counteract any negative effect that higher wages might have on employment, the SASL statement calls for the adoption of new polices, which include

> measures to expand the overall number of relatively high quality jobs; relief from excessive foreign debt payments; raising worker job satisfaction and productivity and the quality of goods they produce; and improving the capacity to bring final products to retail markets. (SASL 2001)

"Shifting the demand curve for labor outward," says economic sociologist Peter Evans (2002), "is almost the definition of economic development-making people more valuable relative to the commodities they need to live." This "high road" approach to development, adds Evans, has the additional benefit of augmenting the demand for the commodities that workers produce.

Historical Change and Social Improvement

A labor code that requires multinational corporations and their subcontractors to pay a living wage, provide safe and healthy working conditions, and allow workers to organize would be likely to have yet more profound effects on these developing economies. On this point, the antisweatshop activists and their critics agree. What they disagree about is whether these broader effects will be a help or hindrance to economic development and an improved standard of living in the developing world (Freeman 1992).

Mainstream critics argue that labor codes are likely to have widespread debilitating effects. The institutionalization of these labor standards proposed by activists, they argue, would derail a market-led development process (Irwin 2002, 214; Sengenberger 1994, 10–11).

As they see it, labor-intensive sweatshops are good starter jobs—the very jobs that successful developing economies and developed countries used as "stepping-stones" to an improved standard of living for their citizens. And in each case, these countries outgrew their "sweatshop phase" through market-led development that enhanced productivity, not through the interventions of an antisweatshop movement (Krugman 1994, 116).

These economists often use the Asian economies as examples of national economies that abandoned "sweatshop practices" as they grew. Their list includes Japan, which moved from poverty to wealth early in the twentieth century, and the tiger economies—South Korea, Hong Kong, Singapore, and Taiwan—which grew rapidly in the second half of the century to become middle income countries (Irwin 2002; Krugman 1994; Krugman 1997; Lim 1990; Weidenbaum 1999). Paul Krugman (1997) allows that some tigers relied on foreign plant owners (e.g., Singapore) while others shunned them (e.g., South Korea). Nonetheless, he maintains that their first stage of development had one constant: "It's always sweatshops" (Meyerson 1997).

For anyone who doubts that market-led development that begins with a sweatshop phase produces intergenerational progress, Murray Weidenbaum (1999) invokes the personal story of Milton Friedman, the Nobel Prize–winning economist. "If his parents were not willing to work so long and hard under sweatshop conditions, they could not have earned the money to invest in his education," writes Weidenbaum. "We should all be grateful for that investment by a previous generation of Friedmans and for the circumstances that enabled them to make that enlightened choice."

But these arguments distort the historical record and misrepresent how social improvement is brought about with economic development. First, the claim that developed economies passed through a sweatshop stage does not establish that sweatshops caused or contributed to the enhanced productivity that they say improved working conditions. Second, in the developed world, the sweatshop phase was not extinguished by market-led forces alone but when economic growth combined with the very kind of social action, or enlightened collective choice, that defenders of sweatshops find objectionable.

Even Nobel Prize–winning economist Simon Kuznets, whose work did much to inspire economists' faith in the moderating effects of capitalist development on inequality, would find the mainstream economists' story of market-led social progress questionable. Kuznets based his famous hypothesis—that after initially increasing, inequality will diminish with capitalist economic development—not on the operation of market forces alone, but on the combined effect of economic growth and social legislation. For instance, in his famous 1955 *American Economic Review* article, Kuznets writes,

> In democratic societies the growing political power of the urban lower-income groups led to a variety of protective and supporting legislation, much of it aimed to counteract the worst effects of rapid industrialization and urbanization and to support the claims of the broad masses for more adequate shares of the growing income of the country. (1955, 17)

The labor codes called for by the antisweatshop movement would seem to be an example of the "protective and supporting legislation" that Kuznets says is key to spreading the benefits of economic growth more widely.

To be sure, labor standards in the absence of economic growth will be hard put to make workers better off. Economist Ajit Singh and Ann Zammit of the South Centre, an intergovernmental organization dedicated to promoting cooperation among developing countries, make exactly this point in their article opposing compulsory labor standards (Singh and Zammit 2000, 37). As they note, over the last few decades, wages in rapidly growing South Korea increased much more quickly than those in slowly growing India, even though India had much better labor standards in the 1950s than South Korea did.

[...]

Finally, no matter how mistaken these mainstream economists might be about how societies have rid themselves of sweatshops, they are perhaps right that past economic developments have gone through a sweatshop stage. On that score, I would reply exactly as one well-known economist did to a 1997 *New York Times* article that made the same point. His letter read this way:

> Your June 22 Week in Review article on sweatshops quotes some prominent economists to the effect that sweatshops, which they confuse with "low-wage factories," are "an essential first step toward modern prosperity in developing countries." Sweatshops indeed existed in 19th-century Britain during early industrialization, leading to a burst of social legislation to rid the country of these ills. But nothing requires us to go that route again. Nations should join nongovernmental groups like the International Labor Organization to rid the world of sweatshops. In addition, we can require multinationals to apply our own labor, safety and environmental standards when they manufacture abroad. In Rome, they must do not as Romans do but as we do. Their example would spread.

Surprisingly, the author is none other than Jagdish Bhagwati (1997). I would only add to Bhagwati's powerful pre-ACIT letter that the student-led antisweatshop movement has increased the likelihood that future economic developments might avoid the sweatshop stage. Unlike earlier periods, when labor standards were imposed in response to the demands of labor organizations and an urban population of the developing world alone, first-world consumers today are also pushing multinational corporations to improve the working conditions in the factories of their subcontractors (Brunett and Mahon 2001, 70).

Fastidiousness or Commodity Fetishism?

Mainstream economists have one last probing question for antisweatshop activists: Why factory workers?

Krugman (1997) asks the question in a most pointed way: "Why does the image of an Indonesian sewing sneakers for 60 cents an hour evoke so much more feeling than the image of another Indonesian earning the equivalent of 30 cents an hour trying to feed his family on a tiny plot of land, or of a Filipino scavenging on a garbage heap?"

It is a good question. There are plenty of poor people in the world. Some 1.2 billion people, about one-fifth of the world population, had to make do on less than U.S. $1 a day in 1998 (World Bank 2001). The world's poor are disproportionately located in rural areas. Most scratch out their livelihood from subsistence agriculture or by plying petty trades, while others on the edge of urban centers work in the informal sector as street-hawkers or the like (Todaro 2000, 151). In addition, if sweat is the issue, journalist Kristof (1998) assures us that "this kind of work, hoeing the field or working in paddies, often involves more perspiration than factory work."

So why has the plight of these rural workers, who are often poorer and sweat more than workers in the world-export factories, not inspired a first-world movement dedicated to their betterment?

"Fastidiousness" is Krugman's answer. "Unlike the starving subsistence farmer," says Krugman, "the women and children in the sneaker factory are working at slave wages *for our benefit*–and this makes us feel unclean. And so there are self-righteous demands for international labor standards" (1997; emphasis in the original).

Ironically, Krugman's answer is not so different from the one Marx would have given to the question. Marx's answer would be commodity fetishism or that commodities become the bearers of social relations in a capitalist economy (Marx 1967). Purchasing commodities brings us in contact with the lives of the factory workers who manufacture them. Buying jeans, t-shirts, or sneakers made in Los Angeles, Bangkok, or Jakarta, or the export zones of southern China and Latin America, connected students in my seminar to the women and men who work long hours in unhealthy and dangerous conditions for little pay in the apparel and athletic footwear industries. And it was the lives of those workers that my most political students sought to improve through their antisweatshop activism. Beyond that, as consumers and citizens they are empowered to change the employment practices of U.S. corporations and their subcontractors.

Krugman's complaint is no reason to dismiss the concerns of the antisweatshop movement. Historically, the organization of factory workers has been one of the most powerful forces for changing politics in the democratic direction that Kuznets outlines. Krugman's complaint does, however, suggest that the plight of sweatshop workers needs to be seen in the context of pervasive world poverty and the gaping inequalities of the global economy.

The global economy, to the extent that we live in a truly unified marketplace, connects us not just with sweatshop workers, but with oppressed workers outside the factory gates as well. By pointing out these connections to my students, I hoped to demonstrate the need to build a movement that would demand more for working people across the multiple dimensions of the world economy. Campaigns to improve conditions in the world-export factories should, of course, be part of that movement. But that movement must also tackle the often worse conditions of low-wage agricultural workers, poor farmers, street vendors, domestic servants, small-shop textile workers, and prostitutes. Only when conditions for both groups of workers improve might economists be able to say honestly, as something other than a Faustian bargain, that more world factory jobs are good news for the world's poor.

POSTSCRIPT

As John Miller mentions in his article, a number of fairly active transnational advocacy networks have organized around the issues of child labour and sweatshops. These campaigns are essentially a subset of a larger network of advocacy groups focusing on issues of corporate accountability. The strategies of these groups vary, ranging from efforts to tighten international labour standards and pressuring multinational corporations to voluntarily adopt codes of conduct for their operations in developing countries, to more aggressive public awareness campaigns aimed at organizing boycotts of products believed to be produced under sweatshop conditions.

While such campaigns have certainly raised awareness of these issues, some analysts have asked whether the results have always been beneficial. As the previous debate illustrates, the issues surrounding sweatshops are complex and cause-and-effect relationships are not always clear cut. Stories that may work great for grabbing public attention and sympathy may not necessarily accurately reflect the economic and social dynamics of what is taking place. Some researchers have even suggested that boycott campaigns frequently lead to detrimental results such as situations where child labourers thrown out of work due to a boycott campaign are forced to turn to more dangerous forms of work or prostitution in order to earn income for their families. This has led some to suggest the need for NGOs to take the issue of research on such issues much more seriously and to invest in building up their research capacity. For a discussion of these issues as they relate specifically to child labour and sweatshops, see Caroline Harper, "Do the Facts Matter? NGOs, Research, and International Advocacy," in Michael Edwards and John Gaventa, eds., *Global Citizen Action* (Boulder: Lynne Rienner, 2001).

Does Outright Debt Cancellation Ignore the Real Problems of Africa?

✔ **YES**

GEORGE AYITTEY, "Smart Aid for Africa," *African Dialogue Series,* no. 773 (2005). www.utexas.edu/conferences/africa/ads/773.html

✘ **NO**

MOSES OCHONU, "The Case for Debt Cancellation and Increased Aid to Africa," *The Nigerian Village Square* (2005). www.nigeriavillagesquare. com/content/view/1137/55/

In the run-up to the G8 Summit scheduled for Gleneagles, Scotland in 2005, a group of high-profile celebrities gathered to present the case for debt relief as a solution to the problem of poverty in African states. A campaign for broad-based debt relief for all developing nations had been gaining steam at the grassroots for several years. The Jubilee 2000 Campaign, based in the United Kingdom and spreading to dozens of other countries, had been working hard to publicize its case for massive debt elimination as a means of giving developing nations a leg up. In 1998, it had mobilized a massive group of demonstrators for the G8 Summit in Birmingham. In the years following, a series of networked groups began to press "drop the debt" campaigns in order to redress the massive dislocations that had come of debt accumulation and structural adjustment throughout the global South.

There had been policy responses to these debt campaigns. Back in 1996, the IMF had launched the Heavily Indebted Poor Country (HIPC) Initiative. The initiative offered debt restructuring and eventual reduction of debt to heavily indebted countries that displayed an ongoing commitment to reducing their dependence on sustained debt. Amid complaints that the criteria for the HIPC Initiative were overly stringent, the program was modified in 1999 and supplemented by the Multilateral Debt Relief Initiative (MDRI) in 2005. Outside debt relief programs, the United Nations' set of Millennium Development Goals (MDGs) laid out in 2000 committed the world to addressing some of the chronic problems of poverty and underdevelopment.

Likewise, previous G8 Summits had occasioned hope for consideration of African economic problems. In 2001 in Genoa, African leaders had presented the New Africa Initiative (NAI), a pledge to own up to African leadership on economic issues while seeking a financial partnership with developed nations. The following G8 Summit held in Kananaskis, Alberta in 2002 had been billed as the summit for African development, featuring an updated version of the NAI known as the New Partnership for African Development (NEPAD), whereby government aid and debt forgiveness would come with demonstrated improvements in governance and curtailment of corruption. However, African development had been consigned to secondary status in the 2003 and 2004 summits and it was not clear that poverty would remain a significant point in the agenda of the organization.

So in the months previous to the Gleneagles Summit, debt relief activists and concerned celebrities combined to organize a live around-the-world series of concerts in combination with a campaign that came to be known as "Make Poverty History". The key spokesmen for the cause were Bob Geldof and U2 frontman Bono, both of whom came to become the public faces of the global drop-the-debt campaign. Well-known actors, musicians, and entertainers lent their time and their images to publicize the event and a multinational petition was launched to be proffered to host Prime Minister Tony Blair at Gleneagles. The "Live 8" concerts held on July 2, 2005 were pitched not as a worldwide benefit as in the case of 1985's Live Aid so much as a means to bring public pressure to bear on the leaders of the G8 to make debt relief a priority.

Despite the remarkable public attention brought to the debt relief campaign, economists and policy makers are by no means united on the utility of debt relief as a means of improving the lot of developing nations in Africa and other areas of the global South. In particular, the G8 and IMF initiatives reflect the general feeling that it is inappropriate to reward developing nations with debt relief if the underlying governance and economic dysfunctions are not addressed. For this reason, debt relief has largely been tied to improvements in the record of transparency, respect of human rights, and financial management on the part of third world governments. Many argue, however, that conditions of such relief have largely remained inconsequential and ineffective. By contrast, others suggest that debt relief programs still reflect the colonial assumptions that developing nations need to be improved through Western intervention and tutelage, and that Western states have not yet come to grips with their own role in promoting the underdevelopment and dependency of the global South.

In this exchange, George Ayittey argues that the improvement of governance through a policy of "smart aid" is a better strategy than outright debt relief. On the other hand, Moses Ochonu points out that the problem of governance is more deep-seated and requires a solution that combines debt relief with reformation of Western aid and development agencies.

✔ **YES**
Smart Aid for Africa
GEORGE AYITTEY

Mired in grinding poverty and social destitution, Africa cries for help. A cacophonous galaxy of rock stars, anti-poverty activists, and heads of state are calling on the G-8 countries to cancel Africa's $350 billion crippling foreign debt and double aid to the continent. British Prime Minister Tony Blair will make aid to Africa the centerpiece in Britain's presidency of the G-8 meeting in Gleneagles, Scotland in July. Live 8 is planned for July 2. After meeting with President Bush on June 10, modalities are being worked out to cancel at least $34 billion in debt of 27 of the world's poorest nations, mostly African. Will this African Marshall Aid Plan work?

Africa's plight follows a ten-year attention deficit cycle. Every decade or so, mega-plans are drawn up and rock concerts held to whip up international rescue missions for Africa. Acrimonious wrangling over financing modalities ensues. Years slip by, then a decade later, another grand Africa initiative is unveiled. Back in 1985, there was Live Aid and a "Special Session on Africa" held by the United Nations to boost aid to Africa. Then in March 1996, the U.N. launched a $25 billion Special Initiative for Africa. In September 2005, the plight of Africa will again take center-stage at a U.N. conference with clockwork precision. Expect another major initiative for Africa in 2015.

Helping Africa of course is noble but has now become a theater of the absurd—the blind leading the clueless. A recent IMF study estimated that Africans in the diaspora remit $32 billion annually back to Africa, with the main destinations being Ghana, Nigeria, and Kenya. About $7 billion is sent to southern Africa (Ghana News Agency, Accra, May 31, 2005). The amount Africans abroad remit back exceeds the $25 billion Tony Blair seeks to raise.

Nigerian President Olusegun Obasanjo says corrupt African leaders have stolen at least $140 billion (£95 billion) from their people since independence. The World Bank estimates that 40 per cent of wealth created in Africa is invested outside the continent. Even the African Union, in a stunning report last August, claimed that Africa loses an estimated $148 billion annually to corruption—or 25 percent of the continent's Gross Domestic Product (GDP). Rather than plug the huge hemorrhage, African leaders prefer to badger the West for more money. And the West, blinded by its own racial over-sensitivity and guilt over the iniquities of the slave trade and colonialism, obliges. This is the real tragedy of Africa.

Between 1960 and 1997, the West pumped more than $450 billion in foreign aid—the equivalent of four Marshall Aid Plans—into Africa with nothing to show for it. Contrary to popular misconception, foreign aid is not free but a soft loan. Outright debt relief and massive inflow of aid without any conditionalities, safeguards or monitoring mechanisms is absurd. It is akin to writing off the credit

George Ayittey, "Smart Aid for Africa" *African Dialogue Series*, No 773. (2005), http://www.utexas.edu/conferences/africa/ads/773.html.

card debt of a drunken sailor and allowing him to keep the same credit cards. No African government has been called upon to give a full public accounting of who took what loan and for what purpose since many of Africa's foreign loans taken in the past were misused and squandered. No government official has been held accountable; instead, irresponsible past borrowing behavior is being rewarded.

More distressing, much of the new aid money will flow directly into an African government budget—a huge black maze of vanishing tax receipts, extra-budgetary expenditure items, perks and off-budget "presidential privy accounts," redolent with graft, patronage and waste. Over the past few decades, African budgets have careened out of control. State bureaucracies have swollen, packed with political supporters. Back in 1996, 20 percent of Ghana's public sector workforce was declared redundant by the Secretary of Finance and Guinea's 50,000 civil servants were consuming 51 percent of the nation's wealth. In Kenya, civil service salaries take up half the budget; in Uganda, it is 40 percent. Zimbabwe has 54 ministers; Uganda with a population of 35 million has 70, while Ghana, with a population of 22 million, has 88 ministers and deputy ministers. With bloated bureaucracies, soaring expenditures and narrow tax bases, budget deficits have soared.

They are covered with World Bank loans and foreign aid (Ghana's budget is 50 percent aid-financed and Uganda's is 60 percent). If the aid is insufficient, the rest of the budget shortfall is financed by printing money. Even when aid is available for "budgetary support," there is no guarantee that it will be used productively to generate a return to repay the soft loan. It could well be "consumed" when it pays for the salaries of civil servants. Writing off Uganda's debt does not eliminate the aid dependency. In fact, when the World Bank canceled $650 million of Uganda's debt in 1999, the first item President Yoweri Museveni purchased was a new presidential jet!

The British Prime Minister thinks he can cajole or browbeat African leaders into curbing corruption and ensuring that resources released by debt relief are put to some good use—such as increased spending on education and health care. But the push for good governance and reform must come from within—from African civil society groups, organizations and the people. However, in country after country, chastened by diabolical restrictions, these groups have no freedom or political space to operate.

Carlos Cardoso, an investigative journalist, was murdered in November 2000 for uncovering a bank scandal in which about $14 million was looted from Mozambique's largest bank, BCM, on the eve of its privatization. The official in charge of banking supervision, Antonio Siba Siba, was also murdered while investigating the banking scandals. Such was also the fate of Norbert Zongo, a popular journalist in Burkina Faso, who was gunned down on Dec 13, 1998, while investigating official corruption. In September 2001, [Eritrean] President Isaias Afwerki closed down all the independent media and arrested its staff, quashing calls for democratic reforms. In all, the government shut down eight private newspapers and arrested its journalists, picking them up in their newsrooms and homes and from the streets. They were held in a central jail until April 2002, when they threatened to begin a hunger strike to protest their detention. They were then transferred to an undisclosed location.

In neighboring Ethiopia, President Meles Zenawi, a member of Tony Blair's Africa Commission, just held fraudulent elections. Anticipating public outrage, he banned street demonstrations for one month and assumed full control of the country's security forces. When the opposition rallied to protest the results dribbling in, the police opened fire, killing 26; opposition leaders have been placed under house arrest. Witness the election machinations in Egypt.

The paucity of good leadership has left a garish stain on the continent. Worse, the caliber of leadership has distressingly deteriorated over the decades to execrable depths. The likes of Charles Taylor of Liberia and Sani Abacha of Nigeria even make Mobutu Sese Seko of formerly Zaire look like a saint. In an unusual editorial, *The Independent* newspaper in Ghana wrote: "Most of the leaders in Africa are power-loving politicians, who in uniform or out of uniform, represent no good for the welfare of our people. These are harsh words to use on men and women who may mean well but lack the necessary vision and direction to uplift the status of their people" (*The Independent*, Ghana, July 20, 2000; p. 2).

The crisis in leadership remains a major obstacle to poverty reduction and has many manifestations. It is characterized, among others, by the following dispositions and failings: the "Big Man" syndrome, subordination of national interests to personal aggrandizement, super-inflated egos, misplaced priorities, poor judgment, reluctance to take responsibility for personal failures, and total lack of vision and understanding of even such basic and elementary concepts as "democracy," "fairness," "rule of law," "accountability," and "freedom"—among other deficiencies. In some instances, the leadership is given to vituperative utterances, outright buffoonery, stubborn refusal to learn from past mistakes, and complete absence of cognitive pragmatism.

Believing that their countries belong to them and them only, they cling to power at all costs. Their promises are worth less than Al Capone's. They stipulate constitutional term limits and then break them: Angola, Chad, Gabon, Guinea, and Uganda. African leaders themselves drew up a New Economic Partnership for Africa's Development (NEPAD) in 2001, in which they inserted a Peer Review Mechanism (PRM), by which they were to evaluate the performance of fellow African leaders in terms of democratic governance. What happened? To be fair, they acted in reversing the "military coup" in Togo in February but went on vacation when elections were stolen in Zimbabwe and Togo.

Ask them to cut bloated state bureaucracies or government spending and they will set up a "Ministry of Less Government Spending." Then there is the "Ministry of Good Governance" (Tanzania). They set up "Anti-Corruption Commissions" with no teeth and then sack the Commissioner if he gets too close to the fat cats (Kenya) or issue a Government White Paper to exonerate corrupt ministers (Ghana in 1996). To be sure, multi-party elections have been held in recent years in many African countries but the electoral process was contumaciously manipulated to return incumbents to power. Four such "coconut elections" have so far been held this year: Zimbabwe, Togo, Congo (Brazzaville), and Ethiopia.

Ask them to place more reliance on the private sector and they will create a Ministry of Private Enterprise (Ghana). Ask them to privatize inefficient state-owned enterprises and they will sell them off at fire-sale prices to their cronies (Uganda). Or ask them to move a foot and they will demand foreign aid in order to do so. In 2003, some 30,000 ghost names were discovered on the payroll of the Ministry of Education, costing the government $1.2 million a month in salaries heisted by living workers. When Ghana demanded foreign aid to purge the payroll of these ghost names, Japan coughed up $5 million.

The reform process has stalled through vexatious chicanery, willful deception, and vaunted acrobatics. Only 16 out of the 54 African countries are democratic, fewer than 8 are "economic success stories," only 8 have a free and independent media.

No amount of debt relief and increased aid will help Africa until Africa cleans up its own house. But the leadership is not interested in reform. Thus, without new leadership and genuine reform, debt relief and increased aid would compound Africa's problems and more African countries will implode. The continent is stuck in a veritable conundrum. What can Western donors do?

Smart aid would do one of two things. One, bypass the vampire state and target the people, who produce Africa's real wealth. An African economy consists of three sectors: the traditional, informal, and the modern sector. The people who produce Africa's real wealth—cash crops, diamonds, gold and other minerals—live in the traditional and informal sectors. Meaningful development and poverty reduction cannot occur by ignoring these two sectors. But in the 1960s and 1970s, much Western development aid was channeled into the modern sector or the urban area, the abode of the parasitic elite minority. Industrialization was the rage and the two other sectors—especially agriculture—were neglected. Huge foreign loans were contracted to set up a dizzying array of state enterprises, which became towering edifices of gross inefficiency, waste and graft. Economic crises emerged in the 1980s and billions in foreign aid money were spent in an attempt to reform the dysfunctional modern sector. Between 1981 and 1994, for example, the World Bank spent more than $25 billion in Structural Adjustment loans to reform Africa's dilapidated statist economic system. Only 6 out of the 29 "adjusting" African countries were adjudged to be "economic success stories" in 1994. Even then, the success list was phantasmagoric. Ghana, declared a "success story" in 1994, is now on HIPC life-support system.

At some point, even the most recklessly optimistic donor must come to terms with the law of diminishing returns: that pouring in more money to reform the modern sector is futile. Greater returns can be achieved elsewhere—by focusing on the traditional and informal sectors.

Second, smart aid would empower the African people (African civil society groups) to monitor how the aid money is being spent and to instigate reform from within. Empowerment requires arming the African people with information, the freedom and the institutional means to unchain themselves from the vicious grip of poverty and oppression.

Africa already has its own Charter of Human and Peoples' Rights (the 1981 Banjul Charter), which recognizes the right to liberty and to the security of his person (Article 6); to receive information, to express and disseminate his opinions (Article 9); to free association (Article 10); to assemble freely with others (Article 11); and to participate freely in the government of his country, either directly or through freely chosen representatives in accordance with the provisions of the law (Article 13). Though the Charter enjoins African states to recognize these rights, few do so. When President Thabo Mbeki called on June 3, President Bush should have handed him a signed copy of this Charter to be delivered to President Robert Mugabe of Zimbabwe.

The institutional tools Africans need are an independent central bank (to assure monetary stability and stanch capital flight), an independent judiciary (for the rule of law), a free and independent media (to ensure free flow of information), an independent Electoral Commission, an efficient and professional civil service, and a neutral and professional armed and security forces.

Recent events in Ukraine (November), Ghana (December), Zimbabwe (March), Lebanon (April), and Togo (April) unerringly underscore the critical importance of these institutions. Without them, President Bush's plan to spread democracy may stall. Democracies are not built in a vacuum but in a "political space" in which the people can air their opinion, petition their government without being fired on by security forces and can choose who should rule them in elections that are not rigged by electoral commissions packed with government goons.

On May 13, thousands of Egyptian judges, frustrated by government control over the judiciary, agitated for full independence from the executive in their oversight of the electoral process. "The institutions are presenting Mr. Mubarak with an unexpected challenge from within, one that will be difficult to dismiss. The fact is, major changes in this country are going to come out of those institutions, not from the streets," said Abdel Monem Said, director of the Ahram Center for Strategic Studies in Cairo.

In the past 24 years, Egypt has received more than $55 billion in U.S. aid in direct government-to-government transfers. Smart aid would assist civil society in instigating institutional reform. Since this approach carries some risks, the same objective can be achieved by funneling aid through diaspora Africans and their organizations, as was the case with Soviet dissidents during the Cold War.

Africa's long term growth prospects do not lie in rock concerts and increased dependency on Western aid but on the ability of the African people or civil society groups to instigate reform from within. Assistance to such groups—both at home and abroad—constitutes much smarter aid to Africa than all the LIVE AID concerts Bob Geldof can organize.

✗ **NO**
The Case for Debt Cancellation and Increased Aid to Africa
MOSES OCHONU

Since the announcement, in 2003, of debt cancellation to a select group of highly indebted African countries who are said to have met some of the conditions for such a gesture, the gesture has been criticized by a motley intellectual crowd of African and non-African commentators. These critics of the Tony Blair initiative, if I may conveniently call it that, argue that Africa neither deserves what is commonly called debt relief or debt forgiveness nor has it proven itself worthy of increased aid. Extending debt cancellation and increasing aid to African countries, the critics argue, would simply be rewarding bad debtor behavior and would also be providing money to corrupt African governments that, they claim, mismanaged aid money in the past. What is needed in Africa, these critics contend, is not debt cancellation but a thorough reform of African states with the aim of eliminating wastage and avenues of corruption.

Some critics have gone so far as to ask that increased aid be conditional upon the completion of, so far, largely elusive political reforms, or that aid be channelled outside governmental control directly to what they call the civil society, a supposedly autonomous domain of mobilization and civic action that is free from the problems that plague the state in Africa. In their effort to focus attention squarely on the internal dimension of the African economic predicament, some of these critics also seek to minimize the impact on African economies of unfair and hypocritical Western trade practices and of so-called free market conditionalities, which are often attached to Western aid or written into reform recommendations of Bretton Woods organs and debt negotiators. Finally, the critics denigrate the efforts of Western anti-poverty groups, especially Bob Geldof's Live Aid, which is critiqued as a feel-good, self-justifying jamboree of naive Western entertainers and their equally naive fans.

In this essay, I take on some of these criticisms, outlining their faulty premises, commenting on their weaknesses, and suggesting alternative paradigms for evaluating both governmental and non-governmental Western efforts to remedy Africa's poverty problem. Let me start by deconstructing the idea of "debt relief" or "debt forgiveness," two innocuous but ideologically weighty and suggestive concepts that have come to dominate discussions on the debt cancellation package agreed upon at the 2012 G8 summit in Scotland. The two concepts betray the extent to which notions of Western magnanimity have converged in current analyses of Africa's problems. Even African scholars and intellectuals have

Moses Ochonu, "The Case for Debt Cancellation and Increased Aid to Africa," *The Nigerian Village Square* (2005) http://www.nigeriavillagesquare.com/content/view/1137/55/

allowed themselves to be seduced by the faulty foundational assumption that the West is altruistically lifting a burden of debt off of Africa. We should reject such misleading assumptions. Instead of the concept of "debt forgiveness," I subscribe to the more appropriate and neutral concept of debt cancellation.

To people unschooled in the politically powerful art of using words and concepts to shape political discussions and reality, this distinction may seem like a pedantic semantic obsession. Far from being so, it is a distinction around which the current discussion of Africa's debt problem revolves; it may even help determine what African negotiators are able to exact from ongoing negotiations. Concepts deployed in international political discussions are hardly neutral; they are often carefully and strategically crafted to shape perceptions and discussions that emanate from such perceptions.

In fact, in this particular case, the medium is the message, to use mass communications terminology, for the concepts of debt relief and debt forgiveness suggest that Africans do not deserve the gesture and that it is a magnanimous act of minimal or no self-interest on the part of the West. The two concepts also efface the nature and archaeology of these debts, which, as we know, emanate from dubious loans knowingly provided to African governments who, it was known, would, with the active assistance of rapacious Western business executives, economic hit men, and financial institutions, embezzle funds to benefit themselves and their Western collaborators.

You do not forgive bad loans; you write them off or cancel them. The gesture of debt cancellation (as opposed to debt relief) connotes, more than anything else, an important willingness on the part of Western governments to be self-critical and to admit a certain degree of culpability on their own part and on behalf of Western actors in the aid-corruption-Swiss-bank-accounts racket. The concept of debt cancellation, then, speaks both to a present programmatic imperative and a need for analytical and historical accuracy in the matter of African foreign debt. The concept of debt forgiveness, on the other hand, re-inscribes the same obdurate insistence on the part of the industrialized world that it is merely coming to the rescue of a self-destructive Africa—an Africa racked by a crisis devoid of Western culpability.

THE BLAIR PLAN AND ITS CRITICS

Most critics have argued that the Blair plan simply endorses throwing money at a bad situation. This is a gross disservice to and a crude mischaracterization of the Blair plan; it reduces the plan to yet another attempt to raise and throw money at Africa's myriad problems. It is an unfair caricature of a three-pronged, nuanced proposal, of which aid is only one aspect. Debt cancellation, which the plan calls debt relief, is another aspect. The most important aspect of that proposal—and this is what makes it radical in an unprecedented way—is its courage in calling for the abolition of many anti-Africa Western trade practices, not the least of which are the agricultural subsidies that not only close Western markets to African producers but also belie the West's rhetoric of free trade and globalization. The failure of the G8 to reach an agreement on the issue is not an indictment of the Blair plan's weak proposal regarding it; it is an indictment of the unrelenting Western commitment to its global economic hegemony.

Critics such as Professor George Ayittey of American University argue that Africa has already received and absorbed the equivalent of several Marshall Plans, and that this invalidates calls for an African Marshall Plan, for more capital infusion. Comparing Western aid to Africa to the Marshall Plan of post-World War II Europe is misleading. The $450 billion purportedly "pumped" into Africa between 1960 and 1997 was not free money but a plethora of soft loans, with conditions that are anything but soft. The Marshall Plan, on the other hand, was direct, free American aid, the only condition being that the nations of Europe had to form a collective and devise a comprehensive plan on how to spend the money. One could say the world has changed and that the political threats and goals that made the case for the Marshall Plan no longer exist today. That may be so, but who is to say that global hunger, disease, destitution, and anger in Africa pose a lesser threat to the United States than did the advancing wave of Soviet socialism?

It is also argued that no African government has been made to account for how it expended past aid money. This is a fair statement, for state accountability is indispensable to any transparent regime of aid disbursement. I have no doubt in my mind that the day of reckoning is coming for all the leaders who mortgaged Africans' collective patrimony and destiny by taking foreign loans on behalf of expectant and needy compatriots and squandering the funds. But I have no illusions that the West will be the champion of such a project of accountability. The West will not demand such an accounting, not because of their anxieties and guilt over historical injuries inflicted on Africans; as anyone can see, the West has since shrugged off the guilt of the slave trade and colonialism, and mainstream revisionist histories that exonerate the West and assuage its conscience regarding these historical injuries now proliferate in academic and non-academic circles. Rather, the West will not pursue such a project because a full accounting will inevitably indict a cast of Western actors and complicit financial institutions, not to mention some respectable Western figures who do business with African leaders, and who are either in power in Western countries or have politicians in these countries that are beholden to them. Such a process of accounting will open the proverbial Pandora's box and reveal the underbelly of the fraudulent, duplicitous poverty-producing machine of aid, loans, and corruption. This is why the West will not demand full public accounting. They will not investigate their own institutions and practices.

Analyses that harp only on the misdeeds and corruption of African governments are, at best, one-sided. If African kleptocrats have yet to be held accountable for collecting and misusing dubious aid, no Western contractors and economic hit men (apologies to John Perkins), who callously pushed dubious waste-pipe projects on greedy African bureaucrats and politicians, have been called to account for their destructive adventures on the continent. Neither group must go scot-free.

Perhaps the most contentious argument offered so far against increased aid and debt cancellation is the claim that until Africa "cleans its house," Western gestures will be meaningless to the continent's peoples. On the surface, this appears to be a reasonable claim, and it would be a noble assertion were it not for the fallacy that inheres in it. How can Africa not be better off, even with all the corruption and waste, if it no longer has to pay the billions of dollars that it pays annually to service debts that were dubiously incurred, debts that ended up for the most part in the West with the active collaboration of Western institutions and persons? The example of Nigeria, where the country has spent more than four times the amount of the original loan in servicing, penalty, and interest payments, and was still left with a rapidly appreciating principal, shows that repayments of foreign debts and the withholding of so-called debt relief are immoral. Nigeria was eventually made to make a whopping one-off payment of $12 billion in exchange for "debt forgiveness." Nigeria's example is a microcosm of the African debt situation. Is it morally acceptable for a country to continue to pay interest and service charges on dubious debts for which servicing payments alone have eclipsed the original debt amount? If only the critics would temper their economics with some morality and humanity, it would be easier for them to lend a sympathetic understanding to the clamour for debt cancellation.

I do not subscribe to the notion of aid as *aid*. These payments—which need to be shorn of their soft loan character and the imprisoning strings that make them tools of hegemonic economic control—should be seen as token restitutive and compensatory measures *deserved* by Africa and Africans as a negligible material compensation for the ongoing devastation of the continent. Such devastation results from the wanton extraction of the continent's resources by environmentally nonchalant Western companies, and the consequent destruction of African ecologies, agricultural traditions, livelihoods, and lifestyles, not to mention Western mavericks' instigation and exacerbation of armed conflict and their repatriation of tax-evading profits to Western capitals. No amount of Western aid will adequately compensate Africans for these schemes and their devastating aftermaths.

It sounds good to call for a complete reforming of African state institutions as a prelude to increased aid and debt cancellation. Without discounting the need for transparency, is this complete cleansing feasible or possible—in Africa or anywhere in the world? Is this insistence on cleansing as a condition for aid in the interest of the suffering (and innocent) mass of Africans, some of whom depend solely on foreign aid handouts for survival? Is this not tantamount to withholding food and medicine from a child until its parents "clean up their acts" and start being financially responsible?

It is a good thing that the critics of increased aid and debt relief offer some alternatives. The most bandied-around of such alternatives is what the *New York*

Times calls smart aid. Smart aid, it is argued, would bypass the predatory African state and deliver help directly to Africans in the traditional and informal sectors through civil society organizations. This is a sensible alternative, one that does not punish innocent Africans for the sins of their leaders and does not insist on elusive governmental cleansing as a condition for helping Africa's needy populations. But this alternative makes a naive and crucial assumption: it fetishizes civil society and ignores the organic connections and appendages that unite the governmental sector and the so-called informal sector.

The idea that civil society organizations and the informal sector are corruption-free and could thus serve as an accountable, efficient, and effective channel for aid distribution and implementation reveals a mindset that is hopelessly out of touch with realities on the ground in Africa. It is a fiction of self-congratulatory Western development experts who are symbiotically linked to careerist Western NGO personnel, whose organizations mentor local NGOs and need to justify their relevance in order to have access to a steady flow of funds. The redundant bureaucracies, inefficiencies, and wastage that have resulted from this bureaucratic detachment from African grassroots problems and from the veneration of African civil society for its own sake, are now part of the problem of the failure of aid to improve situations in Africa.

Moreover, since the African state is quite ubiquitous in terms of power, the smart aid proposal may not work, as state officials will resist or undermine this usurpation of what they consider their jurisdictional prerogative. It is illusory to expect that state bureaucrats will not invade or interfere with the implementation of such a smart aid package.

CRITICISM OF LIVE AID AS A DISTRACTION

I disagree with certain hypercritical views on the Live Aid movement in the West, which compare it to the Berlin Conference or the Scramble for Africa that crystallized there. The analogy is a little far-fetched. The Scramble was animated by a different set of historical forces and was characterized by a brazenly explicit social Darwinist and racist ethos disguised as a humanitarian intervention. It would be a stretch to characterize the present global non-governmental initiatives on Africa in the same terms. What is more, the Scramble endorsed and formalized a process of physical conquest and rule, while the present movement, condescending as it sometimes is, portends no such scheme.

Certainly, one can sense some rhetorical congruence between the grandiose redemptive proclamations of the G8 summit and the "save Africa" rhetoric of mid to late nineteenth century Europe. The spectacle of a self-righteous and arrogant Europe (this time joined by Japan, Canada, and the U.S.), pontificating on the failings and supposedly intractable problems of Africa is quite disturbing and reminiscent of similar proclamations in the past. It does conjure up images from a not-so-distant history of Africa's interaction with Europe. And, of course, no self-respecting African would find palatable the television and radio sound bites about do-good white men and women once again raising money to help Africa's needy and hungry. One would wish not to encounter such images. But life involves tough trade-offs, and tolerating a little unflattering imagery is a good trade-off for solving real economic needs of real people.

However, while I remain very critical of, among other things, the G8's unacceptable failure to make a deal on fair trade and Africa-friendly trade practices, I personally would not extend my criticism of the G8 summit of global political leaders to the Live Aid initiative. I have serious problems with the occasional cacophonous proclamations of the G8 regarding Africa's problems, declarations that are not usually accompanied by sincere and comprehensive plans for redress, recompense, and amelioration. Indeed the forum is more a gathering for Africa bashing and the repetition of an almost pathologized notion of Africa's hopelessness and dependence than it is a meeting for an honest quest for comprehensive solutions to the African predicament.

But I cannot honestly analyze Live Aid in the preceding terms. The Live Aid initiative is different in that it casts itself as a purely humanitarian and pressure-generating intervention. That such humanitarian interventions are always targeted at Africa is a cause for concern. The ways in which these initiatives are packaged and the rhetoric deployed to publicize them can be quite disturbing, paternalistic, and patronizing towards Africa and Africans. They are sometimes the stuff of media sensationalism. But these images are also the unfortunate products of the reality of the African situation. The truth is that certain parts of the continent are in dire need of humanitarian intervention. It is sad but true that Africa is still the world's poorest continent and thus the face of global poverty. Let me hasten to add that my definition of poverty here rests purely on macro- and micro-economic indices and not on the presence or absence of resources and wealth-generating capacity. This reality of poverty is not the fault of Bob Geldof, Bono, or Madonna. It is the fault of a multitude of actors and circumstances ranging from corrupt African leaders, to lethargic and indifferent African civil societies, to Western corporations and governments who participate in and tolerate shady schemes and policies that worsen the continent's economic fate.

Western anti-poverty activists have, for the most part, earned their livings honestly from their creative expressions, even if one could argue that they have benefited from the structural blessings in their societies that are partly sustained by their governments' predatory economic behavior in Africa. They do not have to care about poverty in Africa. They do not have to do anything. After all, they are not the Western politicians, bureaucrats, bankers, and business executives who have contributed and continue to contribute to the impoverishing of the continent through dubious schemes, intolerable environmental and ethical practices, the fuelling of conflicts, and hypocritical trade practices. These young musicians are not the Western politicians and corporations who will benefit from a prosperous and stable Africa or suffer the adverse but logical consequences of a poor, unstable, and badly governed Africa. They are not the ones invested in the emergence of an Africa made safe for Western investment through the revitalization of civil society and the empowerment of a restive rural and urban underclass.

We Africans gain nothing for ourselves or for our struggle for basic human comforts and dignity by mocking or trivializing the efforts of the anti-poverty movement in the West. This focus is, at best, a distraction from the challenge of awakening major stakeholders in the African situation to their obligations and responsibilities. We can point out the near-revolutionary naivety and utopian idealism, which inevitably colour Western anti-poverty movements. But in the end, the Bonos and the Geldofs deserve praise and commendation for their extraordinary humanity, for using a private anti-poverty initiative to put pressure on Western officialdom (which, so far, is behind Oxfam, Bono, Geldof, and others in appreciating the dire need for action and change on the continent), and for a departure from faulty premises of problem solving.

There is room in Africa for both the grandiose, bureaucratic (elusive and pretentious) plans of the G8 and the humanitarian gesture of Live Aid. The former, if it ever materializes, is a long-term systemic initiative calculated, at least in rhetoric, to generate economic growth, curb corruption and bad governance, and increase responsible social spending. The latter is aimed at providing immediate relief for Africans whose lives may depend on such help and who cannot afford to wait for the ever-elusive international Marshall Plan for Africa to materialize, if it ever will.

Small, ad hoc, and target-specific steps like Live Aid (Live 8) should not be derided; they go a long way, and fill niches that often get ignored in highfalutin international discussions on African problems. Live Aid does not remove from the table the need to devise feasible developmental plans for Africa; it does not obliterate the need to encourage and fight for democratic reforms in Africa or the need to curb corruption and its internal and external props. In fact Live Aid complements these goals and draws a popular, showbiz attention to them.

For good or ill, entertainment has proven to be a great tool of activism and awareness in our world. Caring, if self-righteous, Westerners who recognize this convergence of entertainment and social consciousness and are willing to put their showbiz celebrity status at the disposal of the movement to fight poverty in Africa deserve a lower critical standard than the Western politicians who have so far refused to do the right thing regarding Africa because of a plethora of economic and political pressures from their countries.

For all these laudable efforts I am willing to forgive the problem of image and rhetoric, which plagued the last Live Aid installment and which admittedly is hurtful to African pride. I am willing to subordinate my African pride to the imperative of saving and nurturing a few African lives where possible. Africa is not a concept whose honour should be preserved at the expense of its human inhabitants.

POSTSCRIPT

The debate surrounding debt relief inevitably veers toward deeper issues surrounding the prescription for underdevelopment in marginalized countries. For every developing country that succeeds in improving governance along the lines set out by multilateral lending agencies another is unable or unwilling to pay the political and social costs. While improvements in the stability of governing institutions in places such as Nigeria and Liberia have contributed to a great deal of optimism, the descent of Zimbabwe into virtual economic chaos has dealt a blow to optimism for other parts of Africa.

There is no question that longstanding debt servicing has held back many parts of the developing world for decades. In the most marginalized countries of Africa and other reaches of the developing world, it stands as an insurmountable burden with or without improvements in governance. Efforts at debt forgiveness are therefore only the tip of the iceberg when it comes to addressing the broader problems of underdevelopment and poverty.

Can Genetically Modified Food Help Solve Global Food Needs?

✔ **YES**
GREGORY CONKO AND C.S. PRAKASH, "Can GM Crops Play a Role in Developing Countries?" *PBI Bulletin, Issue 2* (2004)

✘ **NO**
DR. MAE-WAN HO AND DR. EVA SIRINATHSINGHJI, Ban GMOs *Now*: Health & Environmental Hazards, Especially in the Light of the New Genetics

The question of whether world food production levels are adequate to meet the expected demand for food, especially in developing countries, is a subject of ongoing debate. While some analysts have focused on the political and economic obstacles to an adequate and fair distribution of existing food production, others have looked at ways that scientific research can contribute to future food availabilities. In this issue, we look particularly at the promise of biotechnology research to resolve the problem of food availability by technological advances in production. Can genetically modified food provide a vital weapon in the fight against hunger in developing regions, especially in regions like Africa? Advances in biotech research now make it possible for scientists to genetically modify seeds, allowing drought- and disease-resistant crops to be grown even on previously infertile lands. In addition, genetic modifications can be used to significantly improve the nutritional levels of existing crops.

Proponents of genetically modified food argue that only by supporting and investing in biotechnical innovation will developing countries have a reasonable chance of becoming agriculturally self-sufficient and achieve a sustainable level of food security. Biotech crops can produce multiple benefits, including the improvement of crop yields, higher nutritional values from existing yields, and overall reduced cost of production. By using newly engineered disease- and drought-resistant varieties, less effort and expense are needed for irrigation, fertilizers, and pesticides. Thus, the new high tech breeds of crops will also contribute to an environmentally sustainable level of agricultural production capable of meeting future food needs without putting undue stress on the ecosystem.

Despite these promises, the issue of genetically engineered food crops has become intensely controversial, perhaps more so in Europe than in North America. On the one hand, critics are concerned that the high cost of research and development and the tendency for biotechnological control to be held by a small number of firms raise important questions of accessibility and equity. Biotechnology is an area where the use of patents and commercial licences are all pervasive, giving the firms undertaking the research the legal means to protect their investments. By asserting their intellectual property rights, a few biotech firms, largely controlled by large Western corporations, can seriously limit the access that poorer, developing countries have to the new seed types.

Since the biotech research field is driven by desire of corporations to enhance their profits, critics argue that the research often focuses on developing new varieties of crops like wheat, corn, and other temperate crops, grown by more affluent farmers in the North who can pay for the higher cost of genetically modified seeds. GM research has focused less on common staples, such as yams and plantains, which are widely used in developing countries. Intellectual property rights laws restrict the access that poor countries have to these new technologies while the high costs of research reduces the possibility for developing country scientists to develop their own alternatives. Because a relatively small number of GM companies, like Monsanto, control the biotech research, it is feared that these companies may too easily control seed markets and force many local farmers out of business altogether. Thus, it is argued that better means need to be developed to ensure that developing countries have affordable access to these new emerging technologies.

Other critics have focused on the safety concerns relating to the development of GM crops. Genetically modified foods are unnatural and they introduce genetic alterations that cannot be achieved by conventional breeding techniques. These innovations potentially introduce changes in foods that may have unknown long-term side effects on our health. By shifting away from conventional plant breeding techniques toward synthetically created breeds, the degree of biodiversity needed for long-term sustainable agriculture may be undermined. Anti–GM food activists make two points: traditional farmers lose their livelihoods and long-term health risks will exist.

Others contend that the GM debate misses the main point altogether. The problem of hunger is not the availability of food. The world can produce already what it needs. The problem of hunger is more related to distribution and unequal economic and political power structures. Poverty, not an absolute lack of food, is the real issue. Even if biotechnological innovations significantly boost the world's food production, unequal distribution of economic power will still prohibit large numbers of people from being able to purchase the food they need.

At the heart of this issue is the question of the extent to which technological innovations can help us address development problems that also have complex economic, political, and environmental dimensions. In the following debate, we have two sharply contrasting positions. Gregory Conko and C.S. Prakash are co-founders of AgBioWorld Foundation. This is a non-profit organization, based in Auburn,

Alabama, which "aims to provide science-based information on agricultural biotechnology issues to various stakeholders across the world." AgBioWorld's purpose is to demonstrate the benefits that biotechnology holds for improving living conditions in developing countries. In their essay, Conko and Prakash set out to show how biotechnology is effectively assisting in the struggle against global hunger.

The second reading is the Executive Summary of a longer report issued by a group called the Independent Science Panel, based in London, England. The ISP states that it brings together "scientists working in genetics, biosciences, toxicology and medicine, and other representatives of civil society who are concerned about the harmful consequences of genetic modifications of plants and animals and related technologies and their rapid commercialisation in agriculture and medicine without due process of proper scientific assessment and of public consultation and consent." The reading presents a summary of the arguments that the ISP developed in a 136-page report released in 2003.

✔ **YES**
Can GM Crops Play a Role in Developing Countries?
GREGORY CONKO AND C.S. PRAKASH

In 2002, while more than 14 million people in six drought-stricken southern African countries faced the risk of starvation, efforts by the U.N.'s World Food Programme were stifled by the global "GM" food controversy. Food aid, containing kernels of bioengineered corn from the United States, was initially rejected by all six governments, even though the very same corn has been consumed daily by hundreds of millions in North and South America and has been distributed by the World Food Programme throughout Africa since 1996.

Four of those governments later accepted the grain on condition that it be milled to prevent planting, but Zimbabwe and Zambia continue to refuse to this day, and recently Angola also joined this group. Zambian President Levy Mwanawasa said his people would rather starve than eat bioengineered food, which he described as "poison." The actually starving Zambian people felt differently, though. One news report after another described scenes of hungry Zambians rioting and overpowering armed guards trying to release tens of thousands of tons of the corn locked away in warehouses by the government.

This is one of the tragic consequences of global fearmongering about recombinant DNA technology and bioengineered crops. Although many varieties that are of use to resource-poor farmers in less developed countries are at very early stages of the development process, even ones that have already been commercialized in such countries as Canada and the United States are being kept from farmers by governments skeptical of "genetic modification".

In the most fundamental sense, however, all plant and animal breeding involves—and always has involved—the intentional genetic modification of organisms. And though critics of recombinant DNA believe it is unique, there have always been Cassandras to claim that the latest technology was unnatural, different from its predecessors, and inherently dangerous.

As early as 1906, Luther Burbank the noted plant breeder said that, "We have recently advanced our knowledge of genetics to the point where we can manipulate life in a way never intended by nature. We must proceed with the utmost caution in the application of this new found knowledge," a quip that one might just as easily hear today regarding recombinant DNA modification.

But just as Burbank was wrong to claim that there was some special danger in knowledge or technology, so are today's skeptics wrong to believe that modern genetic modification poses some inherent risk. It is not genetic modification per se that generates risk. Recombinant DNA-modified, conventionally modified, and unmodified plants could all prove to be invasive, harm biodiversity, or be harmful to

Gregory Conko and C.S. Prakash, "Can GM Crops Play a Role in Developing Countries?" *PBI Bulletin*, Issue 2 (2004).

eat. It is not the technique used to modify organisms that makes them risky. Rather risk arises from the characteristics of individual organisms, as well as how and where they are used.

That is why the use of bioengineering technology for the development of improved plant varieties has been endorsed by dozens of scientific bodies. The UN's Food and Agriculture Organization and World Health Organization, the UK's Royal Society, the American Medical Association, and the French Academies of Medicine and Science, among others, have studied bioengineering techniques and given them a clean bill of health. Moreover, bioengineered crop plants may be of even greater value in less developed countries than in industrialized ones.

In a report published in July 2000, the UK's Royal Society, the National Academies of Science from Brazil, China, India, Mexico, and the U.S., and the Third World Academy of Science, embraced bioengineering, arguing that it can be used to advance food security while promoting sustainable agriculture. "It is critical," declared the scientists, "that the potential benefits of GM technology become available to developing countries." And an FAO report issued in May 2004 argued that "effective transfer of existing technologies to poor rural communities and the development of new and safe biotechnologies can greatly enhance the prospects for sustainably improving agricultural productivity today and in the future," as well as "help reduce environmental damage caused by toxic agricultural chemicals."

Today, some 740 million people go to bed daily on an empty stomach, and nearly 40,000 people—half of them children—die every day due to hunger or malnutrition-related causes. Despite commitments by industrialized countries to increase international aid, Africa still is expected to have over 180 million undernourished citizens in 2030, according to a report published this year by the UN Millennium Project Task Force. Although bioengineered crops alone will not eliminate hunger, they can provide a useful tool for addressing the many agricultural problems in Africa, Asia, Latin America, and other poor tropical regions.

Indeed, recombinant DNA-modified crops have already increased crop yields and food production, and reduced the use of synthetic chemical pesticides in both industrialized and less developed countries. These advances are critical in a world where natural resources are finite and where hundreds of millions of people suffer from hunger and malnutrition. Critics dismiss such claims as nothing more than corporate public relations puffery. However, while it is true that most commercially available bioengineered plants were designed for farmers in the industrialized world, the increasing adoption of biotech varieties by underdeveloped countries over the past few years demonstrates their broader applicability.

Globally, bioengineered varieties are now grown on more than 165 million acres (67.7 million hectares) in 18 countries, such as Argentina, Australia, Brazil, Canada, China, India, Mexico, the Philippines, South Africa, and the United States, according to the International Service for the Acquisition of Agri-Biotech Applications (ISAAA). Nearly one-quarter of that acreage is farmed by some

6 million resource-poor farmers in less developed countries. Why? Because they see many of the same benefits that farmers in industrialized nations do.

The first generation of biotech crops—approximately 50 different varieties of canola, corn, cotton, potato, squash, soybean, and others—were designed to aid in protecting crops from insect pests, weeds, and plant diseases. As much as 40 percent of crop productivity in Africa and Asia and about 20 percent in the industrialized countries of North America and Europe is lost to these biotic stresses, despite the use of large amounts of insecticides, herbicides, and other agricultural chemicals. Poor tropical farmers may face different pest species than their industrial country counterparts, but both must constantly battle against these threats to their productivity.

That's why South African and Filipino farmers are so eager to grow bioengineered corn resistant to insect pests, and why Chinese, Indian, and South African farmers like biotech insect-resistant cotton so much. Indian cotton farmers and Brazilian and Paraguayan soy growers didn't even wait for their governments to approve biotech varieties before they began growing them. It was discovered in 2001 that Indian farmers were planting seed obtained illegally from field trials of a biotech cotton variety then still under governmental review. Farmers in Brazil and Paraguay looked across the border and saw how well their Argentine neighbors were doing with transgenic soybean varieties and smuggling of bioengineered seed became rampant.

When the Indian government finally approved bioengineered cotton in 2002 for cultivation in seven southern states it proved to be highly successful. A study conducted by the University of Agriculture in Dharwad found that more insect damage was done to conventional hybrids than to the bioengineered variety and that the bioengineered cotton reduced pesticide spraying by half or more, delivering a 30–40 percent profit increase.

During the 2002–2003 growing season, some Indian cotton farmers saw no increased yield from the more expensive biotech varieties, but droughts during that year generated harsh conditions throughout India's southern cotton belt. Many growers of conventional crop varieties also suffered unanticipated and tragic crop losses. Most of the farmers who grew bioengineered cotton decided to plant it again in 2003, however, and total planted acreage grew from approximately 1 million acres in 2002–2003 to an estimated 3.3 million acres in 2003–2004.

When the planting of bioengineered soybean was provisionally legalized in Brazil for the 2003–2004 growing season, over 50,000 farmers registered their intent to plant it—including almost 98 percent of the growers in the southern-most state of Rio Grande do Sul, where the soybeans originally bred for Argentine climatic conditions will grow best. What is especially noteworthy is that the government decree did not legalize commercial sales of the biotech soybean, it only authorized the planting of illegal seed already in the possession of farmers. Thus, by registering their intent to grow the bioengineered variety, farmers were informing the government of their prior guilt.

There are few greater testaments to the benefits of biotechnology than the fact that thousands of poor farmers are willing to acknowledge having committed a crime just to gain access to the improved varieties. The clear lesson is that, where bioengineered varieties become available (legal or not), most farmers themselves are eager to try them.

"When the Indian government finally approved bioengineered cotton in 2002 ... it proved to be highly successful."

There is even evidence that biotech varieties have literally saved human lives. In less developed nations, pesticides are typically sprayed on crops by hand, exposing farm workers to severe health risks. Some 400 to 500 Chinese cotton farmers die every year from acute pesticide poisoning because, until recently, the only alternative was risking near total crop loss due to voracious insects. A study conducted by researchers at the Chinese Academy of Sciences and Rutgers University in the U.S. found that adoption of bioengineered cotton varieties in China has lowered the amount of pesticides used by more than 75 percent and reduced the number of pesticide poisonings by an equivalent amount. Another study by economists at the University of Reading in the U.K. found that South African cotton farmers have seen similar benefits.

The productivity gains generated by bioengineered crops provide yet another important benefit: they could save millions of acres of sensitive wildlife habitat from being converted into farmland. The loss and fragmentation of wildlife habitats caused by agricultural encroachment in regions experiencing the greatest population growth are widely recognized as among the most serious threats to biodiversity. Thus, increasing agricultural productivity is an essential environmental goal, and one that would be much easier in a world where bioengineering technology is in widespread use.

Opponents of biotechnology argue that organic farming can reduce pesticide use even more than bioengineered crops can. But organic farming practices are less productive, because there are few effective organic controls for insects, weeds, or pathogens. Converting from modern, technology-based agriculture to organic would mean either reducing global food output significantly or sacrificing undeveloped land to agriculture. Moreover, feeding the anticipated population of eight or nine billion people in the year 2050 will mean increasing food production by at least 50 percent.

As it is, the annual rate of increase in food production globally has dropped from 3 percent in the 1970s to 1 percent today. Additional gains from conventional breeding are certainly possible, but the maximum theoretical yields for most crop plants are being approached rapidly. Despite the simplistic claims made by critics of plant technology, providing genuine food security must include solutions other than mere redistribution. There is simply no way for organic farming to feed a global population of nine billion people without having to bring substantially more land into agricultural use. Dramatically improving crop yields will prove to be an essential environmental and humanitarian goal.

We have already realized significant environmental benefits from the biotech crops currently being grown, including a reduction in pesticide use of 20 million kg in the U.S. alone. A 2002 Council for Agricultural Science and Technology report also found that recombinant DNA-modified crops in the US promote the adoption of conservation tillage practices, resulting in many other important environmental benefits: 37 million tons of topsoil preserved; 85 percent reduction in greenhouse gas emissions from farm machinery; 70 percent reduction in herbicide run-off; 90 percent decrease in soil erosion; and from 15 to 26 liters of fuel saved per acre.

And, as we have seen, while the first generation of bioengineered crops was not designed with poor tropical farmers in mind, these varieties are highly adaptable. Examples of the varieties that now are being designed specifically for resource-poor farmers include virus-resistant cassava, insect resistant rice, sweet potato, and pigeon pea, and dozens of others. Chinese scientists, leaders in the development of both bioengineered and conventional rice have been urging their government to approve commercialization of their biotech varieties that have been thoroughly tested and ready for market for several years.

The next generation of products, now in research labs and field trial plots, includes crops designed to tolerate climatic stresses such as extremes of heat, cold, and drought, as well as crops designed to grow better in poor tropical soils high in acidity or alkalinity, or contaminated with mineral salts. A Mexican research group has shown that tropical crops can be modified using recombinant DNA technology to better tolerate acidic soils, significantly increasing the productivity of corn, rice and papaya. These traits for greater tolerance to adverse environmental conditions would be tremendously advantageous to poor farmers in less developed countries, especially those in Africa.

Africa did not benefit from the Green Revolution as much as Asian and Latin American nations did because plant breeders focused on improving crops such as rice and wheat, which are not widely grown in Africa. Plus, much of the African dry lands have little rainfall and no potential for irrigation, both of which play essential roles in productivity success stories for crops such as Asian rice. And the remoteness of many African villages and the poor transportation infrastructure in landlocked African countries make it difficult for African farmers to obtain agricultural chemical inputs such as fertilizers, insecticides and herbicides—even if they could be donated by aid agencies and charities. But, by packaging technological inputs within seeds, biotechnology can provide the same, or better, productivity advantages as chemical or mechanical inputs, but in a much more user-friendly manner. Farmers could be able to control insect pests, viral or bacterial pathogens, extremes of heat or drought and poor soil quality, just by planting these crops.

And the now-famous Golden Rice, with added beta carotene, is just one of many examples of bioengineered crops with improved nutritional content. Indian scientists have recently announced development of a new high protein potato variety available for commercial cultivation. Another team of Indian scientists, working with technical and financial assistance from Monsanto, is developing an improved mustard variety with enhanced beta carotene in its oil. One lab at Tuskegee University is enhancing the level of dietary protein in sweet potatoes, a common staple crop in sub-Saharan Africa. Researchers are also developing varieties of cassava, rice, and corn that more efficiently absorb trace metals and micronutrients from the soil, have enhanced starch quality, and contain more beta-carotene and other beneficial vitamins and minerals.

Ultimately, while no assurance of perfect safety can be made, breeders know far more about the genetic makeup, product characteristics, and safety of every modern bioengineered crop than those of any conventional variety ever marketed. Breeders know exactly what new genetic material has been introduced. They can identify where the transferred genes have been inserted into the new plant. They can test to ensure that transferred genes are working properly and that the nutritional elements of the food have been unchanged. None of these safety assurances have ever before been made with conventional breeding techniques. We have always lived with food risks. But modern genetic technology makes it increasingly easier to reduce those risks.

Societal anxiety over the new tools for genetic modification is, in some ways, understandable. It is fueled by a variety of causes, including consumer unfamiliarity, lack of reliable information on the current safeguards in place, a steady stream of negative opinion in the news media, opposition by activist groups, growing mistrust of industry, and a general lack of awareness of how our food production system has evolved over time. But saying that public apprehension over biotechnology is understandable is not the same as saying that it is valid. With more than thirty years of experience using recombinant DNA technology, and nearly two decades worth of pre-commercial and commercial experience with bioengineered crop plants, we can be confident that it is one of the most important and safe technologies in the plant breeder's toolbox. It would be a shame to deny biotechnology's fruits to those who are most in need of its benefits.

✘ NO

Ban GMOs *Now:*
Health & Environmental Hazards, Especially in the Light of the New Genetics

DR MAE-WAN HO AND DR EVA SIRINATHSINGHJI

EXECUTIVE SUMMARY

Since the first commercial growing began in 1996, the global area of genetically modified (GM) crops is reported to have increased 100-fold. However, nearly 90 % are confined to 5 countries, with top grower the US accounting for more than 40 %. GM crops have been largely excluded from Europe and most developing countries because opposition has been growing simultaneously as widespread agronomical failures of the GM crops as well the health and environmental impacts are coming to light.

GM remains limited to three major crops – soybean, maize and cotton – and two traits: herbicide (mainly glyphosate) tolerance (HT) at nearly 60 % and insect resistance with toxins from the soil bacterium *Bacillus thuringiensis* (Bt) at 15 %, with the remaining stacked traits (HT and one or more Bt) at 25%.

The failures and hazards of glyphosate and glyphosate tolerant crops and Bt crops are reviewed respectively in Chapter 1 and Chapter 2. Chapter 3 reviews the range of hazards resulting from the uncontrollable, unpredictable process of genetic modification itself in the light of advances in molecular genetics within the past decade, which tells us why the technology cannot be safety applied to grow our crops or produce our food.

GLYPHOSATE & GLYPHOSATE TOLERANT CROPS

Glyphosate use has gone up sharply worldwide since the introduction of glyphosate-tolerant GM crops. Herbicide use per acre has doubled in the US within the past five years compared with the first five years of commercial GM crops cultivation, the increase almost entirely due to glyphosate herbicides. Glyphosate has contaminated land, water, air, and our food supply. Damning evidence of its serious harm to health and the environment has been piling up, but the maximum permitted levels are set to rise by 100-150 times in the European Union with further hikes of already unacceptably high levels in the US if Monsanto gets its way.

1. Scientific evidence accumulated over three decades documents miscarriages, birth defects, carcinogenesis, endocrine disruption, DNA damage, general

toxicity to cells, neurotoxicity, and toxicity to liver and kidney at glyphosate levels well below recommended agricultural use.

2. The major adjuvant POEA in glyphosate Roundup formulations is by far the most cytotoxic for human cells, ahead of glyphosate and its metabolite. It also amplifies the toxic effects of glyphosate.

3. A recent review blames glyphosate for practically all modern diseases as its general chelating action affects numerous biological functions that require metal cofactors. It is the most pervasive environmental chemical pollutant that also inhibits enzymes involved in detoxification of xenobiotics, thereby increasing *their* toxicity. In addition, it kills beneficial gut bacteria that prevent pathogens from colonizing the gut and promotes the growth of the pathogenic bacteria, leading to autism and other diseases.

4. Rats fed Roundup contaminated and Roundup tolerant maize beyond the required 90 days showed a startling range of health impacts. Females were 2 to 3 times as likely to die as controls and much more likely to develop mammary tumours. In males, liver congestions and necrosis were 2.5 to 5.5 times as frequent as controls, while kidney diseases were 1.3-2.3 times controls. Males also develop kidney or skin tumours 4 times as often as the controls and up to 600 days earlier. The harmful effects were found in animals fed the GM maize that was not sprayed with Roundup, as well as those that were, indicating that the GM maize has its own toxicities apart from the herbicide.

5. Livestock illnesses from glyphosate tolerant GM feed including reproductive problems, diarrhoea, bloating, spontaneous abortions, reduced live births, inflamed digestive systems and nutrient deficiencies. Evidence has also emerged of chronic botulism in cattle and farmers as the result of glyphosate use.

6. Glyphosate is lethal to frogs and Roundup is worse; it increases toxic blooms, and accelerates the deterioration of water quality. It use also coincides with the demise of monarch butterflies.

7. Glyphosate poisons crops and soils by killing beneficial microorganisms and encouraging pathogens to flourish. Forty crop diseases are now linked to glyphosate use and the number is increasing.

8. Glyphosate-resistant weeds cover 120 million ha globally (61.8 m acres in the US) and continue to spread; it is a major factor accounting for the enormous increase in pesticide use since herbicide tolerant GM crops were introduced.

9. Contamination of ground water supplies, rain, and air has been documented in Spain and the US. Berlin city residents were found to have glyphosate concentrations above permitted EU drinking water levels.

BT CROPS

Bt crops were sold on the premise that they would increase yields and reduce pesticide use; instead they have resulted in too many crop failures, and the introduction of Bt cotton is now acknowledged to be responsible for the escalation in farm suicides in India.

1. Bt crops' claim to reduce pesticide use is based on excluding the Bt produced in the crops in total 'pesticides applied'; but the Bt toxins leach from the plants and persist in soil and water, with negative impacts on health and the ecosystem comparable to conventional pesticides.

2. Fungicide use and insecticide treatment of corn and soybean have gone up dramatically since the introduction of Bt crops.

3. The breakdown of Bt traits due to target pest resistance and secondary pests has resulted in increasing use of conventional pesticides; and pesticide companies are reporting 5 to 50% increase in sales for 2012 and the first quarter of 2013.

4. Contrary to industry's claim that Bt is harmless to non-target species, independent studies showed that Bt toxins elicit immune response in mammals in some cases comparable to that due to cholera toxin. This is consistent with farm workers' reports of allergic symptoms affecting the eyes, skin and respiratory tract.

5. A new study found Bt proteins toxic to developing red blood cells as well as bone marrow cells in mice.

6. Toxicity to human kidney cells has been observed *in vitro*, consistent with *in vivo* experiments in lab animals showing toxicity to heart, kidney and liver.

7. Bt crops fail to control target pests due to insufficient expression of Bt toxins, thereby promoting the evolution of resistance.

8. Bt crops promote the emergence of secondary pests when target pests are killed. Primary and secondary pests are already huge problems in the US, India and China, and are now hitting multiple crops in Brazil since Bt maize was introduced.

9. Stacked varieties containing multiple Bt toxins are predicted to hasten the evolution of multiple toxin resistance, as resistance to one toxin appears to accelerate the acquisition of resistance to further toxins.

10. Bt toxins harm non-target species including water fleas, lacewings, monarch butterflies, peacock butterflies and bees, which are showing worrying signs of population decline across the world.

11. Bt toxins leach into the soil via the root of Bt crops where they can persist for 180 days; this has been linked to the emergence of new plant diseases and reduced crop yields.

12. Bt toxins also persist in aquatic environments, contaminating streams and water columns and harming important aquatic organisms such as the caddisfly.

NEW GENETICS & HAZARDS OF GENETIC MODIFICATION

The rationale and impetus for genetic engineering and genetic modification was the 'central dogma' of molecular biology that assumed DNA carries all the instructions for making an organism. This is contrary to the reality of the fluid and responsive genome that already has come to light since the early 1980s. Instead of linear causal chains leading from DNA to RNA to protein and downstream biological functions, complex feed-forward and feed-back cycles interconnect organism and environment at all levels, marking and changing RNA and DNA down the generations. In order to survive, the organism needs to engage in natural genetic modification in real time, an exquisitely precise molecular dance of life with RNA and DNA responding to and participating fully in 'downstream' biological functions. That is why organisms and ecosystems are particularly vulnerable to the crude, artificial genetically modified RNA and DNA created by human genetic engineers. It is also why genetic modification can probably never be safe.

1. Genetic modification done by human genetic engineers is anything but precise; it is uncontrollable and unpredictable, introducing many collateral damage to the host genome as well as new transcripts, proteins and metabolites that could be harmful.

2. GM feed with very different transgenes have been shown to be harmful to a wide range of species, by farmers in the field and independent scientists working in the lab, indicating that genetic modification itself is unsafe.

3. Genetic modification done by human genetic engineers is different from natural genetic modification done by organisms themselves for the following reasons: it relies on making unnatural GM constructs designed to cross species barriers and jump into genomes; it combines and transfers genes between species that would *never* have exchanged genes in nature; GM constructs tend to be unstable and hence more prone to further horizontal gene transfer after it has integrated into the genome.

4. Horizontal gene transfer and recombination is a major route for creating new viruses and bacteria that cause diseases and spreading drug and antibiotic resistance. Transgenic DNA is especially dangerous because the GM constructs are already combinations of sequences from diverse bacteria and viruses that cause diseases, and contain antibiotic resistance marker genes.

5. There is experimental evidence that transgenes are much more likely to spread and to transfer horizontally.

6. The instability of the GM construct is reflected in the instability of transgenic varieties due to both transgene silencing and the loss of transgenes, for which abundant evidence exists. *Transgenic instability makes a mockery of 'event-specific' characterization and risk assessment, because any change in transgene expression, or worse, rearrangement or movement of the transgenic DNA insert(s) would create another transgenic plant different from the one that was characterized and risk assessed. And it matters little how thoroughly the original characterization and risk assessment may have been done. Unstable transgenic lines are illegal, they should not be growing commercially, and they are not eligible for patent protection.*

7. There is abundant evidence for horizontal transfer of transgenic DNA from plant to bacteria in the lab and it is well known that transgenic DNA can persist in debris and residue in the soil long after the crops have been cultivated. At least 87 species (2 % of all known species) of bacteria can take up foreign DNA and integrate it into their genome; the frequency of that happening being greatly increased when a short homologous anchor sequence is present.

8. The frequency at which transgenic DNA transfers horizontal has been routinely underestimated because the overwhelming majority of natural bacteria cannot be cultured. Using direct detection methods without the need to culture, substantial gene transfers were observed on the surface of intact leaves as well as on rotting damaged leaves.

9. In the only monitoring experiment carried out with appropriate molecular probes so far, China has detected the spread of a GM antibiotic resistance gene to bacteria in all of its major rivers; suggesting that horizontal gene transfer has contributed to the recent rise in antibiotic resistance in animals and humans in the country.

10. GM DNA has been found to survive digestion in the gut of mice, the rumen of sheep and duodenum of cattle and to enter the blood stream.

11. In the only feeding trial carried out on humans, the complete 2 266 bp of the epsps transgene in Roundup Ready soybean flour was recovered from the colostomy bag in 6 out of 7 ileostomy subjects. In 3 out of 7 subjects, bacteria cultured from the contents of the colostomy bag were positive for the GM soya transgene, showing that horizontal transfer of the transgene had occurred; but no bacteria were positive for any natural soybean genes.

12. The gastrointestinal tract of mammals is a hotspot for horizontal gene transfer between bacteria, transfer beginning in the mouth.

13. Evidence is emerging that genomes of higher plants and animals may be even softer targets for horizontal gene transfer than genomes of bacteria.

14. The CaMV 35S promoter, most widely used in commercial GM crops, is known to have a fragmentation hotspot, which makes it prone to horizontal gene transfer; in addition. it is promiscuously active in bacteria, fungi, as well as human cells. Recent evidence also suggests that the promoter may enhance multiplication of disease-associated viruses including HIV and cytomegalo-virus through the induction of proteins required for transcription of the viruses. It also overlaps with a viral gene that interferes with gene silencing, an essential function in plants and animals that protects them against viruses.

15. The *Agrobacterium* vector, most widely used for creating GM plants is now known to transfer genes also to fungi and human cells, and to share genetic signals for gene transfer with common bacteria in the environment. In addition, the *Agrobacterium* bacteria as well as it gene transfer vector tend to remain in the GM crops created, thereby constituting a ready route for horizontal gene transfer to all organisms interacting with the GM crops, or come into contact with the soil on which GM crops are growing or have been grown.

16. In 2008, *Agrobacterium* was linked to the outbreak of Morgellons disease. The Centers for Disease Control in the US launched an investigation, which concluded in 2012, with the finding: "no common underlying medical condition or infection source was identified". But they had failed to investigate the involvement of *Agrobacterium*.

17. New GM crops that produce double-stranded RNA (dsRNA) for specific gene-silencing are hazardous because many off-target effects in the RNA interference process are now known, and cannot be controlled. Furthermore, small dsRNA in food plants were found to survive digestion in the human gut and to enter the bloodstream where they are transported to different tissues and cells to silence genes.

18. Evidence accumulated over the past 50 years have revealed nucleic acids (both DNA and RNA) circulating in the bloodstream of humans and other animals that are actively secreted by cells for intercommunication. The nucleic acids are taken up by target cells to silence genes in the case of double-stranded microRNA (miRNA), and may be integrated into the cells' genome, in the case of DNA. The profile of the circulating nucleic acids change according to states of health and disease. Cancer cells use the system to spread cancer around the body. This nucleic acid intercom leaves the body very vulnerable to genetically modified nucleic acids that can take over the system to do considerable harm.

CONCLUSION

The serious harm to health and the ecological and agronomical impacts of glyphosate and glyphosate tolerant crops are the most thoroughly researched, and for which there is little remaining doubt. The same kind of evidence has now emerged for Bt crops and Bt toxins. Evidence that genetic modification *per se* is harmful is also convincing, and can be attributed to the uncontrollable process of genetic modification itself as well as the dangers from the horizontal transfer of the GM constructs, which can spread antibiotic resistance, create new pathogens and trigger 'insertion carcinogenesis', as well as taking over the body's natural nucleic acid intercom to do harm.

There is a compelling case for banning all environmental releases of GMOs *now*, and with that the glyphosate herbicides. Action can be taken locally in communities, villages, towns, municipalities, regions, as well as nationally and globally. It must be done now; for time is running out. We need to shift comprehensively to non-GM sustainable ecological farming in order to feed ourselves under climate change. We the people need to reclaim our food and seed sovereignty from the corporate empire before they destroy our food and farming irreversibly.

POSTSCRIPT

From the previous discussion, it is clear that the role of genetically modified organisms (GMOs) as a potential solution to the food deficits of developing countries remains highly contentious. An equally contentious issue is the role of the genetically modified food should play in international food aid programs. The United States, the world's leading food aid donor, is also the largest donor of genetically modified food aid. In 2002, it shipped significant amounts of such food aid, particularly maize, to southern Africa. Despite experiencing serious food shortages, a number of southern African countries refused to receive the food aid. Part of the reason was over concerns about the negative health risk of GMOs. But they were also concerned that the genetically modified food aid would contaminate local crops, thus making it difficult to export to Europe in the future. In Europe, the opposition to GMOs has been much stronger and the European community has banned imports of genetically modified food. In turn, the United States refused to provide the countries that refused the maize with alternative non-genetically modified food aid.

Some accused the United States of using their food aid program to create markets for the new strains of food that they could not market in Europe. In response, the United States criticized African leaders for their shortsightedness and suggested that they had acted irresponsibly in refusing much needed aid at time when many were suffering from starvation conditions. At the same time, the US complained the Europe's moratorium of GMO food imports was unnecessarily contributing to hunger in Africa.

Given the contentious nature of GMO foods, what is an appropriate food aid policy to follow? If large numbers of people are vulnerable to starvation, would it not be better to use the food aid to save their lives? Or, does the imposition of GMO foods on recipients governments constitute another form of imperialism?

Do Current World Bank and IMF Lending and Aid Models Alleviate Poverty?

✔ **YES**

BRIAN AMES, WARD BROWN, SHANTA DEVARAJAN, AND ALEJANDRO IZQUIERDO, *Macroeconomic Policy and Poverty Reduction.* Prepared by the International Monetary Fund and World Bank, August 2001

✘ **NO**

ADAM DAVIDSON-HARDEN, "An 'Empty Glass': How the Bretton Woods Institutions Sustain and Exacerbate Poverty"

In the 1990s, major international lending agencies began a fundamental re-examination of how grants and loans are delivered, particularly to the poorest of the developing countries. The impetus for this review was the ongoing criticism of the lending policies of the International Monetary Fund (IMF) and the World Bank undertaken within the framework of their "structural adjustment programs" (SAPs), which many argued had failed to adequately address the needs of the poorest populations. Evaluation of the SAPs had shown that they had produced only limited results in terms of promoting sustained growth of the economy, while poverty and social inequalities often increased as a result of their implementation. Critics suggested that there needed to be greater attention to social reforms that made a more coherent linkage between macroeconomic, structural changes, and more equitable social policies. In addition, studies had shown that the conventional poverty reduction strategies pursued by many development countries have produced disappointing results because of their failure to adequately engage civil society actors and allow for more participatory forms of governance.

As a result of these discussions, in 1999 the World Bank and IMF adopted a new set of policies and procedures to guide their lending to developing countries. This approach, known as the Poverty Reduction Strategy Paper (PRSP), set out a process that very poor countries would need to follow in order to access any of the concessionary lending facilities of either of the agencies, including debt relief under the Highly Indebted Poor Countries Initiative (HIPC). IMF and the Bank saw these changes as constituting a significant departure from their previous way of dealing with low-income countries.

According to the new procedures, each country wishing to receive assistance from the World Bank and IMF is expected to develop a Poverty Reduction Strategy Paper (PRSP). This document sets out a national strategy for integrating poverty reduction into the macroeconomic policymaking of recipient governments. In preparing this document, the recipient government confers with a broad base of stakeholders in the civil society and private sectors in regards to the formulation, implementation, and monitoring of the PRSP. The hope is that this will give the recipient country a greater sense of ownership and legitimacy of the reforms measures that are agreed to. By fostering a stronger ownership of the strategy and participation among a broader range of stakeholders, it is hoped that a more successful and sustained implementation will occur than was the case for the previous Structural Adjustment Programs.

Proponents of the PRSP also contend that the new approach will enable a shift away from the SAP's top-down approach to a more bottom-up approach that would more successfully include the poor. In explaining the new approach, the World Bank argued that by increasing the voice and participation of the poor in decision-making, not only would the new poverty reduction policies be given more legitimacy, but also the popular input would actually improve the quality and the policies and services provided. Such popular participation would ensure that a stronger political basis for the pursuit a "pro-poor growth strategy" would be built.

Both the Bank and IMF have been careful to emphasize that they are not proposing a single template for a PRSP, a common criticism of the former SAP agreements. Rather, they suggest that each nation should develop its own unique PRSP around the following five core principles. Each PRSP must be:

- country-driven and owned, founded on broad-based participatory processes for formulation, implementation, and outcome-based monitoring;
- results-oriented, focusing on outcomes that would benefit the poor;
- comprehensive in scope, recognizing the multidimensional nature of the causes of poverty and measures to attack it;
- partnership-oriented, providing a basis for the active, coordinated participation of development partners (bilateral, multilateral, non-governmental) in supporting country strategies; and
- based on a medium- and long-term perspective for poverty reduction, recognizing that sustained poverty reduction cannot be achieved overnight.

Each recipient country is expected to take the lead in designing and implementing its own development strategies. A broad level of consultation and participation among civil society and private sectors is intended to ensure both a wide consensus on policies and a more effective integration of local values into the policy initiatives. A well prepared PRSP would lay out a plan to both reduce poverty and increase sustainable economic growth. Rather than just addressing macroeconomic and structural changes designed to produce economic growth, the PRSP would address improvement in participatory governance, sectoral policies for reducing poverty, and realistic and appropriate funding levels for social programs.

Both the World Bank and IMF claim that the PRSP approach represents a radical departure to their previous lending policies. In particular, they argue that the new approach demonstrates their sensitivity to criticism and ability to adapt to demands to make their programs more focused on poverty reduction and the fostering of popular participation.

But to what extent do the current lending policies represent a new and radical departure from the past? In the first reading, a group of economists from IMF and the World Bank set out the case for the new Poverty Reduction Strategy approach. In the second reading, Adam Davidson-Harden provides a careful reading and critique of this approach. He argues that elements of the neoliberal focus on economic growth, which typified the era of structural adjustment, still undergirds the new approach. As a result, he suggests that the PRSP should be seen as more of an effort at "rebranding" of old policies that have already been called into question rather than a radically new departure.

✔ YES
Macroeconomic Policy and Poverty Reduction
BRIAN AMES, WARD BROWN, SHANTA DEVARAJAN,
AND ALEJANDRO IZQUIERDO

1. INTRODUCTION

Poverty is a multidimensional problem that goes beyond economics to include, among other things, social, political, and cultural issues (see Box 1). Therefore, solutions to poverty cannot be based exclusively on economic policies, but require a comprehensive set of well-coordinated measures. Indeed, this is the foundation for the rationale underlying comprehensive poverty reduction strategies. So why focus on macroeconomic issues? Because economic growth is the single most important factor influencing poverty, and macroeconomic stability is essential for high and sustainable rates of growth. Hence, macroeconomic stability should be a key component of any poverty reduction strategy.

Macroeconomic stability by itself, however, does not ensure high rates of economic growth. In most cases, sustained high rates of growth also depend upon key structural measures, such as regulatory reform, privatization, civil service reform, improved governance, trade liberalization, and banking sector reform, many of which are discussed at length in the *Poverty Reduction Strategy Sourcebook*, published by the World Bank. Moreover, growth alone is not sufficient for poverty reduction.

BOX 1

DEFINITION AND MEASUREMENT OF POVERTY

The World Bank's 2000 World Development Report defines poverty as an unacceptable deprivation in human well-being that can comprise both physiological and social deprivation. Physiological deprivation involves the non-fulfillment of basic material or biological needs, including inadequate nutrition, health, education, and shelter. A person can be considered poor if he or she is unable to secure the goods and services to meet these basic material needs. The concept of physiological deprivation is thus closely related to, but can extend beyond, low monetary income and consumption levels. Social deprivation widens the concept of deprivation to include risk, vulnerability, lack of autonomy, powerlessness, and lack of self-respect. Given that countries' definitions of deprivation often go beyond physiological deprivation and sometimes give greater weight to social deprivation, local populations (including poor communities) should be engaged in the dialogue that leads to the most appropriate definition of poverty in a country.

Brian Ames, Ward Brown, Shanta Devarajan, and Alejandro Izquierdo, *Macroeconomic Policy and Poverty Reduction*, International Monetary Fund, August 2001.

Growth associated with progressive distributional changes will have a greater impact on poverty than growth that leaves distribution unchanged. Hence, policies that improve the distribution of income and assets within a society, such as land tenure reform, pro-poor public expenditure, and measures to increase the poor's access to financial markets, will also form essential elements of a country's poverty reduction strategy.

To safeguard macroeconomic stability, the government budget, including the country's poverty reduction strategies, must be financed in a sustainable, noninflationary manner. The formulation and integration of a country's macroeconomic policy and poverty reduction strategy are iterative processes. Poverty reduction strategies need first to be articulated (i.e., objectives and policies specified), then costed, and finally financed within the overall budget in a noninflationary manner. The amount of finance, much of which will be on concessional terms, is, however, not necessarily fixed during this process: if credible poverty reduction strategies cannot be financed from available resources, World Bank and IMF staff should and will actively assist countries in their efforts to raise additional financial support from the donor community. Nonetheless, in situations where financing gaps remain, a country would have to revisit the intermediate objectives of their strategy and reexamine their priorities. Except in cases where macroeconomic imbalances are severe, there will usually be some scope for flexibility in setting short-term macroeconomic targets. However, the objective of macroeconomic stability should not be compromised.

2. THE LINKS BETWEEN MACROECONOMIC POLICY AND POVERTY REDUCTION: GROWTH MATTERS

Economic growth is the *single most important factor* influencing poverty. Numerous statistical studies have found a strong association between national per capita income and national poverty indicators, using both income and nonincome measures of poverty. One recent study consisting of 80 countries covering four decades found that, on average, the income of the bottom one-fifth of the population rose one-for-one with the overall growth of the economy as defined by per capita GDP (Dollar and Kraay, 2000). Moreover, the study found that the effect of growth on the income of the poor was on average no different in poor countries than in rich countries, that the poverty–growth relationship had not changed in recent years, and that policy-induced growth was as good for the poor as it was for the overall population. Another study that looked at 143 growth episodes also found that the "growth effect" dominated, with the "distribution effect" being important in only a minority of cases (White and Anderson, forthcoming). These studies, however, establish association, but not causation. In fact, the causality could well go the other way. In such cases, poverty reduction could in fact be necessary to implement stable macroeconomic policies or to achieve higher growth.

Studies show that capital accumulation by the private sector drives growth. Therefore, a key objective of a country's poverty reduction strategy should be to establish conditions that facilitate private sector investment. No magic bullet can guarantee increased rates of private sector investment. Instead, in addition to a sustainable and stable set of macroeconomic policies, a country's poverty reduction policy agenda should, in most cases, extend across a variety of policy areas, including privatization, trade liberalization, banking and financial sector reforms, labor markets, the regulatory environment, and the judicial system. The agenda will certainly include increased and more efficient public investment in a country's health, education, and other priority social service sectors.

Macroeconomic Stability Is Necessary for Growth

Macroeconomic stability is the cornerstone of any successful effort to increase private sector development and economic growth. Cross-country regressions using a large sample of countries suggest that growth, investment, and productivity are positively correlated with macroeconomic stability (Easterly and Kraay, 1999). Although it is difficult to prove the direction of causation, these results confirm that *macroeconomic instability has generally been associated with poor growth performance*. Without macroeconomic stability, domestic and foreign investors will stay away and resources will be diverted elsewhere. In fact, econometric evidence of investment behavior indicates that in addition to conventional factors (i.e., past growth of economic activity, real interest rates, and private sector credit), private investment is significantly and negatively influenced by uncertainty and macroeconomic instability (see, for example, Ramey and Ramey, 1995).

[...]

Macroeconomic Instability Hurts the Poor

In addition to low (and sometimes even negative) growth rates, other aspects of macroeconomic instability can place a heavy burden on the poor. Inflation, for example, is a regressive and arbitrary tax, the burden of which is typically borne disproportionately by those in lower income brackets. The reason is twofold. First, the poor tend to hold most of their financial assets in the form of cash rather than in interest-bearing assets. Second, they are generally less able than are the better off to protect the real value of their incomes and assets from inflation. In consequence, price jumps generally erode the real wages and assets of the poor more than those of the non-poor. Moreover, beyond certain thresholds, inflation also curbs output growth, an effect that will impact even those among the poor who infrequently use money for economic transactions. In addition, low output growth that is typically associated with instability can have a longer-term impact on poverty (a phenomenon known as "hysteresis"). This phenomenon typically operates through shocks to the human capital of the poor. In Africa, for instance, there is evidence that children from poor families drop out of school during crises. Similarly, studies for Latin American countries suggest that adverse terms-of-trade shocks explain part of the decline of schooling attainment (see, for example, Behrman, Duryea, and Szeleky, 1999).

Composition and Distribution of Growth Also Matter

Although economic growth is the engine of poverty reduction, it works more effectively in some situations than in others. Two key factors that appear to determine the impact of growth on poverty are the *distributional patterns* and the *sectoral composition* of growth.

If the benefits of growth are translated into poverty reduction through the existing distribution of income, then more equal societies will be *more efficient transformers of growth into poverty reduction*. A number of empirical studies have found that the responsiveness of income poverty to growth increases significantly as inequality is lowered. This is also supported by a recent cross-country study that found that the more equal the distribution of income in a country, the greater the impact of growth on the number of people in poverty (Ravallion, 1997). Others have suggested that greater equity comes at the expense of lower growth and that there is a trade-off between growth and equity when it comes to poverty reduction. A large number of recent empirical studies, however, have found that there is not necessarily such a trade-off and that equity in its various dimensions is growth enhancing.

The *sectoral composition* of growth can determine the impact that growth will have on poverty. Conventional wisdom has been that growth in sectors of the economy where the poor are concentrated will have a greater impact on reducing poverty than growth in other sectors—indeed, this is almost a tautology. For example, it is often argued that in countries where most of the poor live in rural areas, agricultural growth reduces poverty because it generates income for poor farmers and increases the demand for goods and services that can easily be produced by the poor. Various country-specific and cross-country studies have shown that growth in the agricultural and tertiary sectors has had a major effect on reducing poverty, while growth in manufacturing has not. This reinforces the case for duty-free access to industrial country markets for agricultural exports from low-income countries. The links may be more complex over the long run, however. While faster growth in agriculture may address rural poverty in the short-term, reliance on agricultural activity may also intensify output variability, which, in turn, would contribute to increasing rather than decreasing poverty. A more diversified economy with a vibrant manufacturing sector might offer the best chances for a sustainable improvement in living standards in the long run.

What are the implications of these empirical findings for macroeconomic policy? First, in light of the importance of growth for poverty reduction, and of macroeconomic stability for growth, the broad objective of macroeconomic policy should be the establishment, or strengthening, of macroeconomic stability. Policymakers should therefore define a set of attainable macroeconomic targets (i.e., growth, inflation, external debt, and net international reserves) with the objective of maintaining macroeconomic stability, and pursue macroeconomic policies (fiscal, monetary, and exchange rate) consistent with those targets. In cases where macroeconomic imbalances are less severe, a range of possible targets may be consistent with the objective of stabilization. Precise targets can then be set within that range, in accordance with the goals and priorities in the country's poverty reduction strategy (see the section on fiscal policy later in this [essay]).

Second, most developing countries will likely have substantial scope for enhancing the quality of growth, that is, the degree to which the poor share in the fruits of such growth, through policies aimed at improving income distribution. These policies (e.g., land tenure reform, changes in marginal and average tax rates, increases in pro-poor social spending, etc.) often are politically charged, and usually require supporting structural and governance reforms that would empower the poor to demand resources and/or ensure that resources intended for them are not diverted to other groups of the population. As these topics pertain more broadly to political economy, rather than exclusively to macroeconomics, they are beyond the scope of this [essay]. But they reinforce the point that economic growth alone is not sufficient for poverty reduction and that complementary redistributional policies may be needed to ensure that the poor benefit from growth.

Finally, while issues regarding the composition of growth also go beyond strict macroeconomics, several general policy observations can be made. There is a general consensus that policies that introduce distortions in order to influence growth in a particular sector can hamper overall growth. The industrial policies pursued by many African developing countries in the 1960s have long been discredited (World Bank, 1982). Instead, strategies for sector specific growth should focus on removing distortions that impede growth in a particular sector. In addition, policymakers should implement policies that will empower the poor and create the conditions that would permit them to move into new as well as existing areas of opportunity, thereby allowing them to better share in the fruits of economic growth. The objectives of such policies should include creating a stable environment and level playing field conducive to private sector investment and broad-based economic growth; removing the cultural, social, and economic constraints that prevent the poor from making full use of their existing asset base and accessing markets; and increasing the human capital base of the poor through the provision of basic health and education services. Using these policies, and the redistributive policies described above, policymakers can target "pro-poor" growth—that is, they can attempt to maximize the beneficial impact of sustained economic growth on poverty reduction.

[...]

Sources of Instability

There are two main sources of economic instability, namely exogenous shocks and inappropriate policies. Exogenous shocks (e.g., terms of trade shocks, natural disasters, reversals in capital flows, etc.) can throw an economy into disequilibrium and require compensatory action. For example, many low income countries have a narrow export base, often centered on one or two key commodities. Shocks to the world price of these commodities can therefore have a strong impact on the country's income. Even diversified economies, however, are routinely hit by exogenous shocks, although, reflecting their greater diversification, shocks usually need to be particularly large or long-lasting to destabilize such an economy. Alternatively, a disequilibrium can be "self-induced" by poor macroeconomic management. For example, an excessively loose fiscal stance can increase aggregate demand for goods and services, which places pressure on the country's external balance of payments as well as on the domestic price level. At times, economic crises are the result of both external shocks and poor management.

Stabilization

In most cases, addressing instability (i.e., stabilization) will require policy *adjustment*; whereby a government introduces new measures (possibly combined with new policy targets) in response to the change in circumstances. Adjustment will typically be necessary if the source of instability is a permanent (i.e., systemic) external shock or the result of earlier, inappropriate macroeconomic policies. However, if the source of instability can be clearly identified as a temporary shock (e.g., a one-time event) then it may be appropriate for a country to accommodate it. Identifying whether a particular shock is temporary or is likely to persist is easier said than done. Since there is often a considerable degree of uncertainty surrounding such a judgment, it is usually wise to err somewhat on the side of caution by assuming that the shock will largely persist and by basing the corresponding policy response on the appropriate adjustment.

In most circumstances where adjustment is necessary, both monetary (or exchange rate) and fiscal instruments will have to be used. In particular, successful adjustment to a permanent unfavorable shock that worsens the balance of payments will often require a sustained tightening of the fiscal stance, as this is the most immediate and effective way to increase domestic savings and to reduce domestic demand—two objectives typically at the center of stabilization programs.

Adjustment policies may contribute to a temporary contraction of economic activity, but this contingency should not be used to argue against implementing adjustment policies altogether, as the alternative may be worse. Attempting to sustain aggregate demand through unsustainable policies will almost certainly aggravate the long-run cost of a shock, and could even fail in the short run to the extent that it undermines confidence. In the long run, greater benefits to the poor are to be had as a result of the restoration of macroeconomic stability. The appropriate policies to protect the poor during adjustment are to maintain, or even increase, social expenditures and to adopt, where feasible, compensatory measures that would insulate or offset temporary adverse impacts to the fullest extent possible. This is best done by devoting resources to the establishment of effective social safety nets, as an enduring part of a country's poverty reduction strategy, rather than as a response to crisis. Countries that lack such resources/safety nets could be forced to either subject their poor to the short-term adverse effects of stabilization or to delay the pace with which macroeconomic adjustment proceeds (and put off the corresponding long-term benefits to economic growth and poverty reduction).

Countries in macroeconomic crisis typically have little choice but to stabilize quickly, but for countries in the "gray" area of partial stability, finding the right pace may prove difficult. In some cases, a lack of financing will drive the pace of stabilization. Where financing is not a constraint, however, policymakers will need to assess and carefully weigh various factors on a case-by-case basis in choosing the most appropriate pace of stabilization.

Elements of Macroeconomic Stability

Macroeconomic policies influence and contribute to the attainment of rapid, sustainable economic growth aimed at poverty reduction in a variety of ways. By pursuing sound economic policies, policymakers send clear signals to the private sector. The extent to which policymakers are able to establish a *track record of policy implementation* will influence private sector confidence, which will, in turn, impact upon investment, economic growth, and poverty outcomes.

Prudent macroeconomic policies can result in *low and stable inflation*. Inflation hurts the poor by lowering growth and by redistributing real incomes and wealth to the detriment of those in society least able to defend their economic interests. High inflation can also introduce high volatility in relative prices and make investment a risky decision. Unless inflation starts at very high levels, rapid disinflation can also have short-run output costs, which need to be weighed against the costs of continuing inflation.

By moving toward *debt sustainability*, policymakers will help create the conditions for steady and continuous progress on growth and poverty reduction by removing uncertainty as to whether a government will be able to service new debt. By keeping domestic and external debt at levels that can be serviced in a sustainable manner without unduly squeezing nondebt expenditure, policymakers can also ensure that adequate domestic resources are available to finance essential social programs.

Inappropriate exchange rate policies distort the composition of growth by influencing the price of tradable versus nontradable goods. Household survey data for a number of countries indicate that the poor tend to consume higher amounts of nontradable goods while generating relatively more of their income from tradable goods (Sahn, Dorosh, and Younger, 1997). Hence, in addition to distorting trade and inhibiting growth, an overly appreciated exchange rate can impair the relative incomes and purchasing power of the poor.

By building and maintaining an *adequate level of net international reserves,* a country can weather a temporary shock without having to reduce essential pro-poor spending. External shocks can be particularly detrimental to the poor because they can lower real wages, increase unemployment, reduce nonlabor income, and limit private and net government transfers. The level of "adequate" reserves depends on the choice of exchange rate regime.

[...]

Fiscal Policy

Fiscal policy can have a direct impact on the poor, both through the government's overall fiscal stance and through the distributional implications of tax policy and public spending. Structural fiscal reforms in budget and treasury management, public administration, governance, transparency, and accountability can also benefit the poor in terms of more efficient and better targeted use of public resources. As indicated above, there is no rigid, pre-determined limit on what would be an appropriate fiscal deficit. An assessment would need to be based on the particular circumstances facing the country, its medium-term macroeconomic outlook, and the scope for external budgetary assistance. The terms on which external assistance is available are also important. There is a strong case, for instance, for allowing higher grants to translate into higher spending and deficits, to the extent that those grants can reasonably be expected to continue in the future, and provided that the resources can be used effectively.

With regard to the composition of public expenditure, policymakers will need to assess not only the appropriateness of the proposed poverty reduction spending program, but also of planned nondiscretionary, and discretionary nonpriority, spending. In so doing, they will need to take into particular consideration the distributional and growth impact of spending in each area and place due emphasis on spending programs that are pro-poor (e.g., certain programs in health, education, and infrastructure) and on the efficient delivery of essential public services (e.g., public health, public education, social welfare, etc.). In examining these expenditures, policymakers should evaluate the extent to which government intervention in general, and public spending in particular, can be justified on grounds of market failure and/or redistribution.

Policymakers must also ask themselves whether the envisaged public goods or services can be delivered efficiently (e.g., targeted at the intended beneficiaries) and, if not, whether appropriate mechanisms and/or incentives can be put in place to ensure such efficient delivery. Countries should begin by assessing in a frank manner their administrative capacity at both the national and subnational levels to deliver well-targeted, essential public services in support of poverty reduction. In this regard, policymakers should consider the extent to which both technical assistance and the private sector can play a role in improving the delivery of these services.

In the context of medium-term budget planning, policymakers should consider the scope for reallocating existing government spending into priority areas and away from nonproductive spending, including areas where a rationale for public intervention does not exist. Operation and maintenance expenditure tied to capital spending should also be reviewed with a critical eye. The quality of public expenditure could be assessed in the context of a public expenditure review with the assistance of multilateral and/or bilateral donors. Policymakers could then assess the new poverty reduction projects and activities that have been identified in the context of the poverty reduction strategy and integrate them into the preliminary spending program. In so doing, they should attempt to rank the poverty programs in order of relative importance in line with the country's social and economic priorities, the market failure/redistribution criteria identified above, and the country's absorptive capacity in the light of existing institutional and administrative constraints. If spending cuts are deemed necessary in the context of the integrated poverty reduction/macroeconomic framework, policymakers should refer back to the ranking of the spending program based on the relative importance and priority assigned to each activity.

A key aspect of any poverty reduction strategy will be an assessment of the impact of the present tax and nontax system on the poor. An important medium-term objective for many developing countries will be to raise domestic revenue levels with a view to providing additional revenue in support of their poverty reduction strategies. The existing revenue base should be reviewed relative to its capacity to provide for the poverty spending requirements from nonbank domestic financing. Revenues should be raised in as economically neutral a manner as possible, while taking into consideration equity concerns and administrative capacities.

In a developing country, taking account of allocational effects means that the tax system in particular should not attempt to affect savings and investment—experience indicates that aggregate savings and investment tend to be insensitive to taxes, with the result that the tax system typically only affects the allocation of those aggregates across alternative forms. As regards equity, the tax system should be assessed with respect to its direct and indirect impact on the poor. It is difficult to have a tax system that is both efficient and progressive, particularly in those countries without a well-developed tax administration. Therefore, governments should seek to determine a distribution of tax burdens seen as broadly fair rather than use the tax system to achieve a drastic income redistribution.

[...]

The scope for domestic budgetary financing will depend on a number of factors, including the sustainable rate of monetary growth, the credit requirements of the private sector, the relative productivity of public investment, and the desired target for net international reserves. Sacrificing low inflation (through faster monetary growth) to finance additional expenditure is generally not an effective means to reduce poverty because the poor are most vulnerable to price increases. At the same time, since private sector development stands at the center of any poverty reduction strategy, governments need to take into account the extent to which public sector borrowing "crowds out" the private sector's access to credit, thereby undermining the country's growth and inflation objectives. At times, public sector borrowing can also "crowd in" private sector investment by putting in place critical infrastructure necessary for private enterprise to flourish. Given that at any point in time there is a finite amount of credit available in an economy, policymakers must therefore assess the relative productivity of public investment versus private investment and determine the amount of domestic budgetary financing that would be consistent with the need to maintain low inflation and support sustainable economic growth.

The amount and type of available external resources to finance the budget will vary depending on the particular circumstances facing the country. Countries that have access to external grants need to consider what amount is available and sustainable under the present circumstances. The same is true in the case of external debt, but policymakers also need to determine whether the terms on such borrowing are appropriate and whether the added debt burden is sustainable. To the extent that a country is benefiting from, or may benefit from, external debt relief under the enhanced Heavily Indebted Poor Countries (HIPC) Initiative, net resource flows—flows that are predictable over the medium term—will be freed up to finance poverty-related budgetary expenditure. Domestic debt reduction could also represent a viable use of additional concessional foreign assistance, since it would both free up government resources to be directed at priority poverty expenditure, as well as free up additional domestic credit for use by the private sector.

There may be a limit to the amount of additional external financing that a country would deem to be appropriate, however. For example, there may be absorptive capacity constraints that could drive up domestic wages and prices, as well as appreciate the exchange rate and render the country's exports less competitive, thereby threatening both stability and growth. The extent of such pressures will depend on how much of the additional aid is spent on imports versus domestic nontraded goods and services. There may also be uncertainty regarding aid flows, especially over the medium term, as well as considerations regarding long-term dependency on external official aid. In the absence of medium-term commitments of aid, policymakers may therefore wish to be cautious in assuming what levels of assistance would be forthcoming in the future.

[...]

External Shocks and the Choice of Exchange Rate Regime The choice of exchange rate regime—fixed or flexible—depends crucially on the nature of the economic shocks that affect the economy, as well as the structural features of the economy, which may either mitigate or amplify these shocks. Choosing a fixed exchange rate regime when these underlying features of the economy are not supportive leaves a country more exposed to the possibility of an external crisis, which can result in the ultimate abandonment of the peg. In addition, shocks to output can have a strong impact on the poor. Since different exchange rate regimes have different insulating properties vis-à-vis certain types of shocks, choosing the regime that best insulates the economy will serve to moderate fluctuations in output, and thereby best serve the poor.

For example, if the predominant source of disturbance to an economy is shocks to the terms of trade, a flexible exchange rate regime may be best because the nominal exchange rate is free to adjust in response to the shock and bring the real exchange rate to its new equilibrium (see, for example, Devarajan and Rodrik, 1992). Alternatively, if domestic monetary shocks predominate, such as shocks to the demand for money, output may be best insulated by a fixed exchange rate that allows these shocks to be absorbed by fluctuations in international reserves. Of course, one of the challenges facing the policymaker is to identify which shocks are in fact predominant in a particular economy.

The structural features of the economy may also affect the impact a particular shock has on the economy, as well as the insulating properties of exchange rate regimes. For example, if an economy is characterized by a significant degree of nominal wage rigidity, wages will not fully adjust (at least in the short run) in response to small real shocks, and hence the effect of those shocks on output will be amplified. In these circumstances, even if domestic monetary shocks are important, a flexible exchange rate regime may well be preferable (in contrast to the conclusions above). Another important structural feature is the degree of an economy's openness. Typically the more open an economy is, the greater is its exposure to external shocks. This would argue generally in favor of a flexible exchange rate regime. However, if an open economy is sufficiently diversified (i.e., it trades a wide range of goods and services) and if its prices are sufficiently flexible, then a fixed exchange rate may be preferable because the volatility of flexible exchange rates may impede international trade, and thus lower external demand (although the evidence on this is mixed). In conclusion, these various pros and cons of fixed versus flexible exchange rate regimes need to be carefully assessed and weighed on a case-by-case basis—again, there is no universal "right answer."

Policies to Insulate the Poor Against Shocks

Given that the poor are adversely affected by macroeconomic shocks, what should governments do about it? The question can be divided into two parts: How should economic policy be designed to cushion the impact of shocks on the poor, in particular during times of crisis and/or adjustment? What specific policies can governments undertake to insulate the poor from the consequences of shocks by removing existing distortive policies?

Social Safety Nets Sound macroeconomic policies will help a country to reduce its exposure to macroeconomic shocks, but there is no cost-effective policy that will insure against *all* possible shocks. It is therefore crucial to have *social safety nets* in place to ensure that poor households are able to maintain minimum consumption levels and access to basic social services during periods of crisis. Social safety net measures are also necessary to protect the poor from shocks imposed on them during periods of economic reform and adjustment. Safety nets include public work programs, limited food subsidies, transfers to compensate for income loss, social funds, fee waivers, and scholarships for essential services such as education and health. The specific mix of measures will depend on the particular characteristics of the poor and their vulnerability to shocks and should be well-targeted and designed in most cases to provide temporary support.

Equally important, the resources allocated to social safety nets should be protected during economic crises and/or adjustment, when fiscal tightening may be necessary. Governments should have budgetary guidelines approved by their legislatures that prioritize and protect poverty-related programs during periods of crisis and provide a clear course of action that ensures access of the poor to basic social services during periods of austerity (see Lustig, forthcoming). As will be discussed below, countercyclical fiscal policies can also ensure the availability of funds for financing safety nets during crises.

Another important factor to consider is that safety nets should already be operating before economies get hit by shocks so that they can be effective in times of distress (for a more detailed account, see World Bank, 2000). However, if a shock occurs before appropriate safety nets have been developed, then "second-best" social protection policies may be necessary. For instance, food subsidies have been found to be inefficient and often benefiting the non-poor, and most reform programs call for their reduction or even elimination. However, after a severe shock such as the 1997–98 East Asian financial crisis, when countries like Indonesia lacked comprehensive safety nets, existing food subsidies were probably the only means of preventing widespread malnutrition and starvation. In the context of a country's reform process, however, these subsidies should be replaced with better targeted and less distorting transfers to the poor.

[...]

Finally, and most important, governments can do a lot to reduce the pro-cyclical nature of their fiscal policies by saving rather than spending windfalls following positive shocks and ideally using those savings as a buffer for expenditures against negative shocks. A cautious approach would be for the government to "treat every favorable shock as temporary and every adverse one as permanent," although judgment would also depend on, among other things, the availability of financing (Little, and others, 1993). However, even this rule of thumb may not be enough. Governments need to find ways of "tying their hands" to resist the pressure to spend windfall revenues (Devarajan, 1999). For example, when the source of revenue is publicly owned, such as oil or other natural resource, it may be appropriate to save the windfall revenues abroad, with strict rules on how much of it can be repatriated. Countries such as Colombia, Chile, and Botswana have tried variants of this strategy, with benefits not just for overall macroeconomic management, but also for protecting the poor during adverse shocks, since saved funds during good times can be applied to financing of safety nets during crisis.

✗ NO

An "Empty Glass": How the Bretton Woods Institutions Sustain and Exacerbate Poverty

ADAM DAVIDSON-HARDEN

INTRODUCTION

As the international community continues in a project of seemingly earnest self-scrutiny concerning the feasibility of reaching the modest targets reflected in the Millennium Development Goals (MDGs)—the successor to earlier, failed benchmarks—citizens of both the global South and North remain the principal witnesses to the track record of the Bretton Woods Institutions (BWIs), the World Bank and International Monetary Fund (herein referred to as the Bank and Fund), in their stated intentions and associated efforts to alleviate global poverty. The outstanding question casting a long shadow on these institutions is whether the proverbial glass is seen as "half-full" or "half-empty" in this regard. With respect to the track record of these international financial institutions (IFIs) as arbiters of development finance and policy, culpability of the Bank and Fund for their failures in helping to address global poverty has been routinely dismissed along with promulgated visions of progress "around the next bend" or "over the next hill". With only that further commitment to initiatives of trade liberalization, privatization, or investment deregulation, it is argued by the BWIs that paradise is seemingly around the corner. Skeptics question both the earnestness and truthfulness of the Bank and Fund (as well as the northern economic and political powers behind them), however, and see these institutions' potential for development as an either nearly or completely "empty glass," to follow the saying.

In particular, the term "structural adjustment" stands as a damning icon for the destructive social impact and legacy of the BWIs in the global South. With increasing global recognition—including within the BWIs themselves—that structural adjustment policies have hurt rather than helped the world's poor, the turn of the 21st century has seen a momentous "re-branding" of the way the Bank and Fund seek to manage the odious debts of the global South and its beleaguered citizens. The term "poverty reduction" is now as ubiquitous as "structural adjustment" once was in the lexicon of the BWIs, and its use as a mantra to help legitimate and justify the current modus operandi of these institutions has been well established. Though ever-eager to take advantage of any meagre concessions in terms of debt relief and allowance for social policy shifts favouring investment in crucial social services such as health and education, both observers of and participants in the deliberately inclusive Poverty Reduction Strategy Paper (PRSP) processes in heavily indebted countries continue to grapple with a set of core

Adam Davidson-Harden, "An 'empty glass': How the Bretton Woods institutions help to sustain and exacerbate poverty." © Nelson Education Ltd., 2007.

conditions that act as an unalterable foundation for the Bank and Fund, rooted in policies and economic ideologies of "free trade" or global economic integration, as well as financial liberalization, privatization, deregulation, and restrictive regimes for social spending (a policy recipe known to critics and proponents as economic neoliberalism, or colloquially, the "Washington Consensus"[1]). This set of prescriptions—known among insiders as "structural conditionalities" on loans and aid—remain consistent with the policy-based lending formulas stubbornly adhered to by the BWIs throughout the "era" of structural adjustment. This regime of conditionality, referred to as the "Washington Consensus," is very much alive and continues to act as a frustrating barrier toward effective models of human development. Through the ideological furtherance of unfair rules and systems of debt, aid, and trade, the Bank and Fund work to sustain and exacerbate global poverty, particularly in the countries that are most susceptible to imposed conditionalities. This article will briefly touch upon two essential characteristics of the BWIs' ideological framework, which, if unchanged, will continue to be responsible for the immiseration of a substantial portion of humanity into the 21st century. These are a) the proffering of false arguments concerning the state of global poverty and the role of the BWIs' preferred policies in alleviating it; and b) the ongoing entrenchment of market-based or "neoliberal" solutions for development as conditions for loans and aid within current BWI frameworks for "poverty reduction," in the context of an unfair global trade system.

COMING TO TERMS WITH THE NUMBERS ON POVERTY AND THE BWIs' CULPABILITY

The approach to development finance espoused by the BWIs remains rooted in essentially myopic approaches to measuring "success" with respect to outcomes related to poverty. Despite musings and discussions about more holistic measures, the Bank and Fund remain committed to more simplistic economic definitions of poverty as opposed to multidimensional and comprehensive interpretations. In addition, the principal criterion underlying all of the BWIs' methodology in evaluating poverty reduction programs remains the consideration of aggregate economic growth as a precondition for addressing poverty. Consequently, a standard set of macroeconomic adjustment policies are assumed to be the only means of achieving such growth by the BWIs, policies that themselves are contributors to poverty and inequality, as this article will endeavour to show. A principal paradox of this stubborn approach to development economics is evident in the fact that economic growth measures themselves are insufficient, indeed incapable, of constituting any valid measure of social or ecological progress, because of the simple fact that economic growth rates (whether measured through changes in Gross National [or Domestic] Income/Product) only take into account aggregate economic output. Indeed, this is their only purpose. However, inequality, poverty, or ecological degradation may all increase along with positive economic growth.[2] Measures of aggregate economic growth are at best an extremely limited means of measuring progress in development, and at worst, a completely misrepresentative tool for this goal, one continually taken for granted by the BWIs in current strategies and planning around policies for "poverty reduction".[3] Consequently, the piece by Bank and Fund authors included in this volume, "Macroeconomic Policy and Poverty Reduction,"[4] is an excellent example of how the discourse of the BWIs concerning poverty remains rooted in disingenuous arguments about the effectiveness of these institutions' policies in the global South.

Associated with an ongoing, drawn-out debate surrounding economic growth and its relationship to global poverty, a sharp, detailed, and comprehensive critique of the BWIs' proffered numbers and statistics suggesting a decline in global poverty rates has surfaced in recent years.[5] Through pointing out the fact that data used to calculate rates of poverty by the Bank and Fund are insufficient, inaccurate, and based on incommensurable sources and datasets, it has been suggested that the BWIs consistently obtain lower global poverty rates than could be expected from more effective, comprehensive, and comparable measurements. For instance, accepting an arbitrarily low international poverty line based on a crude figure of U.S. dollars per day, per capita income, Pogge and Reddy effectively argue that the purchasing power of those in poorer countries is erroneously conflated with that of citizens of richer countries by the Bank and Fund. One example of this error is evidenced by the necessity of the global poor to rely on purchases of basic necessities such as food and water to survive, whereas aggregate measures conflate more expensive commodities and services—which only the comparatively wealthy can afford—along with commodities necessary for survival, thus making poverty as measured by crude income seem less prevalent.[6] An alternative measure of poverty might focus, it is suggested, on attempts to measure for multiple dimensions through more qualitative rather than economic and purely quantitative tools. For instance, multidimensional conceptions of poverty can focus on levels of human deprivation seen through the lenses of lack of access to basic needs (shelter, food, water, health services, education, a clean environment), or lack of fulfillment of basic human "capabilities" (in terms of malnutrition, life expectancy, literacy rates, etc.).[7] Economistic conceptions of poverty preferred by the BWIs in the main focus myopically on inaccurate measures of income in dollars per day, per capita, and as such paint a much too optimistic appraisal of the state of global poverty today.[8] Still more accurate measures come from consultation with those affected by BWI programs and policies; one important example of such research will be discussed below.

Considering that the deficiency of the IFIs' predominant method of measuring poverty relates to essential dynamics of global inequality (for instance, in terms of purchasing power), it is perhaps unsurprising that other researchers have forcefully argued that the BWIs employ a related "glass mostly full" approach when it comes to assessing purported progress in levels of within- and between-country inequality during the period of their growing ascendancy in financing development in the global South. Branko Milanovic, himself a Bank researcher, argues in this case that contrary to the dominant discourses of the BWIs, in fact global inequality has been on the rise in the past three decades.[9] In both cases of numbers around poverty and inequality, data from India and China serve to skew the global picture somewhat, which, along with the methodological deficiencies touched on here, lead to a far more sober and grim picture of the reinforcing effects growing global poverty and inequality. A 2006 study undertaken by the World Institute for Development Economics Research (WIDER, affiliated with the United Nations University) confirmed—using comprehensive household survey methods—that 2 percent of the world's wealthy own more than half of all global household wealth, and that the richest 1 percent on their own hold 40 percent of global assets, while the poorer half of the global adult population owns not even 1 percent of household wealth.[10] The phenomenon of such vast social polarization on a global scale accompanied with trends toward worsening poverty is deplorable on its own, even without the evidence linking such trends with increased vulnerability and incidence of violent conflict.[11]

THE TERMS OF THE "DEBT SENTENCE": UNFAIR TRADE, ODIOUS DEBTS, AND A RE-BRANDED NEOLIBERAL "TOOLKIT" FOR "POVERTY REDUCTION"

The previous discussion of the debate around numbers lacks a concrete social or historical context to make the reality of growing poverty and inequality apparent to the reader. However, even this general body of evidence facing us prompts a natural line of questioning concerning how the BWIs—institutions with a stated commitment to alleviating poverty—could be culpable for a precipitous deterioration of the global situation during the same time in which their influence in development agendas has become all the more pronounced. The key to understanding frustration and regression in achieving even modest levels of adequate and ecologically sustainable human development—understood through essential indicators such as health, education, employment and livelihoods, food security, access to safe water, preservation of biodiversity, etc.—lies in appreciating the fact that uneven development today is an outgrowth of a continually uneven and asymmetrical world system with colonial roots. The massive, disproportionately unequal distribution of wealth and attendant severe discrepancies in quality of life in the world today are reflected in the politics of the "debt sentence" that continue to immiserate a substantial portion of humanity. The politics of the debt of the global South have been directly responsible for the imposition of a set of failed, destructive, and still-preferred economic policies that continue to sustain and exacerbate poverty today.

At the same time, the debts themselves are questioned by many as being illegitimate or "odious."[12] The BWIs themselves were initially intended to solve short-term balance of payments problems in the post-WWII context.[13] With the U.S. dominating lending to post-war Europe under the Marshall Plan, the Bank and Fund, particularly beginning under Robert McNamara in the 1970s, began a program of lending to poorer countries. Several exogenous economic shocks, however, contributed to the precipitous ballooning of the debts of these new recipient countries—among which the oil shock of 1973 and the interest rate fluctuations of the early 1980s deserve special credit, raising the level of total external debt among developing countries from $70 billion U.S. in 1973 to approximately $540 billion by 1982. Today, the figure has mushroomed to approximately $2.8 trillion U.S.[14] As a consequence, the estimated $100 billion (an optimistic figure) in debt relief that has been disbursed to recipient countries during the years 1989–2005 does not even equal half of the amount hemorrhaged from sub-Saharan African countries alone in the form of debt service payments between 1980 and 2000, an estimated $240 billion U.S.[15] When one considers—as does a recent report[16]—that the "odiousness" and illegitimacy of such transfers and debts not only stems from unpredictable exogenous shocks but also from the actions of occasional money-hoarding, corrupt dictators (from Galtieri to Mobutu or Marcos, and many others who enjoyed support from the BWIs in their time[17]), the validity of these debts in the eyes of the publics of affected countries can be roundly called into question. In the meantime, the Fund and particularly the Bank have continued to use a discourse of anti-corruption and governance reform as important justifiers for their particular approach to poverty reduction strategies, helping to entrench, as is argued here, the same dynamics that have worsened the situation of poverty in poorer countries.[18]

The reality of the disjuncture between BWI promises of development and the effects of their preferred policies on the ground began to become apparent as the "lost decade" of the 1980s took its cruel course in the global South. Under a neo-liberal ideological policy cookie cutter, a "one-size-fits-all" recipe emphasizing trade liberalization in all sectors, currency devaluation, financial liberalization, privatization and deregulation (there are privatization "toolkits" for a variety of sectors, including water and sanitation), and austere and restrictive regimes of social spending in public services such as health and education, countries of the global South watched as structural adjustment took its toll. With the advent of the "strict fiscal discipline" of the BWIs, domestic manufacturing industries suffered and collapsed, domestic finance and investment in critical small- and medium-sized businesses languished,[19] economies were restructured toward export of primary agricultural and natural resource commodities whose value steadily plummeted, and the vital—if meagre—social safety nets in vulnerable states were either emaciated, destroyed, or left to stagnate for lack of funding. In addition, the position of workers was made more tenuous with "flexibilization" of the workforce through changes and relaxations in labour laws. In all cases, women, as the principal caretakers of households in the global South, were disproportionately affected, and the precarious position of indigenous peoples was made even more so. There are obviously regional variations in these trends, though, in the main, the pattern holds. Ironically, the developing states that are most often held up to be contemporary success stories are those which adhered the least to the prescriptions on offer from the BWIs, countries such as China, India, and Singapore, for example (though we must take "success" with a grain of salt here beyond simple economistic terms).[20] Meanwhile, in the unfortunate, debt-ridden countries that had no choice but to accept the strings attached to loans and aid brokered by the Bank and Fund, a fundamental transformation of the state's role in the economy gained pace, one that oriented the state toward facilitation of the market as a principal role, with involvement in service provision (from water, to health and education) also mediated through market mechanisms. In health and education, this neoliberal transformation meant (and continues to mean) the encouragement and demand of the use of "cost-recovery" methods and "demand-side financing" (or user fees, in every day terms) in service provision, while in water, transportation, and other infrastructure (that existed) privatization was (and is) the preferred vehicle for delivering "efficiencies" to "public expenditure management".[21]

Civil society actors and organizations have helped to track and document the impact of these reforms, and their contribution to deepening effects of poverty and inequality as structural adjustment took its course. One such path-breaking and comprehensive research project was the Structural Adjustment Participatory Review Initiative (SAPRI) (SAPRIN, 2004). SAPRI tracked experiences of structural adjustment from the perspective of a large constituency of citizen-driven, participatory review exercises in conjunction with civil society organizations in 12 countries subject to BWI programs. Many core themes emerged from this research, although they coalesced significantly around the shared experience that the standard prescriptions of structural adjustment—and the core conditionalities on loans and aid that enforce it—were directly culpable for increased poverty and inequality in the countries studied (chapter 9, SAPRIN, 2004). Initially undertaken in cooperation with the Bank in the late 1990s under then-President James Wolfensohn, the SAPRI report produced damning evidence of the ongoing and lasting legacy of an ideological adherence to a set of development policies that continues to sustain and exacerbate the poverty affecting the most vulnerable among us.

Of course, given the effects of adjustment as described in brief above, it seems logical that poverty and inequality would be worsened as a result. One need not see too much evidence to realize that increases in fees for access to critical and life-sustaining public services and human needs—from water to health and education—increasingly dictated that access to these goods would be stratified according to one's ability to pay for them in the absence of state investment in providing subsidized or free access. In tandem with these more stark effects of structural adjustment were the more insidious effects in economic terms in sectors such as agriculture, for instance, which—as alluded to above—saw steadily falling prices for primary export goods such as coffee (a staple export of many African and Latin American countries), making small-scale farmers unable to eke out a livelihood in a global market dominated by large-scale, often corporate producers and distributors from the North who enjoy heavy subsidies and advantages that the BWIs refuse domestic small-scale agricultural producers in the South. Nevertheless, debtor countries remain beholden in this context to continued policies of maintaining an economy predicated on exports of primary commodities that can earn sufficient foreign exchange to service debts. In India—a country not looked at in the context of SAPRI—these globally unfair terms of trade have marginalized small-scale farmers to the extent that suicide rates among rural farmers have skyrocketed in recent years, along with enforced global trade rules entrenching below-living wage rates of return to small-scale producers for staple crops such as rice, and related trade rules that make traditionally saved and harvested seed the intellectual property of northern corporations, a trend described as "biopiracy".[22] Such trends and related questions have led more observers to wonder whether the BWIs are simply acting as the latest arbiter of a politics of (neo)colonial dependency economics, as both cheap raw materials and commodities as well as debt interest payments are continually siphoned from the global South for the good of the global North and its consumers.[23]

Ironically, just as the Bank began to distance itself from the findings of SAPRI report, the evidence and bad PR of the "era of structural adjustment" had finally, it seems, sunk in. At the turn of the 21st century Bank President James Wolfensohn would introduce the new discursive wrapping or "re-branding" of structural adjustment in the new emphasis on "poverty reduction," along with a re-branded and deliberately inclusive and participatory process for mediating BWI-sanctioned development plans, in the form of Poverty Reduction Strategy Papers (PRSPs). PRSP processes sport several positive attributes relative to their predecessors in the National Development Plans—namely in the direct mandate of incorporating elements of a debtor country's civil society in consultation processes around what poverty reduction strategies should entail. However, a significant number of organizations in affected countries have cited difficulties in becoming engaged in the process,[24] while other observers note that the essential "veto power" remains with the BWIs to vet and authorize the policy directions inherent in PRSPs through various mechanisms.[25] Finally and most damning is the necessity for PRSP countries (HIPC countries must complete the process to qualify) to adhere to previous neoliberal conditionalities attached to existing debt commitments, as well as new sets of neoliberal conditions for further debt relief or cancellation.[26] A report by the World Development Movement sums up this dilemma in terms of condition-alities emphasizing water privatization attached to existing loans brokered by the BWIs:

> There are three reasons why it has been extremely difficult, if not impos-sible, for the poorest countries to truly determine their own development strategies. First, the content of PRSPs is influenced by pre-existing World Bank and IMF programme conditions. Rather than start afresh, these IFI determined policies are generally 'cut-and-pasted' into the PRSP with no further analysis or scrutiny. For example, in the Gambia, Ghana, Guinea, Malawi, Mali, Mozambique, Nicaragua, Sierra Leone and Yemen, water pri-vatisation was already a condition of a Bank and/or Fund programme *before* being included in the PRSP. These countries had little choice but to include water privatisation within the document. In theory then, IMF and World Bank policy conditions are determined by the content of PRSPs, but in practice, in many cases the PRSP content is determined by already existing IMF and World Bank conditions. (Hardstaff & Jones, 2006, p. 43)

These effects of a self-sustaining mode of re-branded structural adjustment remain a critical area of concern when it comes to the BWIs' present tactic of advocating, requiring, and brokering the privatization of water, a basic necessity for life in a world characterized by severely unequal access.[27] Across all areas of crucial social services, the Bank, for instance, retains the status of its "private sector development strategy" by requiring and advocating for various forms of privatization of social services such as health and education and other infrastruc-ture.[28] User fees remain a rampant and evident feature of social systems across the heavily indebted world, despite public assertions on the part of the Bank and Fund that user fees in education, for example, are not preferred. Years of starvation-level financing for social services in Africa, southeast Asia, and Latin American poorer countries has entailed a continued reliance on user fees of various kinds to help support public services such as health and education (or other types of infrastruc-ture, including water), making the situation all the more pressing, and all of this in spite of the assertion within countless human rights instruments and conven-tions that such services should be free.[29] Terry McKinley of the United Nations Development Programme suggests that the replication of neoliberal conditionali-ties constitutes more of a form of continuous economic imperialism than an attempt to address poverty (McKinley), particularly in the context of obvious chal-lenges and frustrations toward achieving modest—and critical—development tar-gets such as the MDGs. Though the IMF's Independent Evaluations Office produced a review of conditionality in IMF programs in 2005,[30] the focus of this report and the continued operational mandate remain focused on core tenets of neoliberal conditionality, albeit carefully phrased through a discursive wrapping of country "ownership" of "poverty reduction strategies".

REVISITING PRIORITIES OF DEVELOPMENT AND HOLDING THE BWIs ACCOUNTABLE

In the context of an unfair global trade system premised on maintaining the advantage of northern (and now southern) capitalists[31] to continue exploiting the resources of the poorer global South, the ongoing debt crisis has served to further impoverish the world's poor rather than lift them out of poverty as per the mantra of "poverty reduction" repeated by the BWIs. Given the fact that the debts of the nations in which the most impoverished peoples of the world are citizens are arguably odious and/or illegitimate, and that so much of the wealth of the South has already flowed into the coffers of Northern banks and corporations at the behest of the BWIs, it seems patently unjust, for example, that debt servicing obligations represented 417 percent of health care outlays in Angola in 2003, and 352 percent in the Democratic Republic of the Congo in the same year.[32] These are the consequences of a drastic misalignment in priorities on the part of the institutions that wield so much influence and power with respect to the development agenda impacting the world's poorest and most vulnerable people.

Ironically and even pitifully, despite the change in public relations strategies on the part of the BWIs, they still cling to the same core conditions of neoliberal macroeconomic policy that have served to sustain and exacerbate the problems of inequality and poverty that persist today. Current poverty reduction strategies endorsed by the Bank and Fund have been roundly criticized for furthering immiseration in sub-Saharan Africa[33] and the world over. Announcements regarding full multilateral/BWI-related debt cancellation for the 18 HIPCs (heavily indebted poor countries, according to the BWIs' criteria) are an important precedent, but exclude 40 other countries that are heavily indebted while maintaining a stubborn affinity for policies of neoliberal conditionality. With soft-edged internal review processes having been undertaken at the BWIs, recently the U.K. has joined a chorus of critical voices calling for an end to these conditions, although a threat of cancelling funding because of the issue fizzled (see endnote 18 for further discussion). Recently at the time of writing, a conference in Norway reviewing policy conditionality attracted representatives from several countries as well as the dedicated critical civil society organizations that have helped to keep these issues on the public radar.[34] A global call for action against poverty from global civil society organizations and citizen movements (GCAP), rooted in a confrontation of unfair systems of debt, trade, and aid, has garnered incredible global support from global citizens across the planet,[35] and another global call for action against the IFIs points a finger more concertedly at where a good share of the blame lies for the present crisis.[36] This author wholeheartedly endorses both campaigns and particularly the latter for its specific demands of the BWIs. The time is long past due for a thoroughly critical revisitation of the role, mandate, structure, and operation of these institutions[37] and a re-orientation of development away from the benefit of the creditors of odious debts, northern corporations, and the wealthy toward the betterment of all.

NOTES

* I am indebted to both Fraser Reilly-King, co-ordinator of the Halifax Initiative, Ottawa, Ontario, Canada, and Patrick Bond, Director of the Centre for Civil Society, University of KwaZulu-Natal, Durban, South Africa, for their useful comments on this work.

1. Cf. George (1999); Demartino (2000). This neoliberal "toolkit" or policy recipe is well evidenced in a 2005 speech by Danny Leipziger, the Vice-President, Poverty Reduction and Economic Management, of the Bank, to the sixth session of the World Trade Organization Ministerial meeting in Hong Kong in December of that year.

2. For one exploration of this seeming contradiction, see Woodward & Simms (2006).

3. One particularly vicious example of this incapability of aggregate economic growth to measure anything related to progress against poverty can be found in Angola. A civil society organization report put the case of Angola in the following way: "... there is the problem that even if an economy grows—something that you can measure by looking at its gross domestic product (GDP)—that doesn't mean that poor people within it are better off. GDP doesn't account for distribution of wealth within an economy. GDP can grow if an economy sells arms or requires the clean up of a major environmental disaster. GDP will also grow if a few companies generate high profits, but these factors don't mean that the economy's poor people are benefiting. Angola is a perfect example of this dichotomy. Thanks to oil and diamonds, Angola's economy has grown significantly in 2000. Yet a third of Angolan children still die before their fifth birthday; the Human Development Index rates the country 160th [161st as of 2006] of a possible 171, and UNICEF considers it "the worst place in the world to be a child." Angola's GDP is growing even as most of its people derive no benefit from oil or diamonds. Indeed, it is growing even as many people are further impoverished. (CCIC, 2001, p. 6). The most recent World Bank Independent Evaluations Group review of development effectiveness (2006) acknowledges that growth remains uneven and untied to any substantial reductions in poverty apart from the crude income changes in the rapidly growing "emerging markets" of China and India.

4. Ames et al. (2001).

5. Pogge & Reddy (2006).

6. The Bank reproduces these critical flaws and limitations in depicting supposed progress in declining poverty rates in a recently updated website portraying poverty issues "at a glance": http://web.worldbank.org/WBSITE/EXTERNAL/NEWS/0,,contentMDK: 20040961~pagePK:64257043~piPK:437376~theSitePK:4607,00.html.

7. This work will operationalize a more multidimensional approach to poverty as deprivation of basic needs and capabilities. These types of measurements are employed in the construction of the United Nations Development Programme (UNDP)'s Human Development Reports (http://hdr.undp.org/). Two papers, one by Boltvinik (1998) and another by Lok-Dessalien (1998) of the UNDP, offer an accessible introduction to

different approaches to conceptualizing and measuring poverty. A more in-depth study is offered by Laderchi et al. (2003), who compare four approaches and the weaknesses of each along with methodological issues and difficulties.

8. Pogge & Reddy, *op cit.*

9. Milanovic's (2005) analysis of ways of measuring inequality is comprehensive in its scope and a good introduction to methodological controversies in this area.

10. UNU-WIDER (2006). This picture of a massive global gap between rich and poor is complemented by a broader perspective that takes into account the lack of progress in ameliorating inequality since the 1970s. Developing countries have 80 percent of the world's people but share in only a fifth of global GDP. Meanwhile, global GDP has increased in the past 30 years from $3 trillion to $30 trillion. The richest 20 percent of the world's people control 82 percent of world export trade and 68 percent of world foreign direct investment, while the bottom poorest 20 percent share barely more than 1 percent of these categories. Continuing a two-century trend, the same 20 percent of the world's richest people in OECD countries in 1997 had 74 times the income of the poorest 20 percent, up from a 30:1 ration in 1960. Astonishingly, the world's richest 200 people's net worth increased to $1 trillion from $440 billion between 1994 and 1998, and the assets of the world's three richest people totalled to an excess of the GNP of the world's 43 poorest or "least-developed" countries combined. This information is adapted from the United Nations Development Programme's Human Development Report for 1999, pp. 25–37.

11. Kofi Annan affirmed this line of research and its implications for the conception and policy model of "human security" in his report, *A more secure world* (UN, 2004).

12. Mandel (2006); see also Mutasa (2005).

13. Interestingly, John Maynard Keynes had a rival vision of an institution not tied directly to the U.S. dollar but instead to a neutral currency, a proposal which was trumped by the U.S. For an accessible introduction to this historical contextualization of the BWIs, see the World Development Movement (WDM) "Out of time: The case for replacing the World Bank and IMF" (2006).

14. Ferraro & Rosser (1994); CETIM et al. (2006, p. 5). See also the data from the most recent *Global Development Finance* report of the Bank (2006), at http://web.worldbank.org/ WBSITE/EXTERNAL/DATASTATISTICS/EXTGLODEVFINVOL2/0,,contentMDK:20915314~ menuPK:2459328~pagePK:64168445~piPK:64168309~theSitePK:2459286,00.html.

Current total external debt for developing countries in Africa amounted to 91.2 percent of the value of trade in goods and services in 2005. For "net debtor" countries according to the IMF's criteria, this statistic is more than 166 percent, while debt service payments constitute over a fifth of the value of traded goods and services in these countries (IMF, 2006, pp. 251–253).

15. Dembele (2005, p. 390). For a post-mortem analysis on the comparatively meagre promises of debt relief at the much-vaunted Gleneagles G8 summit in 2005, see a recent report by the European Network on Debt and Development (2006).

16. Mandel, *op cit.*

17. Cf. Mandel, *op cit;* another notable example of a power-hungry regime that enjoyed the full support of the BWIs is that of Habyarimana's in Rwanda up until 1993; see Storey (2001).

18. Tensions flared in September 2006 as the U.K.'s Department for International Development, under Hilary Benn, threatened to withhold £50 million in protest of the Bank's "aggressive agenda" concerning anti-corruption strategies under current

President Paul Wolfowitz. Joseph Stiglitz, for one, draws attention to the fact that anti-corruption strategies can be but one more potentially blunt "stick" for cutting aid where it is desperately needed (http://www.globalpolicy.org/socecon/bwi-wto/critics/ 2006/1027stiglitzcorruption.htm); while at the same time not enough attention is paid to transnational corporations and other business who may benefit from corruption, bribery, and "kickback" schemes associated with neoliberal privatization and trade liberalization reforms. Transparency International (http://www.transparency.org/) is a global civil society organization that attempts to track these, and related trends.

The U.K. backed down on its threat in December of the same year, although not before the Bank moved to withhold funds from Chad, India, Argentina, Congo, Kenya, Ethiopia, and Bangladesh under its new guidelines purportedly aimed at combating corruption. The U.K. has, in 2005–6, begun to join a chorus of international civil society voices in decrying the BWIs' persistent focus on certain forms of neoliberal policy conditionality. This stated focus, however, rings somewhat hollow while U.K. Trade and Investment continues a strong push for trade liberalization and neoliberal policies in the developing world (cf. http://www.ukinvest.gov.uk/10415/en_GB/0.pdf). Meanwhile, Wolfowitz—an architect of the 2003 war on Iraq—embodies a critical fusion of neoliberal and neoconservative politics for the Bank's leadership. For a synopsis of the debates around corruption and the BWIs, see http://www.globalpolicy.org/socecon/bwi-wto/bankind.htm.

19. Estimates concerning levels of short-term, speculative international currency and other forms of trading are up to 2 trillion dollars per *day* today, severely dwarfing "productive" forms of global, regional, and local investment. Liberalization of finance has meant the freer movement of speculative capital and its disconnection from productive investment. Social movements have arisen around the possibility of a "transaction tax" on the massive amounts of speculative capital criss-crossing the world daily; one prominent advocate was the late Nobel Prize for Economics winner James Tobin, a Canadian. See the website for ATTAC, a global social movement based in France pushing for a transaction tax to provide development funds (http://www.attac.org/), the Halifax Initiative (http://www.halifaxinitiative.org), as well as Tobin (1996) and Haq et al. (1996). The U.S. has historically opposed this kind of move, representing the interests of powerful finance capitalists.

20. Cf. Kiely (2004). Kiely's study also instructively points out that "globalizing" countries—those which most faithfully implemented BWI prescriptions for trade liberalization and integration with global markets—show poorer rates of productivity than do countries that protect domestic industries and sectors.

21. This topic comes up below and other useful works are referenced. Cf. Mehrotra & Delamonica (2005).

22. Shiva (2005). See also a documentary and resources produced by the U.S. Public Broadcasting Service entitled "Seeds of Suicide," available at http://www.pbs.org/frontlineworld/rough/2005/07/seeds_of_suicid.html. For one among many other critics and observers, Shiva also contends that implication of poorer countries in the global agricultural trade exacerbates poverty by turning attention away from food security on a local and regional basis, or "food sovereignty" (2002).

23. In addition to sector-specific effects of an unfair global trade system, international trade regimes acting in tandem with the neoliberal orientation of the BWIs—such as the World Trade Organization and its sub-agreements, and many Regional Trade Agreements as well as bilateral agreements—serve to reinforce patterns of

entrenchment of neoliberal social and economic policy from a supranational basis. The General Agreement on Trade in Services (GATS) of the WTO is an interesting case in point in this regard, used as a lever by richer states in demanding market access into services relating to water, education, and health, for example.

24. Wood (2004).

25. Alexander (2004); Hardstaff & Jones (2006).

26. World Development Movement (2005); McKinley (2004). These represent a mere sample of a pattern of criticism that has emerged along with the evolution and observation of the PRSP processes at work. Many civil society organizations agree that the rhetoric surrounding "country ownership" in the end seems but a façade for an edifice of neoliberal conditionalities in a different guise.

27. There are several adequate primers on the topic of the global water crisis and problems of equity of access for proper nourishment and survival, *vis-à-vis* unlimited access by corporations and industry at little to no cost, for profit. See Barlow and Clarke (2005) for one such critical introduction. The UNDP's Human Development Report for 2006 is built around a theme of the global water crisis (UNDP, 2006), although Bond and Ruiters (2006) argue that even the UNDP remains mired in a neoliberal approach to water management that serves to frustrate progress toward ameliorating poverty through improving access. For a primer on the Bank's involvement in water privatization schemes in developing countries, see a resource developed by the Halifax Initiative (2004).

28. cf. World Bank (2004).

29. For a discussion of the prevalence of user fees in global education systems as of August 2006 as a form of "human rights violation," see the work of Tomasevski (2003; 2006). Tomasevski was UN Special Rapporteur on the Right to Education from 1998–2004. For a sampling of literature on how user fees persist in health care systems—including those in heavily indebted countries—see Homedes & Ugalde (2005), van Doorslaer et al. (2005), as well as Gilson & McIntyre (2005).

30. IMF Independent Evaluations Office (2005).

31. Increasingly in Africa, for example, the interests of "southern capitalists" in the form of Chinese interests in oil and other commodities has also taken centre stage, highlighting ongoing structural problems in indebted countries vulnerable to whatever form of foreign direct investment chooses to look their way. The cases of Sudan, the Democratic Republic of the Congo, and Zambia, for example, are germane in this regard. Each are the source of invaluable commodities in global markets, and both nations' citizens have been caught in a literal and figurative crossfire between competitors seeking to exploit valuable resources such as oil, gold, coltan, tin, and timber among others, while poverty continues to worsen. Angola's dependence on oil "resource rents" from American TNCs are another example; Africa abounds with examples of these dynamics. These points highlight the fact that BWI encouragement and imposition of neoliberalism comes in tandem with unfair and unaccountable trade dynamics involving capital in the North and South.

32. These statistics and related analyses can be found at the website of the International Debt Observatory: http://www.oid-ido.org/en.ratio.php3?id_article=96. IDO compiles ratios of debt servicing obligations relative to various other expenditure categories, including health and education, in the most indebted countries.

33. Lewis (2005); Bond & Dor (2003); Bond (2004).

34. Cf. http://www.eurodad.org/articles/default.aspx?id=747; with the tensions raised through critics from global civil society and now government quarters, however, many acknowledge that outwardly, at least, the stance on conditionality has softened; the roots and operationalization of conditionality, however, remain firmly in place. For a recent synopsis of the BWIs shape-shifting in this respect, see Bull et al. (2006).

35. http://www.whiteband.org. The four goals of the global campaign are "just governance, accountable to the general public, and the fulfilment of human rights; trade justice; a substantial increase in the quantity—and quality—of aid, and financing for development; and debt cancellation".

36. http://www.cadtm.org/article.php3?id_article=1893. The goals of this campaign are more specific than those of the GCAP:

    1. Immediate and 100% cancellation of multilateral debts as part of the total cancellation of debts claimed from the South, without externally imposed conditionalities.
    2. Open, transparent and participatory External Audit of the lending operations and related policies of the International Financial Institutions, beginning with the World Bank and IMF.
    3. Stop the imposition of conditions and the promotion of neoliberal policies and projects.
       a. In this 50th anniversary year of the International Finance Corporation (IFC), the IFIs must end the promotion of privatization of public services and the use of public resources to support private profits.
       b. Stop IFI funding and involvement in environmentally destructive projects beginning with big dams, oil, gas and mining and implement the major recommendations of the Extractive Industries Review.
       c. Immediately stop imposing conditions that exacerbate health crises like the AIDS pandemic and make restitution for past practices such as requiring user fees for public education and health care services.

37. As another program for action, I also support the essential restructuring of the BWIs along the lines suggested by both the World Development Movement (in Hardstaff & Jones, 2006) and the Halifax Initiative (http://www.halifaxinitiative.org). Although this work has limited itself to probing the effect of the Bank and Fund on poverty in a broad sense, cross-cutting issues with respect to the BWIs like their domination by the U.S. and U.K. under current voting rights, their lack of transparency to those affected most by related programs, and the fundamental links between northern capitalist interests and the modus operandi of the Bank and Fund are issues that require systematic attention in any attempt to come to terms with unfair systems of debt, trade, and aid. Finally, with respect to the future of the Bank and Fund, the current and ongoing debate in global civil society revolves around whether to reform or reject the BWIs, to "fix" or "nix" them. This author gravitates substantially toward the latter in favouring a complete re-tooling of the uneven and hyper-liberalized global financial architecture that continues to ensnare the globally poor. Two works that may assist the reader in formulating their own opinion are those of the WDM (2006) and another paper by Bond (2006). Soederberg's (2006) book puts these matters in the context of controversies surrounding the BWIs and related institutions of "global governance".

POSTSCRIPT_____

For several decades, development NGOs have worked at building stronger transnational advocacy networks for holding the major development funding agencies like the International Monetary Fund and the World Bank more accountable. Clearly, there have been shifts in the development discourse coming from these two agencies. The adoption of the PRSPs approach, they argue, shows that the Bank and IMF have been sensitive to criticism from the development community. The two agencies claim to have moved away from the standard "cookie cutter" approach of their previous SAPs and have instead adopted an approach that is both more sensitive to the specific needs of each country and more encouraging of national participation and ownership of the planning process.

Does this mean that the years of lobbying by the NGO sector paid off? In light of Professor Davidson-Harden's critique, have the World Bank and International Monetary Fund conditionality really significantly changed? Or, has this simply been a "rebranding" exercise that leaves the same fundamental assumptions in place? Given the G8 Summit commitments to significantly increase aid in order to meet the UN Millennium Development Goals, the PRSP process will ensure that the World Bank and IMF continue to function as the primary gatekeepers to development aid and debt relief for some years to come. In light of this, what strategy should NGOs now take to ensure great accountability of these two critically important agencies?

Has the Adoption of a Rights-Based Approach to Development Failed?

✔ **YES**

PETER UVIN, "On High Moral Ground: The Incorporation of Human Rights by the Development Enterprise," *Praxis: The Fletcher Journal of Development Studies,* XVII (2002)

✗ **NO**

HUGO SLIM, "Making Moral Low Ground: Rights as the Struggle for Justice and the Abolition of Development," *Praxis: The Fletcher Journal of Development Studies,* XVII (2002)

Following the Second World War, the discourses on human rights and development emerged simultaneously but largely independent of each other. Development discourse focused on the notion of development as a problem of promoting economic growth. Whether this meant increases in the Gross National Product, meeting "basic needs," or promoting "structural adjustment policies," human rights were largely absent from the equation.

Within the human rights field, debates focused on the appropriate balance between traditional civil and political rights and the more collectivist-oriented economic, social, and cultural rights. The dichotomy between these two sets of rights was formally institutionalized by the adoption in 1966 of two separate international agreements–the International Covenant on Civil and Political Rights and the International Covenant on Economic, Social, and Cultural Rights.

During the Cold War, debates on the appropriate balance between these two sets of rights were largely shaped by the ideological divisions of the Cold War. Western nations, led by the United States, argued that civil and political rights should always be given priority and that true development could be achieved only when civil and political rights are first recognized. Many developing states, led by China, argued that social, economic, and cultural rights needed to take precedence. If someone is starving, what good does a guarantee of freedom of speech do? Some pointed to the so-called Asian Tigers–South Korea, Taiwan, Malaysia, and Singapore–as examples where authoritarian governments were successful in promoting development. Human rights might have to take a secondary place until economic development and growth is achieved.

The artificial distinction between these two sets of rights came under increased challenge in the 1980s. The first significant step in this process was the 1986 adoption by the United Nations General Assembly of the Declaration of the Right to

Development. True development, it was argued, ensures that all human rights are realized—civil, political, economic, social, and cultural. According to this concept, the two sets of rights formed an integral whole.

Acceptance of this notion gained momentum with the end of the Cold War. The 1993 UN Conference on Human Rights in Vienna made the case that all human rights form an undivided, interdependent, and non-hierarchical whole. This theme was picked up in subsequent UN meetings, such as the Copenhagen Summit on Social Development in 1995, which focused attention on the importance of human rights in meeting the goals of social development. A growing number of UN agencies began identifying the promotion of human rights as a part of their development agenda. For example, UNICEF takes the UN Convention on the Right of the Child and the UN Convention on the Elimination of All Forms of Discrimination Against Women as the reference point for all their programming. The United Nations Development Programme (UNDP) has promoted the development agenda, but focused its *Human Development Report 2000* on "Human Rights and Human Development." As its report noted: "Human rights and development share a common vision and a common purpose—to secure the freedom, well-being and dignity of all people everywhere" (p. 1). As noted in the discussion on Issue 9, the adoption of the Millennium Goals was also framed in the context of human rights commitments to ensure the establishment of a development process through which all humans could reach their full capacities.

As a result of these developments, a growing number of both official government development agencies and non-governmental organizations have integrated human rights discourse into their development programming. Proponents of a "rights-based" approach to development argue that this helps to establish a clearer normative framework for orienting development cooperation. It links development efforts to an internationally agreed set of norms that are backed by international law. As a result, citizens have a stronger basis for making claims against their own states, and civil society groups can more effectively hold states accountable for their actions and policies.

In addition, a rights-based approach marks an improvement in the "basic needs" strategies that many advocated a decade ago. Needs-based approaches tend to focus on the securing of new or additional resources for delivering services to the identified "needy" groups. Such an approach can be driven primarily by charitable or even paternalistic concerns which may overlook some more fundamental issues of social justice. Instead, rights-based approaches shift the focus to a more equitable sharing and distribution of existing resources, with greater attention to those groups and individuals who are particularly marginalized and vulnerable. As a result, some feel that the adoption of rights-based approaches give legitimacy to more progressive, even radical, approaches to development rather than the technocratic, managerial approaches that dominated in the past. Many of the quantifiable measures of development used in the past are no longer relevant. Instead, development success may now be measured in terms of the empowerment of people and communities to take greater control of their futures.

A growing number of intergovernmental development organizations, governmental development assistance agencies, and non-governmental organizations have adopted the discourse of human rights in their development programming. But, is all this just new window dressing? Has the fundamental way in which development agencies operate been significantly altered? In the following essay, Peter Uvin raises several questions regarding the widespread adoption of rights-based approaches. While he applauds the intentions, he is ultimately fearful that the changes have been primarily rhetorical and amount to not much more than "fluff." Hugo Slim responds by acknowledging some problems with the concept, while arguing that Uvin should not underestimate the importance of the "prophetic" use that many NGOs make of human rights discourse to hold governments and development agencies accountable.

✔ **YES**

On High Moral Ground: The Incorporation of Human Rights by the Development Enterprise

PETER UVIN

Until quite recently, the development enterprise operated in perfect isolation, if not ignorance, of the human rights community.[1] This does not mean that all development practitioners are undemocratic people or lack personal interest in human rights. Rather, it means that development practitioners did not consider human rights issues as part of their professional domain: they neither weighed the implications of their own work on human rights outcomes, nor sought explicitly to affect human rights through their work. This tendency continued until well into the 1990s, allowing the organizers of a prestigious UN-sponsored 1999 Conference on Nutrition and Human Rights to state that "the human rights approach to nutrition is not even on the radar screen"[2] and that "interaction between the [UN human rights machinery] and the UN development agencies has been essentially non-existent."[3]

This intellectual and operational gap began to close slowly from the early 1990s onwards. There is nowadays a significant and growing literature, mainly of the 'gray' kind, on the relationship between development and human rights: policy declarations and exhortations of the need for further integration, mainstreaming, collaboration, and analysis are commonplace.

While much of this is to be applauded—at the very least, a major departure from the previous policy of complete blindness and acquiescence seemed overdue—there is still much to worry about in this context. Two issues stand out: 1) much of this work risks being little more than rhetorical, feel-good change, further legitimizing historically created inequalities and injustices in this world, and 2) the many faces of power reveal themselves, as they always do, when the powerful and the rich voluntarily set out to collaborate and redefine the conditions of misery and exploitation for the rest of the world, and fund the resulting solutions.

I intend to critique some of the typical ways in which human rights have made their way into the development agenda. Specifically, I will discuss three levels that are part of a continuum from the most status-quo oriented approach to the most radical. At the lowest level, I will describe the incorporation of human rights terminology into classical development discourse. As this is purely rhetorical, the traditional discourse is not challenged at all. On the contrary, it is validated by its occupation of yet another plane of high moral ground. At a second level, human rights objectives are added to a range of goals and criteria for development agen-

---

Peter Uvin, "On High Moral Ground: The Incorporation of Human Rights by the Development Enterprise," *Praxis: The Fletcher Journal of Development Studies*, XVII (2002). Reprinted with permission of The Fletcher School–Tufts University.

cies, thus allowing for the establishment of new programs with specific human rights aims. A perfect example thereof is the fashionable good governance agenda. At the third and highest level, the mandate of development itself may be redefined in human rights terms, potentially bringing about a fundamental rethinking of the development paradigm itself—a so-called "human rights approach to development." In this context, the work of Amartya Sen stands out. The following discussion investigates each of these approaches in greater detail.

THE RHETORICAL-FORMULAIC INCORPORATION

During the 1990s, bilateral and multilateral aid agencies published a slew of policy statements, guidelines and documents on the incorporation of human rights in their mandate. An enormous amount of this work was little more than thinly disguised repackaging of old wine in new bottles. As Frankovits rightly states:

> With an increasing demand for economic and social rights to be a major factor in development assistance, donors have tended to reformulate their terminology. Beginning with the World Bank's statement at the 1993 Conference on Human Rights in Vienna, followed by frequently heard assertions by individual donor agencies, the claim is made that all development assistance contributes to economic and social rights. Thus agricultural projects—whatever their nature—are claimed to contribute directly to the fulfillment of the right to food.[4]

A few additional quotes on the issue will get my point across nicely. There is the World Bank, claiming that its "lending over the past 50 years for education, health care, nutrition, sanitation, housing, environmental protection and agriculture have helped turn rights into reality for millions."[5] Or UNDP, declaring that it "already plays an important role in the protection and promotion of human rights.... Its program is an application of the right to development."[6] Essentially, these statements colonize the human rights discourse, arguing—as Moliere's character, who discovered he had always been speaking prose—that human rights has been the focus of these development agencies all along. Case closed; high moral ground safely established.[7]

Interpreted more benignly, this wordplay constitutes the first step towards a true shift in vision. Indeed, much scholarship argues that discourse changes have real-world impacts: they slowly reshape the margins of acceptable action, create opportunities for redefining reputations and naming and shaming, change incentive structures and the way interests and preferences are defined, and influence expectations. This is, after all, a key proposition of all international law: even in the absence of enforcement mechanisms, international law does matter by affecting actors' perceptions, calculations, reputations, and norms. The same insight is also a key tenet in so-called sociological, institutionalist, and social-constructivist schools of thought in the academic discipline of international relations.

Hence, the kind of rhetorical incorporation discussed in this section, while it may change few of the immediate actions undertaken, may make a real difference in the longer run. How much of a change this will amount to is a matter of time.

There are, however, some serious problems with this habit of rhetorically incorporating human rights. Typically, until now, what this approach has produced is not only a simple sleight-of-hand; it is also wrong, for it overlooks the tensions between the logics of human rights and development.[8] As Donnelly convincingly argues, referring to the UNDP's new work on human development:

> Human rights and sustainable human development "are inextricably linked" only if development is defined to make this relationship tautological. "Sustainable human development" simply redefines human rights, along with democracy, peace, and justice, as subsets of development. Aside from the fact that neither most ordinary people nor governments use the term in this way, such a definition fails to address the relationship between economic development and human rights. Tensions between these objectives cannot be evaded by stipulative definitions.[9]

Working out the relationship between development and human rights requires more than simply stating that one automatically implies, equals, or subsumes the other. Michael Windfuhr, founder of Food First Information and Action Network, one of the world's foremost human rights organizations devoted to an economic right (the right to food), correctly adds:

> Besides the general misconceptions related to ESC-Rights[10]—that they are costly to implement, that implementation can only be done progressively and that they are therefore not rights at all but rather political objectives— one additional basic misunderstanding often comes up in discussions on how to integrate ESC-Rights into development cooperation, the concept that development cooperation automatically implements ESC-Rights because it is oriented to improve health or food situations of groups of the population. A rights-based approach means foremost to talk about the relationship between a state and its citizens.[11]

There is a real danger in this kind of rhetorical discourse. Far from constituting the first step towards a fundamental re-conceptualization of the practice of development cooperation, it seems merely to provide a fig leaf for the continuation of the status quo. By postulating that development projects and programs by definition constitute an implementation of human rights, the important distinction between a service-based and a rights-based approach to development is obscured.

Another pernicious tendency to manipulate words exists as well. In the previous paragraphs, the rhetorical sleight of hand consisted of arguing that the development community has always—automatically and axiomatically—furthered human rights, and everything is thus fine and dandy. The exact opposite rhetorical trick is sometimes employed as well. It consists of suggesting that major, epochal changes are now underway in the development enterprise, and they follow directly from the blinding realization of the crucial importance of human rights in development practice. The key human rights contribution to development practice, as repeated in countless documents, is the need for the engagement and participation of the poor in the processes that affect their lives.[12] This argument is breathlessly presented as a major breakthrough that we all ought to feel truly pleased about, as if development practitioners have not been proposing exactly the same thing for decades now, with very little to show for it. When human rights specialists, most of whom are lawyers, write this kind of nonsense, one can forgive them on the grounds of their ignorance. When development practitioners write such things, however, it amounts to deliberate misrepresentation.

The prime reason why development agencies adopt such language with its deliberate obfuscations is, of course, to benefit from the moral authority and political appeal of the human rights discourse. The development community is in constant need of regaining the high moral ground in order to fend off criticism and mobilize resources. As the development community faces a deep crisis of legitimacy among both insiders and outsiders, the act of cloaking itself in the human rights mantle may make sense, especially if it does not force anyone to think or act differently.

GOOD GOVERNANCE

At a second level we find the concept of good governance, developed by the World Bank in the early 1990s. The Bank identified "four areas of governance that are consistent with [its] mandate: public sector management, accountability, the legal framework, and information and transparency."[13] The good governance notion was an extension and deepening of the Bank's economic conditionality agenda, contained in the structural adjustment programs of the 1980s. It was widely perceived that these programs had not lived up to expectations and this failure was seen as a result of political factors. Economic conditionality had not worked as expected. Governments signed structural adjustment agreements but subsequently failed to implement them correctly, if at all. If only the workings of Third World governments were more transparent and accountable, the thought went, then surely other social groups would demand the right policies and a domestic basis for a stable and liberal policy environment would be laid. As such, the good governance agenda was explicitly designed to be the complement, the political extension, of structural adjustment programs.

The good governance agenda also fulfilled a rhetorical-political function. It allowed the World Bank to discuss the reforms that it proposed as economic and not political matters. In short, it constituted an attempt to de-politicize the concepts of democracy (and *a fortiori* human rights) in order to avoid allegations of undermining state sovereignty, as well as to benefit from the widespread acceptance that economic thinking enjoys in the development community. As the Human Rights Council of Australia puts it: "The use of 'good governance' arises from a perception that governments in developing countries will prove less resistant to such euphemisms than to talk of 'corruption' or 'human rights.'"[14] This apolitical nature is crucial for the survival of international organizations in a world of *de jure*, if not *de facto*, sovereignty.

In some ways the good governance agenda, being defined in a more restrictive fashion, is less politically interventionist than that of democracy and human rights. In other ways, it extends the reach of the international community, for it has almost no backing in international law. Unlike human rights (and some would even argue democracy), not a single international treaty or legal instrument commits governments to transparency, accountability of civil servants, or 'good' public sector management, however defined. State practice, for that matter, differs dramatically even among the rich countries.

The access to public information that U.S. citizens enjoy under the Freedom of Information Act is absolutely unthinkable in most of Europe. Then again, the degree of financial clout exerted by Wall Street on the U.S. Department of Treasury, or by large corporations on the U.S. Department of Commerce, if not on the entire political system in the United States, would be unacceptable to most European citizens. Yet the extent to which French foreign policy, especially towards Africa, is a private presidential matter beyond democratic scrutiny is unimaginable in most other countries. Moreover, the broad-based coalition governments underpinned by corporatist institutions reaching deep into society, characteristic of a number of European countries, are inconceivable in the United States. Indeed, profound differences in the way public institutions are accountable or transparent to citizens, or the way the public sector is managed, exist between rich countries. None of these matters are governed by international legal standards. Although good governance is defined as a technical matter, essentially another term for liberal public sector management, it is a strong extension and imposition of the liberal ideology of its promoters and is also totally unsupported by international legal standards.

More recently, the World Bank has officially converted to 'real' human rights, and its discourse on governance has subsequently become much less technical, at least in documents meant for human rights activists. This produces interesting results. According to the Bank itself, "By helping to fight corruption, improve transparency, and accountability in governance, strengthen judicial systems, and modernize financial sectors, the Bank contributes to building environments in which people are better able to pursue a broader range of human rights."[15] As this quote suggests, and as I have already discussed, much of the human rights conversation still amounts to little more than rhetorical repackaging. Policies that were once justified by their promise to improve investor confidence are now justified for their human rights potential.

Nothing else has changed. It takes more than a few ideological leaps to see how strengthening financial systems is a human rights activity. Certainly the framers of the Universal Declaration and the two Covenants were not thinking of shoring up banking reserve requirements, improving accounting standards, or liberalizing current accounts when they constructed the original human rights edifice.

In such statements, the many faces of power and their associated discourses come together. Human rights, free trade, or the willingness to let multinational corporations (MNCs) buy national assets become conflated, amounting to restatements of the 'good world' as the powerful see it. They are decreed from above, morally self-satisfying and compatible with the status quo in the centers of power. Rich countries remain immune to criticism. Over-consumption in the north, a history of colonialism, environmental degradation, protectionism, the dumping of arms in the Third World, the history of shoring up past dictators, the wisdom of structural adjustment, and globalization are not on the table for discussion. No wonder so many people resent the human rights agenda.

SEN AND FREEDOM AS DEVELOPMENT

At a third level, a new paradigm of rights-based development is emerging in which development and rights become different aspects of the same dynamic. The boundaries between human rights and development disappear, and both become conceptually and operationally inseparable parts of the same processes of social change. Development comes to be redefined in terms that include human rights as a constitutive part: all worthwhile processes of social change are simultaneously rights-based and economically grounded, and should be conceived in such terms. This makes intuitive sense, because at the level of human experience these dimensions *are* indeed inseparable.[16]

Amartya Sen has produced significant and often-quoted reflections on this new paradigm. His latest book, *Development as Freedom,* synthesizes many of his earlier insights. He defines development as the expansion of capabilities or substantive human freedoms for each person, "the capacity to lead the kind of life he or she has reason to value."[17] He rightly adds, "despite unprecedented increases in overall opulence, the contemporary world denies elementary freedoms to vast numbers—perhaps even the majority—of people." He argues for the removal of major factors that limit freedom, defining them as "poverty as well as tyranny, poor economic opportunities as well as systematic social deprivation, neglect of public facilities as well as intolerance or over-activity of repressive states."[18]

An interesting part of Sen's work is his treatment of freedom as simultaneously instrumental, constitutive, and constructive for development. This goes beyond arguing that both development and freedom are nice (so why don't we call them something else altogether). Rather, it sets out the deep and mutually constitutive links that exist between these two concepts and domains in ways that make their inseparability clear for all. As he states:

There is the often asked rhetoric: What should come first—removing poverty and misery, or guaranteeing political liberty and civil rights, for which poor people have little use anyway? Is this a sensible way of approaching the problem of economic needs and political freedoms—in terms of a basic dichotomy that appears to undermine the relevance of political freedoms because the economic needs are so urgent? I would argue, no, this is altogether the wrong way to see the force of economic needs, or to understand the salience of political freedoms. The real issues that have to be addressed lie elsewhere, and they involve taking note of extensive interconnections between political freedoms and the understanding and fulfillment of economic needs. The connections are not only instrumental (political freedoms can have a major role in providing incentives and information in the solution of acute economic needs), but also constructive ... I shall argue that the intensity of economic needs *adds* to—rather than subtracts from—the urgency of political freedoms. There are three different considerations that take us in the direction of a general preeminence of basic political and liberal rights:

1. Their *direct* importance in human living associated with basic capabilities (including that of social and political participation);
2. Their *instrumental* role in enhancing the hearing that people get in expressing and supporting their claims to political attention (including the claims of economic needs);
3. Their *constructive* role in the conceptualization of "needs" (including the understanding of "economic needs" in a social context).[19]

Such ideas have made great inroads in international development discourse. Take this statement, for example, from the UN Secretary-General's *Agenda for Development,* which clearly discusses the first two types of relations between development and human rights:

Democracy and development are linked in fundamental ways. They are linked because democracy provides the only long-term basis for managing competing ethnic, religious, and cultural interests in a way that minimizes the risk of violent internal conflict. They are linked because democracy is inherently attached to the question of governance, which has an impact on all aspects of development efforts. They are linked because democracy is a fundamental human right, the advancement of which is itself an important measure of development. They are linked because people's participation in the decision-making processes which affect their lives is a basic tenet of development.[20]

This was written five years before Amartya Sen's book, by an institution that is not exactly the hotbed of philosophical innovation. And we can go back further in time as well: cannot Wilson's four freedoms be seen as direct precursors of exactly the same ideas? Hence, we have to acknowledge that these concepts have been around a long time in the development field. Rather than congratulating ourselves on how smart and insightful we have become since we all read and talk about Sen's work, we ought to ask why we have not acted on these ideas before. And this is where we encounter the limits of Sen's major contribution to development. There is no politically grounded analysis of what stands in the way of his approach. In addition, Sen does not even try to move beyond the level of broad paradigmatic insight. This is hardly a cause for discarding Sen's major contribution: no man is obliged to do everything. What it does mean, though, is that agencies, by signing up to Sen's vision, remain committed to little more than improved discourse.

Why then the barrage of praise for Sen's seminal contributions to development? The reason is deeply linked to the constant search for high moral ground that preoccupies so many in a field where competition for scarce resources is intense. In the development enterprise money is never made, only spent. The voices of those who receive the services supplied are hardly heard, actions are rarely evaluated, and product quality measures are almost totally unknown. In that world, the creation of attractive visions is a prime mechanism to ensure survival and growth. Such visions combine the appeal of science with the high moral ground of 'doing good.' Indeed, their essential function is just that—providing visions of oneself, markers of identity, trademarks of progressiveness. Many of the ideological changes that the development community goes through are traceable to this imperative, and the glorification of Sen's fine work is no exception. With insightful and stimulating conceptual formulations, but zero practical guidelines or obligations, there is little to disagree with in Sen's thinking: adopting it costs nothing. Aid agencies are left with a pure win-win situation.

In addition, Sen has been able to restate well-known concepts intelligently in *economic-sounding language*. He is an economist by profession, and a good one. Over the years, he has constructed a body of work that is deeply erudite, methodologically and theoretically sound, and empirically rich, as well as—a rarity in his profession—multidisciplinary and informed by a strong ethical vision.[21] Because he is an economist employed by prestigious universities such as Harvard and Cambridge and is therefore certifiably authoritative, the fact that he speaks the language of the dominant ideology of "economism" simply adds to his appeal—an appeal that has come to border on beatification since he received the Nobel Prize. We, the do-gooders working in the margins, need every economist who comes our way! Nevertheless, there are a few limitations in his work that should be discussed.

Specifically, if we believe Amartya Sen is right, what do we do differently when we redefine development along his path? It is interesting here to look at the institution whose discourse has most taken over Sen's ideas: UNDP. Their excellent 2001 *Human Development Report* deals with human rights, human development, and the relations between the two. This report is chocked-full of interesting insights, and has a distinctly different intellectual feeling to it than, for example, a typical World Bank report or even UNDP work a decade ago. Yet the most remarkable finding comes from the section that describes the practical implications of "promoting rights in development."[22] According to the Report, there are five concrete things to be done in the new approach:

1. Launch independent national assessments of human rights;

2. Align national laws with international human rights standards and commitments;

3. Promote human rights norms;

4. Strengthen a network of human rights organizations; and

5. Promote a rights-enabling economic environment.

Four out of the five implications—ensure that governments make references to human rights in their constitutions and remove contrary laws; educate, sensitize, or mobilize people in human rights; create national human rights commissions or ombudsmen—are largely legalistic and technical and will not challenge anyone. These are all potentially useful activities, but they do not reflect any mainstreaming of human rights into development practice. They are simply small, technical add-ons. Only the fifth seems to offer the potential of going further. Allow me to quote from it at more length from the same report:

> How to create an enabling environment in which public policy can most effectively provide resources for advancing human rights? First, the public sector must focus on what it can do and leave for others what it should not do ... Second, with this division of labor, the state can focus on the direct provision of many economic, social, and civil rights.... Third, the major economic ministries, such as finance and planning, need to integrate rights into the economic policy-making process ... Fourth, the private sector also has responsibilities in creating an enabling economic environment. Chambers of commerce and other business organizations should contribute to efforts to further improve human rights ...

This is all the new approach amounts to: a standard repetition of the late 1990s liberal dogma of the sanctity of economic growth combined with a measure of human resource development and pious statements that ministries and corporations ought to think about human rights. Vagueness dominates. Are UNDP's suggestions different from what the World Bank's *World Development Report* would allow? If so, how would they be operationalized? What would the role of external aid agencies be? Not a word on any of these questions. In addition, none of the human rights objectives relate to UNDP, the aid enterprise, or the international community itself. All of them are to be implemented out there, in this separate place called the Third World, but do not require any critique of the global system and our place in it.

CONCLUSION

As could be expected, there is less to the emerging human rights approach in the development regime than meets the eye. Much of it is about the quest for moral high ground: draping oneself in the mantle of human rights to cover the fat belly of the development community while avoiding challenging the status quo too much, cross-examining oneself, or questioning the international system. One can see power at work here, which is to be expected. Most of this rethinking constitutes a voluntary act by people in New York, Washington, London, or Geneva (not to forget Medford, Massachusetts). Smart and well intended, most of them, but not exactly people in great need to overthrow the established order or second-guess themselves. The people in whose name the innovations are adopted did not fight for this change. It is not part of a fundamental reshuffling of the cards of power or a redistribution of resources worldwide: no such dynamic has occurred. As a result, one could expect little more than fluff, self-congratulation, and more or less hidden transcripts of power.

I am aware that I am painting a particularly negative picture in these pages. As someone who has strongly argued that the old development paradigm and associated practice was in need of profound repair,[23] I am certainly not making the case that we should simply leave things alone, or that any alteration of the development mandate in the direction of a greater attention to human rights is by definition a bad idea. I also appreciate how major change always starts small, and how even rhetorical gains sometimes turn out to be the snowballs that set in motion fresh avalanches. I even realize that there are organizations and people, in both rich and poor countries, who are courageously rethinking long-held ideologies and practices in human rights terms. That said, for this paper, I have chosen the uppercut approach to argumentation: pricking through a few balloons in the hope that when they burst, the noise will be enough to rouse academics, policymakers, and practitioners from the comfortable sleep of the just.

NOTES

1. Katarina Tomasevski, *Development Aid and Human Rights Revisited* (New York: Pinter, 1993) and Hans-Otto Sano, "Development and Human Rights: The Necessary, but Partial Integration of Human Rights and Development," *Human Rights Quarterly* 22, no. 3 (2000), 742.

2. Lawrence Haddad, "Symposium Synthesis and Overview," *SCN News*, no. 18 (July 1999), 14.

3. Urban Jonsson, "Historical Summary on the SCN Working Group on Nutrition, Ethics, and Human Rights," *SCN News*, no. 18 (July 1999), 49; David P. Forsythe, "The United Nations, Human Rights, and Development," *Human Rights Quarterly* 19, no. 2 (1997), 334. Note that the right to food is probably the most well developed of all economic, social, and cultural rights; hence, the situation is even worse in all other fields of development!

4. André Frankovits, "Rejoinder: The Rights Way to Development," *Food Policy* 21, no. 1 (1996), 126; see also Human Rights Council of Australia, "Inquiry into the Link

between Aid and Human Rights," Submission to the Joint Standing Committee on Foreign Affairs, Defense and Trade, February 2001, sections 2 and 3.

5. James C. Lovelace, "Will Rights Cure Malnutrition? Reflections on Human Rights, Nutrition, and Developments," *SCN News*, no. 18 (July 1999), 27; World Bank, *Development and Human Rights: The Role of the World Bank*, (Washington DC: World Bank, 1999), 3–4.

6. "Integrating Human Rights with Sustainable Development," *UNDP Policy Document* 2 (1998), 6.

7. See also Katarina Tomasevski, "International Development Finance Agencies," *Economic, Social and Cultural Rights: A Textbook*, eds. Asbjorn Eide, Catarina Krause, and Allan Rosas (Dordrecht: Martinus Nijhoff, 1995), 409.

8. Sano, "Development and Human Rights," 744.

9. Jack Donnelly, "Human Rights, Democracy and Development," *Human Rights Quarterly* 21, no. 2 (August 1999), 611.

10. Economic, social and cultural rights.

11. Michael Windfuhr, "Economic, Social and Cultural Rights and Development Cooperation," in *Working Together: The Human Rights Based Approach to Development Cooperation–Report of the NGO Workshop*, eds. Andre Frankovits and Patrick Earle (Stockholm: October 16-19, 2000), 25.

12. DFDID, *Realizing Human Rights for Poor People* (London: DFID Strategy Paper, 2000), 5; Stella Mukasa and Florence Butegwa, *An Overview of Approaches to Economic and Social Rights in Development in Uganda–Draft report for DANIDA* (Kampala: Nordic Consulting Group, June 2001), 40; Arjun Sengupta, *Study on the Current State of Progress in the Implementation of the Rights to Development*, Commission on Human Rights, 56th sess., July 1999; Arjun Sengupta, "Realizing the Right to Development," *Development and Change*, 31 (2000a), 553–578; Note by the Secretary-General for the 55th session. A/55/306. Aug. 2000b. E/CN.4/1999/WG.18/2.

13. World Bank, *Governance and Development* (Washington DC: World Bank, 1992), *passim.*

14. HRCA 2001.

15. World Bank, *Development and Human Rights*, 3.

16. Craig Scott, "Reaching Beyond (Without Abandoning) the Category of 'Economic, Social and Cultural Rights,'" *Human Rights Quarterly* 21, no. 3 (1999), 635–6.

17. Amartya Sen, *Development as Freedom* (New York: Alfred A. Knopf, 1999), 87.

18. *Ibid.*, 1; see also UNDP, *Human Development Report 2001* (New York: Oxford University Press, 2001), 19.

19. Sen, *Development as Freedom*, 147–8.

20. United Nations, *An Agenda for Development: Report of the Secretary-General* (New York: UN, A/48/935, 6 May 1994), par. 120.

21. Please note that, in the community of his economist peers, the latter qualifiers—all the ones that follow the words "methodologically and theoretically," in fact—are much less appreciated. As a colleague recently remarked: "Sen couldn't get tenure in any good American economics department on the basis of his famous work."

22. UNDP, *Human Development Report 2001*, 112.

23. Peter Uvin, *Aiding Violence: The Development Enterprise in Rwanda* (West Hartford: Kumarian Press, 1998).

✗ NO
Making Moral Low Ground: Rights as the Struggle for Justice and the Abolition of Development
HUGO SLIM

It is always a pleasure to reply to the exciting, broad-brush strokes of a scholar like Peter Uvin. He paints an expressive and important picture of the adoption of human rights speak by powerful sectors of the international development establishment—or "enterprise," as he usefully describes it. Not surprisingly, I find myself agreeing with much of what he says and admiring the way in which he says it. There is indeed "much to worry about" when the powers-that-be adopt the liberationist language of the oppressed and drape their projects in revolutionary garb. Peter Uvin is right to be concerned that much of the new rights agenda in international development circles is really about "fluff and power." In this reply, I would like to amplify some of his main themes. But, above all, I would like to take them further and think about what happens when people other than the development establishment use human rights to talk about poverty.

But first, there are a couple of things that might be usefully added to Uvin's piece. It is slightly inaccurate to say that the development enterprise has lived "in perfect isolation, if not ignorance, of the human rights community." This is partly but not entirely true. Assuming that "the development enterprise" includes NGOs, churches, and community-based organizations (CBOs), then this statement is not correct. For those of us whose work is primarily concerned with Africa, it is easy to forget the experience of Latin America, South Asia, and even South Africa.

In these societies and their polities, the idea of human rights has played a central part in the struggle for development, social justice, and peace. In conflicts and political repression in Latin America, Freireans and liberation theologians conceived of development as a popular movement for social justice. While their analysis was essentially Marxist in many of its aspects, most of them were not averse to the political philosophy of human rights and framed their struggle for land, livelihood, democracy, and peace in rights terms. In this process they radicalized many European and North American NGOs. The highly conflictual experience of the Roman Catholic Church in Latin American politics played an equally major part in the Church's determination to reach a conclusion about the ideology of human rights and to endorse them as an important and acceptable aspect of Catholic teaching. Similar processes took place in South Asia around land and gender rights and in South Africa around the struggle against apartheid.

In reality, therefore, there are perhaps two development traditions—a Latin American–style one and a more paternalistic and scientific one. In NGOs that

Hugo Slim, "Making Moral Low Ground: Rights as the Struggle for Justice and the Abolition of Development," *Praxis: The Fletcher Journal of Development Studies*, XVII (2002). Reprinted with permission of The Fletcher School–Tufts University.

I know best, people have tended to stay in one tradition and seldom move between the two. One exciting possibility is that the introduction of human rights into development might mean that we see a more Latin American flavor to development struggles in future.

Another topic that may have been overlooked in Uvin's piece is the way in which human rights ideology is (perhaps increasingly) contested. This can take three main forms. Particular rights, around gender or childhood for example, can be contested at the periphery of a majority of rights that are generally accepted. In this way, states or groups can argue moral relativism on particular rights. More fundamentally, however, and in a way which Uvin himself comes close to doing, states, societies, or groups can reject the whole way the human rights regime functions as simply a bossy and superior aspect of Western hegemony serving Western interests. In other words, while societies may share many of the values expressed in human rights ideology, they will reject the human rights regime. Finally, of course, others will take cover under both these objections to use them as a means of ignoring international law and opinion while they deliberately violate human rights.

The fact that human rights ideology is contested is important when it comes to rights-based development because inevitably such contest will lead to conflicts that might not arise if a less legal and political discourse were pursued to focus on public goods. So, for example, one could envisage a government refusing to work with UNICEF on a child health program because it cannot tolerate the particular politics of child rights and state obligation that accompanies the program. Such a government could just as likely be a right wing U.S. donor government as well as an aid recipient government. Development pragmatists might argue that using the idea of rights in such situations is a sure way to ensure that nothing gets done for poor people. Thus, rhetoric or not, rights-talk can simply be a bad tactic in certain situations.

But enough about what Peter Uvin may have overlooked in his wide-ranging sketch. Let us now focus on his main point, that the adoption of rights-based development is really all about "fluff and power" and the taking of moral high ground without changing one's practice in any meaningful way. For this is a serious charge and one which is pretty well on target as things stand. In many NGOs advocating a rights-based approach, there is as much confusion as excitement. While most development people have got their hearts around a rights-based approach, they have not yet got their heads around it. Many feel that rights are important, but they may also have a hunch that Peter Uvin is onto something and that reading Sen and talking rights makes for little more than an "improved discourse" which may not be of much use to people enduring poverty around the world.

So, what about rights as fluff? Much of the breathless adrenalin rush of the new rights talk does indeed seem to offer a new way of feeling good. I began to embrace the political philosophy of human rights three years ago and have always noticed how passionate I can become when talking about rights and what a warm glow it leaves me with after lecturing on the subject. Peter Uvin is right. Simply talking about human rights quite literally makes me feel virtuous. At last, rights-talk seems to give the dry, quasi-scientific theory of development a moral and political vision. It can really make one quite excited. Such is the sad life of a British academic! This aspect of rights-talk is a bit like prayer. One mouths escha-tological ideas about human dignity and the coming of heaven on earth. One prays and feels good but has very little idea of its power and effect. It does indeed allow one to walk the "moral high ground" and makes one feel self-righteous.

But human rights don't only do this. They can act socially as well as piously. And rights-talk can function differently from different mouths. Human rights can sound and act very differently when they are spoken from what Gustavo Gutierrez calls "the underside of history"—the muddy side where people pay the price for those walking along the top. The same language of rights that may be rhetorical fluff in one place may be words of extreme courage and radical change in another. The power of speech is the power to name and define things. Rights-talk in Washington or Paris might be used piously as new words for the same old liturgy in the cathedrals of international trade and development. This might indeed be "repackaging" of old wine in new bottles as Peter Uvin suggests. It represents the power of re-dressing rather than power of redress. But from another place (a slum or the scene of a rigged election) and spoken from another voice (that of a poor man or a woman land rights lawyer) the same words of rights-talk could function prophetically as a demand for redress to change and challenge power.

So, I think the shift of development talk from previous discourses of philan-thropy, charity, modernization, and progress to one of human rights can be made to be extremely significant. Most importantly, rights-talk has the ability to finally politicize development between the muddy low ground and the moral high ground. Human rights give a language of political contract to matters of poverty, injustice, and armed violence. Rights-talk stops people being perceived as 'needy,' as 'victims,' and as 'beneficiaries.' Instead, it enables these same people to know and present themselves as rightful and dignified people who can make just demands of power and spell out the duties of power in terms of moral and polit-ical goods. In grammatical terms, it moves them from being the objects in some-body else's sentence to being the subject of their own free speech. This requires courage, knowledge, and organization but it has often happened and it will happen again. Human rights can fire people up. It is a political philosophy that can have deep meaning to people—meaning deep enough for them to risk their lives and die for. This is what happened in Boston in the 18th century. It has hap-pened many times since and is happening somewhere every day.

But does this mean that I have only moved from an idea of rights as fluff to one of rights as prophetic fluff? I hope not! But to be sure it is necessary to look at Peter Uvin's second point about rights-based development talk as simply serving Western power. Power certainly does tend to use ideas to serve its own interests and there is a serious risk that this is happening with rights ideology. As Uvin suggests, neo-liberal economic and political projects of "good governance" are simply being re-packaged in rights terms. There is little evidence that the structural violence and injustice of global power systems are being truly challenged by the philosophy of equal rights now mouthed by power itself. The traffic of change-talk still really flows in one direction only. Human rights in the mouths of OECD governments send a predominant message to the effect that "human rights demand that you—poor countries—must change." As Uvin observes, rights-talk has engendered very little revolutionary analysis of the structures of poverty or serious consideration of the demands these same human rights make for powerful countries to change their ways.

Yet I would like to suggest that the situation is not quite as simple or as bad as Uvin presents it. There may well be a way in which the fact that Western power continues to talk a discourse of rights may increasingly make it accountable to those rights. In welcoming human rights into the citadel of development, I have a hunch that rights ideology may function as something of a Trojan horse for those who really mean what they say about human rights. Peter Uvin's analysis focuses on governments, multilateral agencies, and transnational corporations as the adopters of the new rights talk. But, as noted above, there are others using human rights in a different and prophetic way down in the muddy lowlands. And, there is also a group of international NGOs who straddle the middle hill country between the moral highlands and the muddy lowlands who are also using human rights talk in a slightly different way to mainstream power. While these NGOs can be more pious than most on occasion, they can also challenge Western power extremely effectively from time to time. Between them, the lowlanders and the NGOs might make up an important group who, like the Greeks before them, may be able to leap out of the Trojan Horse and take the real struggle for rights to the heart of politics and policy-making in governments, corporations, and public opinion. Once inside, they may also find that the citadel contains many others who are sympathetic. For, dare I say it, government departments, political parties, and transnational corporations contain people who benefit from living on the powerful upper side of history but who would also like to change the world in pursuit of human rights. Uvin is right to claim that—in the main—the move to rights has not resulted in a thorough analysis of the construction of poverty and a system-wide strategy for its transformation. But some organizations among the powerful are making some connections. For example, the British Government's Department for International Development (DFID) has important policies that see the links between global trade and poverty, arms exports and violence, and energy consumption and ecological crisis.

The challenge for people using human rights prophetically rather than piously is to organize and create a counter-veiling force to the complacency and oppression of those on the moral high ground. (This is the part of the paper where Uvin's feel-good law kicks in as using rights-talk starts to make me feel virtuous again!) In practice, this means producing the analysis that Uvin notes is lacking and making the connections between global power structures and poverty. It means having the courage to build local, national, and global movements that argue for specific duties to be met by governments, corporations, and individuals that will enable all people to enjoy their rights. Above all, it involves abolishing the development enterprise as a neo-colonial program of correction administered from rich to poor and replacing it with a common political project that recognizes everyone's equal rights and judges the behavior of all on the basis of how they realize or violate these rights. This would involve all involved looking in the mirror as well as looking down from the moral high ground.

Then, finally perhaps, we could also do away with the very word 'development.' The common struggle for human rights and social justice would at last bring the end of the era of development. We could begin to talk a proper moral and political language of equality, fairness, social justice, right, and responsibility. This would be an equal discourse that has no notion of some people being whole (developed) and other people being inadequate (under-developed). Rather, everyone would be sharing responsibility and working towards common goals. This would be heaven. But we are encouraged to start making it here on earth or, at the very least, to continue to ensure that the basic moral goods involved in such a vision are struggled for each day. In doing so, rich and poor alike would have to meet on the muddy low ground where they all really live, and make it moral.

POSTSCRIPT

The growing acceptance of "rights-based" approaches to development has been applauded by many working in the field of international development. What it does, they argue, is to put discussions of politics, power, and social justice back into development planning, which too often focuses exclusively on technical and utilitarian economic calculations. Injecting rights talk into development discourse restores a sense of passion and justice and mobilizes people in a way that technocratic economic models of development cannot.

But, is there a danger, as Peter Uvin suggests, that simply shifting the discourse toward human rights will have little effect on the day-to-day operations of development agencies? Is rights talk mere "fluff" as Uvin claims? Is there a need for a greater "mainstreaming" of human rights into development agencies themselves? If so, what changes would this necessitate? How would development agencies operate differently if human rights were more fully integrated into development planning?

Hugo Slim reminds of us of the useful "prophetic" role that rights language provides for critiquing development policies. At the same time, the definition of many of these rights remains highly contested. For example, within many Western countries themselves, the appropriate balance between political/civil rights and social/economic/cultural rights is still subject to considerable debate. What is the appropriate balance between individual and collective rights? If these issues are still contested in donor countries, how can the appropriate balance of rights be incorporated into the policies of development agencies?

MORE ISSUES NOW AVAILABLE

A collection of important issues that concern us today

Are you seeking additional issues for study, debate, or general interest? It is now easier to choose additional issues and to create your own customized reader from the *Crosscurrents* series. All issues follow the same format with an issue introduction, two opposing sides addressing the issue, and a postscript. Build your own text of issues from the total list of available issues below:

Issue	Issue Title
1	Will Conservatism and the Conservative Party Fail?
2	Can Native Sovereignty Coexist with Canadian Sovereignty?
3	Is the Canadian Charter of Rights and Freedoms Antidemocratic?
4	Is a Majority Government More Effective Than a Minority Government?
5	Is the Prime Minister Too Powerful?
6	Is a Mixed-Member Proportional Electoral System in Canada's Interest?
7	Should the Court Challenges Program Be Reinstated?
8	Is Ethnic Diversity an Inherent Cause of Conflict?
9	Can Trade Liberalization Benefit Both the Rich and Poor?
10	Can Sweatshops and Cheap Labour Benefit the Poor?
11	Does Outright Debt Cancellation Ignore the Real Problems of Africa?
12	Can Genetically Modified Food Help Solve Global Food Needs?
13	Do Current World Bank and IMF Lending and Aid Models Alleviate Poverty?"
14	Has the Adoption of a Rights-Based Approach to Development Failed?
15	Are Property Titling Systems the Key to Increased Economic Growth?
16	Is Development Assistance Ineffective?
17	Should Canadian Troops be Deployed to Darfur Rather Than Afghanistan?
18	Are Prohibitions on Private Health Care Inconsistent with the Charter of Rights?
19	Is the Canadian Political Culture Becoming Americanized?
20	Should the Federal Government Play a Leading Role in Health Care?
21	Should Party Discipline Be Relaxed?
22	Should Women Focus on Small-p Politics?
23	Should Religious Beliefs Be Excluded from Consideration of Public Policy?
24	Living Together with Disagreement: Pluralism, the Secular, and the Fair Treatment of Beliefs in Law Today
25	Do Canadian Government Foreign Aid Programs Help to Alleviate Poverty?
26	Is Ethnic Conflict Inevitable?

For more information about *The Crosscurrents Collection*, browse our website at **www.nelson.com/crosscurrents**, or contact your local Nelson Education Sales & Editorial Representative.